THE HUNTING TIME

For every thing there is a season,
And a time for every purpose under heaven.

ecclesiastes

THE HUNTING TIME

Adventures In Pursuit Of
North American Big Game

A Forty-Year Chronicle

JOHN E. HOWARD

Illustrated by
JOHN RICE

ST. HUBERT'S
P r e s s
DEFOREST, WISCONSIN
2002

Library of Congress Cataloging-in-Publication Data

Howard, John E.
  The hunting time : adventures in pursuit of North American big game :
a forty-year chronicle / John E. Howard ; illustrated by John Rice.
    p. cm.
  ISBN 0-9633094-4-7 (hard cover)
    I. Title.

SK40 .H68 2002
799.2'6'097--dc21   2001058866

Printed in the United States of America

First Edition

St. Hubert's Press
P.O. Box 404
DeForest, Wisconsin 53532-0404

For Kelly, my daughter,
who must wonder at times what it is
that possesses her father so;
and for Michael, my son,
who on a few, too brief occasions,
perhaps knew.

And for Ginny.
Always, for Ginny.

Contents

PART IV

Full Page Illustrations

Vignettes

Then Comes The Morning Wind

Have you wandered through the far-off places,
Gone where your passing leaves no traces,
   Gone where wild winds
     And wild waters roar;
Have you seen untamed rivers flowing,
Seen the northern lights aglowing,
   Have you been
     Where no ones ever been before?

Have you caught a whiff of spruce trees,
Smelled the tundra on a north breeze,
   Felt the sting of rain and sleet
     Upon your face;
Have you shivered awake the morning,
Watched the new day's sun aborning,
   Watched the moon wane low
     In some wild and lonely place?

Do you still wonder at the night skies,
Wonder where the river's source lies,
   Long to solve the mystery
     Of what's around the bend;
Do Nature's creatures still delight you,
Her wild places still excite you,
   Do you long to follow trails
     That never end?

Do you feel the need to roam free,
Then you feel the need that finds me,
   In those far-off places
     That beckon with autumn's dawn;
When I see fitful leaves start falling,
When I hear the Red Gods calling,
   Then comes the morning wind
     I will be gone.

PART I

Chapter 1

Beginnings

Fate rules o'er Destinies' sea,
And hapless mortals we,
Like flotsam adrift on the tide,
Fate's fickle whims must need abide.

On a fateful Monday, on his thirty-first birthday, my father decided to go horseback riding. Shortly after he left the stable something shied his horse, causing it to rear up on its hind legs. Almost thrown, my father clung precariously to the reins, fighting to regain control; but he succeeded only in pulling the frightened horse off balance, bringing it crashing down upon him. My alarmed mother ran to his aid. She helped my father struggle to his feet, then rushed him to the nearest doctor, supporting him in her arms to the office door. There he went limp, slipping through her grasp to crumple across the threshold. My father died as the doctor reached him, drained of life by massive internal bleeding.

I was one year old.

After the funeral, my mother found herself with me, my one-month-old brother, and exactly thirty-eight cents to her name. She did then what she would do for the rest of her days. She gathered her children to her, and in her sublime, self-reliant way, took care of her own. Times were hard then, at the tail end of the Great Depression. She took a job in a shoe factory to support us. We were poor, supposedly, but in my childhood world, I did not know it.

From time to time as my brother and I grew up, my mother spoke to us of our father. He was, by her accounts, a devoted husband and a doting parent. He had been an accountant by profession and a musician by avocation, playing piano and organ in supper clubs on weekends. In later years when I asked her, my mother could not recall my father ever hunting, or even talking about hunting. Nor did she.

There must have been earlier ancestors of mine in whom the hunting instinct flourished, for we are shaped by genetic streams flowing through the generations. Who those ancestors were remains a mystery, their identities shrouded in time. But the ageless impulse to hunt that flowed through them endured.

My earliest recollections of hunting take me back to Mrs. Amato's neighborhood garden, a boyhood jungle of towering sunflowers and arbors of grape vine amid terraces of luxuriant flowers. Butterflies abounded there. Regal monarchs and swallowtails flitted about, attended by painted ladies and red admirals. They tantalized me. I had a need to capture them and hold them in my hand. When they eluded my childish grasp, I fashioned a net from a broken broom handle, a wire clothes hanger, and a swatch of discarded muslin. Jim Corbett, stalking man-eating tigers in the jungles of India, glided no more stealthily through the amalta trees than did I stalking tiger swallowtails through Mrs. Amato's rhododendrons.

Even before the butterfly jungle, guns had become a familiar part of my childhood. Toy carbines and six-shooters were commonplace with my playmates and me. How else to ward off the desperados? When the play guns were in time outgrown, I pestered my mother until she finally gave me a classic Red

Ryder BB gun for Christmas. Tin cans and paper bullseyes served as backyard targets, and once I shot at a robin. Surely the robin shared my surprise when it toppled from the tree. Looking at the fallen bird aroused a vague uneasiness within me. I had no idea what to do with a dead robin. I buried it and shot at no others.

As a youth I learned camping and outdoor skills during Boy Scout outings, but little of hunting, except for the subtle lessons absorbed during my summer forays into Mrs. Amato's garden. My horizons gradually expanded. Like some primordial nautiloid, my instincts drew me to water. Rock River and Turtle Creek became familiar haunts, and long summer days saw me bicycling miles west of town to explore the meanderings of Raccoon Creek. There, nervous-tailed gray squirrels chattered high in the white oaks, while startled cottontail rabbits bolted from underfoot. Occasionally, from the grassy creek bank, a gaudy cock pheasant erupted with a raucous cackle. They tempted me like the butterflies, but remained far beyond my grasp.

In my teenage years, along with my ongoing involvement in the out of doors, a compelling interest in the military emerged. At age fifteen, while a sophomore in high school, I feigned a few more years and managed to enlist in an infantry company of the Wisconsin National Guard. As an unexpected enlistment bonus, the recruiting sergeant informed me of a small caliber rifle range in the basement of the Beloit armory where the company trained. I was intrigued to also learn that not only did the Guard provide twenty-two caliber target rifles to use there, but likewise furnished all the ammunition you wanted to shoot. I haunted the place. There was method in their generosity. Practice makes better riflemen. The following summer I qualified expert with the thirty caliber M1 rifle at the Army's Camp Douglas range.

National Guard pay, along with after school and weekend part-time jobs, kept me in spending money and enabled me to acquire my first rifle, a twenty-two caliber Mossberg. The armory range became my second home until the rifle's newness wore off.

Perhaps the stimulus of shooting triggered an ancestral gene deep inside me, for during that period something awakened a latent impulse to hunt. I have no clear remembrance of my first actual hunt, only that it was for squirrels with my Mossberg. I do vividly remember warm September afternoons, making four-hour round trips to the western counties just to hunt the last fleeting minutes of the day, because squirrel season opened two weeks earlier there. I remember sun-drenched days in October, gliding through green-canopied hardwood stands with my twenty-two in hand. I remember frosty November mornings, sitting stone-like beneath towering, russet-leafed oaks. I remember stark December and January woods that lay frozen in an overwhelming silence, where mine was the only movement in the snow-fringed white dawn. I remember I was caught up in the wonder of it all, and could hardly wait to go hunting again tomorrow.

There was no mentor to show me the way. Outdoor magazines became my tutors, but essentially I learned from my own experiences. Squirrels continued to hold a fascination, while an occasional rabbit fell to the Mossburg. A Browning sixteen-gauge was not long in being acquired to better serve the fleet cottontails; and on one memorable, crisp November morning with the new shotgun, a gloriously plumed cock pheasant cackled out of the downed corn behind me to fall with heart-stopping elation to my twisting, rearward shot.

Grouse were discovered, and then ducks, the first being a hen wood duck flushed from a flooded cornfield in the Sugar River Bottoms. I later brought a drake wood duck home in awe of its beauty and had it mounted to preserve the magic. Geese came, in wary vees out of the north, exciting wonder at their wildness. Woodcock flighted through the river bottoms on soft, early autumn nights. On one never-to-be-repeated morning, a limit of five fell to my Browning with as many shots. Occasional coveys of quail flushed from overgrown fence rows. And during one sunlit afternoon, a covey of Hungarian partridge led me on a cross-country chase before a pair was eventually downed.

In the off-season I roamed the river bottoms at night calling fox, and occasionally a bobcat, to a distressed-rabbit call. One moonless night a great horned owl glided silently to my pleadings and brushed my hat off with its wings. I found raccoons in their den trees and followed others through the darkness to the music of the hounds. In the glory days of spring I went often to the woods to learn the wildwood's ways. And sometimes, when nothing else compelled me, I went to the woods just to be there.

Over the seasons I marked a number of favorite covers. One of them was a ten-acre woodlot of mixed softwoods and oaks surrounded by fields of corn and alfalfa. Mostly the squirrels drew me there. On a couple of occasions, however, while walking through the fields to the woodlot with my twenty-two in hand, pheasants flushed within easy range. A shotgun was needed, but stalking squirrels with one held no appeal. I began crossing the fields carrying my Browning sixteen-gauge, with my twenty-two rifle slung over my back. At the edge of the woodlot, the shotgun, along with an occasional pheasant, was secured under a fallen tree and the rifle unslung. The business of squirrel hunting remained a rifleman's business.

A great grandfather of an oak stood paternal guard over the surrounding trees along the north edge of this woodlot. Squirrels favored the oak when the acorns ripened, drawing me regularly to it as the autumn mast fell.

On a particular fall day of glorious color, with the maples still tenaciously clutching their multihued leaves, I found myself on one of many watchful vigils beside the great oak. The crisp dawn had given way to a lazy, warm morning. The squirrels seemed as somnolent as the day, for none made an appearance. The lack of activity eventually dulled my alertness. My gaze began wandering from the dense tree cover to the open countryside beyond.

From the edge of the woodlot that the great oak sheltered, fields sown in alfalfa sloped gently down to a graveled county road a quarter of a mile away. A fence line, overgrown with brambles, followed the western edge of the woodlot north to the county road. Beyond the road ripened fields of corn splashed wide swatches of gold among fallow fields dotted with marshland. Other woodlots showcased their muted fall colors. Birds soared aloft, and from somewhere in the background the disturbed barking of a farm dog echoed faintly in the still morning air.

The barking soon subsided and the farm dog loped silently into view along the edge of a marsh on the far side of the road. It was barely discernable at the distance. The dog ran across the road and through the alfalfa field on the west side of the fence, angling in my direction. I idly watched as it bounded steadily through the field. When the dog reached the fence it did a strange thing. Instead of turning along or crawling through it, the dog gracefully leaped over the fence without breaking stride. Less than a hundred yards separated us.

The dog continued to draw closer, coming on a direct line as though drawn to me by a magnet. I watched it approach, but something was not registering. The image in my mind of a dog and the animal running toward me refused to mesh. Then the realization struck. It was not a dog. It was an animal I had only seen pictures of before.

It was a deer!

The proximity of game triggered a reflex. I brought my rifle to bear. The deer came on. I stood frozen. The deer slowed. Scant feet separated us. The deer stopped, suddenly aware of a strange apparition before it. Her ears began to cock, trying to funnel in a telltale sound. She took a few mincing steps toward me, stretching out her neck. Her nostrils quivered as they sought to draw in a revealing scent. Then she froze, framed in the halo of my rear peep sight, the sharp front bead literally inches from her black nose. Not a quiver betrayed man nor deer. We became as statues locked in a magical sculptured tableau.

The doe finally shattered the magic, either wearying of her role in the drama or sensing some alarm. She bounded away to my left into the shelter of the scrub brush, leaving me in a breathless state of intense exhilaration.

A deer! I had seen a deer! That mythical creature who heretofore existed only in faraway lands or on the covers of outdoor magazines. But now, right here in my squirrel woods, I had seen a deer!

Here was rare game. Previously unattainable game. But no longer. The deer were here. And like the small game and pheasants, and all that came before, I felt an impulse to pursue them, and to bring one to hand.

Chapter

First Deer

The Sugar River rises in south-central Wisconsin a few miles below the hamlet of Pine Bluff, flows east a short distance before picking up a feeder stream, then swings south past Paoli into Green County. There it adds volume from Sylvester Creek before slicing through the southwest corner of neighboring Rock County. The twisting waterway continues south through the county before crossing into Illinois where it joins the Pecatonica River seven miles below the Wisconsin state line.

That portion of the river flowing through Rock County traverses a series of wooded lowlands dotted with potholes and sloughs. In years of minor flooding, farmers coax corn and soybeans from the drier fields, but for the most part the lowlands grow wild. All manner of animal life resides there, and in the fall the resident duck population is swelled by the northern flight. This game-rich area is known locally as the Sugar River Bottoms. Like the woodlot where my first deer was sighted, it became one of my favored hunting grounds.

Unlike the woodlots modest ten acres, however, the river bottoms encompassed several hundred acres of wild, secluded country. Deer reportedly sheltered there. The more I considered where to hunt for a deer, the more my thoughts turned toward the Bottoms. It is true I had never seen a deer there. But after the initial euphoria of my first deer encounter wore off, the little woodlot in which it occurred began to seem too confined. Big game presumedly required big country. The river bottoms loomed large.

The 1959 Wisconsin deer season opened November twenty-first at six-thirty in the morning. Well before that appointed hour my flashlight beam was guiding me deep into the heart of the Bottoms. One constant in all I read about deer was that they were especially active in the early morning. A hunter well-positioned before dawn, the authors advised, stood a greater chance of seeing deer than did those who arrived after first light. The authors also offered earnest advice about watching for deer near rubs and runs and scrapes, which no doubt would have been helpful had I any idea what a rub or a run or a scrape looked like.

The wind, however, I understood. As the eastern light began to displace the darkness, I faced into the whisper of a breeze and began a silent watch.

There seemed little to distinguish deer hunting from squirrel hunting except that the ground drew my attention rather than the trees. A few scattered shots echoed faintly in the distance as the morning progressed, but whether they were at deer or some other game was impossible to determine. Inevitably the habits of past seasons took hold. I caught myself on more than a few occasions scanning the trees for squirrels. None were in evidence.

The hours passed with nothing breaking the stillness except a few more distant shots and the occasional quacking of a hen mallard from the direction of the river. At last, tiring of the inactivity, I began still-hunting through the deeper cover, moving slowly and pausing often. Nothing stirred.

At noon I came out on the river bank just as a low-flying flock of mallards whooshed around an upstream bend. They flared skyward when they spotted me. I swung on them with my shotgun but they were safe from the ponderous slugs it carried. The darkened trees stretched solidly along the opposite bank of the river. I watched there for a time, giving idle thought to how a deer might be retrieved through the swift current.

I resumed still-hunting and by late afternoon had circled back to my stand of the morning. One lone gray squirrel answered for the only game seen during the evening watch. When the dark shadows announced closing time, I turned eastward and followed the deepening dusk out of the Bottoms. Night settled down along the way.

Night was still with me as I retraced my steps well before daybreak. The dawn came with its expectations but it passed into the morning without even the hint of a deer. The afternoon mirrored the previous empty afternoon and my brief first deer season ended with the close of the second day.

Wisconsin hunters registered 105,596 deer that season, of which 164 were registered in Rock County, one of the lowest county totals in the state. Many northern counties registered deer in the thousands. While planning for the next deer season, my thoughts turned increasingly toward the north.

Deer and the north country had likewise been on the mind of my friend Dick Mason, with whom I had shared a number of small game hunts. Black bear could also be hunted in the north during the deer season. No additional license was required. Over five hundred had been taken in 1959. The odds of a bear remained long, but just the chance of seeing one added extra excitement to the hunt. Dick and I laid our plans for the north.

Two other friends joined in during the summer, enabling us to apply for a party permit. This special license allowed a group of four hunters one additional deer of either sex. An armband was issued with the permit and only the hunter wearing it could legally fill the party tag. Since none of us had shot a deer, we decided to rotate the armband. We drew cards to set the order of rotation. I drew high card.

Highway 64, the dividing line beyond which black bear could be hunted, runs east and west across northern Wisconsin, passing at the halfway point through Medford, a town noted in the 1960's for its thriving mink industry. Ten miles west of Medford, Highway 64 begins marking the southern boundary of a two hundred and fifty square mile block of the Chequamegon National Forest. This ranging wilderness drew us, for black bear were said to roam there along with deer.

We reserved sleeping rooms over a tavern in downtown Medford for the opening weekend, planning to arrive there Friday after work. The night was well-advanced by the time we pulled into town and the tavern was awash in a sea of red-coated hunters. Wisconsin, per capita, was the number one beer drinking state in the union, and the stalwart souls there assembled were struggling manfully to assure that Wisconsin maintained that exalted ranking. Purely to fulfill our patriotic duty to the state, we joined in a few rounds before climbing a narrow staircase to the sleeping rooms above. After a full day of work and a two hundred mile drive, sleep came easily in spite of the blaring jukebox and the rumble of the hunters below.

Five o'clock Saturday morning saw the town again awash in red coats, although the local restaurants rather than the taverns were now profiting from the influx of deer hunters.

After breakfast we headed west on the highway, then angled north on a darkened county road into the Chequamegon.

Dawn was barely a glimmer in the eastern sky when Dick stopped the car near a prominent boulder chosen to mark my later pick-up point. I loaded my rifle as the other three drove off and waited in the semidarkness for the six-thirty opening.

That time was still minutes away when a muffled shot far off to the north broke the stillness, possibly announcing the early closing of some lucky hunter's season. A shiver started through me with the realization that deer must be moving. Suddenly anxious, I took a hasty compass bearing on the road, and in the half-light of the dawning eased into the woods.

A series of far-off, scattered shots came with the growing light. I had no idea where my three friends were hunting and could only speculate as to whether any of the shots were theirs. I continued deeper into the woods, moving slowly and pausing often to peer intently into the pockets of screening brush.

After an hour I came to a fallen tree at the edge of an extended thinning in the dense forest cover. I sat on the tree enjoying the expanded vista, thankful to be holding a rifle instead of the short-range shotgun that had served me the preceding deer season. Shotguns were required in the southern counties and I had picked up an old double-barreled J.C. Higgins twelve-gauge from an acquaintance who needed some quick cash. Even after fitting the shotgun with a makeshift peep sight, the groups it shot convinced me that old Higgins was a fifty-yard weapon at best. I searched for a rifle during the summer and settled on a Winchester Model 70 in .270 caliber. Fitted with a Lyman peep sight, the rifle shot inch-and-a-half groups at one hundred yards.

An hour passed in silent watching from the fallen tree with only a pair of flittering chickadees bringing life to the scene. The lure of distant cover prompted me to resume still-hunting.

Another hour elapsed during my silent passage through the gray woods. Deer presumably were still being sighted since occasional shots continued to break the forest stillness, but except for some encouraging tracks, none were evident in my section of the woods.

At nine-thirty I paused to take my bearing. My presence back at the road was required in two hours in order to transfer the party-permit armband. I checked my compass, turned on a heading to the road, and began to hunt in that direction.

Half an hour later found me again pausing to recheck my heading. I slung the rifle over my left shoulder, then held the compass in my extended right hand and waited for the needle to settle. When it held steady, I looked up to take a bearing, and was awestricken by an astonishing sight.

A deer was standing there! Facing straight at me! Thirty yards away!

Shock overwhelmed me. Adrenaline surged in response. My right hand glided slowly to the sling, easing it off of my left shoulder. No reaction from the deer. I lowered the rifle with infinite care until my left hand could close around the forearm. The deer watched intently. I eased the rifle across my body, my right hand with the compass still in it closing awkwardly around the pistol grip. The deer still stood there. I raised the rifle butt to my shoulder in muscle-tensing slow motion and peered through the peep sight. The front bead wavered through a distressingly wide arc. Desperately willing my quivering muscles to be still for an instant, I settled the front bead on the deer's neck and squeezed the trigger.

The deer collapsed instantly to the ground.

I began to tremble. My right leg shook uncontrollably. Raging emotions engulfed me. A flood of intense elation overwhelmed my senses. I had shot a deer! By all the Powers! I had shot a deer!

I waited with the rifle still bearing on the animal, fearful it might rise and vanish like a sorcerer's illusion. But the deer did not rise. My trembling gradually subsided. When a measure of control returned, I walked the thirty paces to the deer and stood gazing down at it in silent wonder, lost in a reverie of dreamlike fulfillment.

Finally, with still quivering fingers, I tagged the deer using the party permit and began the mundane chore of dressing the animal. In spite of my experience with small game, the size of the task gave me pause.

One of the outdoor magazines had published an illustrated, twelve-step article on dressing deer a few months earlier. That article, clipped from the magazine, lay beside the deer while I proceeded through the twelve steps, pausing after each one to admire my progress. Skilled surgeons would have wept in envy at my scalpel-like precision.

After the deer was dressed, I fastened the middle of my drag rope around its neck, made a loop at each end, slipped the loops over my shoulders, and following my compass, dragged the deer to the road. When my companions arrived they were at first incredulous, then congratulatory, over my good fortune. They had seen nothing all morning.

I hunted the same area in the afternoon on the theory that where there was a doe there should also be a buck. But none appeared. My friends likewise reported no sightings.

We hunted a new area the following day. The morning passed in careful watching and searching, but with the exception of distant scattered shots and a few chickadees, I neither heard nor saw a thing. The afternoon duplicated the morning. When we gathered in the final light, my first deer remained the only deer seen through the two days.

The close of the weekend ended our hunt. Jobs required our presence Monday morning. Within half an hour of dark we were retracing the two hundred mile route home. In the long quiet of the night we settled into our thoughts and my mind replayed the still vivid sequence of opening morning. The passing images melded into images of hunts to come and I dreamed of other game, and of magical days, and of distant lands beyond my memory. And in the dreams, in the fleeting, passing visions, when time and place took form, I saw myself in those distant lands. And I saw a time when those lands would be a dream no more.

To The North

In the months following my first successful deer hunt, I began to plan for other big game. Black bears roamed Wisconsin's North Country, monsters too if rumored weights were to be believed. But except for a limited early bow season, bears could only be hunted during the regular deer season. While making inquiries, I discovered that the Canadian province of Ontario had a black bear season that ran from early September through the end of June, practically the entire year. A nonresident license cost a manageable ten dollars and fifty cents. And incredibly, there was no limit.

Ontario lived in my dreams during the long winter months. I queried my deer hunting friends about a Canadian bear hunt in the spring, but they were less than enthusiastic. Unresolved questions about how to hunt spring bear, along with concerns about exactly where to go in Ontario's vast wilderness, dampened their interest.

It was true that I knew nothing of bear hunting. It was also true that I had no clear idea of where to go. And it was rapidly becoming apparent, given the tepid responses of my friends, that my dreamed-of bear hunt would be a solo venture. These along with a number of other compelling reasons to defer the hunt were bantered about. Sensible concerns, one and all. I give them careful consideration, then decided on the only course of action that seemed reasonable. I went.

Early spring of 1961 saw southern Wisconsin basking in delightful weather. Nature's bursting renewal of life sent surges of restlessness through my winter-wearied soul. It was time to go.

I gathered my equipment. It seemed meager indeed as I loaded it into my car. An army issue pup tent, a sleeping bag and air mattress borrowed from a friend, an army surplus five-gallon container for water, and a small hand axe. No cooking utensils were included. Canned food heated over a fire would suffice.

My way north took me through Wisconsin and well into Minnesota before weariness compelled me to stop. Rather than bother with the tent, I slept in the car, curled up in the sleeping bag. The cold induced me to run the car heater several times during the night. My borrowed sleeping bag provided uncomfortably scant insulation.

By noon the following day I was well into Canada, still with no clear destination in mind, but, as though guided by the pole star, driving irresistibly north. The narrowing gravel roads, pinching tighter where Bailey bridges crossed rushing streams, stretched like slender ribbons through an endless expanse of pristine forest.

About the time my gas gauge began suggesting a limit to my northern travels, a few scattered houses centered around a small general store came into view. The single gas pump in front of the store provided a welcome sight.

I pulled up to the pump. A woman emerged from the store and asked if she could help me. I told her to fill it up and went into the store to wait. The crowded interior was lined with shelves of canned and packaged goods. An assortment of gardening tools hung from ceiling hooks. Behind the small counter a grouping of pictures flanked a large portrait of England's Queen Elizabeth. The Empire still reached far.

The woman finished filling my tank and came into the store. I withdrew a bill from my wallet and handed it to her. An odd expression crossed her face. She turned the bill in her hands, examining it curiously.

"What's this?" she asked.

"Why it's a twenty-dollar bill," I replied.

"No it isn't," she countered, pulling a multicolored Canadian bank note from her cash drawer. "This is a twenty-dollar bill."

And indeed it was. The only kind of twenty-dollar bill of any value to this Canadian store owner. She had no familiarity with American money and as far as she was concerned my strange looking piece of paper was worthless.

Money exchange never crossed my mind. An oversight suddenly turning into an embarrassing dilemma. I was vainly trying to convince the store owner to accept my twenty dollars when a young man about my age entered the store. He turned out to be a local resident. Fortunately the young man intervened and explained that American money was not only good in Canada, but might even be worth a little more than face value.

This last bizarre revelation was more than the store owner could accept. She did, however, eventually agree to an even conversion and carefully counted out my gas purchase change in Canadian dollars while looking a bit like someone throwing good money after bad.

Relieved to have my money problem solved, and with several good Canadian dollars secure in my pocket, I soon left the tiny hamlet behind and continued north. Hours passed without another sign of civilization. My intention was to continue on until half my gas remained, then set up camp wherever the moment found me.

The road gradually deteriorated, turning into little more than a forest track. Ruts and protruding boulders slowed my progress to a crawl. The wisdom of proceeding farther was turning in my mind when a high mound of dirt across the road settled the matter. Directly behind the mound a wide river swept steadily northward. No bridge spanned the river and the far bank remained an unbroken wall of trees. I literally had reached the end of the road.

The intense sound of silence, disturbed only by the faint murmur of the river, held me awhile before camp chores called. When dusk began to press, I moved downstream to a small opening on the bank of the river, cleared a section of ground, and set up the pup tent, pounding the stakes in with the back of my hand axe. The air mattress and sleeping bag filled half of the tent's interior. My spare clothes, canned goods, and water can filled the other half. I scooped out a circular fire pit, lined it with rocks, and gathered a supply of wood from the downed timber around the tent.

I built a fire and warmed a can of beef stew, then watched the river and listened to the silence while I ate. The stars glittered in the darkening sky. The flicker of the fire barely held back the night from the tiny, glimmering circle of my existence.

The pleasure of the evening was rapidly dispelled as the night cold seeped through my lightweight sleeping bag. The borrowed air mattress had come with a leak and my continuing attempts to keep it inflated only resulted in growing frustration. The cold ground coupled with the cold air quickly drained my body heat. The night passed miserably.

Dawn at last sent its diffused light through the tent. I crawled out of the sleeping bag and tried to start a fire, but with my hands shaking uncontrollably from the cold, it was impossible even to hold a match, much less strike one. The car heater tempted me, but using it might not leave enough gas to get back to the little general store. My shaking became violent. In desperation I began to run through the woods, trying to generate body heat from the exertion. My shivering gradually subsided. I returned to camp and soon had a roaring fire underway. The morning brightened.

Some other sleeping arrangement would have to be made to avoid another bitter night. I set to work remaking camp. I converted the pup tent into two shelter halves and arranged the halves into a lean-to. A steady fire tended through the night in front of the lean-to would provide reflected heat. I cut a generous quantity of evergreen boughs and piled them high inside the lean-to. The springy boughs would provide a cushioned, off-the-ground bed. Between the fire and the boughs, the nights promised to pass more comfortably.

I put a few finishing touches on my rearranged camp, loaded my rifle, and set off into the woods. The morning held cloudy and gray, prolonging the chill of the night. I followed the river downstream, still-hunting slowly along the bank. Neither animal nor bird enlivened my passage. Half the morning drifted by before I angled beyond hearing of the murmuring waters and began a wide circle into the woods.

Silence reigned away from the river. The deep forest seemed almost forboding in its gray stillness. Life seemed to shun the stark forest depths. A few hushed hours turned me back to the cheery murmur of the river. My lean-to appeared like a welcome haven through the thinning trees.

Camp held me long enough to heat a can of beans over a hasty fire. Then, with the warming sun making a belated appearance and a full afternoon before me, I set off to explore upstream.

The afternoon continued sunny, intensifying the pleasure of roaming unfettered through the wilderness. But still, no sign of wildlife appeared during my quiet passage.

Midafternoon found me easing through a dense stand of pines when an opening became visible ahead. I broke into the opening to an unexpected sight. A small lake, partially covered with ice, glistened in the afternoon sun. And beside the lake, nestled in a cutover clearing, stood a tiny cabin.

I approached the cabin and noticed the door closed but without a lock. Curiosity drew me inside. The interior was Spartan. A built-in bunk filled one wall, crude shelves lined another. A rough-hewn table sat across from the door with a sawn tree stump serving as a chair. A metal-drum stove occupied the center of the dirt floor. One small window let in a shadow of light. The logs cut down to construct the cabin created the clearing in which it stood. The cabin probably served as an overnight stop for a trapper running his winter trap line. It appeared not to have been occupied for some time.

I stepped outside the cabin. The partially frozen lake danced and sparkled in the sun. A nearby bubbling spring added a steady flow to the lake's thawing surface. I followed the shoreline a ways in both directions, discovering moose tracks but no hoped-for imprints to mark the presence of a bear.

I finally left the pleasant setting and retraced my steps through the pines. The waning afternoon called me back to the river and to camp. A generous supply of firewood was gathered before supper and bed. The night passed tolerably, although a bit restlessly, the chilling air awakening me from time to time as the fire died down. A quick rekindling from the wood pile soon set me dozing from the renewed warmth, only to repeat the waking cycle when the fire ebbed.

In the morning I decided to move camp to the trapper's cabin. The country around it possessed more allure and the game sign, modest though it appeared, held more promise than the sterile woods of the preceding day. Of course, purely as an afterthought, there was that metal-drum stove.

I had no pack so I made one out of my sleeping bag, filling it with most of my food and some spare clothes. A rope served to secure it and make two shoulder loops. The five-gallon container could remain behind. The spring would provide a reliable source of water.

By midmorning I was settled in the cabin, with a supply of firewood from a pile of cut logs split and stacked near the stove. I made two sandwiches to carry for lunch, then set off to hunt around the lake and along a ridge rising in the distance.

Occasional moose tracks showed where sun-thawed mud touched the lake's shoreline. A number of vague impressions other than those of a moose were also evident, but none my unpracticed eye dared proclaim to be that of a bear. I turned into the woods at the far end of the lake and hunted toward the ridge that had been visible from the cabin.

The weather held sunny and pleasant. By the time I topped the ridge my unneeded coat was slung in a tight bundle over my back. A captivating vista rewarded my climb to the ridge top. A primal forest, sprinkled with blue-shimmering lakes, spread unbounded to the horizon. Not a sign of civilization marred the jeweled greenwood setting, but the grandeur of the scene was tempered with bewildering thoughts of how and where, in all that immense wilderness, a bear could ever be found.

The puzzle of it stayed with me as I crossed the ridge and hunted to the nearest lake. A stand of poplar bordered the edge of the lake, offering an enticing setting in which to enjoy lunch.

Several downed trees, showing unmistakable patterns of the hourglass chiselling's of a beaver, offered welcome choices of shoreline seats.

During lunch I noticed a large beaver swimming along the shore of the lake. Apparently it also was the beaver's lunchtime, for it regularly approached the bank to briefly sample some delectable morsel. The beaver's route in time brought it to the poplar serving as my seat. The hungry animal began chewing on the tender bark of the branch my right foot was resting on, its two, yellowing, oversized front teeth chomping greedily toward my toes. The novelty of the scene was too fascinating to spoil by moving. The beaver remained oblivious to my presence as it gnawed steadily closer to my boot. Novelty was about to give way to a judicious withdrawal of my foot, when suddenly a sharp crack resounded over the lake. Something had disturbed the beaver's heretofore unnoticed mate, and the warning splash of its broad tail sent my lunch companion instantly underwater.

The rest of the afternoon passed without incident, the beaver furnishing my sole wildlife sighting of the day. The little cabin in the clearing provided a welcome shelter for the night. The metal-drum stove blazed cheerfully, although my initial generosity with the wood created a sauna-like atmosphere in the close quarters, temporarily driving me outside. Once properly banked, the little stove served well through the night.

The following day I hunted the near ridge, crossed through a broad valley to a parallel ridge, then followed that a considerable distance before turning in a wide circle back to the cabin. The weather continued pleasant and the venue remained grand, but no bear or even a suggestion of a bear was discovered.

In the morning of the fourth day I struck away from the ridges into a lower country. Shortly after leaving the cabin something went crashing off through a cluster of willows. I brought my rifle half to bear in startled surprise. The sound faded quickly. I watched intently but could see no movement in the dense thicket. I continued forward with keyed alertness.

An hour into the morning, along a narrow trail skirting a marsh, moose tracks traced in the soft earth. I followed the trail until it faded into a spongy depression edging a small swale. And there, along the edge of the swale, the ground revealed the unmistakable impression of a bear's paw, distinguishable even to my unpracticed eye. Here at last lay definitive sign. Where the elusive creature that left the sign now roamed remained hopefully to be discovered, but at least one tantalizing reality became confirmed. A bear was in the area.

I continued in the direction the bear's tracks led. Long stretches of hard ground confused the trail, interrupting my progress. My chances of overtaking the bear, whatever they might have been, grew slimmer with each delay. Still I pressed on, hoping with every new perspective to sight the bear.

Hours passed and the trail became hopeless, the hard ground leaving no discernable sign. I continued in the general direction the bear seemed to be going, pausing frequently to scrutinize the woods ahead.

The trail had long been cold when movement ahead suddenly caught my eye. Something appeared to be stirring alongside a distant tree. I eased down to one knee to better see beneath the intervening branches. Nothing. Then, there it was again. A slight movement of indistinct black on the ground right next to the tree. I waited, trying to define the object.

The more I stared the more my mind began to trace the image of a bear into the movement. I began to suspect that this might even be the bear who's tracks had led me this way. It appeared as though the bear was laying down alongside the tree, shifting occasionally for whatever reason. The longer I stared, the more firmly the aspect of a bear took shape. The continuing movements accentuated the image.

I raised my rifle and looked through the peep sight. All that could be seen to sight on was an indeterminate black mass. I dared not consider a shot without certain definition. I had to get closer.

I began crawling forward, carefully removing sticks and debris from my path. The distance slowly closed. The bear remained undisturbed, although it stirred from time to time.

An intervening evergreen screened me as I crept nearer. I paused behind the evergreen, then carefully peered around it. A new perspective opened. The bear alongside the tree resolved itself.

It was a curled-away piece of black bark, hanging loosely by a fiber hinge, swaying gently with the slightest breeze.

Once on the Sugar River Bottoms, I conducted a brilliant stalk on a flock of mallards only to discover that they were decoys. I felt incredibly foolish then, and I felt incredibly foolish at that moment watching the black bark sway mockingly in the breeze. The rest of the afternoon passed in a desultory fashion.

The low country drew me back at first light the next morning. Bear and moose sign had been seen there. During the first hour a faint flicker in the woods gave hint of a possible presence. In the midmorning hour, an impressive set of moose tracks was discovered, showing huge in comparison to the dainty imprints of a deer. A startled red squirrel scolded me from the safety of a pine limb as I hurried out of its noisy presence. Even a ruffed grouse put in an appearance. The morning had come alive. Of bears, however, there was no sign.

The early hours passed in hopeful expectation, but they passed without that hope being fulfilled. At noon I sat along the shore of a small lake and ate lunch. The day continued pleasant, tempting me to tarry, but my time was running short. Five days were all I could hunt. My job waited impatiently.

I followed along the edge of the lake, crossed over a ridge, and hunted carefully through another lower area. A few birds were the only residents that made their presence known.

I returned to the cabin in midafternoon, packed my belongings in the sleeping bag, and struck out for my lean-to by the river. The time had come to begin my journey home.

I stocked up on wood at the lean-to and piled a few more boughs on my bed. There seemed little doubt that the snug cabin would be missed, but two long days of driving required an early start, and the car was there. I stoked up the fire and warmed my last can of beef stew as night descended. The north wind sighed gently. I huddled close to the warmth, involved in the night and the flickering flames until weariness engulfed me. Then I lay down on the springy boughs and soon drifted off to the crackle of the fire and the whispering murmur of the river.

My gas gauge still showed a tiny space between the needle and the empty mark when I pulled into the little general store. The proprietress smiled in recognition. She seemed pleased to see me. I asked her to fill it up and she wondered if I planned on paying her with more of that American money. I said no, I still had some real Canadian dollars left. She laughed and I laughed and we both stood there grinning at each other with little more to say.

When she finished filling the tank, I followed her into the store, noticing nothing out of place from the week before. The crowded shelves were still well-stocked with goods, and if one of the tools hanging from the ceiling hooks had been sold, a replacement hung in its stead. Queen Elizabeth still looked out regally from her portrait behind the counter, but I noticed one of the pictures in the group surrounding the Queen had been changed. Some presumably valued relative had given up their place of honor above the portrait of Her Majesty. In that person's place, prominently displayed for all to admire, beautifully framed and highlighted, was my former twenty-dollar bill.

Chapter 4

To The West

Wyoming drew me next. The enticement of new country, along with an impressive big game list, proved an irresistible lure. After inquiries to the Game and Fish Department, I settled on a combined antelope and mule deer hunt for September of 1961.

Two acquaintances from work joined me in making plans for the Wyoming hunt. Between us we were able to assemble a respectable camping outfit. Splitting the expenses three ways would ease the financial requirements. Unfortunately, while Irv and I were waiting at my home for our companion to arrive so we could start on the hunt, he called to cancel. The reason had something to do with his wife. He also belatedly informed us that since he was not going, we would have to do without his tent.

Irv and I set off for Wyoming, resigned to sleeping in the car should it rain. With only two of us our expense money might get a little tight. But Irv and I were of the same mind. We would work it out along the way.

Our introduction to Wyoming came at first light as we crossed the border from Nebraska. We had driven straight through for nine hundred miles. I was dozing in the back seat after my turn at the wheel when I sensed the car come to an abrupt halt.

"Wake up!" Irv exclaimed. "Deer crossing the road. Must be mule deer."

My foggy brain cleared to register the sight of three does followed by a truly impressive buck trotting across the highway. The three does quickly bounded out of sight over a small ridge, but the buck paused on the crest, majestically skylined in the early morning light. We watched him for fully a minute as he proudly stood less than fifty yards away. Then slowly, almost disdainfully, as though aware of the fact that our permits were not valid in that area, the buck walked out of sight over the ridge.

We saw no more mule deer that morning. In their place antelope began appearing near and far across the rolling prairie. A single buck came into view a hundred yards to our right, followed by a pair of does on a near rise. Then three more does began pacing our car on the driver's side, gliding along in effortless motion. We matched their impressive gait for a considerable distance. Suddenly, with an unexpected burst of acceleration, the trio dashed across our front and ducked under a line fence on the other side of the road. The does raced away over the prairie in a revealing display of speed and grace, their rosette rump patches flaring white above the green-clad sage.

The rolling terrain merged into irregular sagebrush flats cut with washes and gullies. Rocky hills lay in the background. Groups of antelope dotted the flats, paying little attention when we stopped to glass them. Distance apparently represented safety. As long as several hundred yards separated us, the animals showed little concern.

The day had dawned sunny with a few cumulus clouds in the west. The clouds increased by midmorning, defusing the sun into a patchwork quilt of light and shadow across the sagebrush flats. Numerous herds of antelope gamboled through the patchwork, as though engaged in an immense game of checkers on the broad mosaic. Hundreds of the animals excited our gaze as we tried to absorb the remarkable sight.

The highway continued across the boundless prairie. We came to a fork in the road and turned to the right, for it appeared the way less traveled. Sagebrush grew to the roadway, obliterating any suggestion of a shoulder. In many places the sage encroached upon the road, threatening at intervals to reclaim portions of it as prairie. Off to the west lay the Rattlesnake Range, and to the east, the North Platte River. Antelope sightings began to take on added excitement. We had entered our permit area.

We hunted in what obviously was the most practical way. We continued down the road. There seemed little point in wandering off through the prairie when antelope practically surrounded us where we were. They were there. And in numbers. A grand, wondrous sight to our novice eyes.

We continued on. Soon a single antelope appeared off to our right, while spread out on a distant hillside twenty more browsed contentedly on the bitter sage. A good buck fed among them. We weighed the possibility of stalking within range, but the odds seemed long. Two does appeared close to the road a short way past the group of twenty. Beyond them a lone buck stood enticingly broadside. We debated the buck through the binoculars. He settled any questions by ambling off well out of range.

A buck and a doe appeared next about three hundred yards away, both standing broadside facing right, with the buck on the left. We eased out of the car to better glass them. They stood watching us, cautious but not alarmed. The buck appeared equal to any we had seen. We continued glassing. The choice was left to me. I decided to take a look through my scope, still not sure.

I raised my rifle and centered the buck in the field of view. The crosshairs settled behind his shoulder just above the blending of tan and white on his side. Heat waves shimmered in the magnification. The antelope danced a little in the mirage, but the crosshairs still held steady. I studied the buck. He studied me back. My breathing remained controlled. I became immersed in the sight picture, letting the image absorbed me. Nothing registered beyond it. No decision was weighed. Resolution became subliminal. There was a simple crossing into acceptance. A subconscious willing. The rifle recoiled and the antelope fell to the ground.

And it was over. Almost before it began. A look at my watch revealed that only twenty-two hours had passed since leaving home a thousand miles away. And in little more than a heartbeat, my antelope hunt was over. It seemed too embarrassingly easy. Then I thought back to my bear hunt that spring, a week of persistent dawn to dusk effort with only a few tracks sighted to show for my labors. I decided to just gratefully accept what fate had offered.

The walk to the downed buck confirmed the distance, three hundred yards. He had been taken cleanly through the lungs. Irv drove the car to the antelope. I lifted the ten-gallon milk can used to carry water out of the trunk and dressed the buck, thankful for the cleansing liquid. With that task completed, we set off to find a buck for Irv.

One was not long in coming. Within half an hour a twin to mine presented itself. Irv dropped him with a single shot. The antelope part of our hunt was complete and it was not even noon of the first day.

The heat of the midday sun required that we take care of the antelope quickly. We picked up Highway 287 and drove south into Rawlins where the two bucks were dropped off at a locker plant. Then we continued south toward Saratoga and our mule deer area beyond the North Platte.

The valley of the North Platte River runs between the Medicine Bow Range and the Sierra Madre Range. Saratoga straddles the river. From the bridge north of town, on a clear day, you can see Medicine Bow Peak rising twelve thousand feet off to the east. Highway 130 turns toward the mountains south of Saratoga, crosses the river, then ascends four thousand feet from the valley floor before crossing Snowy Range Pass, 10,847 feet above sea level. The pass is closed for the winter when the first heavy snow falls. Rolling foothills grade from the river into the mountains. Cottonwoods line the river mixed with aspens that climb through the foothills to the high country where Engelmann spruce and subalpine fir predominate. The golden leaves of the aspens quake in the fall with the slightest breeze. Pockets of the gilded trees shimmer like grounded suns among the stately evergreens.

Mule deer roam the Medicine Bow Country, from the river to the pass. One has only to find them.

We started our search along the river, for it was pleasant there. Towering cottonwoods invited us to shelter from the glaring sun. We found a shady place to leave the car, then set out to scout the lower hills.

We walked only a short distance through the scattered bushes along the river when movement ahead attracted us. A turkey was feeding through the cover. We stopped. Several more appeared, pecking industriously along the ground. Here was an unexpected sight. We held our place as the plump fowl advanced. Suggestions of roast turkey were voiced. Temptation traipsed lightly between us.

The unwary fowl pecked away without concern, oblivious to our dinner deliberations. Temptation tugged again. We steadfastly refused to yield. On the birds came. One of us began to waver. The turkeys began to eye us suspiciously. We assumed an innocent air. The turkeys would have none of it. They suddenly began to fear for themselves. In ones and twos they lumbered mightily toward the sky, their flailing wings struggling to lift their ponderous bodies. The turkeys clambered off through the brush in a thunderous din. Finally the commotion subsided. Silence returned. Irv sighed. He wore the unfathomable look of a condemned man denied his last meal. I had no idea Irv was so fond of turkey. The tempting vision faded. We saw the great birds no more.

We stood for a time in thoughtful contemplation, then split up and headed into the hills. The afternoon continued hot, with layered clouds providing occasional shady relief. Tee-shirts became the hunting garb of the day. The country rolled away to the distant, green-clad mountains. Cottonwoods hugged the water courses. Tall alpine bushes of undetermined variety clustered among scattered copses of trees.

It was a relief to be free of the car. The unrestrained pleasure of roaming in the open drew me deeper into the hills. I halted on vantage points and glassed the far ranges. After the hundreds of antelope sighted in the morning, the empty hill country appeared strangely desolate despite the glory of the aspens. Other than their quaking leaves, nothing was moving in the afternoon sun.

Irv and I met in the cottonwoods at dusk. He had seen no deer. We decided to camp where we were and hunt the hill country again in the morning. The evening continued warm with no threat of rain. Irv elected to sleep in the car while

I found a comfortable spot on the ground. Being an inch near six feet, a car seat gets a bit cramped. I heard my first coyote in the night.

There were deer along the river in the morning. Our cottonwood camp was barely out of sight when a small doe walked out of a heavy clump of bushes to stand quartering toward me. I tested her through the scope, for our permits allowed her taking, but this was not the time.

The cottonwoods and alpine bushes held a few more does, but no bucks were in evidence. I followed the river south for a considerable distance before swinging into the hills. The more open terrain intrigued me. The deer evidently did not share my fascination, for once in the hills none were seen. The morning passed with glorious weather and I tasted a bit of the pioneer's pleasure in the discovery of new country. It was good to be wandering free in a land that stretched to the mountains.

We met back at the cottonwoods at noon to compare notes. Irv had seen a few deer in the early hours, none of which were bucks. An afternoon hunt was considered but the midday heat sapped our enthusiasm. The notion also was dawning on us that deer were not particularly active in the heat of the day. We decided instead to drive into the hills and explore toward the higher ranges.

We came upon a dirt track that wove through the foothills and followed it for several miles. It seemed to go on forever. We loafed along, enjoying the day along with the novelty of new terrain. At a point that overlooked several connecting valleys, we halted and set up our modest camp, then split up to watch for deer. If they were moving, they did not move around us. We slept in the foothills that night. Irv curled up in the car while I choose a bed on the ground under a canopy of brilliant stars. Coyotes yipped again in a discordant serenade.

We watched from our vantage points in the morning before hiking our separate ways through the valleys. Ten o'clock saw us back at camp with no deer to report. The river began to look like our best bet. We broke camp and headed back down the track.

Breaking camp basically meant throwing our sleeping bags in the back seat, loading our ten-gallon water container, two-burner Coleman stove, and small collapsible table in the trunk, then driving off. We were not heavily encumbered.

We reached the main road and continued into Saratoga to replenish a few supplies and get something cold to drink. A car in town with two impressive bucks tied to the roof immediately caught our attention. The successful hunters were only too happy to relate their experiences. When pressed as to where the bucks were taken, they waved vaguely toward the Medicine Bow Range. The high country was where most of the deer were at this early part of the season, they agreed, and if big bucks were in our plans, we definitely best get to the mountains.

There was authority in their advice. The two big bucks provided it. We set out for the mountains.

After Highway 130 crosses into the Medicine Bow National Forest, climbing east toward Snowy Range Pass, a number of graveled and dirt roads branch off to the north and south. The better ones are lake access roads. The lesser ones are forest service roads. And the miserable ones are old logging roads. On the assumption that an old logging road would lead us to less disturbed country, we turned north on the first one that looked promising and began to climb into an evergreen forest of spruce and fir.

Old Chevrolets were not designed for rough mountain work. The rock-strewn logging road tested the car severely. The trail, for road soon became a misnomer, crawled along a steep embankment with a clear-water stream running below. Farther on, the trail skirted a beaver pond in an open meadow. Evidence of the beaver's industriousness lay everywhere. Not all their work was profitable, however. A large tree gnawed past the falling point lay tightly wedged against its neighbor. The thought of dropping the supporting tree and thus salvaging both apparently had not occurred to the beavers, for the other tree bore not a tooth mark.

The trail steepened beyond the beaver pond, squeezing at times between the mountainside on our right and a sharp drop-off on our left. We crawled on, coming at last to a level stretch where we stopped to make camp.

We cooked a hasty meal on the Coleman stove, anxious to set off into the inviting forest. A pair of Canada jays, more colorfully known as whiskey jacks or camp robbers, became attracted to our food preparation. The jays were quite bold, swooping very close to us looking for a handout. One pranced warily around my feet as I teased it with pieces of bread.

We finished eating and prepared to explore our new hunting grounds. Irv elected to hunt ahead while I decided to swing around through the spruce and come out above the beaver pond, planning to watch the meadow there until dark.

I followed the trail back a few hundred yards to where a secondary logging trail swung off into the spruce and began hunting along it. The cooler mountain air made a sweatshirt welcome. The forest there was not unlike some of the northern regions of Wisconsin, only steeper. The chattering red squirrels were the same. One quickly discovered me and incessantly announced to the forest at large the presence of an intruder.

I soon left the noisy red squirrel behind and was quietly moving along the trail when, in the trees ahead, the semblance of a deer materialized. The outline was indistinct, but the image caught and held my gaze. I halted, then raised my rifle to get a better look through the scope.

Yes! It was a deer! Standing broadside behind a screening of second growth. The body showed clearly but the head remained a vague impression. If there were antlers, they were indistinguishable from the screening branches. I eased down to one knee to change my perspective. The branches still obscured the head. A little movement by the deer would have been helpful, but it remained a shadowy statue.

A thinning in the branches opened up a clear shot to the lungs. The crosshairs held steady. The deer appeared large, certainly larger than the does seen along the river. Still, without seeing more of the animal, there was too much of a question. I waited.

Deer probably are never pressured by time. A minute or an hour likely registers without consequence to them. Their lives play out in the present, and the present is not time sensitive. Not so with humans. At least not with the human in that standoff with the deer. The minutes began to weigh heavily. Patience fought a loosing battle with a growing impulse to action. Perhaps a different angle would reveal the deer's head. I began a careful shift to the left.

The deer exploded across the narrow trail and was immediately swallowed up in the dense spruce on the other side. A second was all I had, and a second was not enough for a shot. It was enough though to see the broad upward sweep of the deer's antlers. They made a regal crown.

A lingering disappointment, yet tempered with the excitement of knowing we had found the right country. I hunted even more cautiously, hoping to come across the buck again, but he had vanished into the mountains.

I continued on to a vantage point overlooking the beaver pond meadow and sat there until dusk. When the crosshairs blended with the dark, I arose and followed the logging trail back to camp.

Irv had seen no live deer but did find a recent kill, possibly made by some animal, for little remained of it. He claimed the skull and antlers which were already tied to the front of the car. A large rack with four points on each side. Another encouraging sign. We slept where we were that night, high in the mountains. I heard no coyotes.

The morning brought me again to the beaver pond meadow. The mountain chill surprised me after the mild valley nights. I put the hood up on my sweatshirt and shivered through the early dawn. I watched until the sun flooded the meadow but saw neither deer nor beaver.

The secondary trail of the preceding day drew me back with hopes of again coming across that big buck. As I eased around a slight bend, I came face to face with a deer walking down the trail toward me. But it was not the buck. A large doe was approaching instead. She stopped hardly thirty yards away. We watched each other until her patience wore thin. Then she bounded off down the mountain with that peculiar pogo-stick gait.

Irv reported no deer when we met back at camp. Higher up toward the mountain summits we noticed some larger open areas, probably clearings left from earlier logging operations. The second growth there might hold some deer and also give us more glassing area than the dense evergreens surrounding our present location. We decided to move our camp higher.

The logging trail did not improve with elevation. At one point seepage from springs created a wide area of impassable boggy ground. The loggers had built a corduroy roadway with peeled logs sunk in the mire. Probably when they used it the logs were covered with planking. Now they just presented a washboard path. We tested it by walking across. It seemed solid. But our weight hardly compared to the weight of the car. The trail beyond appeared passable. We debated. Then we went.

The car bounced across the logs at an exaggerated crawl. The other side was reached without mishap. We continued upward. Another barrier soon halted us. Three trees had fallen close together across the trail. The size of the larger one made my little hand axe look painfully inadequate. But we took turns chopping and after an hour of steady labor rolled the last tree out of the trail.

On we climbed, hoping no more surprises awaited us. We were bumping along watching for oversize rocks when up ahead a blue grouse appeared. Here was a welcome surprise. And one we could legitimately accept. We stopped. I loaded my twenty-two revolver and began stalking the unwary bird. The blue grouse acted almost tame in comparison to the jittery ruffed grouse back in Wisconsin. I closed the distance while the grouse pecked away unconcernedly. At the shot, the grouse fluttered briefly, then was still.

The trail ended in a large clearing. We came to an opening in a small grove of spruce and set up camp. I cleaned the grouse while coffee perked, fried it with some potatoes, and warmed a can of green beans. We ate, then loafed under a shady spruce with a cup of coffee. The mountains were warm in the midday sun. The whiskey jacks entertained us with their begging. We fed them scraps while watching fleecy clouds bump into the mountains and wondered just where else we could possibly want to be at that moment.

We hunted the second growth and high meadows that afternoon and evening, and again early the next morning, after which we began to question the wisdom of our moving, for we saw not a deer. We met in camp for late-morning coffee and decided to hunt some of the offshoot trails below the meadows. One of those trails branched off into the spruce a few hundred yards beyond camp. It branched again shortly after leaving the main trail. We chose to start there.

When we reached the fork of the offshoot trail, Irv continued down the right branch while I swung off on the left one. I followed the trail fifty yards before it unexpectedly turned and began running parallel with the trail Irv had gone down. That meant Irv was somewhere to my right front, although he was not visible through the heavy cover.

I continued along the trail expecting it to eventually turn left again. The spruce limbs hung close to the narrow pathway, limiting visibility. I moved slowly, peering into the thick evergreen growth.

The trail occasionally ran through small clearings where the second growth had not yet taken hold. I paused briefly at the edge of one of those clearings and then began to follow the trail through it when a deer broke from the cover and started to run across the clearing to my right.

It was a buck! A big buck!

I released the safety and shouldered my rifle, bringing my cheek down to that familiar spot that centered my eye in the scope. I swung the rifle to pick up the deer. It bounded into the scope.

Irv was somewhere ahead.

The deer settled into the crosshairs.

Irv was somewhere ahead.

I swung with the bounding deer.

Irv was somewhere ahead.

I held the final pressure on the trigger.

Irv was somewhere ahead.

The deer disappeared into the trees.

Silence.

Ka-BOOM!

A pause.

Ka-BOOM!

Silence.

I waited, rifle ready, eyes fixed on the clearing, anticipating, hoping, wishing for the return of the deer, but he did not come.

The forest remained silent. There was no sound from Irv. I started through the dense spruce in the direction of the shots and broke out on the other trail to find a beaming Irv looking down on a beautiful mule deer buck sporting two long double forks on each side.

"He darn near run me over. I dropped him with the first shot but I didn't want to take a chance so I gave him a finisher."

I will confess to a twinge of envy. The deer was most impressive.

Irv dressed the buck and we dragged it out to the main logging trail, which we followed into camp. Our little campsite took on a far more cheery aspect with the mighty buck showing proudly from a stout spruce limb.

I combed the trails and high meadows the rest of the day as well as the following morning, but Irv's big buck was the last one either of us saw.

The time finally arrived to break camp. Our trip down the mountain, with gravity favoring us, went smoothly except for one stretch of boggy ground where we managed to get stuck. A couple of muddy hours ensued while we jacked the tires up far enough to jam small logs and branches under them, only to have to repeat the process when the spinning tires bogged down again. Our only mishap on a rather adventurous mountain trail.

We reached the valley and drove into Saratoga. The mountains of the Medicine Bow and the Snowy Range loomed imposingly over the town. I knew that grand deer still roamed those lofty heights. And I knew the coming year would find me in search of them again.

Chapter 5

Wyoming Days

The aspens of the Medicine Bow and Snowy Range shimmered in my mind through that winter and the following spring. Irv remained content with his first mountain hunt, but my brother, Bud, and his friend, Bill, entered into plans for a return to that grand country.

-1-

Early fall 1962. We chugged Bill's heavily ladened Chevrolet up the familiar mountain logging trail of the previous year, bumping over rocks while Bill hung tight to the right watching the ever-deepening valley drop off to the stream bed below. A corduroy roadway across boggy ground gave us a few anxious moments, but the groaning Chevrolet bounced cautiously across without mishap. We arrived well after midday at the end of the trail in a clearing surrounded by spruce and lofty mountain peaks. We set up the tent, arranged our camp, then hiked out on separate paths to scout the rest of the afternoon for next morning's hunt.

The snow started as we gathered back in camp. Heavy, wet, slow-settling flakes. Bud and Bill voiced some apprehension. I reminded them that it was still early in the season. The snow would likely dissipate in a few days and in the meantime would be a boon to our deer hunting.

The snow continued, sent swirling with gusty winds that began to howl down from the mountaintops. We huddled in our sleeping bags listening to the tent bellow and snap. A lull held for a few minutes. I took a quick glimpse out the tent flap. Moisture-laden flakes clouded the night and clung heavily to the evergreens. Windrowed drifts obscured the ground. The car stood outlined in white silhouette, blanketed under an eerie, frosted shroud.

The wind roared again, sending the flakes into a chaotic dance. I tied the flap shut and nestled back into the warmth of my sleeping bag. The mountains bellowed.

The clinging, heavy snow piled high through the night. We awoke in startled confusion when the tent collapsed under its weight. We struggled in the pitch dark to fight our way out from beneath a bewildering, intimidating confinement. A raging blizzard met our escape from the tent. We battled in the wind to clear away the wet-packed snow, fighting against the piercing blasts to re-erect the tent into some semblance of shelter. At last we made our frigid way back into our sleeping bags, dozing in fitful spurts. The wind raged.

In the first light of morning we peered outside to find a daunting blanket of white covering the mountain. Bill's Chevrolet was an indistinct mound, the trail down the mountain obliterated. For two hours we cleared snow, spun tires, pushed and rocked, measured success in feet gained, and finally admitted defeat with the car barely fifty yards from where we started.

We needed help to get the car down off that mountain before additional snow locked it in for good. We stuffed our pockets with candy bars, raisins, and other handy foods, then began our trek through the sometimes knee-high, wet, clinging snow. Mile after mile we slogged, taking turns breaking trail, legs stiffening from the cold, penetrating moisture. An exhausting, miserable descent.

An unplowed Highway 130 confronted us in the fading light of afternoon, closed for the season over 10,847-foot-high Snowy Range Pass. The name struck us with grim irony. We pushed through the snow down the undisturbed highway until we saw a light in a small cabin off to our right. Two hunters were butchering a deer. They took us in, thawed us out, and gave us a ride into Saratoga where we rented rooms in the hotel. I spent a couple of hours keeping the hotel's water heater at full throttle soaking in a sauna-temperatured tub.

The hotel keeper tried to encourage us the following morning by advising us not to worry about our car and equipment. He assured us we would get them down come spring.

Two days passed before we located a four-wheel-drive owner willing to risk the mountain trail. Fifty dollars was his price. My brother volunteered to accompany him, there being room for only one passenger. They made it, retrieving Bill's car and our equipment. After their return the driver informed us that had he known the treacherous condition of that mountain trail, he never would have agreed to go. When we pooled our fifty dollars to pay him, he advised us the price was fifty dollars apiece. We felt disinclined to argue.

We salvaged one partial day of hunting. In keeping with the tone of the trip, not a deer was seen.

-2-

The following year when I broached the subject of another Wyoming deer hunt to my brother, he answered with a pained expression saying he thought he'd had about all the deer hunting fun out west that he felt entitled to. Bill just rolled his eyes and muttered something about the vengeance of heaven.

I made plans to go alone until a friend, hearing of my earlier success on antelope, singular though it was, expressed a desire to join me. Jack had no particular interest in mule deer, being satisfied with Wisconsin's whitetails, but the uniqueness of an antelope hunt intrigued him. So I changed my plans from the mountains to the prairies, settling on an area around Gillette, the self-proclaimed Antelope Capital of the World.

The claim was not without merit. When Jack and I headed south from Gillette on the first of October, we soon encountered herds large and small. But they seemed skittish, quickly bolting whenever we stopped to glass. We saw many antelope from afar, including several good bucks, but our attempts at stalking them ran afoul of their alertness.

At midmorning we came upon a herd of fifty feeding in the middle of a flat tableland half a mile away. Two respectable bucks, along with a few smaller ones, showed temptingly in our binoculars. The antelope watched us cautiously for a couple minutes, then resumed feeding, although our presence remained under scrutiny.

A dry wash angled in their direction, but how close it came to the herd the glasses failed to reveal. We loaded our rifles, and under a few still watchful eyes, nonchalantly disappeared into the dry wash.

For part of the way we could stand upright, allowing us to trot in single file a hundred yards toward the herd. Then the dry wash began to grow shallow, forcing us to proceed in an ever-increasingly stooped position.

We paused often to relieve the stress on our backs. Once I chanced a brief look over the edge, my face obscured by a sagebrush. The antelope continued to feed peaceably.

We gradually became reduced to crawling on hands and knees, rifles slung over our backs. Soon even that would not do. We wriggled a short distance closer on our elbows before an alert doe spotted us. We were stuck, still out of range.

With nothing to loose we decided to simply stand up and start walking toward the herd. All eyes came instantly upon us. At the quarter-mile point we crossed their comfort threshold and the antelope trotted off, although not in an alarmed state. They settled down half a mile away and resumed feeding.

We tried our direct approach again, and again when the comfort threshold was reached the antelope reopened the distance. Hoping to confuse them, we tried approaching at an oblique angle. Our effort met with the same futility. It seemed as though an invisible quarter-mile alarm system surrounded them. They would tolerate no closer encroachment.

We looked longingly across the flat prairie. Not a hint of a contour offered any closer approach. I sat down, turned my scope to eight-power, and centered on one of the bucks. The range was long, surely four hundred yards. My Weaver scope incorporated range-finder crosshairs that subtended five inches at one hundred yards. With an average buck measuring fifteen inches from back to brisket, one fitting exactly between the crosshairs was three hundred yards away. Considerable light showed between the antelope and the crosshairs.

Dropping into a prone position revealed that the sagebrush prevented a clear firing lane. Jack had the same problem. We decided to try the shot sitting, giving each other time to sight in before firing individually when the hold seemed right.

I had discovered when practice shooting from a sitting position that a cord tied in a loop around my knees helped steady me and began using one when hunting. I took the cord I was carrying, looped it in place, wrapped into a tight sling, and locked my forearms into my tension-relieved knees. The scope still wavered but the arc seemed manageable.

My world condensed into a magnified circle. A buck antelope stood in the middle of the circle quartering slightly to the right, his clean lines distorted by shimmering heat waves. His pair of eyes met my eight-power scrutiny. I concentrated on trying to hold the horizontal crosshair one-half the buck's body depth above his back, knowing the bullet would drop fourteen inches at four hundred yards. The wind remained calm. The sight picture did not. The distance and the eight-power magnified every nervous quiver, sending the crosshairs shimmering in and out of the proper placement. Each time they shimmered in, I increased my pressure on the trigger. Finally the pressure broke the three-pound trigger pull, the rifle recoiled, and the buck crumpled to the ground. Jack's shot came almost simultaneously from my right.

The herd raced away, alarmed now. Jack and I stood up. The downed antelope lay hidden in the sage. Jack was not certain of his shot. Bucks ran mixed in with the departing herd but whether one was his or not remained unclear. I placed my hat on a sagebrush and walked toward the antelope. He lay cleanly shot through the lungs. With my buck accounted for, we carefully searched the surrounding area for Jack's, but ultimately concluded that he had missed.

After dressing the antelope, Jack and I paced back to my hat, then back to the buck. An average of four hundred paces. Forty paces short of a quarter-mile.

With one buck down and one to go we resumed our search. The antelope remained skittish, spoiling several of Jack's stalks. A small herd eventually came into view in rolling terrain that allowed Jack to make a close approach. A clean shot on a nice buck ended our hunt.

-3-

The coming of autumn the following year found me once again on a western route to Wyoming. After a two-day drive the large billboard proclaiming Gillette as the Antelope Capital of the World beamed out its now familiar welcome. Another handwritten sign on the outskirts of town also caught my attention. Free Venison Barbecue. A tempting reminder that I had not eaten since breakfast.

The sponsoring tavern was enjoying a brisk business. The noisy crowd seemed to be a mixture of locals and visiting hunters. A jukebox in the corner blared out a sad lament of lost love over the din of jumbled voices. A card game held its participants in rapt attention at a rear table. For a moment I wondered if I really had left Wisconsin, so reminiscent of there was the scene. But the profusion of cowboy hats gave a graphic reminder that I was indeed a thousand miles away.

I joined the barbecue line, built a tangy sandwich, and ordered a tap beer to wash it down. The card game intrigued me, as they always do. I wandered over to watch. I expected poker but found instead a game of euchre.

The locals, as they turned out to be, played a respectable game. When one of the pairs broke up, the table asked if anyone wanted to sit in. Temptation smiled seductively. The stakes were modest, but my funds were severely limited, totaling only a few minor-emergency dollars and gas money to get home.

Beats there the heart of a gambler who does not believe he will walk away a winner? I was well on the way to recovering my minor-emergency money when my partner sluffed off on my low suit lead, then covered my suit ace with the right bower after watching the deciding trick fall to a low trump. I dipped into the gas money to pay off the bump, the game, and my share of the winner's drinks.

I dipped slightly deeper to award myself a consolation beer before slipping quietly into the night, pondering whether my partner's card sense had suddenly deserted him or had the game not been as friendly as I presumed. Then, to add injury to insult, the free barbecue gave me heartburn.

I camped a few miles south of Gillette on a fenceless stretch of prairie. The clear skies led me to forego my tent. The stars glimmered bright overhead. I lay on my back in my sleeping bag and fancied I could see the constellations dancing their slow dance around Polaris. The faint aroma of sage scented the night. I wished for a coyote to howl, but none did.

In the morning I ate a quick breakfast, then commenced my search for antelope. The multiple herds of the previous year were apparently grazing far from their earlier haunts, for the prairie showed stark in its emptiness. I settled in at one observation point with my eight-power binoculars and began a methodical search of the far ranges. A small herd came faintly into view through the early morning light. They were not visible with the naked eye. In fact, they were barely discernable through the eight-power binoculars. Yet every one of the faint figures was staring intently at me. There seemed little chance of a stalk.

The morning progressed with only that distant herd offering a glimmer of hope. I moved from point to point, carefully searching the rolling prairie. Hours passed before, skylined on a far ridge, six antelope appeared. They spooked when they spotted me, disappearing over the ridge. I walked rapidly to just below the crest, then dropped to my knees and began to crawl forward. The far slope came into view. I lowered myself to my stomach and squirmed behind a small sagebrush that shielded my cautious gaze over the crest.

The antelope were moving single file toward the next hill. A small buck brought up the rear. I eased into a steady prone position and tried to estimate the range to the moving animals. They showed over three hundred yards through the scope. How much over it was hard to estimate due to their movement. I captured the buck in the scope, swung gently with him holding just over his back, and fired. He dropped instantly. The other five antelope spurted into a run, quickly disappearing over the far hill.

Three hundred and twenty-five paces brought me to the buck. The bullet had pierced his spine.

After dressing and skinning the buck, I wrapped the meat in cheesecloth and carried it the mile back to my car. I drove into Gillette, filled my gas tank, then counted my dwindling resources. It had cost me more in gas money coming than I had left to get home on, and there still remained a mule deer license to be filled. I decided to hunt and figure out how to get home later.

The treeless prairie south of Gillette suggested country more suited for antelope than for mule deer, so I headed north where my map showed a series of presumably treelined creeks with intriguing names like Wildcat, White Tail, Spotted Horse, and Crazy Woman.

The creeks turned out to be creeks in name only, mostly dry beds fostering just a few stingy cottonwoods. One canyon-shaped area did show promise but a careful hunt around its rim produced nothing.

I swung west toward the Powder River. Trees began to show along its shallow waterway. I turned to follow the river's course, driving south through Arvada. Several miles beyond the little town a ranch house appeared in a grove of cottonwoods that stretched far and deep along the river.

I stopped at the ranch house. A stunning young woman about my age answered my knock on the door. I suddenly became embarrassingly self-conscious of my rather disreputable appearance—unshaven, a little bloody, and likely fragrant from the antelope. I barely began asking permission to hunt when an older woman, presumably the younger woman's mother, protectively filled the doorway. She eyed me disapprovingly but nevertheless assented to my hunting along the river. The young woman smiled.

A faint track past the ranch house took me deep into the cottonwoods. I followed the wheeled impressions until they disappeared close to the river, then set about making camp. The tent served me there, for the setting was pleasant.

With camp made, I heated some water over a small fire and cleaned up, then warmed a supper of stew. I ate to the accompaniment of cottonwoods murmuring softly overhead and watched the broad river flow sluggishly through its shallow, twisting channels. A brief hunt along the river before dark revealed numerous tracks but no deer.

A savage wind came in the night, waking me with its ferocity. A roaring, howling demon charging down from the distant mountains. My little tent billowed and snapped, straining frighteningly at its peg ropes. I shifted my bedroll to the windward side to help hold down the tent and spent a fitful night while the gale whipped my fragile shelter. Heavy limbs crashed eerily close around.

Calm returned with the morning. I looked out upon a scene as peaceful as the afternoon before and wondered had it been a dream. Fresh blowdowns, some uncomfortably close, confirmed that it had not.

Deer began to appear as I finished breakfast. A doe with her fawn slipped teasingly through the cottonwoods off to my left. I gulped down the last of my coffee, loaded my rifle, and hunted cautiously in their direction.

Three more deer appeared, seventy yards ahead, alert, watching me. Does. They stood in place while I scrutinized the surrounding trees. No other deer were visible. A few minutes passed. The does moved off, showing no alarm.

The calm hush of early morning seemed almost surreal after the frenzied roar of the night. In spite of the wind's debris, I was able to move through the cottonwoods in silent harmony with the morning. Deer moved with me. A pair of does to my left. Next a group of four. Then a single gray shadow through a denser stand had me dreaming buck until the antlerless head resolved itself in my scope.

Three more does stood unaware in the trees until they suddenly discovered me too close for security and bounded away in their high, stiff-legged gait.

Then a buck appeared. A young buck. Within easy range. The crosshairs hovered temptingly above his heart.

I had yet to take my first mule deer, but the image of the impressive mountain buck taken by my companion on our initial Wyoming hunt held me. Two more deer came. Both does. They joined the buck. The trio stood beautifully framed in the soft dawn before slowly moving off.

The passing up of the shot ushered in a dearth of deer sightings, as though the Fates had grown spiteful with my refusal of their offering.

An hour elapsed with only a fleeting glimpse of a group of four ghosting through the cottonwoods an impossible distance ahead. Another hour passed with none showing. The young buck began to loom larger as it gradually dawned on me that the river cottonwoods were harboring only smaller bucks and does. If I wanted a mountain buck, I would have to go to the mountains, but they lay far beyond my permit area.

I came with my waning hopes to a narrow mound of earth that paralleled a portion of the river. It rose modestly in imitation of a man-made dyke. Grass grew lushly on its top and along both sides. I walked quietly on its grassy surface, pausing often to scan the cottonwoods. Halfway along the small prominence, a form took shape ahead to my right. A deer lay bedded in the taller grass, barely discernable, less than forty yards away.

I eased forward ten cautious yards. The deer remained unaware. Another five yards. Still no movement. Then five more yards before the deer took definition through the grass, alert, looking toward the river.

It was no mountain buck. But it was there. I considered the shot and the dearth of deer since passing up the earlier shot. There seemed an almost involuntary willing as I eased the rifle to my shoulder, found the deer in the scope, and fired. There was no movement after the rifle's report.

I dressed and skinned the deer, wrapped the meat in cheesecloth, and carried it to camp. I ate, then broke camp and drove out the track, stopping at the ranch house to extend my thanks.

I drove into Gillette, found the Western Union telegraph office, and made arrangements to have some money wired to me. When it had not arrived by closing time, the clerk informed me that the money could be forwarded to any Western Union office along my route.

I camped in South Dakota that night and reached the Wisconsin state line the next day before the gas gauge required a halt. The Mississippi River held me while I waited for my funds to be rerouted to La Crosse. They arrived the next morning minus a substantial rerouting fee. Nonetheless, enough remained to see me home, where I began planning for next season's hunt. Somewhere in the mountains.

-4-

Mid-September 1965. Near the Grand Tetons. The earliness of the season induced Bill to join Dick and me on a mountain hunt for mule deer. Bill's earlier foray into the Snowy Mountain Range with my brother and myself had resulted in his Chevrolet threatening to spend the winter in the high country due to an untimely blizzard. Its retrieval had initially been questionable and in the end painfully expensive, given our strained budgets on that trip. As a consequence, Bill was prone to keep a sharp weather eye on the mountains to the west.

The clouds gathered in the night. Bill kept us well-informed as he made regular inspection trips outside the tent where we were dining on fresh tenderloin from the nice-antlered buck he had taken, his first mule deer. Dick also displayed a nice set of antlers, a very respectable four by four, still in velvet. We had struggled mightily bringing the two bucks into camp, packing them in quarters and halves down the rugged mountainside. The meat hung cooling in the pines sheltering our tent.

The wind sighed peacefully in the night but a threatening sky cautioned us in the morning. I climbed early into the higher country. From a vantage point above the valley in which we were camped, the Idaho mountains to the west showed freshly white. Flurries came in the afternoon, light flakes that gradually built a patina of white upon the mountains rimming our camp. Bill's concern grew as the flurries increased. His experience in the earlier blizzard still haunted his memory. Nor were Dick and I unmindful of the possibilities.

Prudence won out. With two deer in camp and three ante-lope permits still to be considered, risking getting stranded in the mountains to hunt for one more deer, even though it was mine to hunt, made little sense. My elusive mountain buck would have to wait for another season.

We broke camp and followed the faint track through the valley out to the main road. The snow continued to fall, has-tening the evening's dusk. We turned to drive out of the high country, planning on following Highway 26 down to the plains, hoping to keep ahead of the snow.

Our way initially took us north into the face of what became a fierce mountain storm. At Moran Junction we picked up Highway 26 east, but the change in direction offered no relief. The wind-driven flakes swirled madly in the eye-numb-ing, reflective glare of the headlights.

Hour after weary hour I drove on, the storm intensifying with every snow-blinding mile. Stretches of the highway lost their definition. The whirling snow covered the road and sur-rounding countryside in a uniform blanket. I struggled to stay on the highway, sensing relief when an occasional clear patch of asphalt confirmed my intuition. A rare oncoming vehicle offered momentary direction, but as we guided on each other's headlights, I had an uncomfortable sense of the blind leading the blind. Then there were no more oncoming headlights.

The stressful miles dragged on through a frantic ballet of pirouetting snowflakes. The hypnotizing effect of the whirling snow, coupled with the constant tension and my increasing drowsiness, at last prompted me to call a halt. A stretch of level ground showed to the right. I turned onto it, forcing my way through the accumulated snow. There was a concern about get-ting stuck, but I dared not stop too close to the highway.

Bill was sound asleep, having contorted his lengthy frame in some comfortable fashion in the cramped back seat. Dick had dozed off and on in the passenger seat while I drove. Being blessed with a shorter frame, he found no difficulty in curling up for a peaceful slumber.

But sleep refused to visit me. In spite of my weariness, the confined driver's seat kept me tortuously awake. My suggestion to set up the tent fell upon impassive ears. The roaring blizzard outside evidently suggested a greater discomfort to my restless companions than their cramped positions. My night wore on in sleep-deprived exhaustion. Finally, realizing I simply could not sleep in my awkward position, I decided to set up the tent by myself.

My attempt met with failure. The wind overwhelmed me. In weary resignation I laid the tent on the snow, folded the heavy canvas in a protective envelope around my sleeping bag, removed my snow-plastered coat, stood on it to remove my boots, brushed off my pants and shirt, then slid quickly into my sleeping bag. The folded tent extended beyond my head. I propped open a breathing vent with my boots, stretched out full in the new-found space, listened to the wind raging impotently over me, and dreamed of bears slumbering contentedly in their dens.

They tripped over me in the morning, Dick and Bill, finding me covered with the same white blanket as the stark surroundings, still dreaming comfortably.

The day dawned overcast. The storm had run its course. We looked out upon a drear expanse of white, the faint outline of the highway a mere suggestion through the undisturbed countryside.

We tentatively tested the car's traction, found progress possible, and began a cautious drive down the indistinct highway, gaining confidence as signs of other travelers began to appear. The snow stretched from the Idaho to the Nebraska borders. A day passed while we traveled east toward our antelope permit area in Niobrara County. We arrived with the last fleeting light of day.

An overcast sky filled the dawn again the following morning. Snow lay moderately over the prairie, drifting occasionally in wind-funnelled areas. My disappointment on deer in the mountains gained me first rights on antelope, an opportunity that turned out to be more promising in the making than in the fulfilling. There were no antelope. We probed diligently through our hunting area, but the desolate, white expanses remained lifeless.

Wind-blown hours elapsed in frustrating search before a small herd, clumped tightly in a protected draw, came into view. They saw us but seemed reluctant to leave their shelter, milling about uncertainly. A single, most impressive buck stood careful watch on the far side of the herd.

Dick and Bill held the herd's attention while I began an approach. I dipped out of sight behind the rim of the draw and hurried over the snow, slowed in places by unexpected drifts. The far side of the draw slowly became visible. The herd was moving at a rapid walk up it toward a sheltering hill, with the buck bringing up the rear.

I began sprinting toward the top of the rim to try for a shot. A few steps and my foot sank into a drifted depression, sending me sprawling. My rifle emerged from the drift encased in snow.

The buck, along with a few does, paused below the crest of the hill. They turned to watch me. I struggled desperately to

clear the barrel and the scope while the antelope stood in silhouette against the snow. The does slowly drifted over the hill.
The buck followed them to the crest where he again stopped,
his curiosity seemingly not satisfied. I managed to clear the
barrel, but my wet gloves only smeared the snow-covered scope
lenses. I tried to sight through the watery lenses, but the buck's
image was too distorted to chance a shot. My handkerchief fared
no better. The quickly soaked cloth left a frosted smear impossible to sight through.

The buck stood there, his imposing black horns seeming to
grow larger with each frantic second. I desperately considered
a shot by simply sighting along the barrel, but the buck removed
that fleeting temptation when he walked over the crest and
dropped out of sight behind the hill. I watched in helpless frustration as his impressive black horns slowly sank, along with
my chances, into a prairie sea of white.

My misadventure turned out to be the only game activity
in an otherwise antelope-devoid morning. The early season blizzard had caused the herds to seek shelter in hidden pockets
well-protected from our gaze. The numerous herds seen earlier
in the week on our way through to our mule deer area were
now conspicuous by their absence.

At noon we drove into Lusk for a warming cup of coffee,
after which we headed back north down a long hill through a
timbered escarpment that offered promise for mule deer. The
lower plains held a lesser snow accumulation, buoying our
hopes for antelope activity. But another fruitless hour elapsed
with the white plains remaining empty.

Then a small herd attended by a medium-sized buck took
definition in the distance. In a reversal of our morning's strategy, I held the observation point while Dick and Bill made the
stalk. The ground favored the hunters. Two shots rang out in

tandem and two antelope fell. Dick had the honors on the buck. Bill elected to fill his license with a doe. We held permits for either sex.

I found myself again in the position of being the last man with an unfilled license. As the afternoon progressed without any more sightings, I began to sense a long, disappointing ride home.

The day was drawing to a close when a dozen antelope, including a small buck, appeared on the distant horizon. This time the ground did not favor the hunter. My approach exposed me at a distance where judging bullet drop became a challenge.

The antelope watched me from afar. I tried to settle the buck in my scope, testing for range, adjusting my hold with the horizontal crosshair to compensate for a distance still undetermined, then raising the horizontal crosshair higher over his back, debating, then gaining confidence in the sight picture, and firing.

The herd bolted into a run, holding in a compact group until the buck began to drop behind, obviously hit. I fired at the slowing animal, but without effect. He continued on, although falling farther behind. The rest of the herd soon fled out of sight. The lagging buck came to a halt, then lay down. I steadied myself and fired again, but again without effect. I could not determine where the bullets were striking. The wet snow absorbed them without a trace.

There seemed little point in continued futile shooting. I started walking toward the buck to close the range but had hardly begun before he was up and away. A short run brought the buck again to a halt, where he lay down. Once more I tried to approach, and once more he moved to maintain the distance before again laying down.

I closed again, and again the buck moved frustratingly out of range, this time coming to rest on the crest of a hill. I walked directly toward him. When the buck arose and moved over the crest, I ran as fast as possible through the snow, following in his tracks. I halted just beneath the ridge to catch my breath, then eased over the crest.

The buck startled from his bed, fifty yards away. I caught the running form in my scope and fired. And it was over.

A swirl of snow whispered across the prairie, funnelling into a gray sky. Evening began its chill. I looked back to get my bearings. The prairie swept away like a rolling, snowy sea. East finally took shape in my mind. With that satisfied, I knelt in the snow and began to dress the antelope.

Then shadowy figures arose from beyond the line of land and sky. Dick and Bill. Welcome help. But they would be a good while in coming. Time to get the dressing done before they arrived. Then time for them to help me get the antelope out before dark. Then time to go, and to began the waiting for the next time.

The Ridge

There are wondrous places that capture one's heart.
Such was the Thunder. And such was the Ridge.
It was the Thunder that brought me to the Ridge.
And it was Fred who brought me to the Thunder.

The pines grow close to the Thunder on the high ground before the cedar swamp. The swift waters flow freely around the swamp only to bump into the beaver dam pool. The little beaver pond holds the waters awhile, enriching the swamp and in high runoff years flooding the low meadow on the far side of the cedars. The pines shelter close again below the porous dam and the Thunder seeps and gurgles through the mud-caulked barrier to once more dash freely around jumbled boulders before spilling into pools cold, and deep, and darkly mysterious. Below the dense pines the Thunder sings merrily through silver-flecked rapids and beguiling pools, dancing lightly in the sun that transforms droplets into diamonds and yields teasing glimpses into the veiled depths. Trout live in this sylvan wonder. Native trout. Speckled trout. Brook trout. The true wilderness trout. For brook trout live wild only in the wild waters. And brook trout live wild in the Thunder.

-1-

May 1962. Trout season in Wisconsin. My friend Fred Klett knew of a brook trout stream deep in the North Woods with a cabin nearby. Trout streams lay an hour west of my home but Fred enticed me five hours north with a vision of secluded, untrammeled waters. The vision was the Thunder. And the vision became real. We paid due homage to the wildwood stream, and the Thunder in turn yielded a full measure of her speckled treasures.

On our second morning I was fishing a stretch of the stream where heavy willows grew tight to the bank, making casting difficult. The willows bordered the approaches to a deep, inviting pool. An elongated, narrow island lay at the end of the pool, of a size that two men lying head to toe would easily cover. It offered clear casting to the pool. I stepped from the willows toward the island when a remarkable sight checked my movement.

A fawn lay on the island!

The tiny creature was so close that had I fallen forward, I would have landed on it. The fawn lay with its legs tucked under a belly showing the same downy white as the rows of spots dappling its reddish-brown coat. Not a movement betrayed it. The fawn's large, liquid eyes, glistening deep lucent-black, watched me without blinking. We remained locked in time, staring at each other in mutual fascination. The rippling waters were all that broke the silence.

Suddenly, as though a secretive urgent command had reached the more sensitive ears of the fawn, it bolted from the tiny island to splash across the stream and vanish into the willows on the opposite bank. The sound of a larger body joined its diminutive rustlings and the combined crashing quickly faded into the dense cover.

The sighting of deer, along with the allure of the surrounding country, decided the location of that year's whitetail hunt. Six months after our brook trout outing, on the day before opening day of deer season, Fred and I again stood on the banks of the Thunder, anxious to scout our new hunting grounds.

We slipped down a steep, snow-covered bank and crossed the icy stream, gingerly balancing ourselves on water-slick boulders. The Thunder ran north and south at that point, after flowing down from the west and making an irregular loop around a large cedar swamp. A dense mixture of brush and second growth bordered the stream. Tall pines and spruce farther in favored the lower contours, while sugar maples blended with stands of birch and poplar on the slightly higher ground. A series of prominent glacial ridges ran north and south half a mile west of the Thunder. Beyond the ridges the mixed hardwoods and conifers flowed unbroken into the vast Chequamegon forest. The brush and second growth continued throughout, screening heavily in places.

During our scouting we came across a small promontory that rose above the forest floor between the Thunder and the glacial ridges. Deer trails radiating from the cedar swamp passed over and around the little knoll. The elevation, although moderate, provided a more open view of the surrounding brushy hardwoods. Its modest dominance also created a natural reference point. As Fred and I circled through the swamps and hardwoods, we found ourselves guiding on the familiar little hill. When we separated in order to cover more country, it became our agreed upon meeting point. A name was needed. We dubbed it, simply, the Ridge.

Deer season in Wisconsin traditionally opens on the Saturday before Thanksgiving. To the faithful that day is, to borrow a phrase, a holy day of obligation.

That hallowed Saturday found me, Fred, and Gib standing in the predawn darkness alongside a landmark birch, readily identified in the black forest maze by a strategically placed bottle hanging from one of its branches. Gib, a friend of Fred's whose family owned the cabin we were staying in, had arrived late the preceding evening.

Fred took a compass bearing from the birch that led us through the dark woods to a stepping-stone crossing of the Thunder, a precarious balancing act with the hypnotizing waters rushing darkly underfoot.

Once across, Fred and Gib continued on toward the Ridge. I followed them far enough to be clear of the noisy rapids and took a stand alongside a shadowy maple. I listened to the sound of crunching footsteps long after Fred's and Gib's shapes had melded into the dark. The crunching gradually faded and I became as one with the intense quiet of the winter woods.

The dark still held. It is a given that on opening morning you will be at least a half-hour too early. There is a touch of incredible magic promising to take place, and like an anxious child awaiting Christmas, we crowd reluctant time.

Night slowly began to give way. Anticipation swelled as the dark shadows lightened. A shivering tremor of excitement matched the shiver from the cold. From far away came the tingle-inducing echo of the first shot. It was beginning.

Nearer tree shapes started to take form. Another shot echoed from afar. I strained to pierce the morning gloom, thinking of how close a deer must be to offer a sensible opportunity. A third shot tempted me to test my crosshairs. They were indistinct against the dense-timbered background.

Night slipped away from the forest. The grays toned to the browns of the woodland brush and the morning dawned clear. I stood in watchful anticipation, focusing eager eyes on the narrow circle of trees and brush I could see into.

A flighting raven came with the silent dawning, a black essence in the gray-toned sky, the whoosh, whoosh of its wings whispering like a gentle murmur before fading into the hush, leaving me lost in the wonder of being enveloped in a silence so absolute that one could hear a far-off bird fly.

A few more scattered shots sounded dimly from the distance as the morning progressed, otherwise the forest lay cloaked in the quiet. Deer no doubt were moving with the quiet-passing hours, but they moved well beyond me.

Ten o'clock came. The cold had seeped deep within. I turned away from the maple and began still-hunting south into the cedar swamp. The chilled stiffness from four hours of standing slowly worked itself out.

The dense ceders grew close, funnelling me onto narrow game trails where they existed. I followed silently along the wending trails, locked into the fastness. Deer sign was plentiful. Buck rubs showed tantalizingly on stripling cedars. Heart-shaped tracks followed and crisscrossed the narrow trails. Fresh droppings glistened. I eased through the lacework cedars with wary caution.

But not wary enough. A startling crashing brought my rifle instinctively to my shoulder. A white flag flashed through the green. A second followed in close tandem. I caught the flashes briefly in the scope before the scope filled with cedars. The crashing faded into silence.

I watched for a few minutes, hoping for a third deer. If others were there, they slipped away unseen.

I turned west and started to circle through the swamp toward the more open glacial ridges. A flurry of shots from the direction of the Ridge halted me. Ka-BOOM! Ka-BOOM! Then again. Ka-BOOM! Ka-BOOM! A pause. Ka-BOOM!

Ka-BOOM! Ka-BOOM! .... Ka-BOOM! Ka-BOOM! It sounded like a military skirmish.

I held my ground, thinking that perhaps the object of all that ordnance might retreat in my direction. Rapid multiple shots typically signify rapid multiple misses. I watched expectantly, but nothing came my way.

I continued up onto the first glacial ridge, found a convenient log, and sat down to watch the swamp edge. A small saddle to my left dipped through the glacial ridge, providing a natural crossing.

I directed my attention toward the swamp and the Ridge area, occasionally glancing toward the saddle. I looked away from one of those cautionary glances only to have a flicker of movement from that direction catch the corner of my eye. I resisted the impulse to turn my head. Slowly, from my left rear, a deer came into view walking through the saddle. It was a doe. Behind her came a second doe, followed by a third. They poked along in no great hurry, browsing on the low shrubs. In time they fed off toward the Ridge and were lost to view.

The welcome presence of deer brightened the midday. I settled down on my log seat hoping a buck might follow the does through the saddle, but midday wore on into afternoon without the sighting of any more deer.

The coming of the final hour sent me toward the Ridge. A compass bearing from it to the stream crossing would make it easier going out in the dark.

The final hour holds a fascination akin to the first. It is a colder hour, after a full day in the winter woods, yet the gathering dusk tempers the cold with its hint at the movement of game. I watched until the dull light faded to gray and the second growth closed into itself to form an impenetrable shield.

A deer went out in front of me as I followed my compass to the stream crossing. Fred and Gib were waiting by the landmark birch. They reported seeing several deer but none were taken.

We entered the woods with daylight a little closer the next morning, the impatience of the first day giving way to half an hour's extra sleep. Still, the dark continued long after Fred and Gib departed.

The inevitable predawn shot sounded in the distance. I concentrated on the dim area close in front, knowing deer must be moving but needing one to be almost on top of me to be fairly seen. My horizon slowly expanded with the growing light. Then with the full light, a deer appeared.

A rush of excitement banished the morning cold. The deer was moving slowly, obscured by brush, scarcely fifty yards away. When it stopped, it seemed to become part of the brown forest background. I carefully shouldered my rifle and tried to pick up the deer in the scope. Brush confused the image. I moved my eye away from the scope and peered intently. The deer moved again. I looked back through the scope and captured the image. It was a doe.

I lowered my rifle. Another deer materialized out of the brush. Again the rifle came to my shoulder. Again the brush obscured the animal. It moved. Another doe. A smaller one.

The two deer were browsing, in no particular hurry. They meandered in and out of view for over half an hour. My attention became divided between the surrounding cover and the two deer. Sometimes when I looked they were gone, only to instantly reappear as if by sorcery. Then they would be invisible again, their brown winter coats blending perfectly with the background. It was a doe and her fawn of the year. I came to hope, and in time to believe, because I wanted to believe, that the fawn was the same fawn bedded on the little island in the Thunder that spring. The island lay less than half a mile away.

After awhile the deer did not reappear. The chill of the morning prompted me to move. I began still-hunting toward the Ridge. The morning air remained crisp and calm, the ground frozen. My crust-breaking footsteps grated on my ears. I came to the ridge, crunched up the short slope, and sat down to the welcome silence.

My vantage point on the Ridge faced east toward the Thunder, with the cedar swamp on my right. I watched the cover in front of me in the direction of the stream. The morning passed without even an illusion of movement disturbing the somber winter woods. I began to consider the glacial ridges.

All at once a sense of motion unfolded to my right rear. A deer was loping toward me from out of the swamp. At first sight, through the brush, I could not determine what it was. But as the deer came closer, antlers became visible.

It was a buck!

An intense rush of exhilaration surged through me. My senses came alive. Concentration banished all.

The buck was closing rapidly. My position bordered on impossible. Sitting down, facing the worse conceivable way for a right-handed shooter. Any movement would spook the deer, but move I must if there was any hope of a shot.

The buck stopped ten yards from me, suddenly aware of an unfamiliar stump on the hill. His curiosity faded quickly as I tried to inch into a shooting position. Within seconds the buck bolted and began racing away to my right rear. I sprang to my feet and whirled around, rushing the rifle to my shoulder. The buck bounded into the scope, running behind an intervening bush. I waited until he cleared, strived to hold his right shoulder in the center of the scope, and fired. A spurt of blood erupted in the instant before the recoil. The buck plummeted to the ground, then rose almost without breaking stride. I bolted in another round and found the racing animal in the scope. The rifle recoiled. Once more the buck fell and rose running, then fell again and remained still.

Then my trembling began. A release of pent-up control. When it subsided, I paced the distance to where the buck first fell. Thirty yards. Then to where he lay. Another forty. The first shot had gone through his heart. A fortunate placement, since the crosshairs were simply tracking the front of the bounding deer.

I stood for a time in pleasant contemplation before tagging and dressing the buck. Then the task of dragging him out intruded. But I was reluctant to leave the woods. It was only a little after eleven o'clock. The entire afternoon lay before me. I decided to wait with taking the buck out until I went out that evening. The deer would keep nicely where he lay in the below freezing temperature. I turned toward the country beyond the glacial ridges and set off to explore new terrain.

And deep I did explore. So deep that when the Thunder at last came into view after a wide circle to the west, then north and back east again, evening had descended with the buck still laying a goodly distance to the south in the dark woods. He would have to wait until the next day.

In the cabin that evening, after a pleasant meal featuring a few hearty toasts to my buck, Fred expressed some kindly concern about my leaving said buck in the cold, dark woods. I suggested the buck was perfectly content in his present surroundings, having lived in them all of his life. Fred reminded me that the buck was no longer living, and what may have been pleasant for him in one state of being was not necessarily pleasant for him in another. In the warm glow of the moment, I conceded a certain logic to his argument.

As the evening and the toasts progressed, Fred's concern for the well-being of my buck grew. Strangely, I found myself beginning to share his charitable thoughts. Gib remained non-committal. He prudently joined in our salute to the buck with only a single toast.

Fred's fatherly concern for the young buck finally moved him to action. We must go to the buck and bring him to the refuge of the cabin. For some reason his suggestion sounded remarkably reasonable. Gib remained noncommittal, pulling on his boots with a bemused look on his face. He did make one comment as we trundled off into the frigid winter woods. Something about his brother's keeper.

In a feat of worthy woodsmancraft, in the dead of night, we found the landmark birch. I recall it was the beverage bottle hanging from one of its branches that Fred homed in on. Our crossing of the Thunder in the daunting dark rivaled Caesar's crossing of the Rubicon in its audacity.

We found the Ridge. Gib was delegated to stay there so we could take a compass bearing from it back to the crossing. I led Fred on a search for the buck. He lay where I had left him. He appeared content. I told this to Fred. Fred grunted.

Gib joined us at the buck. We greeted him warmly. But why had he left the compass reference position on the Ridge? It lay lost in the impenetrable night. Gib muttered something about his brother's keeper.

We set out from the buck to find the Ridge. It did not seem to be where we had left it. We found the buck again, where he should not have been. We decided to bypass the Ridge and strike out on a straight line to the Thunder. We found the Ridge. It was not where we last recalled it to be.

We wandered in the night like the lost tribes of Israel, the buck towed in dutiful submission behind us. We eventually found the Thunder when one of us stepped in it.

The buck came through our return passage in fine fettle under Fred's watchful eye. When the buck was safely settled in the pine tree next to the cabin, Fred bid him well in a fatherly tone, gave him an affectionate pat, then retired to sleep the sleep of the just.

-2-

My buck turned out to be the only deer taken during our first season on the Ridge. Fred and Gib also saw bucks, but circumstances conspired against them.

The next year we were joined by Gib's brother-in-law, Bill, and Fred's brother-in-law, Ernie. Our gathering in the cabin on the Friday evening before opening day was a somber one, as news of President Kennedy's assassination that afternoon left us in a doleful mood.

Opening morning. The Thunder flowed cold in the moody dark before dawn. We made our passage in silence to the swift-flowing stream. Fred, Ernie, and I crossed first, unavoidably splashing the protruding boulders we stepped on. The rocks quickly iced over. Gib began crossing the slippery rocks and in an instant found himself immersed in the frigid waters. Bill returned to the cabin with him as a precaution, for the morning was bitter cold. Several hours elapsed before Gib thawed out enough to hunt.

Once across the Thunder, Fred, Ernie, and I hunted our separate ways. The cold forced frequent movement to maintain some measure of body heat. I alternated between still-hunting and standing, following around the Ridge, through the cedar swamp, and onto the glacial ridges. No deer were seen or heard and opening morning shooting remained sparse.

The afternoon repeated the morning. The long, cold, interminable hours when it seems as though not a single deer lives within a day of the Ridge. Not even a raven croaked by to enliven the gray, wintery sky.

Fred and I met on the Ridge with an hour of daylight remaining. We took stands on opposite sides and began the final watch. The closing minutes were ticking off when a shot by Fred jarred me. I spun around to see him working his bolt and bringing his rifle to bear. My position prevented me from seeing the object of his shot. He held his rifle to his shoulder but did not fire again.

Then a shot rang out close off to our right front, followed by a second and a third. I stood tense with my rifle at ready.

When enough time had elapsed, Fred and I walked in the direction of the three shots and found Ernie dressing out a magnificent ten-point buck. Fred had seen it running through the brushy hardwoods but could manage only one fleeting shot. Fred's shot alerted Ernie, who was coming down off the glacial ridges on his way toward the Thunder. The ten-pointer ran right into him. A beautiful deer. And the only one seen that day.

Ernie's good fortune carried over to the following morning. He was easing through the tag alders along the Thunder when he heard two men talking. Ernie stood quiet in the alders as an eight-point buck came through, sneaking around the talkative hunters. He dropped the buck with a single shot.

The buck did manage to extract some measure of revenge on Ernie. When he started to dress the buck, its right hind leg, in a reflex action, lashed out, hitting Ernie just below his left knee and knocking him to the ground. The buck left a permanent scar as a momento.

The cold morning made stand hunting an unpleasant, short-lived occupation. I sat on the Ridge until my shivering warned me to move, then set off toward the glacial ridges and the country beyond that I had scouted the preceding year.

My movement through the crystal-tinged woods marked a slow pace, but still it warmed me some. I followed my general route of the preceding year, crossing the seamless boundary into the vast Chequamegon. Deer sign showed regularly—tracks, droppings, an occasional buck rub—but the makers of those intriguing marks remained elusive. I circled out on a ridge leading down to the Thunder north of my starting point with night approaching, but managed to find a crossing, saving me a dark march south through the thick stream-side cover to our regular crossing.

Other than Ernie's eight-pointer, not another deer was seen that day.

Monday. The quiet day. The intensity of opening morning and opening weekend gives way to a calm sense of resolute perseverance. The weekend hunters have returned home. A subdued, relaxed atmosphere permeates the forest. It is a good day.

I found the Ridge in the dark, becoming automatic by then, and sat down on the familiar makeshift seat I had cobbled together from downed tree limbs. My stand faced east toward the unseen Thunder. The cedar swamp lay to my right behind a screening of brushy hardwoods. To my left a mixture of hardwoods and conifers stretched unbroken to the north. The glacial ridges began a few hundred yards behind me.

The morning broke cold although not as bitter as the preceding days. I sat enjoying the tempered quietude, watching for hopeful movement between the swamp and the glacial ridges. The silent minutes slipped by in unhurried harmony with the hushed mood of the forest.

Daylight had been full for two hours when the silent woods became disrupted by the sound of voices in front of me. The morning air remained still, making it difficult to tell how close the men were, so well did sound carry. I expected they would shortly move on, but their conversation continued.

The chance of a deer moving in front of me while they talked seemed remote. I dropped off the front of the Ridge and circled to a vantage point close to the saddle where I had seen three does cross the preceding year. Numerous tracks indicated that deer were still using the crossing.

The sound of the voices blissfully faded away. It occurred to me that they might be the same vocal hunters who turned the eight-point toward Ernie the day before. The two men probably were bemoaning the fact that they were not seeing deer. And wondering why.

A convenient rock provided a seat from which to watch the swamp edge leading toward the saddle. Scarcely five minutes passed when a stirring in the brush drew my attention. Something was moving behind the dense screening in the direction of the saddle. A hesitant yet deliberate movement. I strained to see a red coat, thinking it could possibly be one of the vocal hunters. Then, through the tiniest patch of thinner brush, the brown coat of a deer materialized.

I tried to pick up the deer in the scope, but the maze of brown brush closed in a tangle in front of it. I cautiously turned the setting of my variable scope to six-power, and in the illusion of spreading brush, spaces between the tangle became

visible. Parts of deer showed, but none clearly enough to determine whether it was a buck. The deer moved and was hidden
again. I looked ahead for some small opening, but the cover,
although thinning slightly in places, remained unbroken along
the deer's course.

In another tiny thinning the head of the deer at last revealed
antlers. The buck had stopped and turned to observe his
backtrail. I struggled to find a clear shot, but could not. The
deer moved again, and again disappeared. Then a portion of
its body showed clear through the brush, although which
portion even the higher scope setting could not reveal. From
the elation of first recognition I began to sink to the depths
of despair. A good-sized buck stood fifty yards from me, but
a shot seemed impossible.

The deer moved again, gravitating deeper into the hopeless
brush. Once more he stopped, revealing a small portion of his
body in the last thinning before he would vanish forever. I could
faintly trace the hindquarters and a portion of the back. The
rest of the buck remained completely hidden.

I studied the image in the scope, trying to define an aiming
point, knowing the spine lay there, knowing where my handloads would print. I wrapped into my sling, snugged my elbows
tight against my knees, settled the crosshairs, settled my breathing, locked into the sight picture, and squeezed the trigger.

The deer disappeared. Not a sound broke the silence. I
chambered another round, but it would have been useless had
the deer bolted through the brush. I let myself calm down from
the release of adrenaline, then walked to where the deer had
been. He was still there. The spine shot had dropped him in
his tracks. He was a large, wide-beamed six-point. I did not
leave him in the woods for later retrieval.

Mine was the last of the three deer taken by our group that year. Laid out side by side, the six-, eight-, and ten-point bucks were remarkably close in body size. When Ernie registered his ten-point, he had it weighed. It topped out at one hundred and seventy-four pounds.

-3-

After my experience with the deer in the brush, I acquired a custom built 8MM Mauser mounting a scope with a post reticle, for which I handloaded two-hundred-grain, round-nosed bullets at moderate velocity. Conventional wisdom held that this load would treat brush as being nonexistent.

The 1964 deer season saw our group expand to seven with the addition of Bill's brother, Vic, and Ernie's brother, Tom. Gib's family cabin was already bursting at the seams so Fred, Ernie, Tom, and I shifted to a cabin at a small fishing resort nearby, known locally as Satch's Retreat. The resort consisted of half a dozen cabins scattered around a combination tavern and living quarters in which Satch and his wife, Velva, resided. The cabins were closed after fishing season, not being winterized, but reopened for deer hunters willing to get along without running water during the nine-day season. The accommodations were rustic, the cabins dating to 1927, as was the setting in a stand of stately evergreens along the birch-lined Willow River.

Opening morning. The night held close in a starlit sky. Fred and I crunched our way to the Ridge in the predawn dark. Fred stopped on the little prominence while I continued through the dim-shaped trees to the saddle crossing where the previous year's six-pointer presumably had been heading. I waited there in the quiet as the dawning slowly spread its diffused light through the forest.

Half an hour passed when a shot from Fred's direction alerted me. I watched with that extra intensity one feels when he knows deer are moving nearby, but whatever Fred shot at was either down or moving well out of sight.

The day dawned sunny with a scattering of clouds. A light mantle of snow covered the forest floor, opening up the dark woods. The temperature hovered comfortably in the upper twenties. A beautiful opening morning, except for the absence of deer.

But chickadees came. Tiny, flittering bundles of energy, foraging over twigs and branches and pecking under bark scales for insect eggs. Trusting birds, they paid me friendly attention. One alighted for a few seconds on my hat. Another studied me curiously while perched on the end of my rifle barrel. He appeared quite intent. A black cap and black bib framed his white cheeks, suggesting a formal attire that contrasted with the russet buff of his sides. He stayed but a fleeting moment before joining his companions on their restless foray through the woods. When they were finally gone, I felt strangely alone.

No other wildlife brightened the morning. My continuing fruitless vigil turned my thoughts to the country beyond the glacial ridges.

Late morning brought me to an area where seepage formed a small spring hole surrounded by a dense growth of willows. I carefully pushed through the willows, stopping where they thinned out along the edge of a small opening. Ten minutes at most passed in silent watching before the rustle of something moving to my right rear caught my attention. I remained motionless. The faint rustlings drew nearer. I strained to see through the willows. They remained impenetrable.

Rustling again. Closer now. Willows yielding to a passage. Catching a semblance of movement. A shadowy form. Watching the form take faint definition.

It was a deer! And it was a buck!

The buck moved a few more cautious steps, then paused in full alertness scarcely twenty yards from me. I considered a shot through the tangled thicket, but even with my new brush rifle the dense willows gave me concern. The buck was moving toward the small opening. If he entered it, as he seemed destined to do, my chances would improve dramatically.

Twice did the buck offer a fair opportunity, and twice did I hold, waiting for the sure, clear shot.

The buck reached the edge of the opening and paused. I steeled myself. An instant separated us.

And in that instant the buck whirled and crashed away through the willows!

I stared after him in stunned dismay. An unfathomable emptiness pressed down upon me. He was gone. In a heartbeat. And mine beat in bitter disappointment. What alerted him remains a puzzle. He was a splendid buck and the lost opportunity haunted me to distraction the rest of that listless afternoon.

Fred greeted me with a cheerier tale that evening. The shot I heard that morning indeed had been his. He was watching northeast from the Ridge when a spike buck came loping out of a swale to his right. He made a fine running shot through the brush at thirty-five yards and was the proud possessor of the only deer in camp that night.

Sunday morning. The day held still in the early dawning. I watched again from my stand on the Ridge.

The first hour passed with only the faint rising sun showing motion. Chickadees flighted through in the second hour. A small flock. Perhaps my trusting visitors of the day before. But the foraging birds paid me no heed this day and continued indifferently on their way.

An intermittent breeze from the southwest sprang up in the third hour. The eddying wind began to shift through the area I was watching. By ten o'clock the breeze had steadied to the point where it became futile to remain. I decided to hunt down to the Thunder, follow it north, then circle back and still-hunt into the wind.

I began moving slowly off the Ridge, watching to my left front where the wind would not betray me, when the aspect of a deer showed through the second growth. The backdrop of snow faintly outlined the stationary form, but it outlined it enough to send a rush of excitement through me.

It was a buck!

The range appeared to be sixty or seventy yards, but considerable brush intervened. The buck stood broadside, facing right. I carefully eased the rifle to my shoulder and tried through the scope to find a brush-free lane. The cover was not as dense as the willows of the day before, but still I considered waiting for a clearer shot until the cost of waiting on the other buck intruded. I placed the post reticle low along the front shoulder, trusted to my brush loads, steadied, and fired.

The buck jumped, fell, then rose to run ten yards before falling again. He was dead from a heart shot when I reached him.

I dressed the deer in the forest quiet, then began the tedious work of dragging it over the log-strewn ground. The brush hampered ceaselessly, especially the thick tag alders along the Thunder. Crossing the Thunder with a deer in tow always presented a challenge. But once across, onto the higher ground, the brush thinned some, leaving mainly tangled blowdowns to frustrate the way. It was wearisome work, but in all, with success evident in the steady pull of the rope, still pleasant, this bringing out of the deer.

My buck was the only deer brought into camp that day, and remained the last deer taken by us that season.

-4-

Our group held stable the following year. We returned to Satch's rustic cabins and to his genial welcome. Satch's cozy North Woods tavern, centered among the cabins, became a nightly gathering place for area hunters, and many a mighty buck was slain within its agreeable confines.

Opening morning came with me watching a trail that crossed a low break on the backside of the Ridge. Barely half an hour had passed before three deer appeared through the hardwoods, moving rapidly along the trail. They approached to within fifty yards, noticed movement when I began raising my rifle, and stopped.

Two does and a buck.

They stood in a tight cluster, facing directly toward me. The buck centered in the scope as the rifle nestled into my shoulder. The deer seemed tense, nervous to identify the obstruction in their path. The crosshairs settled on the buck's chest. The deer's agitation turned to action. The three deer bolted to my left as I squeezed the trigger. The buck dropped instantly. The two does bounded through the hardwoods toward the glacial ridges and quickly disappeared into the brush.

The buck required a finishing shot. His rapid turning at the instant of my shooting resulted in the bullet hitting near his spine. I was fortunate not to have missed. He was a medium-sized buck with a small-beamed, though beautifully symmetrical, eight-point rack.

My early good fortune answered for our group on opening day, and for the next two days. I continued hunting on our party permit, which allowed the taking of one additional buck or doe among us, but was still waiting for the sight of another deer. The others had yet to see their first deer.

There is this reality about whitetail hunting in the North Woods. The minutes of intense action are momentary interludes in the long, cold, oftentimes wearisome, and sometimes discouraging hours of waiting and watching and searching. Six hundred minutes of daylight fill a late November day, five thousand four hundred fill the nine-day season. The sighting and shooting of a deer, if and when it occurs, typically fills only one or two of those minutes. During the other thousands, the hunter lives on hope.

Hope had ebbed for the hunters in our little cabin after three deerless days. Fred's solution for our doldrums was a change of scenery. On Tuesday morning we set off for an area several miles away that Fred had found and designated the Bowl.

Old logging trails offered an entry into the area for the unfamiliar. I began hunting along one that led me through forest cover thick with conifers and second-growth hardwoods. Still-hunting occupied my morning as I sought to become familiar with the changing terrain.

A shot rang out around ten-thirty, followed a few minutes later by another. I waited with my customary anticipation, facing in the direction of the shooting. But as seems my fortune, nothing came my way.

I wandered on and off the logging trail, circling back to it as a reference point. A swing through a small cedar swamp brought me around again to the trail when motion ahead halted me.

The motion resolved itself into a good-antlered buck. He emerged from a stand of hardwoods and dashed across the trail, quartering in my direction.

The buck continued through the woods, angling to my left, obviously unaware of my presence. The hardwoods were reasonably open and I swung my rifle trying to isolate the bounding deer in the scope. The trees became a blur but there seemed an opportunity and I fired. The buck continued on, offering no possibility for a second shot.

I walked to where the deer had been and found his tracks in the snow. There was no sign of blood, nor did any appear for a hundred yards along the deer's trail.

Curiosity compelled me to try to trace the flight of the bullet. After considerable searching I found where it had entered a small maple. My shot on the maple was quite good. I hit it dead center.

That buck was one of two seen by the group that day. The two shots I heard earlier were taken at the other. Fred had been still-hunting when he paused to check his compass. He looked up to take his bearing and saw a four-point buck watching him seventy-five yards away. At Fred's shot, the buck wheeled into the brush. Fred was following the blood trail when a shot sounded ahead. The buck had run by Ernie and he was waiting alongside it when Fred arrived.

Wednesday morning. Ernie and Tom returned to the Bowl area to see if they could find the buck I had missed. Fred was content with his four-pointer. So armed with my .270—my 8MM was having a back-ordered Timney trigger installed—and the party permit, I ventured back to the Ridge.

The morning dawned overcast. I sat down on my makeshift seat and began another patient vigil. An hour passed before a subtle stirring deep in the second growth between my stand and the Thunder sent me into a charged intensity. A brown form was wisping through the shadows.

The first intimation of deer never ceases to electrify me, so hauntingly like a ghost do they materialize.

I watched for further movement, and when it came, I framed a deer in my scope. A doe was moving slowly to my left a hundred yards in front of me.

The party permit allowed for either sex. Usually we held out for a buck until the last day, then opened up our doe season. We were leaving that afternoon to be home for Thanksgiving. The final morning was upon us. I elected to take the shot if one presented itself.

The second growth screened the deer well. I struggled to define the indistinct form through the shielding branches and brush. Minutes passed as did the deer through the cover, weaving through small openings but invariably pausing with its vital areas obscured until one of its pauses exposed the chest area. I held carefully on the lungs and fired. The deer disappeared from view.

I waited several seconds, then saw a doe running back toward the swamp. The doe stopped and the crosshairs centered behind its shoulder. My shot had seemed true, but the deer in the scope showed no indication of being hit. There must have been two does. I hesitated, then watched the deer disappear into the cedars.

There indeed were two does, and one lay where it had fallen from a clean shot through both lungs. I tagged the deer with the party tag, dressed it, fastened the drag rope, looped it over my shoulders, and made my way through the blowdowns and across the Thunder to the cabin. Ernie and Tom reported no luck at the Bowl. And so ended our season.

-5-

We expanded into two of Satch's cabins for the 1966 season to accommodate Dick and Paul, who brought our group to six that year.

Dick had a remarkable baptism to the Ridge area. On opening morning, around ten-thirty, while hunting along the edge of the cedar swamp below where the saddle crosses the first glacial ridge, he heard the noise of a drive off to the west. Before long a doe came through the saddle, followed by an eight-point buck that Dick dropped with a single shot. He was dressing the eight-point when he looked up to see a forkhorn watching him. Dick reached for his rifle, which was leaning against a nearby tree, and was soon also dressing the forkhorn.

For three days I had hunted well, or such was my presumption, although my results disputed it. By Tuesday morning my favored haunts had failed to produce even the hint of a deer. I considered shifting to other hunting grounds but the Ridge clung to my mind and the gray dawning broke with me seated on my familiar stand watching toward the Thunder.

Two hours into the morning brought the long-awaited sight of two deer moving through the heavy growth toward the cedar swamp. The deer filtered in and out of the screening offering no clear view. I tried to define them in the scope. At times the screening thinned, offering tempting glimpses. They were both good-sized deer, but if they carried antlers the brush hid them well.

Movement continued. A partial opening ahead of the deer seemed to present a reasonably clear lane of fire. I held on it as a doe moved through. The second deer paused in the opening and the post reticle settled solidly on her shoulder, holding there until she disappeared into the brush after the other doe. No other deer were seen that day.

Wednesday. The warming weather had dissipated the modest snow covering of opening weekend. The brown forest floor blended into one with the brown brush, wonderfully camouflaging the deer's winter coat. More than a few may have passed close to my stand on the Ridge that morning. If they did, they passed as ghosts.

I watched until the dense brush wearied me, then shifted to the first glacial ridge where the added elevation allowed better vision into the cover. An hour passed when the faintest of noises drew my attention to the right. A deer was cautiously approaching, moving quietly except for that single giveaway crackling.

It was a buck! And a very nice one!

He moved slowly, head-on toward me, looking neither left nor right. I dared not move. At fifty yards the buck halted with his head partially obscured by a large poplar. I eased the rifle to my shoulder, and when he moved again, he moved regally into my scope. I held the vision, anxious to grasp the opportunity but mesmerized by the wide-beamed eight-pointer looming ever closer. On he came, holding me dreamlike, until anxiousness suppressed my musings. Then a bullet pierced his heart, and the buck fell amidst the odors of the forest and the fading sound of thunder.

I did not go to him for a while, but waited in the woodland hush, holding on to the moment. The morning settled soft around me. The timeless forest drew my gaze. Five seasons of wanderings made all that I viewed comfortably familiar. There was the saddle, and the deep, dark cedar swamp, and the glacial ridges running true to the north. And beyond the timbered swale, toward the Thunder, stood the Ridge, while before me, in solemn splendor, giving lofty meaning to the whole, lay the magic of the deer.

Mighty bucks, and some not so mighty, fell to our rifles during the following years. The trout of the Thunder called us to pilgrimage each spring, like Muslims called to holy Mecca. The glorious autumn reds and golds heralded thunderous flushes of grouse; and when the colors fell, the bluebills came, riding the Canadian winds. And always, when the early snows hushed the forest grandeur, we came again to the Ridge. Always, we came to the Ridge. In those halcyon days before the wind.

The tamaracks fell first when the great wind came, then the black spruce, their shallow roots ripped from the grounded mat of the bogs. The hemlocks followed quickly, the surging wind sucking their root systems from soil leached porous by their own acid litter. The wind roared into the already tangled cedar swamps and in one grand charge rendered them impassable. The yellow birch held longer, but when the onslaught broke through the basswood circles, they toppled like so many ten-pins. Still, the larger maples resisted, and the stalwart white pines. And in scattered pockets, copses of hardwoods held fast.

Then the downburst came. A phenomenon outside of memory. An irresistible one hundred and fifty mile an hour torrential wind. And like the charge of Napoleon's Garde Imperial—The Immortals—committed only at the climatic moment of the battle, nothing could stand against it.

When the great windstorm thundered through Wisconsin on that fourth day of July in 1977, it left a path of destruction ten miles wide from Grantsburg to Rhinelander, a distance of one hundred and sixty miles. Nothing was spared, not even a sixteen hundred acre tract of massive, old-growth, virgin timber that had survived the logging days. The devastation passed beyond comprehension. Meteorologists christened it the windstorm of the century. Grizzled old woodsmen called it the windstorm from Hell.

The deer finally struggled free of the fallen cedar. She teetered on trembling legs, dazed and disoriented. The cedar swamp in which she had franticly sought refuge from the screeching wind had come crashing down around her. A nervous thirst assailed her. She thought of water, but the way to the stream that flowed around the swamp lay blocked by the jumbled cedars. She remembered the little spring beyond the glacial ridges. She had only to follow the trail out of the swamp and around that smaller ridge to reach it. But both the trail and the smaller ridge lay buried beneath an impenetrable tangle of broken, twisted trees. Her world lay in utter desolation. All landmarks had vanished with the passing wind. Nothing existed as it existed before. Nor could it ever again. It was gone. Totally and irretrievably gone.

They were wondrous places that captured my heart. Such was the Thunder. And such was the Ridge.

The Bear Hunters

M ankind's awe of bears is etched indelibly in our genes. In hunting societies down through the ages, bears have held a mystical power. The earliest discovered cult ritual, tracing back to Neanderthal times, involved the skulls and bones of the giant cave bear, the great Animal Master. The rituals of eons stamp their imprint on the generations. Who among us does not sense our ancient ancestors' wonder for the beast that can walk like man?

Bears had been on my mind since my 1961 Canadian hunt. When Wisconsin opened its first early gun season for black bear in 1963, many hunters, myself included, found out too late. Only six bears were taken. When the early gun season opened the following September, my license application was among the first.

My previous futile attempt at still-hunting black bears suggested a different approach. The Wisconsin Conservation Department approved of two other methods, hunting with hounds or over bait. I owned a pair of beagles, but they hardly qualified as bear hounds. Baiting remained an unfamiliar method, although in principal it sounded deceptively simple. So I bought a couple bushels of sweet corn along with a bushel of apples and headed into northern Wisconsin.

My hunt settled into a pleasant routine. I arose before first light, watched my pile of sweet corn and apples for three or four hours, still-hunted the rest of the morning, caught enough trout for an early supper, sat over the bait until dark, then followed the stars back to my tent, crawled into my sleeping bag, and woke up early to repeat the days. At least the trout fishing was good. I dined well on brooks, browns, and rainbows. The bears did not dine on my sweet corn and apples. Still it was an enjoyable week in the North Woods, although I came no closer to realizing my black bear dreams than I did on my Canadian hunt.

But Canada still beckoned, with its offer of a spring hunt amidst a substantial bear population. One hundred and nine black bears were taken during the 1964 Wisconsin early gun season. A modest number when compared to Ontario's one thousand to fifteen hundred taken each spring, with hunters enjoying nearly a fifty percent success rate. And to add to the enticement, there was no limit.

-1-

Ontario became my goal for June of 1965. While preparations were underway, I discussed the upcoming hunt with my friend Dick Holmes. A spring bear hunt greatly intrigued him and he expressed considerable interest in hearing my plans.

I told Dick my plans were simple. I was going to take off into the wilds of Ontario, end up wherever I ended up, and just take things as they came.

Dick thought that sounded like a good plan.

We crossed the International Bridge at Sault Ste. Marie, where Dick and I each parted with seventeen dollars for our bear and fishing licenses, then headed east on Highway 17.

At Thessalon we turned north on Highway 129 and soon were following along the banks of the swift-flowing Mississagi River. We were heading to Aubrey Falls. We in fact had developed a plan.

Our readings about bear hunting suggested a good method in the spring was to hunt around small waterfalls where spawning suckers congregated. Black bears were likely to gather there to feed. Aubrey Falls showed enticingly on the map. It also showed spectacularly when we arrived. A one hundred foot drop into an eighty-foot-wide, sheer-walled gorge. Suckers surely would be halted by the falls. Whales would be halted by those falls. We doubted this was what the authors had in mind.

While Dick and I, along with a few other tourists, were admiring the falls, we struck up a conversation with a man who turned out to be from the area. He suggested we continue north to Peshu Lake. Bears had been reported bothering some campers there.

Peshu Lake turned out to be a fire ranger headquarters complete with a floatplane base. Not exactly a setting conducive to bear hunting. An unimproved, one-lane dirt road branched off of the road to the ranger headquarters. Turning down the road, we began a long, slow journey into a wild, lake-filled country. We bumped and scraped mile after mile through ruts and mud holes and over protruding boulders, uphill and down, on a seemingly endless trek to nowhere. It was a good road. It held promise of solitude. And bear.

The promise of solitude was broken when we finally arrived at the end of the road to find a tent pitched in a clearing on the shore of a lake. We backtracked to another lake, set up our tent, then launched Dick's canoe to find out what we were going to have for supper. We had northern pike.

In the morning we looked out upon a vast wilderness and wondered where to begin. We decided to scout the hills then meet back at camp around noon.

The hilly country was heavily forested. We later learned a massive fire had swept through that area in 1948, ravaging nearly six hundred fifty thousand acres. The succession forest was well under way. Aspen and white birch, along with bracken, fern, bunchberry, wintergreen, and a host of other plants, grew abundantly. Spruce, pine, and balsam were gaining their footholds. The resultant spring foliage reduced visibility to a few yards. To compound that problem the forest was tinder dry and every cautious step crackled out a stern warning. When we met back at camp, the question of still-hunting had been answered with a hopeless no.

We were back to looking for a sucker run, assuming they were still running. Our lake had one outlet but nothing that even remotely resembled a falls. We considered the lake where the tent was pitched. Upon arriving there we met an Ohio hunter named Paul. He and his friend Fred, who was out bear hunting, had been there eight days. Paul had two bears to his credit, but Fred had yet to take his first one.

During our conversation with Paul we were sagely advised that the only hope of bear hunting success in that country lay in baiting. Hardly an unexpected revelation after our morning's scouting. Our problem was that we had neglected to bring anything to use as bait.

Paul very kindly directed us to some baits they were no longer watching. That evening, sitting over two of them, Dick and I painfully discovered another important item we had neglected—insect repellant.

There is a fresh, awakening beauty to the springtime Canadian North. But alas, that beauty is marred by two blemishes—

blackflies and mosquitoes. Swarms of them. Clouds of them. Afflictions of them. The fearsome hordes of Genghis Kahn and Attila the Hun would have panicked into headlong retreat had their adversaries been able to unleash the black armies that assailed me that evening. I endured the onslaught but likely alerted any bait-curious bear with my hand movements in a vain attempt to ward of the attack.

When I removed my boots that night a one-inch circle of raw flesh began where the boot top ended. Blackflies. When blissful sleep began to banish the incessant mosquito bite itch-ing, I was brought rudely back to consciousness as my tossing turned my tender, bloodied ears to the pillow. More blackflies. Dick fared even worse.

Once again Paul came to our rescue with bottles of 6-12 repellent. We were considerably, as well as painfully, embar-rassed by our lack of essentials. Paul responded most graciously in helping out a pair of naive strangers.

Paul's friend, Fred, after nine determined evenings of watch-ing baits, at last got his bear. Paul, remarkably, took a third bear that same evening. After he finished helping Fred skin his bear, Paul decided to check his bait one last time. He returned in a little over an hour to announce to Fred that there was another bear to skin. Paul had no sooner arrived at his bait when a bear obligingly walked in.

Dick and I discussed their success with mixed feelings. Our excitement about being in an obviously excellent bear area was tempered with the fact that four bears already had been taken. We wondered what the chances were for a fifth and a sixth.

The next two days did little to enhance our hopes. Our baits remained undisturbed by bears as they dwindled to the point of vanishing from the constant maraudings of other woodland creatures. We had nothing to replenish them with except for the remains of the fish we caught for supper.

After Paul and Fred left we moved our tent to the lake they had been camped on. The bait Paul shot his last bear over was a half-hour walk from camp. On our fourth day, following his directions, we found it. The bait, consisting of sweet smelling cookie dough, lard, fish leavings, and other odorous food stuffs, remained largely intact.

It was, in truth, the only intact bait left. We considered flipping a coin to determine who would watch it, then decided to watch it together.

We were limiting our bait watching to the evenings mainly because our gifted supply of blackfly and mosquito repellant was running low. At four o'clock we left camp and climbed into the hills overlooking the lake. The walk to the bait took us along a narrow trail through the dense, shaded forest. In places we followed an almost indistinct track across large dolomite outcroppings. We weaved and dipped through the succession growth and the remnants of great pines that had escaped the fire's wrath.

The bait lay forty yards to the right of the trail up a gradual slope. A lane had been cut through the underbrush to view the bait and also to offer a clear path for the flight of a bullet should a bear arrive. A giant white pine stood ten yards to the left of the trail. The pine's base provided a comfortable seat from which to observe. Dick and I settled into position beneath the sheltering branches of the pine and began our vigil.

The warmth of the afternoon made our extra clothing decidedly uncomfortable, but we had discovered that the evening chill was equally unpleasant, so we endured. The blackflies and mosquitoes enveloped us but we came better prepared—pants legs tucked into boots, shirt shelves tied with cords over gloves, hats pulled tight, collars upturned, 6-12 lathering the exposed portion of our faces. The persistent hordes came as they always came. Our defenses held for the most part, but the swarming, buzzing multitudes tested our perseverance.

Red squirrels visited the bait. One in particular found the taste of lard smeared on a tree irresistible. He scampered through the underbrush, up the tree, gulped a quick mouthful, nervously dashed away, then quickly returned for another furtive sample.

A raccoon came but could not penetrate the heavy logs laying over the sweet cookie dough. It trundled away in discouragement. An inquisitive fox tried next, sniffing for a breach in the guardian logs before drifting away unappeased. And always, in background accompaniment to the passing parade, the blackflies and mosquitoes hummed.

Around eight o'clock I heard the brush crackle to my left. I tensed and cautiously turned my head, but saw only a green maze. Time passed and vigilance relaxed. The steady drone of insects soon supplanted the arresting sound.

The forest closed into a nearly impenetrable thicket on the left side of the bait from which the sound came. The forest grew a little more open on the right side. An hour and a half had passed since the crackle to the left when a similar crackle again alerted me. This time to the right. Something was moving through the brush, and it was not a red squirrel.

I eased the safety off and peered into the darkening forest. A movement. Along a fallen log. Steady and determined. Toward the bait. Black in the black shadows. But moving through the shadows. Then forming its own shadow.

A bear! The shifting outline of a bear!

I raised my rifle and was overwhelmed with brush. I swung ahead to the edge of the cut lane where the brush thinned and waited. Seconds dragged. Suddenly the empty scope filled with the image of a bear. I fired and was aware of the bear running into the dense forest on the left.

A crashing through the brush stilled into silence.

Then came a bellowing. An eerie, hackle-raising bellowing diminishing to a low murmur. Then silence again.

"You got him!"

Dick had seen the bear lurch when hit, although the angle through the brush from where he sat to my left hid the bear from his view until the moment of the shot.

I was trembling, the aftereffects enjoying their usual dance with my nerves. We waited ten measured minutes before cautiously walking the fifty yards to the bait, rifles at ready. A blood trail led to a dense thicket. We gingerly approached the edge of the thicket. The impenetrable leaves guarded the interior well.

Dusk had come stealthily upon us. I could not muster up enough courage to enter that thicket in the gathering gloam. Dick nodded in agreement to my whispered suggestion that tomorrow might be a more prudent time to follow the bear.

We returned to camp through the dark forest, my thoughts alive with silent elation. I had shot a bear! Yes! I had shot a bear! He was in the thicket. He had to be in the thicket. The morning would surely find him there.

And so it did. The bear lay a few hidden yards inside the dense greenery. A young boar, hit through both lungs, the bullet angling forward just behind the left shoulder. He ran twenty-five yards after the shot.

I dressed the bear amidst the joy of the blackflies. Then we cut a sapling, lashed the bear securely to it, and carried it to camp.

Skinning a bear offered a new challenge for us. We proceeded carefully and in time had the well-furred hide off, salted, and curing in the shade.

Since neither Dick nor I knew what bear meat tasted like, we decided to have a bear roast. We scooped out a shallow pit, pounded in a stout forked limb at each end, let a fire in the pit burn down to coals, secured the bear to the sapling we had carried it to camp on, and suspended the trussed bear over the roasting fire.

The fire needed constant tending and the bear regular turning. I kept busy with the bear roast while Dick watched the bait that evening. When Dick returned after dark, we stoked up a roaring fire, retrieved two cold beers from our deep-lake refrigerator, then, with an accompaniment of potatoes and beans, dug into our bear roast.

It was awful. We tried various portions but could not get it down. We retrieved two more beers. They did not help. Perhaps the bear had been dining heavily on fish. Perhaps we should have removed all of the fat. Perhaps the overnight stay in the woods before dressing tainted the meat. Perhaps we simply did not know how to roast a bear. Whatever, try as we might, we could not eat it.

I subsequently found bear meat to be quite palatable, but that young boar made a poor first impression.

Dick watched the bait for a final evening but no bear interrupted his lonely vigil. My first bear turned out to be the only bear of our hunt.

-2-

Dick and I were wiser the next year as well as being better prepared. We began gathering meat scraps from butcher shops two weeks before our departure. When we left on June eighteenth, two sealed metal containers of fragrant bear bait reposed in the trunk. Headnets, along with copious quantities of insect repellant, were also packed. My customized brush rifle, a converted 8MM Mauser, was back from the gunsmith with a new Timney trigger. The rifle had also been fitted with a quick-detachable scope mount. The post reticle in the scope stood out sharply against the brush, but standard sights struck me as being more practical for following a bear into thick cover.

We headed north to Ontario on this my fourth bear hunt, and there came at last a comfortable sense of knowing what I was doing and where I was going.

The where was our campsite of the previous year. We delayed our departure a few weeks to avoid interfering with Paul and Fred should they return. We were relieved to find the campsite empty.

Sunday found us preparing baits. We managed to set up three before the time came to begin hunting. One where I had shot the bear. Another two miles away where a game trail wound up a small valley past a rock outcropping. And the third a mile beyond that along another faint trail.

Our baiting procedure was uncomplicated although labor intensive. First a stand was selected, ideally close to a game trail we could approach silently on. Then with axes we cut a lane through the dense brush twenty-five to fifty yards before clearing a small area for the bait. The narrow lane provided a corridor we could see and shoot down. A generous pile of ripe meat scraps was covered with a pyramid of logs to prevent other animals from eating the bait. Each day before noon we checked the log pyramids from the trails. If the logs were askew, a bear had visited. In that case we rebaited. Then one of us essentially camped on that stand, although normally we limited our watching to the evening hours. By ten o'clock, in the forest, it was usually too dark to shoot.

The weather had turned exceptionally warm, into the nineties. The lake offered welcome relief after our labors. At four o'clock Dick trudged up the trail behind camp to watch our successful bait of the previous year while I made my way to the rock-outcropping stand two miles back.

The excessive heat turned the clothing and headnet I wore into a Swedish bath, but the buzzing clouds of blackflies and mosquitoes reminded me that it was either a sauna or a bugfest. I sweated.

The evening passed in measured patience. Hours of inactivity drag interminably, and uncomfortable hours, when you are locked into stillness and silence, drag beyond time. Hope sustains you. The hope of one, intense, heart-stopping moment when the shadows evolve into the form of a bear. For that one moment, the hunter endures.

But so often hope simply fades into the night. By the time all the shadows became one, only a single red squirrel had brought a diversion into my six hours.

The following morning we canoed across the lake and set up another bait, after which we checked the first three. Nothing. The intense heat continued. We fished awhile, ate, then at four o'clock donned clothes we would rather not have and returned to our stands.

Again the long, hot, buzzing, waiting, sweating, vexing, torturous, hope-filled, then hopeless hours before the black shadows bid me return to camp through the eerie, silent, night-dark forest to anticipate tomorrow.

Tuesday we took a long paddle in the canoe around a deep arm of the lake to break our routine and see some fresh country. We came across an old log cabin perched on a small bluff, a trapper's cabin probably. It appeared unoccupied. An intriguing trail led from the cabin into the forest. We followed the trail a fair distance before deciding not to explore farther lest we cut into our hunting time. We fished on the way back, reached camp, ate supper, and trekked out to our respective stands to while away the hours in hope.

The following morning we awoke to company. A family from Michigan had come to fish. Dad, Mom, and two teenagers. When the parents discovered we were bear hunting, they offered to take any meat we might not be able to keep because of the heat. They were well-equipped with coolers, planning on taking home a generous supply of fish.

The dad informed us that we were in the middle of a heat wave. Records that had stood since 1910 were being broken.

The sun must have tried for another record that day. We checked our baits in a heat that sweated through the forest shade. Dick's remained untouched, as did the one across the lake. But when we got to my rock-outcropping stand, we were heartened with the stirring sight of scattered logs and vanished bait. A bear had come during the night or early morning. I rebaited and anxiously began an early vigil.

Watching over an active bear bait vies in teasing expectation with casting over a rising trout. You know one is there. But will it come to your offering?

The bear came at seven-twenty. A black nose and brown muzzle floating out of the green foliage on the left side of the log pyramid. The adrenaline-rushing apparition hung suspended thirty yards away. Only its muzzle showed. Not another inch of the bear could be seen. No sound had been heard. The silence became palpable. The hum of insects ebbed and flowed with the pulse of my labored breathing. The minute was beginning.

The bear came forth with a fluidity of motion like an ebony Neptune emerging from a sea wall of green. So dreamlike did it seem watching the dark form materialize that the bear had reached the pyramid before the image of its muzzle cleared from my senses.

The bear stood angling away, its nose investigating the pyramid. I settled the scope on the front quarters, laid the black post against its black shoulder, and fired. The bear lunged forward while I worked the bolt and disappeared into the thicket on the right as my second shot followed after it. A crashing came, followed by a profound silence. I waited as the adrenaline release began. I let it subside.

The thicket into which the bear had disappeared closed into impenetrableness. I removed the scope from the rifle, practiced a few times bringing the cleared open barrel sights to my eye, eased cautiously to the edge of the thicket, and trailed into it after the bear.

He was dead.

My first shot broke the right front shoulder and punctured the right lung before exiting ahead of the left shoulder. My second shot, taken as the bear was enveloped in the brush, hit its left hind leg. The bear lay just ten yards beyond the edge of the clearing. A good-sized boar but unfortunately heavily rubbed.

It was all I could do to drag the bear from the thicket into the clearing. I dressed him, then returned to camp to wait for Dick's help in getting him out. The heat demanded that the bear be taken care of that night. It promised to be a long one.

I was enjoying a celebratory Molson Canadian Lager from our lake refrigerator when the fishing family pulled up in their boat. They were excited to hear I had shot a bear and offered to help bring it to camp. An offer impossible to refuse. Out we trooped to the bear, Dad, Mom, and both teenagers in file behind me. As we were returning, I suggested to Dad that we carry the bear to their camp if they still wanted the meat. They still wanted the meat.

Dick reported no activity that evening and none of the baits were disturbed when we checked them the following morning. We fished again in the afternoon, then, in keeping with our developing pattern, set off at four o'clock for our respective baits.

After a noneventful evening I returned to camp where Dick greeted me with a harrowing tale. He had walked up the trail and before turning toward his stand had cautiously peered around the edge of the cut lane to find a bear peering back at him from alongside the bait. Dick raised his rifle and fired. The bear began racing downhill directly toward him. Dick quickly chambered another round and dropped the bear with a spine shot at under ten yards.

Upon later skinning the bear, we found the small bronze point of Dick's first bullet just under the hide of the bear's throat. Whether the bear was charging or simply running in the direction he was facing when first hit, as my two had done, could only be surmised. Regardless, that fine boar remains Dick's most memorable bear.

The following morning we checked our baits but found no activity. Dick offered the meat from his bear to the fishing family and they soon had it deboned and packed in their coolers.

That evening Dick elected to hunt over the third bait on the camp side of the lake while I returned to my familiar stand. My vantage point was atop a rock outcropping that sloped up ten feet from a narrow trail. With my traveling up and down the trail, both to reach my stand and to check the bait, I assumed a keen-nosed bear would avoid it. But five hours of burning sun must have dissipated my traces, for shortly before nine o'clock, following in my earlier footsteps along the trail, a bear walked into view. A big bear.

It came in silence, materializing like a black phantom out of the ether, seeming unreal in spite of the tangible presence looming ever closer. An astonishing apparition. I watched as though in a dream. Finally the reality registered. And another minute began.

A rotting log lay alongside the trail, twenty yards from me. The bear ambled to the log, turned it over with a flick of its paw, and began to lap up the grubs and other wriggling delicacies scurrying about in the sudden shock of light. The bear stood facing me, engrossed in feeding, its glistening, heavily furred front shoulders rippling rich and black. Through the scope I watched scuttling bugs trying to escape up the bear's muzzle. The red, lapping tongue nudged them back into the bear's mouth and oblivion.

Time shrank into nothingness until a sense of now brought the rifle's recoil. The bear collapsed to the ground, its head coming to rest upon the log. The echo of the shot faded, and the forest stilled.

I waited in a silence disturbed only by the rhythmic humming of the blackflies and mosquitoes. Five minutes. Eyes locked onto the bear. Watching. Only the insects moved.

The bear turned out to be quite old, given the worn condition of its teeth. A good-sized bear but unfortunately heavily rubbed on one hindquarter and the underbelly, which I had not been able to see. The heat was causing the bears to rub off their winter undercoating, leaving unsightly splotches of naked hide.

The bear was not returning to the bait, which remained undisturbed, but seemed simply to be searching out its normal food supply. No doubt the bait would have been detected, and surely consumed, giving me fresh cause to hope when I checked it the following morning had I not been there for the ultimate fulfillment of that hope that evening.

I detected a fading enthusiasm when informing the fishing family that another bear awaited them. Later one of the teenagers arrived at our camp to announce, "My dad says we got enough bear." And so, Dick and I concluded, had we.

-3-

June 1967. We were brimming with confidence, almost to the point of cockiness. We had spring bear hunting down to a science. We were loaded with bait, with coolers, with salt, with repellant, and all other necessary accoutrements. We sallied forth in smug expectation. We began to feel a brotherly concern for the bears.

Our concern for the bears abruptly left us at the border along with our bait. In spite of our protestations, the adamant Canadian border guard refused to pass us with our fragrant mixture. Our acceptable passage the previous year swayed him not. Back we went to the American side, visualizing a permanent encampment on the International Bridge if United States Customs also turned us away. They did not. We fortunately found a refuse truck whose driver relieved us of our two bait containers at twenty-five cents apiece.

Our smugness vanished with the bait. The hopelessness of the springtime Canadian bush loomed formidably in our minds. Once back into Canada we scoured the grocery stores and bakeries, eventually assembling a replacement bait from meat scraps and outdated bakery goods.

Our old campsite on Rocky Island Lake showed empty. We organized our camp then set out four baits, including one across the lake, and settled into our standard routine. Check and replenish the baits before noon, fish in the afternoon, then watch on our stands from four o'clock until dark.

And so the waiting began. The minutes passing. Patient minutes. Crawling slowly into hours. Holding still through the hours. Locked motionless in the quiet. Memorizing each leave and branch. Memorizing them again. Quickening to shifts in the shadows. Dreaming away in the idleness before rousing again to the passing minutes. Waiting, ever waiting, for that one ultimate moment.

Occasionally a forest animal or a woodland bird filled a minute or two, but for three days they provided the only activity at our stands.

Then the bait on our side of the lake which we had not sat over was hit. A flip of a coin gave Dick the honors. Early that evening, on his stand just off a footpath-wide trail, Dick heard to his left the faint rustling sounds of something coming down the trail. The bait lay forty yards to his front down a narrow cut lane which intersected the trail at right angles. With the exception of the narrow trail and the cut lane, the surrounding forest was clothed in nearly impenetrable green.

The rustling in the dry leaves came steadily closer. Dick was tucked back into the brush, unable to see down the hidden trail. If a bear continued down the trail, Dick's shot would be point blank. He waited tensely, safety off, rifle at ready. The rustling came nearer. Tension mounted. Then a startling, rushing, heart-stopping crashing of brush as Dick brought his rifle to bear and tracked a equally startled ruffed grouse that thundered into flight nearly at his feet.

The following morning my bait was gone. With two stands active, our confidence rose. We were on the stands an hour earlier that afternoon, a sense of renewed hope helping the minutes pass with heightened expectation. But like so many other evenings, hope faded with the fading light, leaving the long, dark trek down the night trail the last chance for a bear encounter.

There was that aspect of the hunt, and an intriguing one it was. Bears used the trails, as did we. The possibility of a nocturnal encounter at close quarters on the dense-canopied forest trail added a stimulating spice to that dark, silent, solitary walk back to camp.

Both baits were gone when we checked the next day. Either the bears were coming during the night or early in the morning. We practically camped on our stands, arriving early in the afternoon, sitting until dark, then returning before first light in the morning after barely four hours of sleep. The bears eluded us.

It quickly became evident that the bears were arriving after dark. They cleaned us out of everything we offered, forcing us to reluctantly admit defeat, our earlier smugness about having spring bear hunting down to a science receiving a rude comeuppance.

We did see two bears. While driving out a pair of cubs scooted up a tree along the forest lane. We stopped but prudently remained in the car knowing the mother bear had to be nearby. The cubs entertained us for a few minutes. We left them undisturbed and drove on before the mother bear put in an appearance.

-4-

We secured our bait in Canada the following year, avoiding the possibility of another challenge at the border, although we could find nothing in the regulations forbidding bringing our own.

We returned to our camp on Rocky Island Lake. Our familiar stands were baited, firing lanes cleared of new growth, and another season of watching began.

That year I brought an 8MM movie camera with the hope of capturing a shooting sequence on film. I constructed a tripod with a plywood platform to hold the camera. The camera rested on the platform which had a strip of wood nailed in front and a simple cam device rigged in the rear. Turning the cam pushed the camera forward, depressing the start bar against the wood strip. The camera whirred away on its own, leaving me free to handle my rifle. Everything worked perfectly when I tested it.

Rain visited us the first day. We trooped out to our stands in spite of the wetting. I covered the camera with a small piece of tarp hoping the dampness would not create a problem. A scampering red squirrel came to sample the bait shortly after my arrival and I practiced turning the cam with my left hand while positioning my rifle. The sequence flowed flawlessly. I waited through the damp evening for the ultimate test. But I waited in vain.

The rain continued on and off the following day, putting a damper on our activities. I took the occasion to read while

Dick wandered down to a creek inlet to seine minnows, luring them by following the biblical admonition of casting bread upon the waters.

We trudged out in the rain to undisturbed baits where we spent a second evening listening to a symphony of dripping trees and humming insects. Not a creature stirred in my vicinity.

Tuesday. The dark clouds hovered. No activity at the baits. We fished in a drizzle, trying for walleyes with Dick's minnows. Apparently it was even too wet for the walleyes. Another dripping evening on our stands, the damp chill seeping to the bone by the final hour. We forced a reluctant fire out of covered wood back at camp. The night skies lay clothed in inky black, although the rain had abated.

The following morning continued overcast, but the afternoon saw the welcome sun make its long-awaited appearance. We stretched some ropes to hang our sleeping bags and clothes out to dry, then basked in the warmth.

The sun brought the blackflies and mosquitoes out in full force, making headnets mandatory on our stands. I wiped off my tripod platform, positioned my camera, and settled down to wait. The insect hordes buzzed in full concert. I watched the little clearing through their enveloping haze.

My evening passed uneventfully. Dick, however, saw hours and days of dampened patience win out when a good-sized bear sauntered in to investigate his bait. A single shot had Dick in possession of a fine boar.

Thursday. We brought Dick's bear into camp then checked the other baits. Still no activity. At least the sun favored us with its presence.

The evening came clear. For the fifth time that week I trudged up the narrow trail toward my stand.

Moose wandered this valley. The rump of one of those great creatures appeared unexpectedly in front of me as I made my silent way up the trail. I tread softly, following surprisingly close behind the unsuspecting animal until I turned off at the cut lane.

My bait still lay undisturbed. The tripod sat in place. I positioned the camera on the plywood platform, checking to make sure the focus centered on the pyramid of logs. Then I situated myself beside it and began the evening vigil.

I watched from a rock outcropping ten feet above and ten yards away from the trail. The bait lay covered by a pyramid of logs twenty yards on the other side of the trail. The trail ran up a narrow valley through which a small rill tumbled toward a sparkling lake where northerns had furnished our supper a time or two. A hundred yards from the rock outcropping, beyond the rill, a sheer dolomite facing rose from the valley floor. The succession growth that clogged the valley climbed the dolomite facing like a continuous green carpet.

An intermittent overcast periodically blanketed the sun, but as my waiting began, the skies cleared. Welcome sunlight appeared, illuminating the darker forest recesses. Biting insects thrived in the warming rays and quickly made their presence felt.

Three hours passed. The sun arced slowly behind me. I stood quietly, hoping for, but after all the empty days, resigned to another evening without the coming of a bear.

And then he came, ghosting up the trail the moose and I had vacated scarcely three hours before, black fur glistening in the sunlight, a phantasmal apparition, drifting through the green, shoulders rippling in fluid motion, drawing closer, great head swaying, steady, steady, closer, closer.

I shrank into motionlessness. The bear flowed effortlessly up the trail to the edge of the cut lane. I held. He paused ten yards from me, then turned away and walked toward the pyramid of logs. I reached my left hand to the cam on the tripod platform. The bear settled his two front paws on the logs. I turned the cam and eased my left hand to the forearm of the rifle. The camera whirred. The bear turned his head toward the sound. My eye found the scope. The bear stared intently in my direction. The post reticle settled behind his left shoulder. I fired.

The scope jarred from the recoil and in that instant I became conscious of the bear running directly toward me. I pulled the bolt back. The bear was coming. I chambered another round. On he came. I tried to find him in the scope. The bear vanished into the small hidden space beneath the curve of the rock outcropping. I lowered the rifle to my hip, pointed the muzzle toward the rock edge a few feet away, and waited for the bear to come over. And waited. And waited.

The bear did not come. Silence reigned. An intense silence. A profound silence. An overwhelming silence. And still the bear did not come.

Insects hummed. A breeze whispered. A throbbing drummed in my ears. The forest green drew close. The rock edge mocked me empty. I waited expectant. And still the bear did not come.

When time that hangs suspended passed, I stepped cautiously to the edge of the outcropping and peered over. Nothing. A blood trail at the base veered to my right into the dense thicket that surrounded me. I eased left through the thicket down to the trail. The scattering of blood led directly from the log pyramid to a stump at the base of the rock outcropping. The stump had turned the bear into the thicket when he hit it. The blood trail led into a tangled tunnel of green.

I removed the scope, settled to my knees, and peered into the twisted tunnel. The blood trail continued through it. I followed on hands and knees. And there I found the bear. A fine boar. Hit through the left lung.

The camera did not work. The rain and dampness warped the plywood platform. When the cam pushed the camera forward, the warping forced it up and over the wood strip set to depress the start bar. The camera ran for a few indistinct frames, then stopped.

I tread silently back to camp awash in mixed emotions, my elation over taking a fine bear tempered with the disappointment of loosing the action sequence of a lifetime.

Dick arrived shortly before dark to announce another bear down. The cessation of rain seemed to have brought the local black bear population out in force. We toasted each other's good fortune, commiserated on my bad, then stoked up a roaring fire, cooked a belated meal, ate, and sat in wilderness delight by the darkened lake watching the flames flicker against the star-intense night sky while the haunting, wild song of a loon echoed across the waters.

The following day was consumed with the chores of a successful hunt. The two bears were brought into camp where the blackflies and mosquitoes were less bothersome, skinned, the hides salted, the meat taken care of, and then ourselves taken care of with a quick, soap-lathered, chilling dip in the lake.

We were debating about going out that evening, wondering if we really needed another bear, when a young man approached us. He introduced himself as Jim, a college student from the University of Wisconsin, in Canada with some friends on summer break to fish and bear hunt. They were camped close by.

Their bear hunting had been fraught with disappointment. They were novices and Jim was seeking advice. Dick and I were not that many years his senior, but with three bears in camp, and no doubt looking a bit rough after a week in the bush, we likely appeared as grizzled old veterans. We dispensed our modest accumulated wisdom in the same fashion that Paul dispensed his to a pair of novices four years earlier, including the location of our stands. Dick and I did not hunt that evening.

Alpha Gamma Rho

9-16-68

Dear John,

Just want to let you know what you did for me. I got our only bear off your friend's stand. We think he weighed about 400-450. When the taxidermist measured this 7 yr old male his skull was 3/8" short of getting in Boone and Crockett.

Thank you much for your help. We learned a lot. Its good to know there are men like you in the woods. I wish you and Dick the best of luck at everything — especially hunting. Maybe see you next spring.

Jim

-5-

Our hunt began with an unexpected encounter the following year. On the highway before our turnoff, a fair-sized black bear came into view, sauntering along the shoulder enjoying his afternoon constitutional. He ambled across the road in front of our car, disappeared briefly into the forest, reappeared, wandered down the other shoulder in our direction, shuffled back across the road, then disappeared for good into the forest on the side where we had first observed him. A favorable omen.

We were close to Mashagama Lake Road so decided to turn down it and set up two backup stands since at least one bear was roaming the area. That done we continued on to our Rocky Island Lake campsite.

The campsite was empty. We wondered if Jim would be returning. The picture accompanying his note showed a beautiful black bear that would be hard to top. None of the seven bears Dick and I had taken appeared to exceed it. Of Paul and his friend Fred, we saw nothing since the first year.

We did have a visitor, however. An Indian named Neos. He emerged from the forest on the trail that led to Dick's stand. We came to discover that the trail continued past the stand and ended at the trapper's cabin we had run across on an earlier canoe trip. The cabin belonged to Neos. His family lived on the reservation but he favored the solitude of the wilderness. He joined us for breakfast, unabashedly polishing off our week's supply of bacon. As recompense, he led us to some secretive brook trout waters.

We found the fishing outstanding, but the bears remained in a reclusive mood. Three days and evenings passed without even a hint of interest in our offerings. On Wednesday we decided to break our routine with an evening on the Mashagama Lake Road stands.

We left early to allow for the hour and a half drive, the distance in miles not being great, but the rutted, rock-strewn lane to the main gravel road a slow-motion challenge. Dick dropped me off at my stand and continued several miles down the road to his.

The clear evening began pleasantly, the attendant biting insects in diminished numbers for a welcome change. I sat just inside the treeline on the edge of a slope overlooking a small cutover clearing surrounded by the dense forest. After seemingly endless hours and days of memorizing every leaf surrounding my rock-outcropping stand, the unfamiliar scenery seemed strangely disorienting.

But the minutes as well as the hours lumbered along the same. A few birds flitted by but no four-footed creatures exposed themselves in the little clearing. The sun continued its steadfast journey to the west, lengthening the dark shadows until they gradually merged into the forest background.

I carried my .270 that year, having shot all my 8MM handloads in practice before discovering my replacement bullets were on back order. I tested the scope and still could faintly make out the crosshairs. The dusk deepened. Finally the crosshairs became indistinct against the darkening background. I eased from my position, then took a few quiet steps toward the road.

A faint noise from below the slope stopped me. I turned around, retraced my silent steps, and was startled to see a bear running from the clearing into the forest. I stood for several seconds, then took a few cautious steps to the edge of the slope and scrutinized the dark forest. The deep dusk rendered it impenetrable. I waited in the closing night, chagrined at timing my leaving just as the bear must have come into the clearing. I brooded, surrounded by gloomy silence, staring at the forest.

Then came a sense of movement as a form took definition. The bear emerged from the trees. He drifted like a phantom back into the clearing, stopping twenty-five yards from me, only his head and shoulders faintly defined against the matching black background. He remained motionless, staring in my direction but likely witnessing a similar formless presence.

I eased the rifle to my shoulder. The bear shadowed into the scope but the crosshairs were lost against him. I let the center of the scope settle naturally against the center of the bear's front and fired.

A rush ensued and the bear was gone. I chambered another round, then listened intently. From the dark forest where the bear had emerged and then disappeared came the eerie sound I remembered from my first bear, the final announcement of a mortal wound through the lungs.

I carried no flashlight so elected to wait until morning to recover the bear. I made my way out to the gravel road and waited for Dick. His arrival brought the relating of an identical experience. A last-minute bear in a small clearing at close quarters. A remarkable coincidence on the first evening on first-time stands. It was well after midnight by the time we reached camp.

We recovered the bears in the morning, both having run only a short distance after the shot. Most of Thursday was spent getting them back to camp and taking care of the meat and hides.

We saw no other bears that spring, but other black bears fell to our rifles in subsequent years. The succession forest continued to slowly hide the scars of the great fire of forty-eight. Aubrey Falls, that scenic wonder that drew us initially to the area, succumbed to the hydroelectric developers in 1969, leaving a trickled remnant of its once glorious grandeur. Still, the wild country sprawls. Brook trout spawn in Neos's secret waters. Northerns and walleyes tempt in the crystalline lakes. Loons send shivers in the eerie quiet of the night. And black bears still wander there in the gloaming.

Chapter 8

In The Big Horns

The pleasure of the mountains and the prairies drew me west each fall. Like most things, the price of that pleasure began escalating. In 1966, Wyoming increased its nonresident license fees from twenty to thirty dollars for deer, and from twenty-five to thirty-five dollars for antelope. Elk licenses, which included deer, bear, birds, and fish, went from one hundred to one hundred and twenty-five dollars.

While planning my 1967 hunt, a business acquaintance put me in touch with two of his elk hunting friends from Newcastle, Les and Vern, with whom I made arrangements for a mid-October elk hunt in the Big Horn Mountains.

I arrived early, intending to hunt antelope and mule deer before joining Les and Vern for the elk hunt. Familiar prairies drew me first, and by one o'clock of the second day a fine antelope hung in the Gillette locker plant.

Mule deer next turned me toward the mountains. I drove west to Buffalo, stopping at a local restaurant to sample the novelty of a buffalo burger before continuing into the Big Horn Mountains along a highway climbing five thousand feet to Powder River Pass. A turnoff several miles up the highway attracted me. I followed the turnoff to a small clearing where a stretch of level ground offered a campsite and set up my tent. The mountains loomed majestically against the evening sky.

First light of the following morning dawned with me climbing toward the summit of my campsite mountain. The way was steep, requiring frequent pauses to catch my breath and rest my unaccustomed leg muscles. On one of those pauses, in an edging of timber bordering a valley opening, two deer appeared. Does. They crossed the opening and wandered casually into the timber on the far side. I waited several minutes, hoping for more deer to follow. None did.

I continued my slow climb. The grade increased drastically near the top of the mountain, prompting me to grasp handholds on protruding brush to pull myself up. Finally the narrow ridge lay beneath my feet and I looked out over peaked horizons. A penetrating wind that rocked me came down off those peaks. I sought shelter from the buffeting gusts behind a large boulder before settling in to glass the surrounding country.

Two hours passed in careful scrutiny. The trees swaying in the wind remained the only movement observed. The slopes continued empty. I turned from them and began to still-hunt along the ridge. The wind still bothered, but a scattering of oversized boulders offered occasional relief.

The narrow ridge widened beyond the boulders into a flat tableland. Pockets of conifers extended out into the flat from a rimming of heavy forest. I hunted slowly along the edge of the denser cover, pausing where evergreen boughs parted to reveal sheltered lanes. Past one of those lanes a small stand of spruce angled away from the cover's edge. I started around it and froze in mid-step.

A deer was moving ahead! Ghosting gray-brown through the trees. A buck! A very good buck!

I brought my rifle to bear. The buck drifted in and out of my scope as he drifted in and out of the trees. No chance for a shot. Then an opening. A chance. Then a tree. Another glimpse. Crosshairs on. Too late. Then again. Moving steady. Not alarmed. Then trees intruding before another opening. Again a fleeting chance. Then a lost chance. Then there again, only to vanish again. Fading into shadows. The scope searching, desperately searching. But finding only shadows, until there were only shadows to find. Then finding only emptiness.

The deer was gone.

I stood there a moment, letting the tension find release, staring into the emptiness, then shook off the disappointment and followed after the buck, hoping to catch another glimpse. But his steady pace soon dashed those hopes.

I resumed still-hunting, circling through the rimming forest, pausing on game-inviting overlooks. No other deer appeared. I hunted back along the ridge, finding myself by early afternoon again seated beside the boulder that had sheltered me from the morning wind. I began glassing.

Far below, on the opposite side of the mountain from camp, a scattering of boulders similar to those along the ridge lay in shadowed relief. I shifted my binoculars from boulder to boulder, scanning in a desultory fashion an area that had shown empty that morning.

A vague suspicion drew my gaze. I looked, and there on the wind-protected side of a large boulder, taking form in its shadow, a bedded mule deer buck came into view.

I glued his image in the binoculars. The buck lay on level ground where the backside of the mountain blended into a flat expanse, facing directly away from me. He turned his head slowly from time to time, watching out over the flat, exciting my wonder with the grandeur of antlers displayed with each turn. A decidedly larger buck than the disappearing buck of the morning.

I studied him through the scope. The range was long. I tried to make a judgement with the double crosshairs but the buck's bedded position rendered them impractical. The steepness of the slope confused my attempts to estimate. That same steepness began intruding as my thoughts turned to packing a deer up the severe grade. The longer I contemplated that rugged mountainside, the more daunting appeared the task.

I watched the buck alternately through my binoculars and my scope, vacillating between the hunter's imperative and the uncertainty of range and retrieval.

The buck lay in blissful unawareness of my deliberations, his position unchanged. I considered the shot, trying to determine a proper hold. The position of the buck helped settle my concern. He lay facing away, directly in line with me. A high hold would offer the entire length of the neck and the front half of the body to compensate for bullet drop. I groaned inwardly at the thought of packing the deer up that formidable mountain, but then, I had come there to hunt.

I took off my wool jacket, folded it over a boulder, rested my rifle on it, and settled into a solid position. The buck held steady in the scope. I placed the horizontal crosshair just above the base of his antlers with the vertical crosshair laying along his left side to compensate for the wind, which was still gusting strongly. I waited for the wind to moderate, then finished my trigger pull.

The buck bounded up at the shot and began racing over the flat. No way to capture him fairly in the scope. He gradually slowed and came to a halt, well out of range. I watched the buck through my binoculars as he began to feed, evidently unharmed. He finally fed out of sight.

Where the bullet struck, I had not seen, obviously close enough to startle the buck into action. The culprit, I like to believe, was the wind. A maddening variable.

Two does moved out unaware as I hunted down the mountain back to camp. Dark was near by the time the little tent showed faintly ahead. I lit my Coleman lantern, gathered a supply of wood, started a fire, and cooked supper. I had taken no food or water onto the mountain. I ate ravenously, then sat in front of my tent in the night, feeding the fire while I sipped hot coffee and contemplated my day as the looming mountains closed dark around.

Stiff legs slowed my early climbing the following morning, muscles rarely used rebelling at the insistence to perform. The morning was well-advanced by the time I reached the ridge and sat gratefully down beside a boulder. The wind whistled, biting through my wool jacket outside the shelter of the rocks.

I focused my binoculars on the scattering of boulders the big buck had bedded in and searched them with mixed feelings, wanting again to see the grand deer but not at the base of that formidable slope. A suppressed sense of relief embarrassed me when my scrutiny did not discover the deer.

An hour passed in careful glassing. The mountain remained empty. I arose and began following the ridge toward the flat tableland where the other buck had eluded me the day before. The morning continued pleasant but windy.

The tableland and rimming forest offered no deer. I came by ten o'clock back to the ridge. The boulders drew my scrutiny again, but if any deer were bedded there they were well-hidden from view.

I followed the ridge a short distance in the other direction, found a sheltered spot from which to observe the camp side of the mountain, and sat down to glass. Four does had wandered through there the day before. Perhaps one of their consorts would follow along the same course.

A warming hour passed. No movement disturbed the ground, but the sky was alive. A flock of unfamiliar western birds flighted nearby, foraging through the trees. Magpies gathered below, worrying something far down the slope. A hawk soared gracefully on the mountain currents, rising aloft in effortless flight, wings rarely adjusting, spiraling free, riding the currents until it became a black speck that hovered over a distant mountain peak.

A motion to my left caught me unaware. I looked away from the hawk. A deer had come up the backside of the mountain and was crossing the ridge fifty yards from me. A spike. I barely registered him before another spike trotted over the ridge, following the first. Next came a third. Then, incredibly, another. I stared mesmerized as yet a fifth buck appeared. But no spike this one. Wide-branching antlers rising tall adorned his head. The sudden appearance of the deer held me frozen for a few seconds. I waited unsure, wondering if the procession would continue, thinking that perhaps a still larger buck might follow.

There were no following bucks. The five deer continued down the mountain in single file, filtering through evergreens that offered fleeting chances in my scope. Then the deer stopped, bunching, disappearing from view in the thickness of trees. I waited breathlessly.

They began moving again, indistinct shadows. A thinning in the evergreens seventy-five yards down the slope began to reveal them. A spike came into view. Another spike followed. Behind him the large-antlered buck broke clear, moving slowly, offering a chance, the crosshairs at last resting on him free of blurring trees. I swung with him for the brief instant needed to match his movement, and fired.

The buck rushed into cover, out of sight. The sound of falling, followed by the cracking of brush, came to me as he tumbled unseen down the mountain. Then silence. I sat while a spike passed fifty yards to my left back over the ridge, then stood up and scrambled excitedly down the mountain.

The buck lay wedged against a bush growing among some small rocks, his tall, wide-branching antlers signaling his position as soon as I cleared the trees. I went slowly to him. The grandness of the creature held me spellbound for a time, absorbed in wondrous admiration.

Three times past did I seek such a deer in the mountains, only to be defeated by the snows and the vagaries of the hunt. But the sun had shone that day, and the Red Gods had held me in the palms of their hands. A primordial contentment flooded through me. I marveled long beside the deer, immersed in the moment, gazing out over the wonder of the mountains, glorying in the wildness, while high overhead, in an exquisite hunter's salute, a hawk soared.

Then came the toil. Small deer have this advantage, they are easier to get down off the mountain. My weary thoughts turned more than once to those spikes as I struggled with that big buck. But the rugged course back to camp steadily grew shorter. The afternoon was shading into evening by the time the welcome tent came into view. Again I took no food or drink onto the mountain. I gulped down copious quantities of water, then rested awhile before building a fire and cooking supper. Sleep came easily with the dark.

I broke camp early the following morning and set off east toward Newcastle. The time for elk was drawing near.

Les, Vern, and I were joined in Newcastle by the fourth member of our party, a University of Wyoming student named Stu, taking a week's break from his studies for the elk season. When we assembled for our foray into the Big Horns, we made a formidable procession.

Vern led the procession in his green Ford pickup, towing a stout metal-framed trailer carrying a four-wheel-drive jeep, foul-weather equipped with a detachable canvas front seat enclosure. Les followed in his GMC pickup, towing our home-to-be in the mountains, a short-based camping trailer with comfortable bunks for four along with a cooking stove and heater. An abundance of equipment from spare gear to game pulleys to snow and mud chains filled the two pickups. For someone accustomed to traveling and camping light, this bounty of vehicles and accouterments was most impressive, a veritable embarrassment of riches.

Our little caravan headed back toward Buffalo, retracing my earlier route west along Highway 16. The steep climb beyond Buffalo tested the two pickups. We labored up the mountain road, passing the turnoff to my mule deer camp of a few days previous, that hunt already assuming the aura of a long-ago adventure as the excitement of new country began building.

The mountains pulled us upward until, coming to an offshoot trail, Vern turned north, with Les following close behind. We climbed through a dense evergreen forest before breaking out into an expansive meadow. Snow dotted the meadow in light patches, grading deeper in the shade of the dark timber that surrounded the extensive clearing. The mountains rose barren in the background showing pockets of cloud-white snow against the gray of the granite. A light overcast exposed wide ribbons of blue sky over the peaks. The air was brisk. The venue grand. We were in elk country.

We followed a faint track along the meadow, splashing through a shallow ford across a narrow mountain stream, sending small trout scurrying frantically away from our disturbance. A grove of pines attracted us. Les backed the camping trailer into the grove, leaving it hitched to the pickup. Vern backed the jeep off of the carrying trailer, then tucked his pickup and the trailer into the pine grove. We busied ourselves with organization for an hour before setting out in separate directions to hunt.

The evergreens rimming the meadow drew me. I climbed slowly through the thick trees, still-hunting cautiously. The trees thinned in places, opening up smaller meadows. I watched each one briefly before moving on, holding just inside the evergreens and aspens surrounding them. In some areas away from the meadows, the thick cover, combined with a jumbled tangle of blowdowns, rendered movement nearly impossible. At times I was forced to retrace my path through the labyrinth when the mazelike pathways closed tight. Elk moved through these thickets, as evidenced by their tracks, but how I could not fathom.

The afternoon continued pleasant. I still-hunted, climbing gradually upward, until a prominence revealed a breathtaking vista below. I sat on a fallen aspen watching the patchwork of timber and meadows. Time floated lazily by like the wispy clouds above. Lengthening shadows began warning me to start back down the mountain. I circled through the openings, avoiding the difficult cover with the down timber, and reached the camp meadow with the last light of day. Supper was already underway when I stepped into the trailer. No elk were reported.

A wild call came in the night. A primal echo, tremoring out of the mountains, floating eerily on the wind, resonating over the meadow, haunting us in the dark. An untamed challenge in an untamed wilderness. Again it came, a single note, pitched high, sending shivers, like the night cry of a loon. Then an answer, responding from afar, a wary rejoinder, tentative, sensing awe. Again the challenge. Fearsome. Resolute. Again the response, but faltering, growing faint. Then a final challenge, echoing unanswered, fading into silence. Then only the sigh of a whisper-breeze in the pines. Then only the dark quiet of the night.

"Elk bugling."

"Yeah."

"Tomorrow."

A suppressed excitement pervaded our preparations in the morning. The serenade in the night confirmed the presence of elk near camp. Les and Vern both agreed that it was a little late in the season for bulls to be bugling, but also allowed that elk kept their own schedule, regardless of what humans thought they should be doing. I had little to contribute to the discussion, my elk hunting experience consisting solely of my brief afternoon still-hunt the previous day.

We climbed early into the heights, each on our separate way, the dawn's air crisp, holding the promise of a clear day. I proceeded again along my route of the previous afternoon, hunting cautiously through timber and opens, heading in the general direction of the prominence overlook.

Each of the small meadows held me for a while. The morning's discussion suggested elk could be feeding in them early. But each meadow continued empty. I skirted their edges, climbing higher. In time I reached the prominence, sat again on the fallen aspen, and began searching the meadows through my binoculars.

The sun rose slowly behind me, shortening shadows, bathing more and more of the meadows in light, spreading a warmth that gratefully replaced the chill of the night. I continued to glass but nothing materialized from the disappearing shadows.

The morning hours passed uneventfully. Restlessness replaced patience. I tucked my binoculars inside my coat, stood up, and began to follow the contour of the mountain south seeking a fresh perspective. As I proceeded along, I came to a stretch of heavy timber that led toward distant meadows. I entered it and quickly became immersed in a jungle of mixed conifers carpeted with a bewildering maze of blowdowns. Visibility was reduced to scant yards in places.

I struggled through, questioning whether to continue. An impasse halted me. I stood, looking for a way around, when the sound of cracking branches brought me instantly alert. The cracking grew louder. Something was moving to my left. Then the sound of a body brushing against branches crackled to my right. Soon a general surge of heavy-bodied animals moving all around enveloped me.

Elk! They had to be elk!

I strained to catch some movement. The dense conifers denied me. I held my rifle at ready, franticly looking left, then right, then back again as the brush and branches telegraphed the passing procession. I knelt down, then stood upon a fallen tree, desperately seeking an opening, but the ghostly clamor flowed unseen around me as though it was passing through the ether.

There seemed to be no mad dash to it, just a steady, unhurried transit. I stood in helpless frustration, listening as the sound came, surrounded me, then passed as invisible as the wind. The last faint rustle receded beyond my hearing, and with its passing, a rising, single note, pitched high, wafted back through the timber.

I followed after the herd, knowing that unless they stopped, my struggles through the blowdowns made overtaking them impossible. Their tracks showed in the disturbed ground, confirming the obvious. They were elk.

I continued after them, but for the rest of the morning they remained as they first had been. Invisible. The hopelessness of my pursuit finally took hold. At a point where their tracks traced close inside a meadow edge, I broke out of the confining cover and climbed toward a promontory, relieved to escape the restrictive closeness.

The noon sun found me high above the tangled timber, perched on another overlook, glassing in the direction the herd seemed to have gone. But they surely had long outdistanced me. An hour passed. The disappointment over the elk gradually gave way to an appreciation for a stirring wild encounter. I ate a sandwich and an apple, then arose and began to circle down the mountainside.

The tangled timber seemed to hold the best promise. Wearisome though it was to hunt through, the thick cover remained the only place elk had been encountered. I dropped down to the closest stand and eased into it.

Straight lines ceased to exist. Devious, convoluted pathways twisted between, around, and up and down a crisscross pattern of fallen trees. Elk obviously felt comfortable in the confusion, their tracks and droppings were in constant evidence. A deep shade pervaded. The air tested still. The cover's denseness likely defused the mountain currents. But fierce gales must have raged at times through these wild mountain forests to have felled the ancient giants that forced me clambering through branch-entangled corridors.

My world became a circle measured in yards, my progress without a halt measured in feet. I wended through the labyrinth, at times forced to sling my rifle across my back in order to free my hands for climbing over deadfalls. The conifers hung close, forming a dense canopy, allowing only rare, solitary rays of sunlight to penetrate. No sound violated the dark sanctuary. Silence reigned. And I struggled to maintain it, picking a careful passage through the dead branches and limbs. Time hung suspended.

I moved slowly along, straining to see into the dark shadows. A lighter opening to my right parted the conifers. I turned toward it, seeking momentary relief from the oppressive closeness. I reached the edge of a clearing and stopped just inside the covering evergreens. The sun showing in the west made me curious about the time. Two-thirty. Still hours to go.

The clearing was an irregular opening some fifty yards in diameter. The tangled forest closed tightly around it except for the downward side where a growth of aspens broke up the deep cover. The prospect of at least fifty yards of tangle-free walking drew me into the clearing as I again continued on.

The entrance into clear sunlight almost startled me, so conditioned had I become to the secretive forest. A strange sensation of exposure came over me. I began to sense game's attachment to the deep, hidden places. By the time I reached the midpoint of the clearing, my newfound sense of exposure intensified. It seemed foolish to have revealed myself after my long, careful passage through the sheltering trees. I began to hurry my steps until a sudden motion to my right brought me to an instant halt.

I looked, and there, forty yards away, on the downward slope of the mountain, through the thinner mixture of aspens and conifers, antler tips were bobbing. Nothing else. Just the steady bob, bob, bob of antler tips. Floating detached. Steadily rising.

An elk! A bull elk!

I franticly settled to my knees, desperately aware of my glaring exposure, hoping I might imitate a wayward stump in the otherwise barren clearing. Rifle at ready. Facing downward. Heart thumping. Tremors threatening.

Then majesty came. A creature of wonder. Rising from the mountain like a spirit incarnate. Resplendent in the haloing sun. Its emergence held me in awe.

The great bull rose full into view with no acknowledgement of my wonderstruck presence. He walked slowly just inside the thinner cover until he came to a stop behind a pine. I dared then to move.

I shouldered the rifle, capturing the left edge of the pine in the scope. Tensing. Waiting. Sensing movement seconds before the elk slowly came forth. Antler tips. The head. More antlers. The neck. The shoulder. The lung area. The roar of the rifle and a frantic rush as the elk ran around the edge of the clearing and stopped behind another pine.

No doubt of the shot, in spite of the uncontrollable shaking that began afflicting my right leg, a reaction rivaling my first deer. I trembled, slightly embarrassed at the release of tension, thinking I had progressed beyond that. Then realized that I probably never would.

The bull remained partially hidden behind the pine with only his hindquarters exposed. Occasionally, through the branches, I could see antlers moving up and down. I waited. Fifteen seconds. Thirty. A minute. Still the bull stood there.

I decided to try a shot through the branches. Laying the horizontal crosshair along his hindquarters, I moved the vertical crosshair forward until, judging from the bobbing antlers, the lungs were centered. A puff of blue smoke erupted in the branches as the rifle recoiled. The bull ran straight away into the dense cover, crashing noisily through the blowdowns. Then the crashing stopped.

I walked cautiously to the pine. A blood trail led me from there. The bull lay thirty yards inside the cover. A wondrous, grand creature. The epitome of mountain majesty. I marveled at his splendor.

The first shot had passed perfectly through the lungs. No evidence existed of the second shot. After dressing the bull, I carefully blazed a trail through the timber to the nearest meadow, then returned to camp.

We retrieved the bull after the next morning's hunt. Vern was able to maneuver the jeep up to the meadow below the timber the bull was in. We rigged a straight-line harness, and while Vern, Les, and I grunted mightily through the timber, Stu guided the antlers through the maze. It was exhausting work. We rested when we reached the jeep. When a measure of strength returned, we lifted the great beast into the back of the jeep and returned with him to camp.

We retrieved a second bull before our week was out, Les having the honors. I saw other elk, and on one memorable morning watched a bobcat stalk a blue grouse pecking away unaware on the ground. Each stealthy step by the bobcat brought it ever closer to the grouse, while each occasional glance around by the grouse found the bobcat a shadowy statue against the mottled background. The outcome was a foregone conclusion.

We at last bid goodbye to our high-country camp and our little caravan wound its way back down the mountains. I returned home with one hindquarter of elk, the rest of my game divided among the others in appreciation for a grand hunt.

The wonder of elk called me to the mountains again and again. Another bull fell to my rifle in the grandeur of Wyoming's Big Horns. I sought them in the untamed wilderness areas of Montana and the glorious Colorado Rockies. The San Juan Mountains of New Mexico once found me hunkered tight in a solitary bush in a clearing watching a heavily tracked up elk-wallow, when a black bear of considerable size emerged from the forest. He stood imposingly on his hind legs for half a minute, then came cautiously across the open meadow toward me, testing the air. I held him in my scope as he stopped at twenty yards and weighed his options. Finally he turned and continued down the mountain, pausing twice to look back. Three other black bear appeared in the half-hour before night-fall. Not surprisingly, I saw no elk that evening. The walk back to my horse in the dark remains memorable.

But in the grandness of those memories there comes always to the forefront that wondrous October day in the Big Horns, when the skies framed the distant peaks in blue, when aspens blended their paleness into the dark conifers, when antler tips ghosted through the shadows, and when majesty came rising up from the mountain.

PART II

Chapter 9

Pronghorn Prairies

The passing ages have witnessed many a wondrous life form on this favored earth. In the great cosmic lottery, most have vanished into eternity. The pronghorn remains.

This singular survivor traces its lineage through a fascinating progression of forebears. Graceful creatures, most of them, bearing exotic names that occasionally stumble across the tongue. Like *Ceratomeryx prenticei*. This slender-legged pronghorn, barely distinguishable from its present day cousins, flourished amid the luxuriant grasslands of southwestern Idaho three and a half million years ago.

Farther back into the ages, another graceful pronghorn with the correspondingly graceful name *Merycodus* thrived on the high plains between the Texas Panhandle and the Missouri River Basin. *Merycodus* roamed the lush prairie flora five to six million years before our time, stepping gingerly in the shadows of giant, shovel-tusked mastodons.

An earlier cousin called *Synthetoceras* prospered on those same high plains. This striking savanna dweller sported a fantastic pair of elongated horns that jutted high above its nostrils, complimenting a smaller pair of horns projecting above its eyes.

Pronghorn-like creatures, such as *Protoceras,* trace back thirty-five million years. But on the hazardous journey through the ages, only one such creature survived the evolutionary winnowing, *Antilocapra americana*, literally, American goat-antelope, a unique North American treasure related to no other living animal. They roam still over the vast prairies of the west. A reminder of epochs merging into eras, when time was measured in the passing of the seasons, and when man was still a stranger on the land.

-1-

October 1970. Ten miles into Wyoming from the Nebraska border. A grand day with a brilliant western sky framing the sagebrush flats and a warm noontime sun shading behind scattered, wispy-white clouds. Twenty antelope does and fawns fed in a loose group before me as I lay scrunched in the sage. No bucks. I laid my rifle across a stunted cactus, pulled my binoculars from inside my shirt, and glassed the area around the feeding antelope. I scanned carefully, hoping to pick up a buck bedded close to the herd.

From my ground-hugging position the sage-covered prairie took on the aspect of a stunted conifer forest. Most of the area around the feeding herd lay obscured. After glassing the scant openings, I carefully raised myself on my elbows and found a level from which more of the surrounding flats became exposed.

The does and fawns fed leisurely, nibbling contentedly on the sagebrush, holding about three hundred yards away. The area to the right of the herd showed empty through the binoculars. I shifted my gaze and scanned between the feeding antelope, looking for black horns above the sage behind them. Nothing.

The aching arch in my back, along with my wearying elbows, prompted me to lay flat for a few minutes. Some of the does began to bed down. The sun drifted behind a fleeting cloud, then reappeared, soothing my back with a lazy warmth.

Several more does and fawns laid down. Siesta time. I began to drift away with them.

Another cloud passed in front of the sun. The shadow helped draw me out of my lethargy. I wriggled back up on my elbows. Half of the herd lay bedded. The others continued feeding. I began glassing to the left of the strung-out animals, and there, fifty yards from the nearest doe, the black horns and black cheek patch of a bedded buck danced in the magnified heat waves among the sage.

The buck lay quartering toward me, most of his body shielded by ground cover. I stuffed the binoculars back in my shirt, eased my rifle in front of me, and carefully assumed a prone shooting position. No good. The low-lying sage blocked the vital area. I shifted a little left, then a little right, to no avail. The buck remained concealed behind the screening of sage.

The standing does continued to feed. The others rested in concert with the buck. The sun warmed. I lay back down, resigned to waiting until the buck eventually stood up. Time drifted lazily by, matching the passing clouds. The feeding does began to bed down. Soon the entire herd lay on the sagebrush flat. Slumber reigned. I watched and waited.

Then impatience stole upon me, encouraged by the unyielding ground where insignificant pebbles began to gouge like volcanic rocks, while tiny cactuses grew into saguaros. The antelope rested in mocking comfort as my discomforts began to magnify. Action whispered her siren's call.

With all the antelope bedded, my concealment in the sage matched theirs. I began to squirm crabwise to my left, discovering, to my added discomfort, new varieties of miniature cactus. As I wriggled along, thinnings in the sage appeared through which some of the does could be partially seen. A lane finally opened where, by lifting myself well up on my elbows, a fair portion of the buck's body lay exposed. The sight picture was awkward, the quartering angle far from ideal. Patience counseled waiting, but the crosshairs held reasonably steady. I fired.

The buck jumped up, obviously hit. The rest of the herd bolted off to the right. The buck stood, watching the fleeing does and fawns. I chambered another round. The buck took a few tentative steps forward. I swung with him, twisting awkwardly on the ground, then fired again. And he was down. The rest of the herd raced out of sight over a distant ridge.

I stood up, momentarily astonished by the wide-open perspective after being so long in a ground-level world of seemingly towering, foot-high sage. I walked slowly to the buck, working off my stiffness. He lay in final repose amongst the sage.

My first shot had been less than perfect. Patience raised an unforgiving reminder.

I dressed the buck, then lingered awhile on the sage-scented prairie. The warm afternoon sun touching on the buck reminded me not to linger too long, but for a short time I gloried in the grand emptiness around me. No sign of life animated the sun-drenched prairie, yet antelope wandered freely there, and that simple realization lent a vibrant perspective to the vacant horizons. They would not remain vacant for long.

-2-

The prairies called me west each fall. The vast open spaces, where one could often stand and gaze toward horizons untarnished by any hint of the passing of man, imparted a grand sense of freedom. Reminders of man lay beyond the horizon, of course, and the illusion remained simply that. But to exist briefly within that boundless illusion found time suspended for a few sublime moments.

The hunting of antelope on those vast prairies became both a simple and a challenging endeavor. The open expanses generally made finding the animals an easy task. If antelope were present, they were visible. But that same openness often frustrated the stalk.

In rolling country the challenges reversed. Then the searching could fill hours with emptiness, while the stalk took on a less formidable aspect. But regardless of terrain, there inevitably came the one constant challenge. The shot.

Summer weekends saw my afternoon hours spent at county gravel pits firing forty to fifty handloads through my .270 at cardboard cutouts of antelope. I also became immersed in ballistics. Terms like sectional density, ballistic coefficient, and the value of Ingalls' "A" skipped lightly over my tongue. I diagramed bullet-drop graphs and plotted wind-drift charts. Knowledgeable rifleman sought my advice. I began to amaze even myself. But embarrassingly, some bullets I fired still went astray. I discovered the glaring flaw in all my precise calculations. A human being is not a stable shooting platform. Yet the practice continued, over varying ranges and from different shooting positions. And although an errant bullet or two still refused to go where the charts promised, the groups tightened.

The hand of man found cause at times to change the pristine aspect of the prairie. Ranchers in western Nebraska and eastern Wyoming discovered the Ogallala Aquifer, an immense subterranean water source, and irrigation came to the plains. Sections of wind-dried prairie that had barely nurtured sagebrush for millenniums suddenly spouted water enough to grow hay. The antelope studied this unaccustomed growth for a season and then did what any enterprising ruminant would do. They began eating it.

October 1972. Thirty-plus antelope fed leisurely in a cut hay field north of Node, Wyoming. The billiard-table-flat field offered no hope of a direct approach. I watched the herd feed an impossible stalk away. The antelope paid me no attention. So far removed as a threat was I, they deigned not even to acknowledge my presence.

Bales of hay stood stacked at the far west end of the field a mile away. The herd fed close to them. I studied a circuitous route to the bales, and deemed it possible.

My watch indicated near noon. The sun favored the day with a benign warmth. I began a roundabout walk to the south, skirting the edge of the field until a modest concave offered cover enough to turn west. I followed the shallow concave at a steady gait, drifting south whenever a slight incline brought the tops of the hay bales into view. My progress finally brought me even with the bales. I dropped to my knees and crawled toward the edge of the field.

The antelope still fed in the cut hay, still out of range, and still close to the stacked bales. I eased back into the concave and continued west until the bales angled sharply behind me. Again a crawling approach revealed the position of the herd unchanged, although an angle had developed in my favor. The bales began to offer screening.

An open stretch still needed crossing before the bales would hide me completely. I duck-waddled part of the way following a shallow depression, stretching little used thigh muscles that would surely punish me later. I came in time to a crawl, rifle slung across my back, then to my stomach, crabbing stealthily toward the shelter of the bales. The antelope remained undisturbed.

The sun fell in shadow as the bales at last surrounded me. The antelope fed spread out over the field, the nearest ones, one hundred and fifty yards away. The shot, from a solid rest over a hay bale, became anticlimactic. The time was one-twenty. Nearly an hour and a half had elapsed.

One more antelope fell to my rifle in a hay field during another season, but after that I hunted the hay fields no more. Although the antelope continued to favor them, I simply favored the sage prairies more.

-3-

My accommodations while antelope hunting were Spartan by choice. Roaming free and setting up camp wherever night found me enabled me to shift my hunting grounds at will, and also put me on them the moment I awoke. A tent remained an option for those rare inclement nights, but typically I just rolled out my sleeping bag and air mattress on the ground. When next the prairies called, however, Ginny accompanied me, and sagebrush beds held no allure for my wife.

My procrastination in seeking a motel resulted in every room in Lusk being already booked. As a last resort, a two-bedroom house turned up that could be rented for twelve dollars a night. Six dollars if we were willing to share with whoever showed up next. Ginny failed to see any humor in my musings about potential house guests.

The accommodations turned out to be as Spartan as my camps. A sagging double bed stood starkly in each otherwise barren bedroom. One metal folding chair sat forlornly in the living room in front of a recycled black and white television. A single bare light bulb cast a harsh light on the unadorned surroundings. The living room opened through an archway into a kitchen with no appliances. The kitchen's crowning glory was a full-sized bathtub sitting in the middle of the floor exposed through the archway. At least there was water. And a woman did show up with clean sheets.

Yet the weather proved glorious and we roamed unrestrained over the prairie. We hunted well, stalking through the rolling, sage-covered hills, crawling along dusty dry washes, bellying through prickly cactus beneath ridges over which wary bucks had been spotted. Chances were offered and chances were taken. But in the grand cosmic scheme the Fates have decreed that the hunters will not always prevail. We wove our day into that fabric, returning gameless to our Spartan quarters in the last fading light of evening.

A cold-water bath in the middle of the exposed kitchen greeted Ginny after a dusty day of crawling through the sage. As she shivered in the cool water, plucking yet another cactus spine out of her elbow, she sweetly commented: "And to think people said you didn't know how to show a lady a good time."

Ginny decided to see the sights of Lusk the following day, while the prairie drew me back. The morning dawned clear, with crystalline skies providing a glorious backdrop to the already shimmering, sage-covered flats. I adjusted a day pack, slung my rifle over my shoulder, and headed out across the flats toward a series of low, rolling ridges.

Time flowed unperceived as the ridges passed in succession. Each gradual incline induced a cautious, step-by-step ascent as binoculars probed the unfolding prairie. The enticing vistas drew me deeper, searching, ever searching, as the sun climbed in measured progression through the cloudless blue.

Far into the ridges, and far into the morning, beyond an incline that raised almost imperceptibly, in the middle of an immense flat, two bedded antelope at last came into view. The binoculars revealed a fair-sized buck and a doe. They also revealed the impossibility of their position.

The antelope had chosen their resting place well. The flat basin, in the center of which they lay, offered no possible route for an approach. I studied the ground again and again, searching for some slight depression, some minor contour, some break in the unvarying flatness that offered hope for a stalk, but none existed. I settled down to wait. The possibility of the pair rising and moving in my direction offered my only hope.

The antelope remained bedded for nearly an hour before the doe stood up and began feeding. The buck watched the doe for a moment then rose to join her. The pair moved slowly as they fed. For several minutes their direction brought a rising hope, but then the general drift of the doe, and that of the buck, steadied away to my right.

From a hidden corner in my memory a drawing in one of my old hunting books emerged. A hunter laying flat on the prairie waving a piece of cloth on his ramrod while a curious antelope drew into range. Flagging, the old hunters termed it.

I had neither ramrod nor piece of cloth. Instead I draped my hat over the muzzle of my rifle, found hopeful concealment behind some sage on the slight backward slope, and raised my rifle, holding the butt on the ground between my hands.

No acknowledgement from the antelope. I moved the rifle back and forth. The antelope continued feeding, drifting farther to my right. I waited until the doe stopped and raised her head, then swayed the rifle again. She instantly became alert, locking in on the movement. The buck followed her gaze. I swayed the rifle gently, fluttering the hat. Both antelope stared intently in my direction.

I moved the rifle again. The buck took a few steps forward. The doe continued staring. Another gentle sway. The buck began advancing toward me in a hesitant manner. The doe followed. Then the buck came on more rapidly while the doe hesitated.

I lay motionless, watching the antelope through a filter of sage. The buck advanced with a steady gait. He reached a point about a quarter of a mile away, stopped, and continued staring. The doe came up to join him.

I moved the rifle again. The buck appeared agitated. He ran to the right a little ways, stopped and stared, then ran back to the left where he again stopped, watching intently in my direction. I lay still. The buck came forward a short distance, then bolted and ran back toward the doe. He reached her, stopped, and looked back. I waved the rifle again. The buck turned toward me. Another slight wave. He retraced his steps to the quarter-mile mark and stopped. The doe followed.

Again the buck pranced in apparent agitation. Back and forth. Then he began a hesitant walk toward me. I stayed motionless. The buck came on. Once more he stopped. I moved the rifle ever so slightly. The buck stared. I moved it again. He began advancing rapidly in my direction. I remained still. The buck continued steadily forward, closing to well within two hundred yards before he stopped and stared again.

I lowered the rifle with infinite care. The buck continued staring. I inched the rifle to my shoulder, found the buck in the scope, steadied the crosshairs, and fired. He crumpled to the ground as the recoil started.

The doe stared for a second when I arose before turning to race across the basin. One hundred and sixty paces brought me to the buck. A distance that seemed impossible to close to when first I saw him.

-4-

In November of 1975, on my birthday, I took delivery of a 1976 four-wheel-drive Chevrolet Blazer, destined to become my hunting and fishing vehicle. After disconnecting the rear seat, some simple carpenter work resulted in a removable bunk covering the wheel well on the driver's side, complete with three storage drawers. The rear of the bunk contained a compartment for a two-burner Coleman stove and cooking utensils, accessible when the tailgate was lowered. Racks on both side windows provided storage for guns and fishing rods. A comfortable foam-rubber mattress promised blissful slumber in a self-contained camp capable of going anywhere.

Or such was my naive assumption before discovering, on a deep-rutted, snow-packed logging trail in northern Wisconsin, that four-wheel-drive benefits one nought when the vehicle is high-centered. I also discovered that getting stuck in a four-wheel-drive gave new definition to the word stuck. The better part of opening day of deer season was sacrificed gaining that hard-won knowledge.

Once the madness of four-wheel-drive-invincibility entered remission, the Blazer and I got along fine, although it occasionally still tempted me into places where other hard lessons were painfully learned.

On my first trip to the prairies with the Blazer in October of 1976, a new .243 Winchester hung on a side-window rack. A rifleman's indulgence, since my .270 continued to serve me well. The .243 performed nicely on that trip, downing both a fine buck antelope and an equally fine buck mule deer.

The following October found me again in Wyoming, pausing beneath a large, black-bordered road sign proclaiming:

```
┌─────────────────┐
│ LOST SPRINGS    │
│ POP.        5   │
│ ELEV.    4996   │
└─────────────────┘
```

A dirt road pointed north toward a distant cluster of weather-beaten wood buildings. I followed down the road, trailing a dust cloud behind. A small, wood-framed general store showed the only sign of life. The interior suggested a time long past. A man appeared and I purchased a cold drink while commenting on the low population number on the sign.

"Oh, that's wrong," he said. "Used to be five but the folks that owned the tavern up and moved away. When they left, the town drunk left with 'em. Now there's just me and the wife."

But there were antelope aplenty, he informed me, waving in a wide arc toward the north. I was not long in taking his leave.

I followed north through a series of low, rolling hills, enjoying a brilliant sky and the pleasure of the prairie. My search for antelope was soon rewarded when a pair of does came into view. They were moving at a slow pace, feeding as they drifted along.

I dropped below a ridge and angled in their direction. The does again came into view. They were slowly feeding over another hill several hundred yards ahead. I waited until they dipped below the far side of the hill, eased over the ridge that had been shielding me, and began a steady jog across the intervening valley.

I slowed to a walk as the reverse side of the hill the does had crossed became visible. The pair came into view. They still fed purposely along, angling around the base of another far hill.

The does gradually drifted out of sight. I crossed into the shallow valley and jogged after them to the curvature of the base of the hill. There I began a cautious stalk, scanning the unfolding prairie before each step. The does appeared, still feeding, moving slowly less than three hundred yards ahead.

I watched as the does fed up the side of a low hill and slowly disappeared over it. Again I jogged after them. The hill they had crossed climbed gently to a broad crest before dipping into another shallow valley. The valley spread open in both directions between the next long ridge half a mile away. I eased up onto the crest, and there in front of me, spread out across the shallow valley, fifty or more antelope were feeding, my two does presumably among them.

But the does no longer held my attention, for bucks fed among the herd. Three with respectable horns. All within comfortable range.

I lay there contemplating the scene. Suddenly another buck appeared from over the far ridge. He moved rapidly toward the feeding herd. The buck reached a small cluster of does and began chasing one of them. The doe broke out of the cluster with the buck in close pursuit. Each time she turned toward the herd the buck cut her off, pushing her in a helter-skelter foot race away from the herd and over the far ridge.

I watched and waited, hoping for the buck to reappear, for he carried a pair of impressive, lyre-shaped horns.

Patience soon brought the hoped-for sight. The buck returned to dash again into a gathering of does and chase a seemingly not too reluctant one back over the far ridge.

Again the waiting, warming some in the flood of sunshine that lighted the intriguing scene. The antelope fed nonchalantly, shifting here and there wherever a delectable morsel lured them. None lay down. Eating had become the vital business of the moment. For all, that is, except the ranging buck.

Once again he appeared from over the hill, like a gallant knight on a hallowed quest. Down the slope and quickly among the does where another lithe, tan and white damsel was spirited away. The other bucks seemed oblivious to their steadily diminishing harem, for none sought to challenge the dauntless cavalier when yet another doe accompanied him over the far ridge.

The lyre-horned buck had chosen his does from the opposite side of the herd. I watched through my binoculars as he sorted among the feeding animals. Occasionally his maneuvers brought him temptingly close and the scope was exchanged for the binoculars. But constant movement remained the buck's forte, and during his rare, brief pauses, a doe inevitably screened him. I resolved to hold for a clear, standing shot or take none at all. So hold I did while the intrepid knight charged through the does and through the image of my scope, never deigning to halt in the clear for those few vital seconds. The herd continued to feed.

Time drifted unconsciously by as the ageless tableau unfolded. Eat. Procreate. Survive. The three absolute imperatives of all life on earth. Unchanged through the eons. And unchanging.

The better part of an hour passed without the buck returning. I considered a stalk around the herd to the backside of the far hill, but the low valley extended into extensive flats on both sides. Crossing it without being seen appeared impossible.

Time did not press me. I watched the grand scene for half an hour more until the herd began to drift toward the extensive flat to my left. Eventually they may have drifted far enough to clear me to the far ridge. But would the buck even be there? He had yet to reappear.

The herd began to slowly feed out of range. A fine buck halted to nip off a piece of sage before following along after the herd. He stood broadside at one hundred and seventy-five yards. I debated. A good hour and a half had passed since the lyre-horned buck's last appearance. The certainty before me tugged against the uncertainty over the far ridge. Certainty won. I centered the buck in my scope. He dropped instantly at the shot. The rest of the herd broke into a run and were soon dashing through the valley and out onto the flat where they gradually faded into the distant horizon.

After I dressed the antelope, curiosity drew me to the far ridge. Only empty prairie was visible from its crest. The knightly buck and his consorts had vanished into the airy reaches of their Camelot land.

-5-

Over the seasons there was time to bide while the locker plant processed my game. The North Platte River often filled that time, for trout generally favored my offerings and later favored me with a welcome change in dinner fare. The mountains also drew me, to wander for a day or two with nothing more pressing than seeking out a blue grouse for supper.

Ancient country abides in the land rolling out from the mountains. To roam it allows one to touch hauntingly beyond the ages. On land where I sought antelope, the archaic bones of horned dinosaurs have come to light. Aboriginal man left his tracings in prehistoric stone quarries known as the Spanish Diggings.

The early days of the West are colorfully chronicled in sites such as the Hog Ranch, a notorious, intriguingly named gambling saloon of the 1880's. And on a lonely stretch of prairie, on one of my many wanderings down faint tracks and roadways, I came across a solitary, weather-beaten gravestone with a poignant, faded inscription.

*HERE LIES
MOTHER FEATHERLEGS
SHEPHARD.
SO CALLED, AS IN HER
RUFFLED PANTALETTES
SHE LOOKED LIKE A
FEATHER-LEGGED
CHICKEN IN A HIGH WIND.
WAS A ROADHOUSE MA'AM
HERE ON THE CHEYENNE-
BLACK HILLS STAGE LINE.
AN OUTLAW CONFEDERATE,
SHE WAS MURDERED BY
DANGEROUS DICK DAVIS,
THE TERRAPIN, IN 1879,
FOR A $1500 CACHE.*

October 1979. The season found me northeast of Lusk where two extremely skittish antelope bolted upon sighting me half a mile away. I continued on until a projecting knoll offered concealment, then followed the knoll around until the open prairie beyond again revealed the antelope. A medium-sized buck and a doe.

They remained well out of range, moving steadily but not as rapidly. The flat expanse extending out from the knoll offered no possibility of closing the distance even if the antelope should stop, but their presence still held me. The pair stayed steady on their course for several hundred yards, then halted, and for some inexplicable reason, reversed themselves and began moving back in the direction they had come from.

I likewise reversed myself and ran back around the knoll, slowing to a walk as the opposite side opened onto the prairie.

The antelope came into view again between five hundred and six hundred yards away. I dropped into a prone position. The pair continued angling slightly toward me. I held the buck in my scope as the range closed. The buck's continued movement forced me to constantly squirm around to keep him in the scope. The sight picture finally held for an instant and I fired.

The antelope burst away in a mad dash. I chambered another round and scrambled into a sitting position.

The doe led the buck in a grand race across the prairie. They flowed gracefully in their flight, their lithe bodies holding level while driving legs flashed beneath them. I strived to pick up the fleeing forms in my scope. The buck at last caught and held. I swung in unison with him. Then ahead. Holding ahead. Farther. Still farther. Swinging well now. Squeezing. Squeezing. Ka-BOOM! Bolt up, back, forward, down. Another round in. Swinging again on the buck as he slows, slows, slows. And falls to the ground.

Three hundred and seventy paces brought me to the buck. A single bullet hole showed in his neck. A fortunate shot and only the second running antelope to fall to my rifle, the other falling two hundred paces closer.

The pronghorn prairies are a rifleman's delight. First the sighting, then the stalk, then the inevitable juncture where the rifle must cover the remaining ground. The ranges are typically long. On all my hunts I made it a practice to pace off my shots, one pace covering one yard. The terrain interfered at times, but the results were still more trustworthy than an imprecise estimate. Of nineteen antelope taken through the sixties and seventies, my average shot was two hundred and sixty yards, the longest being four hundred and the closest just a shade under one hundred. By contrast, that same number of whitetailed deer, taken with a rifle in the dense cover of Wisconsin's North Woods, averaged fifty-five yards. There, one hundred yards covered the longest shot, the closest being seventeen.

The pronghorn and the prairie forever remain entwined. The vast panoramic stage upon which these graceful *Antilocapra* play out the drama of life lends an imposing grandeur to their pursuit. They are the only remaining plains game on this continent. Long may their kind roam free.

Chapter 10

Montana Wild

In a time known as the Mesozoic Era, a supercontinent encompassed most of the land mass on earth and the Atlantic Ocean did not exist. Two hundred million years before our time, great forces began rending the supercontinent apart. This awesome shifting caused the floor of the Pacific Ocean to buckle. A crustal section beneath the ocean's floor began sliding under the western margins of the former supercontinent, forming a bulge on the earth's surface. Enormous masses of granite magma rose from the fiery depths into the bulge. Inexorably and almost imperceptibly these unimaginable forces thrust on until finally, over years measured in millions, great lofts of granite peaks towered majestically into the sky.

The Rocky Mountains had come into being.

Yet the earth was never still. Seventy million years ago, in what is now northwestern Montana, enormous slabs of layered sedimentary rock began heaving upward, creating a massive overthrust that slid relentlessly eastward an inch a year. Then the forces of wind and water spent their millions of years sculpturing the overthrust into spectacular formations with modern era names like the Scapegoat Massif and the Chinese Wall. And in the times that named those brooding sculptures, the earth at last seemed still.

Nearly one million acres of this sculpted Montana wonderland have been set aside as a memorial to Bob Marshall, an avid wilderness advocate and former Chief of the Forest Service Division of Recreation and Lands. This pristine treasure and its contiguous wilderness area can be circled in a four hundred mile road journey, but not a single road crosses it. Elk, mule deer, and grizzly bear roam this striking land of towering cliffs, breathtaking canyons, wild rivers, and dense forests. And in September of 1973, I headed for the Bob Marshall Wilderness Area to journey into that splendid country in their quest.

Swan Valley separates the Bob Marshall Wilderness Area from the Mission Mountains to the west. The rancher I contracted with to outfit me into the wilderness had his ranch in that valley. It was there that I met the five other members of our hunting party, three men from Missouri, and a father with his teenage son from Michigan.

Horses and mules would take us into the mountains. We made an impressive caravan when morning found us on our way—the rancher, three guides, and six hunters on horseback, followed by a wrangler leading a pack string of mules.

We climbed slowly, single file, up a well-defined trail. The horses wheezed and grunted with their early morning exertion. The day dawned clear, the rising sun still a subtle foreshadowing behind the great mountains above. I gloried in the crisp freshness of the morning and the novelty of the unfolding vistas as we climbed steadily higher.

Pines surrounded us as we wended our way upward. At times they closed tightly. At other times they spread out in a lavish green carpet below the bare rock facings we crossed. The horses plodded on, settling into a monotonous, rolling gait. Time sauntered along with them.

We arrived with the midday sun at the summit crossing. The horse riders stopped for a break while the wrangler continued on with the pack mules. The wrangler made regular trips in and out during the elk season. He had boasted earlier of his sure-footed mules and their superiority over horses on difficult stretches of the trail. One of those stretches lay before us—a narrow ledge snaking one hundred feet along a vertical rock facing with a several hundred foot sheer cliff dropping off into a dizzying gorge. The rancher advised us to walk across the ledge first, and if we had any reservations, to lead our horses across instead of riding.

While we were gazing over the intimidating precipice, we noticed a fresh carcass in the rocks below. The rancher informed us that it was one of his mules. When the time came to proceed across the ledge, I thought of that sure-footed mule laying dead in the gorge, and then of my less sure-footed horse. I led my horse across. I was not alone.

We came after the ledge to a steep mountainside covered with loose shale. A narrow ribbon of a trail switchbacked down the rock-strewn slope into a valley. As my horse braked himself descending the abrupt decline, my cinch loosened. When I got off the horse to tighten it, I stepped up.

The valley immersed us in a sea of evergreens. The mountains rose grandly on each side and the sweeping conifers rose with them. Long open swaths, where snow slides had cleared away the trees, scarred down the mountainsides like ski runs. Elk grazed in those grassy opens, the rancher informed us.

We plodded along through the winding valley. Camp in due time showed as a cluster of white wall tents in a pine-encircled clearing. Two tents accommodated the hunters, another the guides, along with the cook, who was already in camp with the evening meal in progress. A larger tent served as the mess. A split-rail corral held the horses and mules.

The sun was approaching the western mountains by the time camp was settled. The cook tent provided welcome warmth as the evening chill descended. Night came with a wonder of stars pulsating in a moon-favored sky.

One of the men from Missouri was paired with me for the week's hunt. Morning's darkness shrouded the valley as he, I, and our guide climbed into stiff saddles and began a slow ride through the pines. Our route took us back along the trail we had come in on the preceding day.

Darkness still enveloped us when the guide dropped me off at the base of one of the slides and continued on with the Missouri hunter. I tied my horse in a sheltering of evergreens, then climbed a short distance up the slide to where a jutting of pines extended into the clearing and waited for the dawn.

It came in shadings of gray, gently across the mountain, revealing an edge of black-green conifers guarding the shadow-hidden slide. Anticipation sent shivers to replace those dispelled by the warming climb. I waited, engulfed in that same intense sense of expectation with which I had greeted so many other dawns. First light remains the most magical of all the magical times.

The fullness of dawn brought definition to the steep slide area. I searched thoroughly through my binoculars, probing the slide's edgings as the shadows receded. No elk or deer. Nor, hope upon hope, grizzly bear, for a coveted license accompanied my elk and deer licenses.

The sun made its slow climb above the rim of the mountain. I returned to my horse, mounted it, and followed the trail to the next slide area where the guide and the Missouri hunter were waiting. Then we set off riding up the valley. The dark evergreens shielded us as we rode along the narrow trail. Each new slide area brought a careful scrutiny before we crossed its base to ride again into the sheltering timber and repeat the process at the next steep clearing. No elk fed upon the slides.

Noon brought us to the steep shale slope that marked our entrance into the valley. We rested the horses and ourselves and ate sandwiches while the horses in turn nipped the sparse grasses. The day had warmed considerably, the sun full above without a hint of clouds. The valley spread invitingly below, with scattered conifers clinging tenaciously to barren higher rocks then deepening into a thick carpet through the lower reaches. Elk regularly roamed this valley, the guide asserted, although the unseasonable warmth could be holding them at higher levels.

Our afternoon hunt followed the morning in reverse. We worked back down the valley hoping to find game resting in the shaded cover. If they were there, they eluded our searching. The descending dusk saw me returned to the same jutting of pines from which I had greeted the dawn. Fading evening shadows brought no elk to graze in the far-reaching meadow above.

No game sightings were reported for the day.

We left before dawn the following morning, shivering in the dark chill that erases all memory of shirt-sleeved yesterdays. Our course took us down the valley into new country, but our hunting tactics remained the same. Another slide kept me in watchful observation until the rising sun brought the return of my guide and a morning ride through the valley. The warming air soon had wool coats tied to the back of saddles. Another grand day. But evidently too grand in the valley for elk. Not even a fresh track showed to perk up our spirits.

Then a track did show. A series of them in fact. Tracks to excite wonder. Fresh over our horse's tracks of the morning. Tracing along the same trail we had followed out and were then following back to camp. Going in our direction. Fascinating tracks. Awesome tracks. Grizzly tracks!

The guide became agitated. When the grizzly tracks turned off the trail toward the mountain slopes and I suggested following in hopes of seeing the bear in one of the slide clearings, the guide would have none of it. We kept on a diverted course back to camp, arriving with good hunting light still showing on the mountainsides.

The two other Missouri hunters reported seeing one mule deer in the high country above camp. No elk had been sighted.

The guides carried no rifles or other arms, but the wrangler carried a holstered, heavy-caliber revolver on his pack trips to and from camp. I noticed my guide in an earnest discussion with the wrangler during breakfast the following morning. When we mounted for the day's hunt, the wrangler's heavy-caliber revolver rested securely on my guide's hip.

The consensus among the guides was that the elk were high. While two guides and four hunters climbed the mountains where the mule deer had been sighted, our little group of three set off in the opposite direction planning to spend the night in a spike camp high above the valley.

No slides traced down the mountain slopes we traversed. We hunted meadows as we climbed. The trail led upward then down into another valley where a clear-water stream dashed sparkling through sunlit openings. The faint track wended back and forth across the stream as we climbed toward distant heights. At one point we struggled up a high bank and came to a series of deadfalls across the trail. Most were smaller trees and the horses took them in stride. At some of the larger trees, however, my horse became skittish, finally balking at one the guide's horse stepped over comfortably.

I tried to prod my horse over the tree but he stubbornly stood fast. I looped the reins around the pommel and reached out to a nearby pine to cut a length of branch for a switch. At my motion the horse suddenly bolted and began running up the mountain alongside the tree. Caught off guard and off balance, I grasped the pommel and reached to unloop the reins. Before I could do so the horse came to the end of the tree and began to run around the upturned roots.

A companion pine stood next to the roots with its branches extending over the fallen tree. My horse chose a confined route beneath the branches as he circled the roots. Other pines hemmed me in. The horse rushed under them. I saw a limb rapidly closing in on my chest. No place to duck. I lifted my elbows as the limb swept me off the horse, locked my upper arms over the unyielding bough, and hung there, feet dangling in the air.

The horse completed his circuit of the deadfall, came to a stop in his accustomed place behind the guide's horse, and turned an inquisitive eye toward me, no doubt wondering why, since I had seemed so anxious to cross the fallen tree, I was now hanging from another one up the mountainside.

The guide and the Missouri hunter broke out in convulsive fits of laughter, laughter which, at that particular moment, I did not feel inclined to share in.

My horse seemed nonchalant regarding his roundabout method of crossing deadfalls and plodded placidly along when I again regained the saddle.

Shortly thereafter a small clearing opened in front of us. Our spike camp. While the other two rested in the tent after lunch, I made my way to an inviting pool in a nearby stream and caught, on a nondescript fly, a bounty of small cutthroat trout. They came heedlessly to my bedraggled fly. A shredding of yarn on a rusty hook would probably have served as well.

The afternoon found us hunting on foot. A welcome change from what seemed to be an excessive amount of riding. We hunted along upper meadow edges, frequently pausing to glass inviting slopes. Our route took us across rock facings that would have been doubtful on horseback. We made a modest circuit through the higher reaches above our spike camp, eventually dropping down to the small meadow we had rode through that morning. The sun already had begun to drop below the western ridges. The last hour would be spent watching the meadow. The deadfall trail would guide our passage back to camp in the dark.

The little stream came down from our spike camp along the timber edge before turning to flow through the meadow, disappearing with its meanderings into deep conifers at the meadow's far side. Dense cover shaded black on the opposite bank of the stream. Gray was replacing green along the forest margins. Dusk began announcing the end of another elkless day.

Then a bull elk bugled! A spine-tingling wild call in the fading light. We instinctively turned toward the sound. Again it came, wafting mysteriously through the evening hush.

The guide, who had been silent up to that time with his elk call, responded. A high-pitched imitation of a bugling elk went out over the silent meadow. We waited, all vestiges of discouraging days banished by another wailing note, an eerie, defiant answer from the dark timber beyond the meadow stream.

Again the guide called. And again the bull responded. We waited in tense expectation. The bull called once more. Closer now. Or was it just a closer wish?

The guide bugled. Silence. Then the bull bugled in response. No doubt now. Closer. Tenseness rising.

The challenge came again, from just across the stream in the dense evergreen cover. The guide answered, a softer tone. Swishing branches broke the silence in the dark timber bordering the trickling waters. We stared intently into the impenetrable tangle, straining to see movement in the closing darkness.

A thrashing of brush startled us, an angry battling back and forth on the other side of the stream. The guide in turn battled with a small shrub beside us. Titan challenging Titan. Back and forth the bull stalked, seemingly upon us so distinct came his grunting. Saplings felt his fury. We waited in the gloam while the bull vented himself on the yielding brush, willing him to the edge of the stream, to an instant of shadow before the night's shadows enveloped the final light.

But the bull would not come. The thrashing subsided. We waited until night closed around us, then walked the silent pathway along the deadfall trail to camp.

We were on the stream bank before first light the following morning. No thrashing or haunting bugles disturbed the hush of dawn, nor did the growing light reveal sought-for forms along the edge of the meadow. We stayed well into the morning, reluctant to abandon the only area where elk had revealed their presence. Or at least an elk. But the warming day brought the guide's observation that probably a wandering bull had come and gone on a rutting search through the valley.

We climbed again into the high reaches above our spike camp and for the rest of the morning followed in reverse the preceding afternoon's hunt. And like that hunt, we saw only empty mountains. We reached camp by noon. While the other two rested after lunch, I again found the cutthroat trout eager for my bedraggled fly. Then came the preparations to leave. The spike camp held an allure, but, we were informed, feed for the horses became a limiting factor, the bulk of it having to be brought in by the wrangler and his mules.

I led my horse around the deadfall on our return down the trail. We tried for several minutes to step the horse across, but he remained obstinate. Some hidden fright held him back. A strange and potentially dangerous trait for a mountain horse.

We hunted the meadows on our return to base camp, but they remained as empty as the meadow of the morning.

My Missouri hunting companion was greeted at camp with the announcement that his two friends were leaving the next morning. They were done with the mountains, done with the rough country, done with the hard work, done with the lack of game, and basically just done with everything in general. Apparently not a complete surprise to my companion, although still a disappointment, since three hunting days remained. But he felt compelled to leave with his friends.

The cook tent rattled half-empty the following morning. The three Missourians and my guide did not put in an appearance.

The Missourians, after supper it seems, had sought to tame the wilds with some soothing Missouri tonic. I gathered that my guide had commiserated long into the night with the Missourians on the sad state of wilderness affairs. And, evidently, had commiserated well beyond his capacity.

Paul would be my guide that day.

I exchanged horses, leaving my log-shy mount happily munching hay in the corral. Our little caravan of two set off down the valley in the predawn darkness. Paul led the way along an offshoot trail that soon began a switchback climb up a steep mountain slope with a canyon growing deeper on our right after each upward loop. We witnessed the dawn at the top where a glorious panorama unfolded with the breaking light. New country. That ever tantalizing promise.

We followed along a ridge for a short distance then tied our horses and eased through the trees until a meadow showed ahead. We sat just inside its edge and began to glass the many little pockets that indented their way down the mountain.

During a pause in glassing, I brought my rifle to my shoulder to check the scope and was dismayed to find it completely fogged up. An examination revealed a deep dent in the metal around the front lens. It seemed improbable that the morning's ride could have caused the dent, and the scope had been fine the previous evening. Someone must have knocked my rifle over during the night.

Since the gas seal was already broken, I unscrewed the front lens, wiped it off, and reassembled the scope. The lens stayed clear for a while. Each time it fogged up the process was repeated. I could only hope that if an elk appeared he would give me time to wipe the lens. Where the scope might place the bullet was another matter.

When the sun rose full to flood the meadow, revealing no elk, I test-fired the rifle. Remarkably that Weaver scope held close to zero. The scope had a fixed reticle, which surely helped. The adjusting screws were located in the mount.

Paul and I discovered no elk during our morning's careful search. We ate lunch on a promontory overlooking a grand sweep of the rugged Bob Marshall Wilderness Area and talked about the wilderness and how it appeals to many in theory but to only a few in its reality. Great passions are excited over wilderness areas, but few seem to enjoy actually immersing themselves in them. The wild apparently remains too wild. A blessing, we agreed, since that helped stay the day when there would be wilderness no more.

Paul was a New Yorker by birth, a dreamer of mountain dreams who finally came west to realize them and found that he could not leave. The mountains had captured him beyond release. One day he hoped to turn his guiding experience into an outfitting business. But he still had elk to guide for that afternoon. And guide he did, through grand, sweeping mountains pocketed with enticing meadows and sweetly running streams that revealed elk imprints in hidden, shallow crossings. The sun attended us gloriously, more gloriously perhaps than we required, for the elk seemed disinclined to move in the excessive warmth. I suggested still-hunting the timber and we did, finding relief in the cool, dark places. The elk likely found similar relief in those dim depths but we failed to find their refuges. We hunted the day in full, coming off the mountain in the dark, switching down a darkened trail that swung perilously close to a deep canyon on its turns, bringing to mind visions of sure-footed mules laying dead in the bottom of gorges.

The rancher was waiting for us in camp. He had left the day after we arrived and returned late that afternoon. The Missourians were gone, as was my former guide, permanently I understood, the rancher taking an intolerant view of guides drinking in camp. The rancher had seen a small herd of elk, including one bull, on a slide area as he rode in. The Michigan father, who took advantage of the rancher's presence to vent his frustration at not seeing game, elected to hunt that area in the morning. Paul and I opted for the higher country. The cook outdid himself at supper that night.

Morning of the sixth hunting day. Grizzly tracks and a rutting bull challenging in the dark timber the only intimation of game so far. Again the stiff saddles in the chill, predawn air, the dark switchback ride up the slender ribbon of a mountain trail, meadows to watch in the shadings of dawn's light, elk calls bugling enticingly over the dark-timbered valleys, then into the dark timber, struggling over blowdowns amidst dense evergreens, tensing as a crackle teases the silence, searching, ever searching, discovering sign but never its maker, hours blending into hours, afternoon passing into shadows, hope ebbing with the ebbing sun, then meadows again in the desperate last light before the long, weary trail ride back to camp, a faint lantern glow in the night quickening the horses as thoughts of home and hay enliven them into the corral, then the warmth of the cook tent and a drowsing meal to settle as sleep settles into dreams.

Then the call in the morning and the saddle and the trail and the meadows and the bugling and the dark timber and the truly desperate last light of the last day and the final ride to camp knowing that it is ended. And still only the dreaming of elk.

Twenty-two percent of Montana elk hunters filled their tags that year. Whoever goes on a hunt not thinking they will be in that twenty-two percent? But weather and the uncertainties of the hunt intrude. A disappointment, especially with mule deer and grizzly bear tags in hand. The grizzly remained an outside chance. But one was there! Montana required a guide for non-residents, hence my first guided hunt. But guides are not guarantees. Even with them none of the six hunters saw elk, although three left with half the hunt remaining. The wild country drew me along with the game, and there certainly was no disappointment in that regard. Grand country, a comfortable wilderness camp, weather presumably too warm, although a bull did quicken the pulse one evening. And always, coming down those dark mountain trails, there lives in the memory, the tracks of a grizzly.

The Passing

We had been an hour in the slough, the canoe slipping easily around the twists and turns of the sluggish backwater. The last oxbow fed us into the main channel. I stopped in the eddy before the current caught us, backing the paddle to hold steady while Mike grasped the awesomeness of the broad, sweeping Mississippi. Grown men sense wonder sitting a paddle thrust away from the inexorable power of the river. To a ten-year-old, the swirling, shifting immenseness must seem overwhelming.

The island lay across a smooth-flowing race that cleaved away from the sweep of the main channel. We eddied in the still water. I let Mike absorb the scene for a moment, then broke the silence.

"You ready?"

"Yeah."

"Paddle steady on your left side."

"Okay."

"We're going to start for the head of the island but we're going to end up farther down."

"Okay."

"Don't worry about the current. I'll handle it."

"Okay."

"Go."

It takes only a thrust to be embraced in the power of the river, and then a steady rhythm to tame that power, to bend it partially to your will. We drifted broadside with the current, closing paddle stroke by paddle stroke on the island that gave the illusion of floating upstream in front of us. Mike paddled steadily, his teenage frame belying his ten and a half years, the youthful energy apparent in the occasional lurch of the canoe. The current slackened as we neared the island. I guided the bow into a quiet flow behind a driftwood pile and tied the canoe to a tree on the bank. Then we unloaded the tent, sleeping bags, and the rest of our supplies.

A great barge was fighting its way upriver in the main channel. While I set up the tent and arranged camp, Mike found a seat on an uprooted tree leaning over the river and lost himself in the fascination of the barge and the grand expanse of the waters. I looked up at one point to see my son in a Mark Twain setting, perched on a tree over the Mississippi, bare feet dangling above the timeless flow as a river boat plied its trade, pushing with lumbering slowness against the current. The appearance of Tom Sawyer and Huckleberry Finn would not have caused a second glance.

The river held us for long, glorious summer days. Other islands beckoned, other sloughs lost us for a time in their twistings. Bluegills snagged our hooks in submerged treetops where crappies also flashed temptingly in the sun-reflected depths. Moon-filled nights found us teasing poppers over largemouth bass. And on a morning sunrise, Mike landed a northern that weighed almost a pound for each of his years. In the wonder of the night we sat in front of our tent, fire flickering in harmony with the stars, sensing the grand power of the mighty Mississippi bending strong around the point of the island. And in the passing of the days, I passed on in a fashion, what lore I was able to pass on.

-1-

Late September of the following year. Ontario. Northland waterways where green pines touch blue-black lakes and swift rivers run free. Home to moose, and Mike's and my destination that fall.

I arranged with an outfitter to fly us to a remote area for a five-day hunt. Camping equipment and supplies along with a boat and motor would be provided by the outfitter. An experienced guide familiar with the area was also arranged for.

Mike and I set out on a grand fall day, heading north through Minnesota along the western shore of Lake Superior. After a two-day journey we arrived at an outpost store on the south bank of the Albany River that served as headquarters for our outfitter. Following introductions, the outfitter informed me that he and my arranged-for guide, who's qualifications he previously praised, had come to a parting of the way. As a consequence, another guide would be provided. He was an Ontario native, although a stranger to the area we were going to hunt.

Not a welcome announcement, especially since the original guide had been highly touted because of his familiarity with the hunting area, which swayed me in my choice of the outfitter. But we were there. So Mike and I found cots in a back storeroom and bunked down with plans for an early rising.

Three other hunters, who were flying to a separate camp, arrived in the night. We met them over a quick breakfast in the chill dawn before starting off to the floatplane pick-up area on a river to the north. The outfitter led, carrying several five-gallon cans of reserve gasoline in the back of his truck. The three hunters followed in their pickup, with my car completing the caravan.

The morning sky remained hidden behind a gray overcast. The close-growing spruce shaded dull in the muted light. We drove silently mile after mile expecting to see the river landing around each new bend. But the bends revealed only the narrow contours of a road weaving ever northward through a somber conifer forest. No mention of distance had been made and my expectation of a short drive gradually became dispelled as first one, then two hours passed. The road became progressively narrower. Branches began whisking against the side of the car.

At last, off to the left, a large clearing appeared on the bank of a broad river. A number of vehicles were parked there, their occupants warding off the morning's chill in small groups around log fires. We pulled in and parked. The outfitter left to pick up our guide while Mike and I settled down to await his return and the arrival of the floatplane.

The morning wore on into the afternoon with neither an appearance by the outfitter nor the floatplane. My patience began to wear thin. A day of our hunt was drifting by while Mike and I wasted it dozing in the car. Eventually wearying of the inactivity, we got out to walk around the clearing. A group of five men invited us to share their fire. Four of the men were hunters waiting for a floatplane. When the fifth man introduced himself, I recognized his name as that of the individual originally booked as my guide. He had a camp farther north where he was scouting in preparation for a group of hunters coming later in the week. The floatplane clearing provided a convenient rest stop while bringing a load of supplies to his camp.

In talking with the hunters, we discovered that everyone in the clearing was waiting for the same floatplane. One group, who had been scheduled to fly in three days earlier, was in the process of pulling out, half their hunt already lost in the waiting. Two other groups, one of which was also getting ready to leave, had been there two days. The four hunters we were talking to were supposed to have flown in the day before. Nobody knew where the floatplane was.

The outfitter returned late in the afternoon. He, likewise, had not been able to obtain any information regarding the floatplane, nor, it developed, about our guide, for when I questioned him about the guide's whereabouts, he became vague in his response. Finally, after pressing him, the outfitter acknowledged that he had no idea where either the guide or the floatplane were.

Something obviously had unraveled in the outfitter's planning. What it was, he refused to explain. Relying on him to get Mike and me into the back country, and more importantly, out again, was beginning to take on the aura of a dark adventure.

I talked with the outfitter again but he would not or could not offer any assurances regarding the floatplane or the guide. He could only suggest that I wait around and see how things developed. I told him this was not acceptable and we thereupon terminated our arrangement.

Mike and I were ill-equipped to hunt on our own, having relied on the outfitter for everything except our sleeping bags, rifle, and extra clothing. A lesson learned and long remembered. I approached the individual originally booked as my guide to see if he could accommodate a couple of hunters until his other group arrived. He was agreeable, but had only three days available. I told him that was three days more than we were presently looking at and we settled on a fee of fifty dollars a day.

Mike and I threw our duffel bags in the back of the guide's pickup, crowded into the front seat, and were soon heading north on what quickly turned into a single-lane track. Mike felt a bit let down from missing out on the flying part of our hunt but he perked up considerably when the guide asked him if he would like to take a turn behind the wheel. With nothing to run into except a possible stray moose, Mike clambered excitedly into the driver's seat and we chugged slowly down what to an eleven-year-old had to be a fascinating forest lane.

Dusk was descending as we made an angling turn to the left that brought us to the end of the lane and to a most pleasant scene. There, tucked into an opening among the hardwoods and evergreens, lay a woodsman's camp. A white wall tent glinted invitingly in the fading light. A smaller A-frame tent close by sheltered supplies. Firewood lay neatly stacked along the hardwood edging and a circle of blackened stones in front of the tent promised a welcome blaze in the evening chill.

We soon had the supplies transferred to the A-frame tent and our duffel and sleeping bags situated comfortably in the wall tent. After a simple meal from campfire-warmed pans, we huddled close to the blaze in the starless night, sipped steaming coffee from hand-warming cups, and discussed the prospects for moose.

While the surrounding area was familiar to the guide, he had not hunted there previously, having generally flown in to remote outpost camps. His plans for the year became altered due to some disagreement with my former outfitter, which he, like the outfitter, choose not to discuss. His scouting had revealed enough fresh sign in the area to warrant setting up camp, although he had yet to see his first moose.

A gray dawn was breaking when we awoke. We built a small fire to make coffee, ate a simple breakfast, doused the flames, and set off into the forest. The guide's plan was to hunt west for half a mile to a nearby river, where he had seen moose tracks, then follow north along the river, eventually swinging inland to explore a number of small ponds and lakes before circling back to camp.

The morning air continued brisk, but the clearing skies promised a warming sun. Towering conifers held back the dawn's light as we wended along a faint pathway toward the river. The woodland's day creatures had awakened with the sunrise. A diminutive red squirrel scolded us severely from its perch. Startled scurryings in the undergrowth announced the departure of some alarmed forest dweller. In a shallow, rain-filled depression, water oozed into the fresh-made tracks of a recent traveler along the trail. A solitary raven croaked hoarsely overhead, highlighting the faint awakening melody of a songbird scaled pleasantly in counterpoint. The day forest was coming alive. We eased silently through the awakening woodland.

The pathway faded out at the river. We stood on the bank in the shelter of a screening spruce and watched in both directions until the sun emerged above the treeline. Moose tracks in the soft mud suggested that stretch of river was being regularly used by at least one moose. But the early hours passed without its appearance.

We turned north and followed single file along the quiet-running waters. No pathway directed our footsteps. The trees funnelled us through a twisting natural corridor. New river perspectives opened as we tread around winding bends. We stopped frequently to scrutinize openings through the evergreens and stalked silently toward boggy clearings showing faint through dense thickets. The morning sun filtered brightly through the cover, exposing hidden niches and forming others in the shifting shadows. A growing warmth banished the morning chill.

Halfway through the morning, during a swing west to bring the river back into view, movement ahead alerted us. We halted. Movement again. Evidently near the river. The remembrance of moose tracks in the mud sent a surge of excitement through me. Once more a glimpse, an indistinct suspicion of form. We tried to discern the object through the dense screening, but the movement remained obscure.

We began easing forward, picking a silent path along the forest floor, holding swishing boughs while skirting brittle-branched deadfalls. Movement appeared then disappeared, seeming to hold in place then shift slightly from side to side. Closer we stalked, tension rising as the screening of trees thinned. I strained to see an outline of a moose. Movement again. A rising from the ground. An object took form through the screening.

It was a man!

We broke into a small clearing and the man looked up in surprise from his task of skinning a bull moose. After acknowledging our unexpected appearance, the man informed us that he and his partner were camped farther north along the river and were hunting the waterway in a boat. He had shot the moose late the preceding afternoon, apparently about the time we left the floatplane clearing. Darkness had forced him to wait for the morning light to finish the skinning and quartering. His partner was hunting along the river.

This information came as surprisingly to the guide as our appearance had come to the hunter. The guide assumed we were hunting undisturbed country, but the other hunter's presence obviously proved otherwise. At least the moose confirmed the guide's scouting skills, although hardly in the manner he desired.

We swung away from the river, resuming our hunt beyond the activity of the other hunters. The morning continued pleasant. The sun highlighted small ponds that sparkled in evergreen frames. Tracks showed along the muddy edges of the ponds, whether from the bull of the morning or from another, we could only surmise.

We circled carefully through the deep forest. Other ponds came into view, and small, boggy openings stayed our passage while we scanned their sunlit edges. At noon we lingered along the shore of a blue-shimmering lake and watched a pair of loons dive in search of their midday meal.

Early afternoon brought us back to our white-tented camp. We soon had a fire kindled with the coffee pot perking merrily above the dancing flames. We dined humbly on sandwiches. The guide built a massive one of thick-sliced, pungent, eye-watering, raw onions, and gulped it down with obvious relish. Mike and I opted for less potent fare.

After lunch, while we were sipping coffee, Mike noticed movement on the woodland floor. A ruffed grouse was casually pecking along the ground a short distance away, obviously undisturbed by our presence. The guide quickly produced a twenty-two rifle. He was about to add the grouse to our camp larder when he turned and asked Mike if he would like to have the honors.

Mike had done some target shooting with my twenty-two rifle but his practice had been limited. With a strange rifle in his hands and two adults hovering over him, it was no singular occurrence to have the first shot miss. The grouse took no alarm at the faint ping. Mike fired again. The grouse remained unfazed.

The guide and I offered our versions of where to aim. Mike dutifully attempted to comply and another shot disturbed the air around the grouse, but not the grouse itself. It pecked unconcernedly along.

Mike sent another missile in search of the brown form in the brown background, and still the grouse, in studied indifference, bravely held his ground. Had that grouse been a combatant under fire, he surely would have been awarded a medal.

Then, in an unexpected maneuver, the grouse hopped onto a fallen log, presenting a perfectly silhouetted target. Mike steadied. The little rifle pinged. A puff of feathers erupted from the grouse and it fell fluttering to the ground. We retrieved the bird and in a matter of minutes Mike was proudly displaying in his hat a tail feather from his first grouse.

After a short rest we set off for the afternoon's hunt. Our route took us south along the narrow track we had driven in on, toward a large, boggy clearing where the guide had seen a number of fresh tracks. He considered the area an ideal place for calling moose, provided the day continued calm.

The afternoon sun filled the forest with a lazy warmth and we quickly succumbed to its cadence. Mike and I followed in single file behind the guide, peering lackadaisically into the screening of hardwoods and evergreens. The restful afternoon seemed to have called the forest creatures to slumber. Not a hint of an animal or a bird did we see during our passage.

We continued in the idle rhythm of the day. Suddenly our attention became riveted on movement ahead. Three animals appeared from out of the forest a hundred yards down the track and trotted unhurriedly across the narrow lane, disappearing into the hardwoods on the opposite side.

"Wolves!" whispered the guide.

We stopped just as a fourth wolf emerged from the trees to halt and stare down the trail at us. We remained motionless, staring back. In the shadows, the wolf appeared black. Time seemed frozen while the ancient antagonists stood in silent contemplation of each other. Then the wolf turned, and with a nonchalant air, trotted across the lane to follow the other three into the forest.

The stimulating encounter rekindled our flagging attention. We continued down the lane with senses alert. Wildlife was on the move. Or so we thought. But the wolves remained the only animals seen by the time afternoon began shading into evening.

The shadows were lengthening when we turned off the lane and angled right into the trackless forest. We walked in single file through the thick woodland. The dense cover began to thin and we left it at the edge of an extensive open bog. Fresh tracks had been observed there. Large ones, according to the guide. Presumably those of a bull.

We settled under the overhanging branches of a tall pine, positioning a few cut boughs in front of us to complete our concealment. The bog stretched empty to the south. Sky-reflecting ponds glimmered dull in the early evening light. Curing marsh grasses hung motionless in the still air. A few scattered evergreens stood like silent sentinels above the otherwise treeless expanse, offshoots from the dense cover surrounding the forest-fringed glade. The ebbing day remained hushed.

The guide produced a rolled cone of birch bark from his pack, brought it to his mouth, and bellowed out a mournful call that wafted rudely over the glade, a discordant sound in the woodland serenity. Again the stillness was disturbed with the hoarse bellow, grading down to a few coughing grunts. The guide lowered his call and we sat waiting in an intense silence.

Young boys are not renowned for their patience. Mike fidgeted in the enforced idleness, whittling a growing mound of shavings from the abundant sticks strewn about as the sun passed slowly into twilight. The plaintive enticement of the birch-bark call drifted at irregular intervals across the open glade, but there came no answering grunts, and no vague illusions emerged from the forest to materialize into the dark form of a bull. The lengthening shadows slowly blended into a single dark. When the pines in the glade lost their definition, we arose stiffly from the ground and made our way through the night woods to the narrow track, where we turned north and walked the long dark walk back to camp. There, under a brilliant canopy of stars, we ate a late supper by the flickering flames of a hardwood fire, spoke quietly of our day and the one to follow, then settled into our sleeping bags and drifted off to the hushed sounds of the night.

We hunted north the following morning, searching the area where tracks had been seen. No new sign was evident. We circled toward the river and hunted along the timbered bank for a considerable distance, but saw nothing of moose, nor of the other hunters or their camp. A long loop brought us back to our tents by early afternoon. Then a southward journey before another watchful evening settled into darkness as the guide echoed his birch-bark call over the dusk-shrouded glade. Silence was the only response.

The following day mirrored the first two, and with the dawning of the fourth our abbreviated hunt came to an end. Not the hunt we had anticipated, but under the circumstances, better than a wasted journey north.

The guide returned us to the floatplane clearing, which stood empty except for my car, and Mike and I in short order were heading homeward.

-2-

The passage of a few years brought the eagerly awaited season when a big game license was proudly tucked into Mike's pocket. One of my business associates also had a son named Mike who turned fourteen that year. John and I made plans to celebrate the two Mike's birthdays with a mule deer hunt in Colorado. The White River National Forest became our destination.

Our route west took us across the boundless plains of Nebraska and Eastern Colorado, tracking along the great curve of the Platte River. The mountains started beyond Denver. We climbed high into the rugged Rockies, my overloaded Blazer laboring at times on some of the steeper slopes. John was of the opinion that one could never have too much equipment and the two Mikes seated in back were almost buried in an excess of gear. We came prepared for any contingency. Had we been launched to the moon, I believe we could have survived.

An offshoot road took us high into the National Forest. We climbed the twisting incline until a level opening in the pines showed to the left. I backed the Blazer into the opening and we cleared an area for our camp. Thin patches of snow covered the ground, making the canvas floor of the sleeping tent most welcome. A shaded grove furnished room for a second tent to shelter our supplies.

With camp in order, Mike and I set off along the mountain ridge, while John and his son scouted lower into the valley. Wispy streaks of clouds drifting like diffused jet trails highlighted the brilliant blue of the sky. A rose-tinted hue capped the mountain ridges across the valley. The air remained brisk, making wool jackets welcome. A glorious day.

Mike and I followed along the ridge. The country spread invitingly below, a grand mosaic of evergreen-clad rolling hills interspersed with great swaths of autumn-brown clearings. The afternoon sun slanted through the trees bordering the clearings, creating shaded pockets on their western fringes.

An indented, dark treeline stayed us as we glassed along its edge. Half an hour passed as we probed the shadows. The play of light and dark created illusory forms that had us staring hard at times, but the glasses inevitably revealed nothing. Half an hour more drifted by in fruitless searching before we moved farther along the ridge to a fresh vantage point. Again the searching. Another hour passed as we hunted along the ridge. Then another as we found new clearings to observe. The waning afternoon suggested movement of game, but the only movements through the clearings were the shadows. We watched as they lengthened and melded into the eastern treeline, then followed the ridge back to camp.

John reported the valley quiet. We built a fire and ate supper while the flames held back the night. The far mountains faded into indistinct outlines. Our world became reduced to the small circle of light flickering off the walls of our tent. We were weary from the long day but the pleasure of the night kept us by the fire until a reminder of the earliness of dawn sent us to our sleeping bags. The wind sighed pleasantly through the pines.

Morning turned us once more toward separate paths. John and his son returned to the valley. Mike and I again followed along the ridge. We settled into a routine of watching and walking, finding lookouts from which to glass the lower reaches and still-hunting slowly through the timbered stretches.

The skies remained clear, and with the dawning, sunlight framed the mountains. We continued our patient search. Parks opened around us and conifers closed us in again. We hunted far beyond our limit of the preceding day, through a country forever changing, yet in its totality, forever the same. Fresh overlooks offered new perspectives. But they offered no sight of game. The country remained grand, but empty.

We came at midday to an outcropping that presented an extensive view and sat there observing the great sweep of the forest while we ate lunch. The weather continued fair. We loafed for a while in the noontime sun, taking a cue from the restful quiet around us. An hour passed before we resumed our hunt.

By early afternoon we had worked our way into a heavily timbered canyon. Snow lay in solid patches where the conifers shaded. We searched the telltale white for hopeful sign, but the smooth expanses remained undisturbed. A pair of blue grouse, their dusky forms showing stark against the snowy background, tempted us as they searched for seeds a dozen yards away. Farther along, another grouse contemplated us from its perch in a pine. We passed silently beneath its watchful eyes.

The vast ranges opened again above the dark-shaded canyon. We rested from our climb, glassing timbered pockets and sweeping distant horizons. If any deer were present, they kept well out of sight. The setting sun lent its final rays to our evening watch. When it dipped behind the western ridges, we turned toward camp. John and Mike reported no deer that day.

The following morning, as we were preparing to set out, I noticed movement just below the summit of a distant mountain. I called attention to it and raised my binoculars. A herd of elk came into view, moving at a steady trot across an open basin. The distance was great but at least one bull appeared to be among them. The herd continued across the basin and finally lost itself in an extensive stretch of conifers.

Mike and I again followed along the ridge, holding there while the gray dawn brightened. We glassed patiently along meadow edges. When the early light disclosed no movement of game, we dropped into the lower elevations and still-hunted through timbered draws. The dawning passed without the sighting of a deer. By the time the sun had us shedding our jackets, the distant elk remained the only game seen.

The morning blended into the afternoon. Another grand day of brilliant skies. Our hunting took us into the timber and onto the heights. When the timber wearied us we found patient use for our binoculars. When they in turn revealed only scenery, we returned to the timber. We discovered occasional sign in the form of tracks and droppings, elk as well as deer, but saw nothing of those that left the sign.

We hunted in the early evening back to the ridge we were camped on and watched from a outcropping until the day faded. No deer appeared.

John and Mike reported a similar day. Grand country, but an absence of deer. The lack of game turned our thoughts toward a change of hunting grounds. We decided to give our area one more try in the morning, and if our luck did not improve, head farther west.

Our luck did not improve. We met back at camp at mid-morning of the following day still waiting to see our first deer.

We broke camp, an unexpectedly monumental task given that our equipment seemed to have expanded in the rarified mountain air. What we had so ingeniously fitted into the Blazer initially, refused now to be forced into the same space.

Unremembered items seemed to have materialized as if by spontaneous generation. We mounded the excess high on the roof while John, ever prepared for the moon, smiled sheepishly. I began to wonder where we could possibly put a deer should the Fates ever present us with one.

Then they apparently did. We saw game. White rumps flashing in the dark shadows of a juniper-covered hill rising from a broad flatland covered with close-cropped grass, with the four of us crammed into the Blazer, coming off a mountain track onto the valley floor, our rifles somewhere in the maze of bedrolls stuffed behind the two Mikes.

We expected deer. Then the white rumps fleetingly suggested antelope, or possibly even elk. Then the binoculars revealed, of all things, sheep. But not domestic sheep. Rocky Mountain bighorn sheep. Thirteen in all. One among them being a grand, well-curled ram nearly half-again as large, and darker, than the ewes feeding around him. We drew remarkably close, within a hundred yards at one point, taking pictures. The sheep paid us scant attention as they fed contentedly in the open. We enjoyed the novel scene for some time before again turning the Blazer westward.

We had no clear idea of where we wanted to hunt, only that we wanted a change of hunting grounds. In time we came to a road that followed along Piceance Creek. A single-lane dirt track across a wood-plank bridge swung off to the southwest. I turned the Blazer down it and followed the track while a rapidly rising dust plume followed us into a scrub growth of junipers.

We were in country less scenic than the mountain grandeur of our first camp, but our second camp still offered a welcome refuge when early afternoon found the tents in place and firewood gathered for the evening. We once again split into pairs and set off to explore.

Mike and I crossed a broad, open valley similar to the one the bighorns had been feeding in. A range of hills, lower than the mountain heights we hunted earlier, climbed steeply from the valley floor. Junipers predominated. We hunted along the base of the hills, taking turns climbing into the cover while the other followed parallel along the edge. The higher country held promise, but we decided to save it for a full day.

Narrow canyons split the hills at irregular intervals. We came upon one that showed a well-used trail running up its side into the high country. We crossed the base of the canyon and climbed up the opposite side until we found a vantage point from which to observe the trail. The sun settled into its final hour.

I informed Mike that deer were likely to descend that trail in the evening to feed in the valley. I cautioned him to keep a careful eye on the upper reaches of the trail, for if a deer came, it would come down from the hills. Mike listened respectfully and fixed his gaze on the heights above.

The deer came from below. In such a manner is a father's wisdom confirmed and passed on to his son.

We saw it simultaneously, a gray-brown figure ghosting up the trail, movement giving the deer form against the dark side of the canyon where night shades were already dimming the deeper recesses. A buck. Branched antlers tracing shadowy in the dull light. Climbing slowly up the trail. Pausing every several steps before continuing on. Unaware of the tense forms against the opposite canyon wall.

Mike brought his rifle to his shoulder, appearing steady. The deer paused, then lunged forward as the rifle's report shattered the stillness. The echo reverberated back. The deer continued on. A second shot. The deer faltered, then stopped. Mike chambered another round. The buck turned to retrace its steps down the trail and collapsed with Mike's final shot.

We held in the dusk, watching the fallen buck through our scopes. Quiet descended. The echoes of the shots faded into memory. Darkness gathered in the canyon. The form on the trail began to blend into the surrounding boulders. Yet we watched a few more minutes.

In the aftermath of my first deer an uncontrollable tremor nerved through my right leg. That same tremoring right leg afflicted me on a number of other occasions. But I remained calm when the deer went down, though sensing excitement for Mike. I lowered my rifle and looked toward him. Mike was still watching the deer, intent on the fallen form, steely nerved in his appearance. Steely nerved, that is, except for his right leg. It was tremoring uncontrollably.

We dressed the deer in the dark, then each of us grasped an antler and dragged it down the trail and across the starlit valley to camp. John and Mike were there and joined in a round of congratulations. The dry spell was finally broken. But, as it turned out, only for Mike. His first deer holds the sole honors for our hunt.

A fine Wyoming antelope and an equally fine Wisconsin whitetail later added to Mike's Colorado mule deer memories. His teenage years also found us in Ontario for spring black bear, and Manitoba, as well as Ontario, for moose. Of course, there was some small game. And we fished a little.

The lore passes down. Mostly in just the doing. A reminder of a timeless process in the natural order. Experiences shared. Lessons learned. Knowledge won. A reminder always of glorious days and magical nights. And a reminder too, that in the evening, mountain deer sometimes come from below.

Chapter 12

In Moose Country

-1-

The great deer of the north turned me toward Ontario in the fall of 1977. I made arrangements with Tom Kuenne to hunt moose using his fishing camp for a base.

Tom's camp lay in the Kenora district of western Ontario, on the isolated south side of Eagle Lake, accessible only by boat across a five-mile passage. Tom remarked that hunters rarely ventured there. A large burned-over area lay close by. The new growth it fostered acted like a moose magnet, said Tom. He had seen a number of them there while fishing.

October seventeenth. I met Tom at a pick-up point on the lake. My duffel was quickly transferred to his boat and we were soon weaving through pine-covered islands that channelled us ever deeper into undisturbed country. Tom pointed out an active bald eagle's nest along the way that dominated a towering pine off to the north. A wilderness reminder that there would be at least one other hunter in the area.

We came in time to the fishing camp, which lay situated on the point of a peninsula jutting into a large bay. A scattering of cabins showed in the evergreens along a shoreline fronted with white rocks. I settled into one of the cabins, ate supper, then sat by the lake listening to the night sounds as darkness stole over the waters.

Morning came clear. Stars began fading in the half-light of dawn as I guided the boat around a series of shoreline shallows and pointed its bow toward an opening separating two islands half a mile to the northwest. The air remained hushed, smoothing the waters to a glassy sheen that wrinkled with my passing into an ever-widening vee. The night sounds had faded and the low throb of the motor struck the only harsh note in the quiet morning. An uncharted day lay ahead. I shivered slightly from a mixture of cold and excitement as the bow parted the yielding-gray waters running deep into the unbounded northlands.

Loons live in these northlands, great seekers-of-wilderness birds that enchant the wilds with quavering, tremulous cries. One cried out in the dawning then and I spotted it ahead on the still waters between the two islands. Its mate revealed itself when I rounded a headland and swung south toward a marsh-sided channel. The pair left me at the headland, diving deep beneath the calm surface as I turned away to watch my bearing.

I came to the channel and proceeded slowly through the reed-lined water. Half a mile brought me to an offshoot channel where I turned right through a narrows to emerge into a large bay. The waters extended calm across its mile-wide surface. I hugged the south shoreline until a rock-free area offered a landing, and there beached the boat. The last cough of the motor brought an overwhelming silence disturbed only by the lapping sound of the boat's wash as tiny wavelets broke and vanished upon the shore.

I sat for a moment listening to the silence, then pulled the boat farther up onto the beach and tied it to a fallen tree. The shoreline angled west. I began searching along it for tracks. They were not long in appearing. Several outsized prints traced clear within a hundred yards of my landing place.

The tracks entered a glade where a rivulet trickled along a pathway. Moose evidently favored the glade, for their prints lay heavy in the soft earth. I followed along the pathway. The tracks continued fresh ahead.

The dawn remained hushed. I sought to blend into the quiet, moving slowly, pausing often, waiting for the forest to forget the disturbance of my arrival. The woodland day sounds came slowly alive. I became a part of the morning.

I entered a deep forest and roamed through the towering stands amid dim shapes of green and brown interspersed with sun-dappled openings. Patterns of dark and light confused me at times, creating moving illusions in the shaded cover. Small glades opened in places, some revealing imprints in their softer earth that vanished in the firmer ground beneath the hardwoods. Larger clearings held me along their edges, their expanded perspective giving relief from the closeness of the forest. I watched the clearings while time passed unmeasured until the hidden woods again drew me on.

The deep woods shaded another dim passage before a lighter tint of blue glinted through the forest. I turned toward the light to emerge on the shore of a small lake. I carefully searched the timbered shoreline, then followed along the edge of the lake until it curved to the south. I paused again to scan the lakeshore before turning west into the sheltering trees.

Midday passed. Shadows and glades and marshy meadows altered my path as I followed the arcing sun. Signs of moose revealed themselves in droppings and tracks, but the moose themselves remained vague suspicions just beyond the shadows.

The chill following the fading sun began to seep through the forest and I circled north, still-hunting along a stream that stepped down in a series of rushing cascades until the far end of the bay came into view. I sat at the edge of the bay watching the timbered margins and a reed-filled inlet across the way. Nothing moved except the shadows. When they finally drifted across the bay, I arose and followed the twisting shoreline east to the boat.

I made a final sweep of the darkening lakeshore, then pushed off and eased through the channel and around the headland. The night shaded my passage between the two islands.

The following morning dawned clear. I returned to the reed-lined channel, bearing left this time to follow up a wide-mouthed creek to where a feeder stream entered from the east. I still-hunted up the feeder stream until I came to a small clearing around a beaver pond. A mounded stick lodge in the pond suggested a possible glimpse of a beaver, but none appeared. Nor did a moose.

I watched by the beaver pond until the rising sun glinted distractingly off the water, then followed the little feeder stream eastward. A willow-choked spring marsh eventually turned me south before a west turning brought me back to the creek. Water plants grew in a shallow widening of the creek. I stopped just inside the trees to watch there as the morning unfolded into a cloudless day.

The forest continued quiet except for the faint murmur of a rapids upstream. Nothing else stirred.

The glinting sun again prompted me to move. I still-hunted past the rapids to the shore of a small lake that fed into the creek. A pair of islands rose above its calm surface. I followed around the lake and came to a portage that led to a larger lake. West around that lake into a darker woods until a high cliff funnelled me into lower ground. Then into dark woods again. And so my day went. Probing lakeshores and waterways and cool, deep places until evening turned me back to the boat. I saw nothing of moose.

First light of the following morning found me tucked into the reeds fringing the channel entering the large bay where tracks had shown so promisingly the first day. I watched from the reeds as the brightening dawn slowly revealed the shoreline, but no sign of moose rewarded my early vigil.

Nor did they reward my later morning search through a channel that stretched for miles to the north. Deep evergreens and pockets of hardwoods shielded the meandering shoreline. Stream-fed inlets entered along the way. I beached the boat on their marshy shores to still-hunt up the streams. Sign remained scarce.

Noon suggested a limit to my northern circuit. I landed on the sandy shore of a small bay, gathered an armful of dead pine branches, fed a growing flame with deadwood from the forest, then boiled some camp coffee and fried fresh walleye fillets while a can of beans warmed.

I sat in the midday sun, eating the walleye fillets and the beans, sipping coffee through the grounds that the sprinkle of cold water after boiling never seems to completely settle, and watched the far side of the bay where two feeder streams lined with marshy opens broke the denseness of the surrounding forest. The little bay sparkled.

The passing sun began suggesting a start to my return. I doused the fire, pushed off the boat, and turned southward, retracing my route of the morning. The familiar shoreline bore a second empty witness to my passage.

In the evening I watched again from the reed-lined channel where my morning had begun. Moose continued to remain elusive. The star-filled night sky guided me to my cabin.

The same star-filled sky guided me in the morning, north again in watchful slow motion through the previous day's channel until an eastward bearing funnelled me into an expansive bay. Then a repeat of my preceding days with an attendant repeat of my success, or rather lack thereof, before another starlit journey back through the night.

The final morning dawned. I returned to the area of the first two days, for moose sign continued most promising there. The woods still held their magic, and no doubt held moose, but the secretive dwellers of those woodlands hid themselves beyond me. I left them there undisturbed and unseen.

-2-

Manitoba became my destination for moose the following year. Woodland caribou also roamed that province's farther regions. I made arrangements with Marvyn McGregor, who owned a fishing camp on Reed Lake, to hunt the first week in October. My hunt would take me deep into the Grass River Country. Marvyn said a guide was required.

The way to the Grass River Country is long. One night had already passed before I reached Winnipeg, an hour and a half into Manitoba. There the road turned northwest before turning north again between the two massive lakes named after the province and its capital city. The largest, Lake Winnipeg, stretches some three hundred miles north to south. I camped for the second night well beyond Grand Rapids, a modest native community and the only one in over two hundred miles along the wilderness road.

My third day of traveling brought me to Marvyn's fishing camp, which consisted of eight cabins and a main building with two impressive sets of moose antlers flanking his sign over the front door. There I met two other hunters, one from South Dakota and the second from North Dakota, along with the two guides making up our hunting party.

Sunday. October first. Windy. The lake a bit choppy. We loaded duffel, rifles, three hunters, and two guides into a fair-sized launch and set off across Reed Lake. The sharp morning wind bit uncomfortably. I raised the hood on my parka as we cleared the lee and entered unsheltered water. Over five hundred islands dotted the expansive lake. We pounded steadily around and between a number of them, heading into a spray-inducing north wind. I huddled deep into my parka and watched the islands pass in silent review.

We reached the far side of the lake and transferred ourselves and our gear to a weary looking old flatbed truck, long past its prime. A battery had been brought across in the launch. The guides hooked it up. The ancient engine coughed into a shaky rumble and we rattled off over a rutted trail through the forest.

A log cabin facing a calmer lake lay at the end of the trail. Once again we transferred ourselves and our gear, this time into two smaller boats, and set off across the lake, holding close in the lee of the north shore.

We reached an isthmus that sloped up and then down to a third lake. Here the two boats were floated one at a time onto a carriage fashioned out of two old car axles and their attached wheels. Two lines of peeled saplings traced across the isthmus like a set of rounded railroad tracks. A steel-cable winch secured at the top of the hill was hooked onto the carriage. We took turns winding each boat up the hill and then carefully lowering it down the sapling tracks into the third lake.

Again the outboards sputtered alive. We crossed the third lake past a narrow channel that revealed another much larger lake off to the north. Whitecaps broke on its surface.

We arrived after the crossing at a landing where a small log cabin sat nestled in the dense conifers. We each made a final transfer of duffel into one of the bunks lining the wall. The guides set about dinner preparations while we organized for Monday's hunt. A cheery log fire in the metal-drum stove soon banished the damp chill. The wind outside whistled a muffled accompaniment to the pleasant crackle of the flames.

The morning dawned cold with the north wind still making its presence felt. The two Dakota hunters left with their guide in one of the boats. My guide, Will, and I climbed into the other boat and eased through the shallow docking area in the half-light of morning.

Once we were clear of the shallows, Will cranked our outboard up to full throttle and we wasted no time in crossing the dark waters to a shadowy bay. There we beached the boat and proceeded to a point overlooking the bay and a marshy feeder stream emptying into it. Will produced a call and the mournful bellow of a moose coughed over the waters.

The wind ebbed into a dawning calm. We watched from the point well into the morning, calling at intervals until the wind picked up again. When it continued steady we returned to the boat and cruised the lake from bay to bay, stopping at each one to search for fresh sign. A few tracks showed in the third bay, suggesting a possibility for the evening should the wind die down. It did not.

The afternoon and evening passed while we searched fruitlessly along the wind-buffeted shoreline. The other hunters reported no sightings.

The following morning opened calm but brisk. The sharp wind from the moving boat soon had me burrowing deep into my hooded parka. We crossed the lake to the bay where tracks had shown the preceding day and Will once more wafted his enticing call across the dawn. No response. We waited in the quiet, calling at irregular intervals, but the bay and the edging forest continued empty.

By midmorning it seemed evident that no bull was coming. We returned to the boat and to our shore-searching routine of the previous day. Evening found us back at the bay with a repeat of our morning calling and a repeat of its results. The lake spread quietly beneath us on our dark return to the cabin.

Two beaming hunters greeted us there, displaying a nice set of antlers from the bull their guide had called in that morning on a connecting lake.

Another calm, brisk morning. We set out in the dark for a return to the bay we had hunted the first day. Will voiced great confidence in that bay, having seen a bull there on several occasions while guiding fishermen.

But once again the morning passed with nothing to indicate that the bull remained in the area, or, if he did, had any interest in the moose Will was trying so artfully to imitate. We stayed longer that morning, having discovered no better sign around the lake except for the tracks in the other bay that had not repeated themselves.

Our lengthened watch continued fruitless. We decided to hunt back to the other bay to see if there might have been some activity during the night or that morning. As we throttled down to round the edge of the fringing reeds, a startling vision jolted us.

A moose was standing in the bay! Feeding. Head underwater. Will cut the motor. We drifted toward the moose. It raised its head from the water, pond weeds dripping from its mouth. Our hopes vanished. It was a cow.

She stared at us for a few seconds, then turned and splashed onto the shore and disappeared into the forest.

We paddled silently back around the edge of the bay, then a little farther before starting the motor, and proceeded at a low rumble along the shore. Moose were accustomed to seeing boats during the fishing season, and while the cow had been momentarily startled, it was doubtful that our brief presence would drive her away. We would return in the evening to see if a bull might be in attendance of the cow. Possibly the bull we so vainly had been trying to call at the other bay. The distance between the bays was not that great.

We decided to scout another area before taking up our evening watch. We crossed the lake and eased through the narrow channel that connected it with a larger lake to the north. The wind became more brisk as we entered the larger lake. A few whitecaps broke toward its center. We crossed the windswept waters, shipping a little spray, and turned into a sheltered bay where we beached the boat. Our walk along the beach disclosed a series of varied imprints. Two, unmistakably, the tracks of a cow and her calf. Another set of tracks suggested the possibility of a bull in the area.

We considered watching there for the evening, but concluded that while the tracks looked promising, the other bay where the moose had been sighted offered greater promise.

Back again through the wind-chopped lake, relieved to reach the sheltered connecting channel and the calmer waters beyond.

We crossed at low throttle to a landing well downwind of the bay, beached the boat, then proceeded along the shore to a point that offered an unobstructed view of the bay and settled down to wait.

The bothersome wind continued, canceling any hope of using the call. We waited in patient watchfulness, listening to the moaning wind play counterpoint to the lapping waves breaking along the shore. The overcast sky shaded the water to iron gray. The day darkened early in the dusky haze. The wind abated some with the coming of evening. We hoped that might induce the cow, and presumably the bull, to venture from the forest. But they did not do so.

Shooting light faded. We returned quietly to the boat and circled away from the bay before pointing our bow campward. The other hunters reported no activity.

Morning of the next day saw us again in position, watching the bay until the rising wind caused us to sense that our vigil would only remain fruitless. We decided to chance a quick look for fresh sign and still-hunted along the edge of the timber until we crossed a set of larger tracks mingled with the tracks we had observed earlier. A bull had evidently joined the cow but the wind was holding them in the dense cover. We considered still-hunting through the cover, but the wind presented too great a handicap. Better to leave the area undisturbed and hope for a calmer day. We chose instead to try the more sheltered, tracked-up bay in the other lake.

The bay may have been sheltered, but the way to it was not. We cleared the connecting channel to find an angry, white-capped lake looming forebodingly between us and the bay. We held in the channel gauging the churning surface, then finally opted to go.

Will turned out of the sheltered water and we began a wild, roller-coaster ride through the breaking whitecaps. The boat thudded and thumped over the waves, rising up on the crests only to crash down into the troughs with a back-jarring jolt. Spray engulfed us and the bow at times parted the waves while the crests folded back above the bounding prow. We shipped water that was soon sloshing disconcertingly over our boots. The raging surface held us transfixed as each successive wave added its measure to the sloshing around our feet. And still we pounded on, committed now with no way of turning about against the facing waves.

The entrance to the bay slowly drew closer. Will turned on a slight quartering angle toward it and our pitching became combined with a rolling that had us both breathing a sigh of relief when we at last entered the calm waters of the bay.

We beached the boat and welcomed the solid land under our feet. After bailing out the water, we retrieved the coffee kettle from the wooden storage box, built a small fire, and ate lunch. The wind still howled over the lake but the surface of the bay lay calm in dramatic contrast.

With lunch finished we proceeded to the head of the bay, found a concealed place to watch from, and sent an occasional call across the sheltered waters. We were answered only with the murmur of the wind in the tops of the spruce.

We did not watch into the dark. Concern about our return through the wind-churned lake caused us to leave early enough to avoid a night crossing. The wind had quieted some but whitecaps still roiled the surface. Will quartered skillfully through the troughs and after a seemingly interminable passage we entered the quiet waters of the connecting channel with the lowering sky still holding on to the faint eastern light. We arrived at the cabin where the Dakota hunters greeted us with news of another moose taken. The bull had come to their guide's call in a sheltered bay.

The following morning we returned to the bay where the moose had been sighted, calling and watching there through most of the day and into the evening, but the track-lined shore continued empty and the single sighting of the cow on Wednesday remained my only view of a moose during the week's hunt.

The next day was occupied in retracing our route back to Reed Lake with the added transport of eight quarters of moose. I did manage to at least see some woodland caribou. A pair crossed the road in front of me on my drive out of the Grass River Country.

-3-

Mike accompanied me on my moose hunt the following year. We had both drawn Wyoming antelope permits and I decided to combine the two hunts into a single trip. I contacted Marvyn McGregor again and made arrangements to hunt the same general area as the preceding year.

We headed north through the fall-tinged cornfields of the Dakotas into Manitoba. The drive was pleasantly familiar and certainly more than pleasant for Mike during his time behind the wheel. Driving was still an all-consuming passion for my high-schooler son.

We camped in the Blazer on the way north, a bit cramped since Mike was already a few inches taller than me. We welcomed the two spacious beds in one of Marvyn's cabins the night of our arrival.

We met our guide the next morning at breakfast. Shortly thereafter we had our duffel loaded in a boat and began tracing a familiar route through the islands of Reed Lake. The north wind blew strongly, kicking up a spray. Mike and I turned our backs to the biting elements and watched the last islands fade behind as we crossed the wind-blown expanse.

The ancient flatbed truck stood patiently on shore. It managed once more to groan into life and transport us through the forest-lined lane to the cabin on the second lake that would be our camp for the week. The plan was to hunt the second lake, which had not been hunted for two years.

The afternoon was well-advanced by the time we stowed our gear in the cabin and set out in the boat toward a distant bay on the south shore of the lake. The ever-present north wind caused me to wonder why we were heading to the south shore, but my question was soon answered when the guide throttled down to enter a calm bay that angled west. Our position along the shore brought a quartering breeze into our faces.

We sat in silence, letting the disturbance from our arrival fade away. The day continued partly overcast. The wind gradually diminished with the coming of evening. As the last sigh whispered through the spruce, a pleading appeal wafted across the bay from the guide's call. The evening became calm. Silence held sway. The call pleaded once more. The forest continued hushed.

We waited in the silent dusk, straining to hear an answer to the call that again echoed mournfully through the stillness. Quiet reigned. A faint whisper of a breeze came and went. Once more the call drifted over the darkening bay. The shadows lengthened. Another mournful call followed the shadows into the gloaming. The dusk deepened. Again the call as the light faded, a closing plea before the night shades fell. We listened until darkness shaded the shore. Silence was all we heard. Then deep night descended and wrapped itself around the silence.

A clouded moon guided us dimly back to camp.

Mike chose to sleep in the next morning since he did not have a moose license, then do some fishing while I hunted. A second boat was available for his use.

The guide and I left before first light and were well-hidden along the shore of the bay we had watched the previous evening by the time dawn broke. The morning opened calm. Once again we began the patient calling, straining to see into the dark forest fringing the sandy shore of the bay. The rising sun gradually pushed back the shadows.

Midmorning came without even a suspicion of a moose. We left our concealing reeds and made a cautious still-hunt along the shore, hugging the treeline. No fresh tracks were in evidence. The guide informed me that a medium-sized bull had been observed around that bay during the fishing season, but the absence of fresh sign suggested that the bull was no longer using the area.

We left the bay and returned to the cabin to pick up Mike, then set out once more, having decided to combine our midday scouting with some fishing.

The fishing provided a pleasant break but unfortunately the guide took it a bit too seriously, for when Mike played a nice northern a little too loosely and lost it, the guide became harsh in his criticism. I told the guide to calm down, puzzled by his outburst.

Later that afternoon, Mike accidently bumped one of the oars against the boat while we were positioning ourselves for the evening hunt. We had not yet started calling so the muffled sound hardly seemed disastrous. The motor and the boat scraping along shore had made more noise a few minutes earlier. But the guide immediately pushed off from the reeds we were hidden in, started the outboard, and returned to camp.

When the motor finally fell silent and I could confront him, he stalked away without comment.

I resolved at that point to be done with the guide and hunt on my own, but in the morning the guide appeared to have recovered his former good humor and we made plans for the day, loaded the boat, and returned to the bay we had so abruptly deserted the evening before.

The morning dawned grand, with the wind still and scattered flights of ducks winging high through the crisp fall air. We sat in the boat, beached among some reeds along the shore, no doubt appearing like a pair of duck hunters trying to entice one of the wary flocks with our call. But our call echoed too hoarsely for the southbound mallards, and we sought our quarry not from the lightened sky but from the darkened depths of the forest. We shivered through the dawning and watched the day come alive in a spreading burst of sunshine that highlighted the green sheen of the conifers and shaded the waters to a sky-tinted blue.

The morning passed as had so many others, with hope fading against the rising sun. The moose call drifted invitingly over the bay, but the moose did not come, if indeed one was even there, for again no fresh sign was in evidence when we checked before returning to the cabin for Mike.

We fished and scouted along the entire south shore during the midday, landing a few northerns but finding no sign of moose. I remembered the tracked-up bay off the windswept lake of the preceding year and suggested it to the guide. He was familiar with it, mentioning also a good walleye area he knew along the way.

When we reached the isthmus separating the second and third lakes, I suggested to Mike that he might enjoy the novelty of winching the boat up and over the sapling rails all by himself. Promising young basketball players benefit from that kind of exercise, or so I tried to convince him. He was not convinced. We shared the winching.

The walleye area proved productive, but the windswept lake was churning whitecaps far too ominous to cross to the bay.

Afternoon brought us back to the second lake, scouting along the north side, where at last, in a small cove funnelling into an inlet, the outsized prints of a recent visitor revealed themselves along the shore.

We set up and called through the evening, watching the day-light fade as the sun sank behind the western treeline. Silence again remained our only answer. The day ended as it began, in a dark journey over the night-stilled waters, with moose still only a wistful dream.

I returned with the guide to the little cove well before first light the following morning. Mike elected to fish along the south shore. The guide and I surrounded ourselves with a screening of reeds and for the umpteenth time the plaintive call wafted out over the silent dawning.

There is a repetition to the seemingly mundane aspects of the hunt that at times in the reciting waxes monotonous, yet in the doing remains ever fresh and intriguing. Such with the calling of moose. For the hunter, caught up in the rhythm of the hunt, knowing a majestic creature could emerge at any moment, the mood is one of suppressed excitement. Expectation fills the passing minutes, and draws the hunter ever back.

The morning slipped by as had the others before it. The pleasure of the woods and waters offered the only compensation for our patient vigil. The first hour had passed, along with a couple more. The guide said it was time to go. But to where, I knew not. That little cove remained the only place on the lake with any fresh sign. Another midday excursion around the lake seemed a futile exercise. I suggested we still-hunt through the cove area but the guide balked at the idea.

"I don't see any point to it. We're not going to see anything back in the bush."

"Well we're sure not seeing anything out here."

"You go ahead if you want, but you'll only be wastin' your time."

I left the guide at the boat and soon lost myself in the quiet of the shoreline woods.

From the little inlet we were tucked into, the sandy-edged cove curved out to the main body of the lake where the shoreline again grew tight against the forest. I decided to hunt the edge to that point and then make a swing through the deeper woods back to the boat.

I followed along the curve of the cove, pausing after every few steps to scan the forest before easing forward another few steps until a fresh perspective bid me pause again. The morning continued calm and I tread lightly along the edge, slipping into the sheltering trees on small half-swings when the conifers blocked my view. The woods grew mostly dense along the edge but opened some away from it. I wove cautiously through the midmorning quiet, holding quiet with it, slow and deliberate, letting the hushed forest guide me along its silent paths.

Time did not disturb me, nor did any other thought save the hope of discerning an antlered form in the soft-lighted forest. Conifers grew thick in places, but little copses of hardwoods offered fairer views, their trunks lining straight like soldiers in file except for the blowdowns that broke the vertical pattern and except for the line that flowed horizontally between a stand of hardwoods sixty to seventy yards away through some second growth that I followed with my eyes until my eyes came to rest upon a palmated object that lay upon an angular shape that flowed back into the horizontal line that materialized into the magical form that held me in stunned wonder.

A moose was standing there! A bull moose! Half-quartering away from me. Antlered head turned in my direction. Staring at the form that was staring at it.

The rifle came smoothly into position. The crosshairs sorted through the second growth, holding steady on the point just behind the shoulder, holding steady while I squeezed, holding steady still at the moment the trigger broke the three-pound tension and the recoil pushed unnoticed with my last view being the crosshairs still locked tight behind the shoulder and the scope coming back down to see the moose vanish in a few steps behind the second growth with the bolt up and back and pushing another cartridge into the chamber but the scope finding only second growth and hardwoods and the quiet closing tight again.

Then the tension release began, a slight tremble in my right leg. My arms tensed down until there was no use trying to hold the rifle to my shoulder. But the need no longer existed. The moose had vanished into the forest.

I waited for the adrenaline rush to subside. The forest continued hushed. I watched and listened for movement. Silent minutes passed.

Pounding footfalls intruded upon the silence. The guide came running toward me along the edge of the cove.

"What happened?"

"I shot a moose."

"Where?"

"There," I pointed.

I led the way toward the spot. Blowdowns detoured us but we came as near to where the moose had been standing as I could determine. No blood or any other sign. I tied my handkerchief to a sapling and we began a careful circle around the spot. Nothing.

"You must have missed."

"No, I don't think so."

"Well, there's nothing here."

We continued searching, but the guide quickly lost interest. I knew the hold was good. But the fact did remain, we could find no sign.

We returned to the spot from where I shot. The guide by then had lost all interest and left to bring up the boat. I studied the woods and the position of the marked sapling, visible through the second growth. Yes. That was close to where the moose had been standing.

I returned to the sapling and began following in the direction the moose appeared to have taken. I could not find any tracks or blood, but the course seemed reasonable and drew me on. I proceeded in silent concentration until a grating noise disturbed the hushed forest. The boat arrived, the motor coughing irritably before finally falling silent.

I continued along the suspected path of the moose. The way led promisingly but no sign confirmed my intuition. The ground seemed undisturbed. Not a single indication of passage offered encouragement.

Then, across a blowdown, glistening deep red along the trunk, a swath of blood sent a surge of hope. Then more blood not far beyond. Then more still, in regular blotches, with the frothy indication of a lung hit.

The guide hollered. I did not want to respond with the moose likely close ahead but he hollered again. I called out simply, "Blood," and waited while the guide came through the forest.

At the sight of the blood trail the guide became all business.

"He'll go to water with that wound. I'll follow the trail. You go down to the shore. He'll likely end up there if I push him out."

I retraced my route to the lakeshore and waited. A few minutes passed. A shot echoed from the forest. I locked my gaze onto the treeline. It remained unbroken.

Another minute passed before the guide called out. I followed the sound to where he stood alongside the moose.

"He was down, but I wanted to make sure."

The need for his shot was questionable. My bullet had pierced both lungs. But no matter. After arduous hours, and days, and seasons, the grand prize lay before me. A magnificent, splendid creature. Even in final repose, noble almost beyond comprehension.

We dressed the moose, then went to pull Mike away from his fishing. We could use all the help we could muster to pack the quarters through the blowdowns to the boat. Most of the rest of the day passed in that task.

We returned to the main camp on Reed lake the following morning where an ice house thoroughly cooled the meat. We packed the meat in boxes, iced them down, secured them on top of the Blazer, covered all with a tarp, and took our leave.

We came down out of the north that year, Mike and I, drifting south from Flin Flon and the Grass River Country through The Pas under a sky cloudy with ducks. We left Manitoba and angled through Saskatchewan on a night crossing into North

Dakota, picking up a south-running highway a little past the Missouri River. The Black Hills of South Dakota drew us up the corkscrew road to Mount Rushmore, then held us along a south meadow while a herd of buffalo paraded before us. We crossed into Wyoming and arrived in Lusk in time to get the moose meat into the locker plant before it closed, completing our two thousand five hundred mile, Grass River Country detour on the way to Mike's antelope hunt.

And a memorable hunt it was. The pronghorns foiled us on a number of stalks before Mike made a fine, three hundred yard shot with his .243 Winchester. My antelope filled the last of our tags, concluding a roundabout, mixed-bag hunt.

A second moose fell to my .270 in the Grass River Country, then my wanderings turned me to other lands. But always memories draw me back to the windswept lakes and the placid bays, where the great monarch of the forest roams in splendid solitude, and the haunting cry of the loon sends wild shivers through the dark-shrouded passages of the night.

Chapter 13

The Ranch

In the days of his youth and adventure, in the year of thirty-seven, a twenty-year-old Nebraskan struck out from his Sioux County home for the cattle country of Wyoming. Within a year a modest acreage with equally modest buildings held the young man's name on the title. The passing years saw other sections of prime grassland added to those initial holdings until the ranch grew to encompass ten thousand acres, nearly sixteen square miles.

The northern half of this sprawling ranch is typical rolling prairie. Cattle graze there, and antelope mingle with them. Cattle also graze in the southern half where the country takes on a more hilly aspect. Some hills rise impressively from the surrounding prairie. One rock-rugged, partially timbered elevation is even grandly named Rabbit Mountain. For a prairie dweller the designation will do, but in reality, Rabbit Mountain remains a pale shadow of the true mountains rising over the western horizon.

South of Rabbit Mountain the prairie rolls away in deeper dips and bowl-shaped draws offering sheltered grazing for cattle and antelope. Canyon Creek marks the southern boundary of the ranch. Conifer-covered rocky hills rise from the grasslands in the southwest corner above the creek. Badlands, they are called, since they offer no grazing for cattle. But mule deer shelter in those broken-country draws, and there may be some who would therefore call those lands good.

In my beginning Wyoming days, I roamed at will through the forests and over the prairies, hunting wherever the mood struck me and the land and my license allowed. The mountain ranges drew me for elk and mule deer. Antelope were found wherever sage and prairie abounded. In time the antelope country around Lusk began drawing me regularly back, for the rolling terrain offered the kind of stalk-hunting that I came to favor. I began scouting north of Lusk for an area holding mule deer as well as antelope. Eventually I came upon the ranch. Rabbit Mountain initially attracted me. At first sight the barren hill seemed an unlikely place for deer, but a covering of evergreens along the north slope drew my attention.

-1-

The first day of October 1976. I looked hopefully toward the prominent hill showing the only sheltering timber on the otherwise treeless prairie. Dark-forested ridges rose off to the southwest, but too far away to be able to hunt before dark.

Open prairie fronted the hill on the north side. A covering of junipers and pines shielded the front of the hill along half of its curved facing. The evergreens ended where the hill bent around toward the west. The rock-strewn hillside lay barren of any further vegetation beyond that point.

I slung my rifle over my shoulder and began the lengthy walk to the east side of the hill. The prairie sloped gently up until the base of the hill drew it rapidly to a sharper pitch. I climbed straight up among the rocks. The steepness of the climb surprised me, making a rest welcome before even half the height was scaled.

The east side of the hill bore south, indented and terraced in a number of places along its several hundred yards. A few scattered junipers relieved the otherwise barren aspect of the boulder-strewn hillside. I began angling up the slope, weary from my straight-ahead assault, then rested again just below the top.

A few seconds passed. The empty slope seemed devoid of life. Then movement flashed through the corner of my eye. Seven antelope emerged from a hidden pocket below, feeding casually within easy range, a good buck among them.

I slowly knelt to the ground, shielded by a screening of rocks, and watched the little band. The buck held steady in my scope, but my antelope license had been filled that morning. Half an hour elapsed before the antelope fed out onto the open prairie.

The sighting of game prompted me to stay on that side of the hill. I began still-hunting among the large rocks and boulders. The terraced, irregular slope provided a surprising number of hidden areas. What from a distance appeared to be a bare hillside offering little concealment, close up turned into a pocket-rich cover that urged caution at every step.

The contour of the hill led gradually upward. The passage around larger boulders and draws determined my route. My caution increased as more of the flattened top came into view. A grassy tableland began to take shape. I continued upward, each added step revealing more of the extensive open. A few steps, a halt, then a few more steps before another halt to scan the unfolding grassland. Another few steps. A halt. Then a few more steps before slowly reversing the last of those steps.

Two deer ahead! A fleeting glimpse in the open.

Some jumbled rocks to my right offered concealment from which to take a protected look. The deer were feeding in a small depression, their forms distorted through the grass and rocks covering the hilltop. A good-antlered buck and a doe. The range was long. I rested my rifle over one of the rocks and tried to capture the buck in my scope, but the intervening ground cover blocked any chance. I shifted carefully into a sitting position, but the small depression the deer were feeding in left the buck only partially exposed. The distance lay beyond a sure offhand shot.

I eased back from the rocks to a point where it was possible to stand and began a stalk along the side of the hill. A steep rock wall began to form. I climbed patiently up the awkward slope to where the rim of the rock wall edged into the tabletop and cautiously raised my head. The deer were still feeding in the depression. The range had closed but the intervening grass and rocks continued to block the sight picture. I dropped back down the slope and continued on. The broken ground impeded my progress. Again I eased up to the rim. The deer continued to feed, offering glimpses but never a reasonable opportunity. At one point the buck raised his head and faced in my direction. He watched for several seconds before he resumed feeding.

I continued the stalk, trying to find some avenue through the grass and rocks that would permit a clear shot. The likelihood appeared bleak. The ground did not seem to improve farther along. Again I peered over the rim. The back of the buck was visible but the doe was no longer in sight. I watched for a while, considering my chances, then decided to try from there before the buck likewise vanished from view.

I stretched on my tiptoes and hung on the rim, supporting my weight on my elbows. The rifle added further muscle strain to an already strained position. I found the buck in the scope and tried to settle the sight picture through the trembling tension of my arms. The range appeared to be about two hundred yards. Only the top half of the buck could be seen above the depression. I held the horizontal crosshair as low on the deer as the ground cover would permit, squeezed the trigger gently through the tightening muscle strain, and saw the buck drop instantly at the shot.

I climbed around to the top of the hill. The doe was gone but three bucks stood lower in the depression looking toward the fallen deer. Two carried antlers considerably larger than those of the downed buck. They evidently had been there all along. I watched the three bucks for several seconds, then began walking along the rim. The bucks came instantly alert, stared briefly in my direction, then turned and were soon bounding away with their pogo-stick gait into the boulder-strewn hillside.

I measured one hundred and eighty paces from the rim to the fallen deer. The bullet had pierced the forward part of his spine. He was a respectable four-by-four and a weary challenge to get off the hill and across the prairie in the dark.

-2-

Four seasons elapsed before my Wyoming wanderings brought me again to the ranch. I followed the mile-long washboard drive from the county dirt road to the ranch house and there renewed my acquaintance with Chuck and his wife, Pauline. Chuck invited me into the kitchen where Pauline graciously served coffee.

The homespun kitchen exuded a warm, well-lived-in atmosphere, as did the rest of their home. A small living room off the kitchen with an adjoining bedroom, and a bathroom off the opposite side of the kitchen, answered for the rooms in the ranch house.

An adjacent dwelling of lesser dimensions and a small trailer permanently parked nearby provided housing for the hired hand and seasonal help. Other buildings and corrals spread out in a seemingly haphazard fashion west and north of the residences. All were rich with the patina of time.

After coffee, Chuck and I walked outside and discussed the hunting prospects. Although not a hunter, Chuck remained keenly aware of the game as well as everything else on his ranch. He suggested Rabbit Mountain for deer, but the hills rising a few miles to the southwest attracted my attention.

"Any deer back there?"

"Yeah."

"Can I get there with my truck?"

"Should be able to if you got four-wheel-drive."

"I do."

"Well that track headin' south leads to an old water tank near the hills, but it cuts through Sawmill Canyon and it's washed out some. You'd want four-wheel in places."

"I'll give it a try. If I get to the hills, I'd like to camp there for a few days."

"Go ahead. Stay as long as you need."

I took his leave and set out in the brilliant sunshine along a track tracing like a matched set of wheel-wide, dark ribbons over the short-grassed prairie. A barbed-wire gate held me briefly just beyond the ranch buildings, then a rise and subsequent dip left the buildings lost to view with only rolling prairie and distant buttes and south-running ridges in sight.

The track followed across easy ground. I picked up speed until a jarring, washed-out stretch cautioned me. I slowed and continued south across the irregular prairie, caught up in the pleasure of wandering deeper into new country. The day unfurled glorious with the azure-blue sky framing the golden browns and deep greens of the conifer-covered ridges rising rugged to the west.

Another barbed-wire gate far into the prairie required a short halt. Beyond it the route traced faint, evidently little used past that section. The track continued southward, leading to the rim of a steep-walled canyon. There it turned east to parallel the rim as though the original maker of the track had been seeking a way across. That way soon revealed itself and I paused to examine the trail leading into the canyon.

A track surely existed at one time, but a rutted, washed-out corridor tracing down the incline was all that remained of it. I studied the rugged descent for a minute, then shifted into low gear, eased the front of the Blazer over the rim, and rode the brakes down the steep-angled slope. A dry creek bed covered with flinty rocks meandered along the bottom. I turned west to follow its course until another rutted corridor traced upward to the other side. The Blazer climbed easily up the rough track, although the steepness of the grade shifted everything that had tumbled forward on the descent back in a clutter to the rear. My rifle hung securely on a side-window rack.

Another barbed-wire gate halted me at the top. The track turned west past the gate toward the timbered heights. I followed along the faint trail in the direction of the now visible water tank, skirting the canyon and the beginning juniper cover that stretched down from the hills. The track ended at the water tank but I continued on, dipping down a gentle slope back into the dry creek bed. Junipers began swishing noisily against the side of the Blazer where they closed tight in level areas before straight-walled banks again rose above me. I wound through the creek bed deeper into the hills until a tangled mass of trees and debris blocked my way.

A steep bank rose to my right. I climbed it on foot and found a small area that offered enough level ground for a camp before the bank again rose sharply to the north. I returned to the

Blazer, maneuvered it at right angles to the creek bed, shifted into low gear, then spun up the steep incline. Dirt and rocks rattled noisily off the undercarriage.

The flat area provided a pleasant campsite. Dense junipers grew tight on the western margin, blending with the pines continuing into the hills. Sparse grass and sage covered the eastern margin for the short distance it remained level before circling up in a continuation of the steep north slope. The effect was one of being enclosed in a deep bowl on three sides. The south opened on a grand view of evergreen-covered hills with the creek bed comfortably below should the rains come surging down through the draws.

I set up camp, which with the Blazer simply meant finding a level place to park, my camp being self-contained within it. A bunk with a comfortable foam-rubber mattress covered the six-foot-long space behind the driver's seat. Three drawers under the bunk held canned food, clothes, books, and other miscellany. A consol cooler fit between the front seats. To cook one simply dropped the tailgate, which served as a table, and opened a rear-facing compartment under the bunk holding a Coleman two-burner stove, pots and pans, and extra fuel for the stove, as well as for a Coleman lantern which served in the dark. Water was carried in a five-gallon container. During fishing season a canoe rode on top, replaced by my duck skiff when the autumn colors came. Breaking camp was as easy as setting up. I simply drove away.

With camp situated, I set off to scout to the south. The afternoon continued warm with the sun highlighting passages through the junipers along the creek bed. Beyond the creek the low-lying hills rose and dipped in succession. Sparse grasses struggled through the flinty rocks covering much of the higher ground. Gip rock, Chuck called it. Numerous draws washed down from the heights, all feeding into the creek bed. Heavy rains must send an impressive surge of water through the narrower confines. Junipers grew dense in and along the draws, mixing with pines near the tops of the hills. A steep, south-running ridge bordered the western edge of the range.

I hunted through the lower junipers, gradually working upward to where an irregular expanse with scattered pines opened onto the higher reaches. I watched there in the pleasant afternoon sun before continuing on. The evergreens grew thick again past the irregular expanse. The ground angled down and back up to open on another tract of scattered pines. The exposed area held me along its edge. Scarcely a minute passed before the motion of a deer crossing through the pines fifty yards away brought me alert. At first appearance the deer seemed to be a doe. Then the supposed doe began angling away and a pair of spikes showed behind its oversized ears. The little buck continued through the scattered pines, unaware of my presence.

I followed south until the evergreens ended and the last flinty-rock slope blended into the grass prairie, then swung east and circled back through the hills, arriving at camp with the last light of day fading over the western ridge.

The night skies held me outside long after I finished the evening meal. The clear, high-plains atmosphere lent an intenseness to the stars that set them glittering like diamonds. A shooting star etched briefly through the dark, a solitary sojourner ending its timeless trek through infinity in a final burst of celestial glory. The night silence matched the intenseness of the stars. I immersed myself in the grand solitude, holding longer in the night, pondering the immenseness and the brilliance of the star-splendored heavens, and the wonder that must exist beyond.

The faint light of morning found me retracing my route of the preceding afternoon. The skies remained clear, the air brisk. I angled east toward a prominent, cone-topped hill, still-hunting through the evergreens. There was no wind.

The junipers and pines grew scattered, leaving open corridors to weave through. The ground covering of pine needles muffled my footsteps. I tread silently along.

Movement ahead began to seep into my consciousness. Something was filtering through the evergreens. I cautiously continued forward, pausing to view around each tree before moving on, careful of the brittle pine cones littering the ground.

Movement again. Brown forms began to materialize. A doe entered the corridor a few yards in front of me. A fawn joined her. The two deer continued slowly through the tree cover. I followed several yards behind, matching their steps and pauses. We wove in file through the evergreens, a fascinating tandem in the hushed dawn. Our little procession continued for a good fifty yards until the two deer slipped out of sight down a dense-covered ravine, still oblivious to the presence behind them.

Beyond the ravine the ground sloped upward to the cone-topped hill. I climbed to just under the crest of the hill and sat down, watching for other deer movement below. The day opened fair. Sunlight began tinging the higher ridge to the west.

The lure of the hills in time turned me southward. I began still-hunting along the contours, holding wherever the trees thinned below. Sunlight shifted down the higher ridge. The warming air brought a breeze from the west. I continued south, facing into the wind whenever it came time to pause.

A convenient rock eventually offered a good perch from which to view a scattering of openings in the evergreens. I sat there enjoying the morning, still caught up in the intenseness of the start of the hunt.

The sun began filling some of the openings below. In one of them the light parted the shadows to reveal an antlered buck easing through it, a fleeting glimpse before the trees closed him in again. Movement continued. Gray-brown patches through the green shadows seventy-five yards away. I locked onto the next opening, waiting for the buck to reappear. He stepped into the opening and stopped. A second buck appeared behind him, a twin to the first. I centered the crosshairs behind the shoulder of the lead buck, and fired. Both deer were immediately lost to view.

The evergreens revealed no movement. I waited a few minutes then worked my way down to the opening. The flinty ground offered scant sign. I followed in the direction the deer were facing and soon began picking up droplets of blood, then a heavier flow leading downhill to a little thicket of junipers. And there the buck lay, a fine four-by-four, taken cleanly through the lungs.

I dressed the deer and began the tedious chore of dragging him to camp. The ground funnelled me farther east than desired, but at least the stretches covered with pine needles made the dragging easier. A last weary lift out of a shallow draw finally brought me to the high bank of the creek bed, still a considerable distance from camp.

I left the deer, returned to camp, then drove the truck to where the top of the straight-walled bank lay level with the roof of my Blazer. A short pull soon had the buck in position to slide from the bank to the top of the truck. After securing him for the ups and downs of the canyon, I followed the twisting route out to the ranch house.

Chuck and Pauline greeted me there, pleased with my early success. I discovered while having coffee that although Chuck did not care for venison, Pauline favored it. When I dropped my deer off at the locker plant, I paid for the processing and had the receipt made out in Pauline's name, giving it to her and Chuck along with the landowner's coupon for the antelope license I later filled.

-3-

Wyoming compensated landowners for game on their ranches by including an eight-dollar coupon on deer and antelope licenses. When a deer or an antelope was taken, the hunter signed his coupon over to the rancher, who in turn redeemed it through the state. The following year, Chuck shared his views on the coupon system, along with his views on a wide range of other topics, as we sat on two straight-back chairs on the small porch in front of his house.

Chuck held strong opinions on just about everything and he was not a bashful man with them. His topic had turned to welfare and how it was ruining the country. Chuck's lack of success in finding good help, he was certain, could be laid directly to the unfathomable practice of the government paying people not to work. How else to explain his hired man quitting and moving into town right when he had a herd of cattle that needed rounding up.

He paused a moment in his discourse, as though pondering another thought, then continued.

"Say, you could help with them cattle."

His tone suggested a settled fact rather than a inquiry.

"Pauline would help but she's not feelin' well. She's doctorin' with some heart pills."

"Oh? I didn't know she had a problem."

"Been botherin' her a long time. She has her good days and her bad."

"I'm sorry to hear that. I'd be glad to help but riding round-up horses is something I've never done."

"Oh, you can ride the ones I got."

"That may be, but I don't know about riding them well enough to go chasing after cattle."

"Come and see."

He led the way to one of the weather-beaten sheds behind the house and there proudly showed me his most recently acquired roundup pony. A motorcycle.

"You can ride one of these, can't you?"

I agreed that I could and we were soon bouncing across the prairie in effective if not classical pursuit of a scattered group of cattle which we herded into a split-rail corral. My job after that was to push the cattle one by one through a stall where Chuck doused them with a liquid solution poured over their backs. The cattle needed little encouragement to return again to the range. They trotted off in quick order when released from the corral.

With my unexpected roundup work completed, I headed south along the track leading to the canyon and the southwest hills. By the time camp was situated the day left little time for scouting. I decided to read awhile before supper and bed.

I sat in the front seat of the Blazer enjoying the pleasant evening, engrossed in my book, when a movement in the side-view mirror caught my attention. A doe was browsing on a low shrub next to the left rear wheel. She snatched a few bites, looked around, took a few more nibbles, then fed across the little clearing before dropping into the creek bed and disappearing into the junipers on the opposite side. Later, in the final dusk, four shadowy forms of deer crossed below the cone-topped hill to the east. They showed too dimly in my binoculars to determine if any were bucks. I fell asleep that night in the pleasant company of deer.

The sightings of the preceding day brought extra alertness as I hunted through the junipers and pines toward the cone-topped hill in the morning dawn. I followed the general route that had brought me to the twin bucks of the previous year, but the early morning passed without any indication of deer movement. The hills farther south drew me. The balance of the morning passed in pleasant wanderings through the evergreens and opens. Midday came as I completed a circle back to camp, still without the sighting of a deer.

After lunch I climbed into the hills to the north and hunted new country. The terrain continued evergreen covered and hilly along the west, grading into flinty-rock opens and steep hill-sides to the east. Farther north, high, elongated ridges, with deep ravines between, graded to the prairie. Junipers hid the ravine bottoms as they climbed into the scattered pines of the upper reaches.

Midafternoon saw me on one of those far ridges, probing the timbered margins. I hunted down a long, angling slope, pausing often to glass into the juniper-and-rock-covered ravines. No deer were in evidence below, but from my height a grand panorama of prairie stretched out to the horizon. The lack of game suggested a break in my hunting and I sat in prolonged enjoyment of the grand view to the north and east. The ranging prairie swept away to distant formations of flat-topped buttes and irregular hills. The ranch showed like a miniature toy-building display far off to the northeast. Other than that reminder, not a sign of humanity marred the pristine aspect of a scene reminiscent of days not so distant, when deer and antelope wandered freely over a fenceless prairie, and great buffalo herds were the only cattle roaming the land.

The west-settling sun begin suggesting it was time to turn campward. I started hunting back along the ridge, watching into a deep ravine that flowed down and up again to top out on a sparsely timbered hill to the south. Junipers grew in scattered array along the steep slope. I proceeded slowly up the ridge, peering into the timber across the way, when suddenly a good-antlered buck crossed out of the trees above and began slanting down the slope to my left front. The buck continued unaware down the slope toward a small cluster of junipers, which he entered. I slowly lowered myself to a kneeling position, held the scope along the edge of the cluster, and waited for him to reappear.

A minute passed. Then two. The buck did not reappear. I raised my head to look over the scope, easing the eye strain and muscle tension. Another minute. And another. Still the buck did not reappear.

He had to be behind the junipers. There was no other place for him to be. The ground lay open around the little cluster except for a few other junipers scattered up and along the hillside.

I waited, holding in long anticipation of the buck's certain reappearance. Minutes ticked by. The sun highlighted the scene. The cluster of junipers stood stark against the rock-covered slope a little over a hundred and fifty yards away. Not a breeze stirred. Not a sound could be heard. I waited in sure expectation of a fair shot. But the shot never came. The buck never reappeared. How he could possibly have vanished remains beyond me, but he was no longer behind the junipers when my careful crossing to them revealed only empty ground.

I puzzled awhile over the buck, trying to determine his escape route, then, still puzzled, resumed my hunt south through the hills. The coming of evening hinted at the movement of deer, but the disappearing buck remained my only sighting for the day.

The following morning sent me again into the northern hills searching for another glimpse of the buck, for his antlers had grown in memory through the night. He remained elusive, as did the other deer no doubt lurking in the timbered draws, the only sign of their presence being the fresh droppings glistening on the flinty rocks.

By late morning my lack of success turned my thoughts toward fresh country. An antelope license remained to be filled, and distant Rabbit Mountain, out of sight far to the north, began to tempt for deer. I broke camp, and once through the canyon, began scouting for antelope. Like the deer, they remained elusive. Rabbit Mountain eventually became the remaining hope for the day.

I approached Rabbit Mountain from the north, walking across the long stretch of open prairie to the west slope of the hill. The warm afternoon made a tee-shirt more than adequate, although a heavier shirt lay tucked in my day pack for the inevitable chill when the sun went down.

The climb up the west slope required a few pauses. The sun beat warmly. The top of the hill at last opened before me. I stopped, took a few sips from my canteen, put the canteen away, and began walking forward.

A chilling burring noise froze me in mid-step. The burring repeated itself. I stared in the direction of the sound and there, coiled in front of a sun-warmed rock, holding me even more frozen, lay a rattlesnake.

We eyed each other while the snake continued its warning burrs. I cautiously eased backward out of striking distance. The snake lay coiled, still burring. I left it there and made a wide circle around the rock.

The south side of the hill dropped down to the prairie in a series of ridges interspersed with grassy draws. A rocky, boulder-strewn stretch east of the ridges swung brokenly around to the north. The prairie encircled the entire hill as it rose up out of the flatland like a monument. A similar rocky expanse rose nearby to the east. Only a few junipers relieved its otherwise barren aspect.

I continued around the hill, seeing no deer by the time the far side above the evergreens was reached. My attempt at still-hunting through the evergreens met with frustration, their denseness offered little chance of sighting deer.

I tried the upper edge with a similar lack of success. Any deer in those junipers and pines remained well-sheltered.

The north side of the hill opened clear where the evergreens ended to the west. A shallow concave, covered with rocks and large boulders, continued into a rock formation near the western end. I found a spot in the rocks just below the crest and cautiously tested for rattlesnakes before sitting down to begin glassing.

The sun was dipping low in the west, creating a slight glaring problem in the binoculars. I patiently searched through the glare among the rocks and large boulders for the form of a bedded deer. Time continued on as did the sun in its journey toward the western horizon. The binoculars revealed only an empty expanse of open rock. I scanned the hillside again. Not a trace of a deer could be found.

Then three does stood up. Then another rose from the barren, rock-covered ground like a spectral spirit rising out of nothingness. That they escaped my careful glassing remains a caution. The four does began climbing toward the western top of the hill. Their presence sharpened the intenseness of my further scrutiny of the slope. Still I could find nothing.

Then a buck stood up, followed by a second one, a little higher.

I locked them into my binoculars. They appeared identical. My rifle lay across my day pack on a rock in front of me offering a steady rest. I nestled into the scope, bracketed the lower buck in the double-crosshair reticle, judged three hundred yards, held steady a little high on the body, and fired.

The buck tumbled down the slope, coming to rest against a rock outcropping. The second buck stared for a moment, then turned and casually followed the does up and over the hill. There was no alarm in their movements.

The light had long faded by the time I got the buck out, a decent three-by-three, and memorable for the refresher course on gray-tinted ghosts hiding among gray-tinted rocks. I stayed there on the prairie that night and finished the second half of my hunt by seven o'clock the following morning with a fine antelope.

-4-

The ranch house was empty when I stopped by to drop off the deer and antelope coupons. I mailed them to Chuck along with a letter expressing my hope of seeing him and Pauline the following year on another hunt. My letter faded from memory until a reply arrived ten months later.

August 8th, 1982

Dear John,

I received your letter in regards to hunting deer and antelope. Yes, you can come and hunt. There is a lot of big bucks around now & I suppose there will be a lot of them around for hunting season.

I had the tough luck of loosing my wife. Pauline passed away on June 8th. This has been an awful summer for me here.

I will be looking for you when the season opens this fall.

Sincerely,
Chuck

Blustery weather confronted me on my return the following year. The somber day before season opened matched the somber contents of Chuck's letter. His pickup was gone when I arrived. I hunted antelope in the mist on opening day and later followed the track through the canyon to my campsite in the hills.

I arrived with only a few hours left in the afternoon. The disappearing buck of the preceding year drew me into the northern hills for the evening hunt. That the buck might still be there was no doubt a wishful dream, but the hills beckoned.

I hunted up the long-running western slope, and at its crest turned north through some timbered draws, coming around to a semi-open area. I watched there for a quarter of an hour, then began hunting through the evergreens edging the open along a draw that dropped off toward the west.

Suddenly a good-antlered buck broke across my right front and disappeared into the draw. So fleeting was the glimpse, the safety had not even been released. I searched into the draw but the denseness of the evergreens offered little hope of again seeing the buck, nor were any other deer seen that evening during my circle back to camp.

The northern hills drew me again in the morning, and again a good-antlered buck thwarted my presumed careful hunting with a sudden burst into cover. I did a little better that time. I at least got the safety off.

Midday found me back at camp without sighting another deer. After a sandwich and coffee, I headed toward the southeast, hunting through the junipers and pines to the cone-topped hill before circling toward the high, western ridge. I climbed the ridge and continued south along its top. The lower hills brightened with the sun finally breaking through the clouds.

At the south end of the ridge the ground sloped away to the prairie. There the flinty rock of the hillside merged into the fragile soil of the plains and the only places offering cover were the deep draws that traced down from the hills like long tentacles of green through the white gip rock.

I came down off the ridge and walked east to the opening of the largest draw. Tracks and droppings revealed themselves in the washed-out dirt. Junipers and pines grew in the draw on its meandering route north toward the hills. I eased into the cover and began still-hunting through the trees. The banks progressively grew higher until they reached well above my head. Side-leaning trees grew out from the banks in narrow places, creating arched, evergreen-ceilinged tunnels. In other places the banks lay far enough apart so that neither side could be seen from the dry watercourse in the center. Locked into the fastness, one became hard pressed to remember that this was a narrow conifer corridor tracking down an otherwise treeless hillside.

The pine needles mixed in with the soft dirt of the watercourse gave silent passage through the green-shrouded shadows. Flickers in the shadows held me at times until they resolved themselves into light playing through the dense-needled branches. Quiet reigned in the deepening confines. I eased along absorbed in my narrow world of encircling green.

Then a movement stilled me. A flicker. Light playing?

Again. Movement. Indistinct. Then gone. Forward in silence. Straining ahead. Another flicker. Holding still. Then a hint of brown ghosting through the green. A momentary glimpse. A sensing of form parting from the shadows.

A deer! Moving ahead. Not alarmed.

Forward once more. Cautious. Form fading back into the green. Eyes straining. Brown flicker again. Farther now. Going away. Still not alarmed. But melding into the green at a pace beyond my quiet pace. No way to match its pace in silence. No way to capture the brown shadow.

I climbed quickly out of the draw, angled a short distance away, then turned parallel to the shielding evergreens and began jogging toward the head of the draw where it flattened out and blended into the south slope. The evergreens ended there before they resumed again fifty yards farther up. That opening offered a chance should the deer continue into the hills. I jogged steadily toward it.

The ground was barren, covered with the flinty, shale-like rock common to the hills. After the closeness of the deep shade the open slope seemed shockingly revealing, but the draw kept the deer hidden, and me from its view.

I jogged in steady rhythm over the open ground, the flinty shale crunching distressingly beneath my feet. The head of the draw drew closer. I slowed and began angling toward the dense trees growing there. A few scattered junipers grew out from the edge. I eased around the last of them. A stirring sight brought me to a sudden halt.

A deer was standing there! A buck!

The rifle came smoothly to my shoulder, safety moving forward in a fluid motion. My cheek touched the stock as the scope settled into position. Sunlight flooded the lens. The deer danced in and out of a confusing haze. The form held vaguely for an instant. I held on the form and fired.

The deer disappeared back into the draw.

I waited, watching and listening. Neither sight nor sound marked the deer's passage. A minute passed before I crossed the fifty yards to where the deer had been standing. The ground revealed nothing.

I peered into the evergreens. They closed around emptiness. I eased into them and began searching the ground for some sign of blood. None showed. I continued carefully down the draw, watching ahead for the deer while scrutinizing the ground. The evergreens continued empty.

I may well have missed. The glare from the west-setting sun had badly confused the sight picture. Still, for an instant, the crosshairs seemed to have held true.

I returned to where the deer had been standing. A stunted bush grew at the spot. Using the bush as a marker, I began a patient circle around it, but the flinty rocks offered no telling traces.

Evening was descending. Time passed pressingly with my continuing futile search. The acceptance of a miss began to take hold. Then, from a fresh angle, a mark on the ground took faint definition. A suggestion of a furrow seemed to trace several inches across the surface. I knelt to examine it. The image of a dragging hoof flickered through my mind.

I searched in the direction the furrow pointed, but no other furrows traced across the flinty surface. Back again and on my knees, searching painstakingly along the furrow's line, eyes wearying in the fading light, time pressing harder now. And then, there, a short distance along, a tiny, russet-brown dot stood out on a small, cream-colored pebble. I licked my finger and touched it. The russet-brown dot dissolved into a red drop of blood.

Elation replaced defeat. The deer had been hit. I marked the spot with a piece of tissue and crawled on. Several yards farther another russet-brown dot dissolved into a red drop of blood. Another piece of tissue marked it. The trail continued laborious, the drops small and scarce. I followed the faint line of dots to the edge of the evergreens and continued into them, but there all sign ended.

I returned to the head of the draw and began searching down the western edge of the evergreens, the only other logical direction the deer could have gone. The pine needles added extra confusion. I weaved in and out of the edging searching for tiny, russet-brown dots, time waning with the fading light.

Then a mark. But no tiny dot this. A series of large drops began to spot the ground inside the edge of the pines. The drops continued, closer together, growing into splotches that led out of the draw onto the open slope down toward another sparsely timbered draw. I followed in haste.

I paused at the edge of the timbered draw and peered intently into the scattered trees. The gathering dusk held the bottom in shadow. I stepped forward.

The buck broke from the shadows in a sudden burst and bounded at full speed down the bottom of the draw. I raised my rifle and caught the deer in the scope just as he disappeared around a bend. No chance.

I broke into a run, sprinting rapidly along the top of the draw toward the turn. I reached it and saw the deer running furiously through the shadows toward another bend. The rifle came to my shoulder, the scope filled with shadows, then a juniper, then the running form of the deer, racing, bouncing in and out, crosshairs bouncing with him, catching hold for an instant, trigger seemingly willing itself back, the deer around the bend before the recoil brought the rifle down again.

I ran at full speed along the top of the draw and reached the next bend breathing hard. The deer was not in sight. I turned my gaze to the bottom and searched the shadows, and there, in the deepening dark, lay the buck.

I sat down on the bank and waited for my heart rate to slow. The buck showed indistinctly in the gathering dusk, but he still showed double forks on an upturned antler. A nice buck. Yes, a nice buck indeed. But then, when did anybody ever shoot a buck that was not a nice buck?

I sat there in the coming night and watched the deer slowly meld into the background, then roused myself to the work at hand. It was wearisome toil in the dark. Night was far advanced by the time camp came into view across the creek bed. I cooked a hasty meal in the halo of lantern light, then settled wearily into my sleeping bag. Consciousness slipped away in a dreamy haze of antlered ghosts floating through an evergreen-shrouded aurora. The morning's dawning passed unnoticed.

-5-

Chuck greeted me warmly when I pulled up to the ranch house the following year. He invited me in for coffee and talked long of Pauline. Even after a year and a half her loss affected him deeply. They had been married a month short of thirty-three years.

But in time his normal demeanor returned and he was soon discoursing at large on the foibles and irritations of the powers to be. His vexation turned to a recent exam required to maintain his pilot's certification.

"The eye doctor said I needed glasses or they wouldn't renew my license. Said it was a puzzle to him how I could land a plane with my eyes the way they were. Nothin' wrong with my eyes. I been landin' planes for thirty years. He just wanted to sell me some glasses. Here look at 'em. Even sold me a fancy case to go with 'em. But I'm not inclined to wear 'em."

With that he put the glasses in the case, slid the case into a corner of the kitchen table, and busied himself pouring coffee before he again sat down.

"Say, you never been up in my plane have you?"

"No I haven't."

"Well its a good afternoon for flyin'. We still got time. Help me push the plane out of the hanger and we'll take a look around the ranch. You'll get a good view from the air."

His new eyeglass case lay forgotten in a corner of the table.

"Chuck, that sounds like it could be a real experience, but I'd like to get back into the hills with some daylight left."

"Well, okay. Maybe another time."

"Yeah. Maybe another time."

The familiar canyon track passed beneath my Blazer, and my campsite above the dry creek bed soon held all in readiness for the afternoon hunt. The hills north of camp attracted me, for good bucks had been sighted there over the years. But the bucks, along with the does, stayed well-hidden for the rest of that afternoon.

The junipers along the south side of the creek bed drew me the following morning. I followed along the course that brought me to the crest of the cone-topped hill and watched from there for a while before continuing south through the eastern fringe of hills. The sun was half an hour over the distant buttes when I came to a ridge that sloped down to a scattered-pine opening. The little lookout kept me for a short watch.

The rising sun began bothering my eyes. I thought of continuing south when movement below held me in place. Deer were filtering through the pines. Many deer.

A procession of does and fawns paraded among the scattered trees. Eight for sure, and likely more. I strained to see antlers, then saw them. Two spike bucks walked out twenty yards below. They spotted me, stared for a good fifteen seconds, and ambled away. The procession through the pines continued, but no other bucks came into view. The last vestige of brown faded and the pines became still again.

The south hills offered no more deer sightings for the rest of the day, nor did a final watch beneath the cone-topped hill before a dark walk up the dry creek bed brought me to camp and a lantern-lighted supper under a starlit sky.

The next morning dawned fair. After a quick breakfast, I began angling through the junipers and pines along the creek toward the southern hills. Less than half an hour passed when movement ahead halted me. The movement resolved itself into a coyote probing cautiously through the evergreens. So intent was the coyote on its hunting that it never noticed the other hunter watching from twenty-five yards away. The wary creature drifted fleetingly through the trees, then paused a moment in an opening before silently slipping away.

Wildlife deserted me after the coyote encounter. Not another creature appeared the rest of the morning. The continuing dearth of deer sightings suggested a shift of hunting grounds. I broke camp and headed north toward Rabbit Mountain.

Early afternoon saw me crossing the prairie toward the western slope of that prominence. The day continued warm and a tee-shirt served adequately under the bright sunlight. I climbed slowly up the rock-strewn hillside. The energy-draining heat brought frequent pauses. My canteen became a welcome companion.

I halted near the crest and glassed the open prairie. Heat shimmers were all that my binoculars revealed. I resumed my climb.

The area beyond the crest of the hill slowly came into view. I eased upward and spotted the head of a doe traced in silhouette against the blue sky. I halted and stared, expecting a mule deer, but an antelope stood up instead. The doe looked back at me from thirty yards, then turned and ran down the grassy hillside onto the prairie and rapidly faded into the distance. An unexpected encounter on the top of Rabbit Mountain.

I followed along the southern crest of the hill toward the east. The ground sloped down to the prairie in a series of small ridges interspersed with wide, grass-filled draws. Rocks and boulders lay scattered about. Granite outcroppings jutted up here and there, adding to the broken nature of the irregular surface.

The ground lay covered in grass. I tread quietly along, watching into the draws. An unusual object in the high grass a short distance beyond the spot the antelope rose from caught my attention. I stared. The form of an ear gradually took shape. I continued staring. Little by little the outline of the head of a mule deer doe came into focus through the deep grass. The doe lay bedded in a shallow depression forty yards below, wonderfully concealed by the grass. The doe held my gaze until an ear flicker to her left exposed the position of a second doe. The indistinct outlines of the heads of four does slowly took definition, all bedded in near perfect concealment, watching downhill. Other deer might lay bedded there, but the grass was too tall to reveal them.

I began to stalk toward the deer. The hillside offered no concealment. My exposure remained glaring. Still each step brought me ever closer to the bedded animals. Half the distance was closed, twenty more paces would put me among them, yet they continued their restful gaze out over the hillside.

Another step, then another, then again, and yet one more before suddenly the four deer were standing and staring intently at me. Their curiosity required mere seconds to satisfy. In an instant they were bounding in great leaps out of the draw, over another ridge, and out of sight.

I climbed back to the crest, sat down, and began glassing east along the south slope, searching for more bedded deer. Draws hid much of the surface but I scrutinized the visible areas, probing with special care into the shadows of larger boulders. Heat waves danced in the magnification. The sun beat steadily down. The blue skies held only the barest wisps of clouds. The warm afternoon suggested restful slumber. Not a sign of life stirred.

The slope remained empty. After a final scan, I arose and began walking along the head of the draw, looking down into areas that had been concealed from my glassing position.

All at once, in a flash of instantaneous recognition, a bedded, good-antlered buck materialized in full relief against a large boulder fifty yards below. He lay in the boulder's shadow, looking downhill. I stood above him on the barren slope, skylined dare he look my way.

The buck watched out over the hillside and the prairie, motionless in the comforting shade. I held in the sun for a few seconds before bringing the rifle to my shoulder. The crosshairs settled forward on the deer. The rifle recoiled. And the antlered head lowered gently to the ground.

I waited a moment, then climbed down to the buck. A fine four-by-five. I dressed him in the afternoon heat. There was a need to get the buck quickly to the locker plant, but the weary work could wait a little while.

I sat down on the hillside beside the buck, gazed out over the grand expanse, and lost myself for a time in the boundless prairie, and the endless, endless sky.

The ranch continued to be my annual Wyoming destination for mule deer and antelope. My only unsuccessful year came in 1986 when a heavy rainstorm sent a rush of water surging down the normally dry creek bed. The ensuing mud and gumbo caked like heavy clay around my boots, making walking a fatiguing, leg-wearying exercise and creating a serious challenge in getting the Blazer out through the canyon. My hunting time unfortunately passed waiting for drier conditions.

During the 1980's, antelope roamed in considerable numbers between the southwestern hills and Rabbit Mountain. More roamed to the north. Licenses were generous then. A hunter could hold two deer and three antelope licenses in a season, and more than three antelope licenses in many areas, including the ranch area. If I filled early on mule deer and antelope, I would pick up additional licenses. Quite often the extra deer licenses were already gone, but several years did find me enjoying a second deer hunt along with another antelope hunt. My English setter, Smokey, thrived on antelope. During the pheasant and quail season he wolfed down half a pound of ground antelope each day before even considering his regular dog food. Whether the antelope meat improved Smokey's nose is debatable, but he definitely was the fastest bird dog in the county.

In the timeless scheme of things, nature moves in cycles. Severe drought conditions began throughout the central Rocky Mountain states in 1988. Within a few years the survival rate of deer and antelope fawns dropped dramatically. Normal ratios of ninety fawns to one hundred does reached as low as thirty fawns to one hundred does. Nonresident deer licenses dropped from forty-five thousand to twenty-nine thousand five years later. Antelope licenses were similarly reduced, as were the drawing odds. The chances of a nonresident drawing a deer license went from eighty-four percent to fifty-three percent. Still, I managed to draw at least a deer or an antelope license every year, and most years ended up drawing both.

The timeless cycles go on. The world will keep on turning and the drought will pass into memory. Deer will still wander the evergreen-clad hills, and the fleet-footed speedsters of the plains will still roam the sagebrush prairies. The hunters, in their turn, will come. And the mornings will dawn with days of wonder waiting for them.

Chapter 14

Antelope In The Mist

In the evening the rain started. It had threatened through Wisconsin and most of Iowa, and now, in the rolling hills before the Missouri River, the heavy-ladened clouds opened to release an incessant patter of drops that drummed rhythmically on the roof of my Blazer. I switched on the windshield wipers and watched the headlights reflect off the shadowing dark of the rain. In the diffused cones of light the dark-shrouded road gave the illusion of being a narrow corridor etched like an undulating ribbon on the rounded contours of the ridges, and I skimmed over its glistening surface aware only of my own, small, headlight-defined moving world, oblivious to the night space surrounding me.

I crested the final Iowa ridge, and in the misty valley below saw the lights of Sioux City glowing like a luminous island in the night sea. The lights shimmered to my right as I crossed the Missouri on a bridge of wet-darkened concrete. The darkness closed tight again beyond the first western hills, and the sense of solitude intensified as the lights flickered out behind.

The plains started after the westward hills. I held steady through the dark hours, slowing only to pass through sleeping Nebraska villages appearing forlorn and lifeless in the gloomy rain. Once beyond the villages the road stretched deserted, with only the growing lights of a rare approaching vehicle relieving the desolate aspect. The night was one easily given to brooding and melancholy, but the somber features stirred me instead and I journeyed through the darkness exhilarated by the solitude.

Somewhere before the Sandhills, weariness overtook me. I peered through the hazy dark, searching for a turnoff, and finally saw a narrow lane running into a grove of tall cottonwoods. I eased down the lane, found a sheltered place to park, and turned off the engine and the lights. The misty blackness engulfed me. I sat for a minute adjusting to the dark, then settled into the back of the Blazer and slipped wearily into my sleeping bag. The rain pattered on the roof while the wind sighed mournfully through the cottonwoods. I lay there, half-awake in the dark, enjoying the night symphony, until the rhythms of wind and rain slowly combined to play a hypnotic melody that soon lulled me fast asleep.

In the morning the rain had subsided, although the sky continued overcast and the damp wind bit uncomfortably. I climbed into the front seat, started the engine, then retrieved a can of grapefruit sections from the melted ice in the cooler. I opened the can, drank off the liquid, and unwrapped some bread rolls. A strengthening breeze set the trees in motion. I sat quietly beneath the swaying cottonwoods eating the grapefruit and bread, and watched wind-loosened leaves flutter fitfully to the ground.

The heater removed the damp morning chill in the short time it took to finish breakfast. I poured a cup of steaming coffee from my thermos, tested it, and put it in the holder to cool. Then, slipping into low gear, I eased the truck back along the rain-slick lane to the highway. There was no traffic. I pulled onto the empty road and settled again into the rhythm of the passing miles, sipping my now cooled coffee while watching the boundless horizon advance before me.

The morning emerged raw, almost cheerless, but in spite of the sullen aspect, the warm, familiar tremor of excitement began building as the sparse cottonwoods gave way to the treeless Sandhills. I was heading west again. It had come a time to hunt.

The sere-brown hills rolled by in hour after hour sameness until, approaching Chadron, ridges of pine began showing green to the south. Farther, along the White River, cottonwoods again flourished, sheltering whitetails in their thickets near Fort Robinson where I had seen them while hunting mule deer on the buttes above Soldier Creek. The road climbed steeply beyond Fort Robinson through a pine forest to the high, west plateau where before long I was slowing through Harrison past a sign proudly suggesting one should "take time to stop at Nebraska's Top—elevation 4880 feet." Another sign eleven miles west of Harrison welcomed me to Wyoming. Half an hour later I crossed the small bridge into the outskirts of Lusk.

The town appeared somber in the drab, cloud-gray afternoon. A chilling mist permeated the damp air, making my wool jacket welcome when I stepped out of the truck for gas. The motel lots were filled with out-of-state car licenses, but only a few orange-jacketed hunters were visible along main street. Most of the hunters were likely seeking refuge from the weather in their rooms or in the restaurants and taverns. I did not linger in town and was soon traveling north on the county road, across the railroad tracks, out past the cemetery, to the rolling prairie beyond.

There was little need to hurry, for an easy hour would bring me to the ranch. I loafed along the narrow roadway, stopping occasionally to glass the far ridges. Antelope were often active along this stretch before the pine breaks, but the miles rolled by without a single sighting.

I rumbled over a cattle guard just past the pine breaks and entered open rangeland. Free-roaming cattle wandered across the dirt road, moving grudgingly out of my way. Often they just stood in statue-like bewilderment, staring dumbly at the approaching vehicle until gently nudged aside. Multihued tags adorned their ears, suggesting images of colorful banderillas placed on the bull's withers before the matador begins his final passes with the muleta. But no fighting bulls these. They were destined for a far less noble demise.

The road cleared after another cattle guard and I resumed glassing the rolling prairie. Still no antelope. I continued down the road and stopped on a slight elevation near the ranch to scan the far ridges. The wind bellowed from the west, occasionally gusting to rock the truck and distort the images through my binoculars. I glassed carefully, covering areas where antelope had often been observed, but not a one came into view.

I focused on the ranch buildings and noticed that Chuck's pickup was gone, then remembered that he, too, liked to be out the day before the season opened, keeping tabs on the activity around his ranch.

After a final sweep with the binoculars, I started the truck and continued north, scouting along both sides of the narrow road and stopping often to glass the distant sage flats for telltale flashes of white. Not a sign of antelope or anything else could be seen. The whirling west wind seemed to have swept the prairie of all life.

I came to the east-west road and turned right, following it to a turnoff where a track wandered south past a stock-watering impoundment tucked between two low hills. I turned down the rutted track and bumped my way to the impoundment. No antelope showed on the way in, and although a multitude of game tracks surrounded the watering area, the maker's of those tracks were nowhere in evidence.

The wind continued to drive droplets with piercing force. I donned my raingear and climbed toward the crest of the western hill, settling to my stomach the last few yards. The rolling landscape beyond slowly came into view. It seemed empty. I lay in the wind-driven mist, carefully glassing to the horizon, seeking some vestige of life on the vast prairie, but only empty, barren land appeared in my binoculars. It was as though the living world had gone to ground to wait out the raw, blustery elements.

I stood up, retraced my steps to the impoundment, climbed the eastern hill, and repeated the process. Still nothing. A succession of ridges ran off to the east. I worked my way through them, cautiously approaching each summit, but not an antelope could be seen in that vast panorama of rolling hills and open prairie.

The lack of game puzzled me. I turned into the wind and began walking the long ridges back to where the truck lay concealed. Gust-driven droplets stung my face while the piercing wind penetrated the weak points in my raingear. Another prolonged gust doubled me forward. It began to occur to me that the antelope were likely sheltering in the lee areas. A section of higher hills interspersed with broken ground lay farther west, hardly typical antelope country, but it offered a number of protected places from the fierce west wind. Perhaps antelope might find it appealing on a blustery day.

The truck offered welcome shelter and I relished the refuge from the wind. I started the engine, and when my chill subsided, followed the impoundment track south, then west to where it connected with the dirt road. From this juncture the start of the broken-hilled area could be glassed. I examined the leeward slopes carefully. The broken terrain contained

many pockets that escaped my scrutiny. If antelope were sheltered there they were as secure from my gaze as from the
probing wind.

The east-west road ran along the north side of the hills and
breaks. I drove up the dirt road to the intersection, turned left,
and continued unhurriedly along, watching south into the few
pocket areas observable from the road. The prairie stretched for
miles off to the north. It was hard to resist stopping occasionally to glass the vast flatlands, although seeing anything on the
windswept opens seemed doubtful.

The ground began to level out as the west end of the break
area drew closer. A short distance before the breaks ended, in
an angulated wash that cut between two barren hills, a brief
flash of the white markings of antelope caught my attention.
They were in and out of my vision quickly. The sharp angle of
the wash provided only a narrow corridor of observation. I continued well past the hidden animals before pulling off to the
side of the road and scrutinizing the area with my binoculars.
From my observation point half a mile away even the wash was
not discernable. Its rim broke away and blended into the background. The antelope were below the rim, out of the wind as
well as out of sight.

The glimpse had been too fleeting to estimate how many
antelope there might be or to determine if a buck was among
them. I needed to get closer.

I got out of the truck, tucked the binoculars inside my
rain jacket, and started walking across the open prairie toward
the hidden antelope. I angled southeast, moving rapidly over
the open ground, pushed along unceremoniously at times
by the strong, quartering wind. The rim began to take definition as I neared the wash, prompting me to proceed cautiously.
Gradually more of the rim-concealed area came into view,

requiring a halt after each step to carefully examine the newly exposed ground.

My advance continued step by cautious step. Then, barely discernable through the sage and bunch grass that fringed the rim of the wash, an antelope materialized. I froze. It was the top of the head of a doe. I slowly sank to the ground and started crawling forward, intently watching the spot where the doe's head had appeared. Once again it came into view. I hugged the ground and began inching forward, carefully easing to the rim of the wash. A low-growing sagebrush concealed me. I peered through it.

The ground before me appeared as though a bulldozer had cut a wide swath through the prairie, gouging out a steep shoulder on the west side while leaving the east side level with no defined edge. A rocky channel, where snow melt and rain water flowed, meandered through the bottom. The surrounding ground was covered by sagebrush mixed with prairie grass. I lay motionless six feet above the bottom, daring only to blink, for below me, bedded in the grass, laying loosely in an elongated oval pattern close to the sheltering west bank, rested at least forty antelope. Most were fully visible, some only partially. Others likely remained out of my field of view, hidden by the angle of the bank. But no compulsion tempted me to search for those hidden others, for toward the upper edge of the group, resting unconcernedly less than seventy-five yards away, lay an impressive, stately horned buck.

There indeed reposed noble prairie game. A pronghorn of rare dimension. Surely the equal, if not the master, of any of the hundreds of grand bucks I had seen over the years. He rested regally, great head alert, attended by consorts and a few tolerated princes—heirs apparent, but seasons away from their reign.

I lay in the misty wind absorbing the scene, wondering if tomorrow would present as favorable an opportunity. My observations continued until the chilling damp persuaded me to leave. Carefully easing away from the rim to a distance where it was possible to regain my feet, I arose and began walking back to the truck. The wind still blew with body-bending force, welcome now, as it would likely keep the antelope bedded beneath the shelter of the bank.

The truck offered grateful relief from the wind. I sat for a time watching toward the hidden wash, contemplating the grand emptiness of the prairie. Antelope with lyre-shaped horns played through my mind.

The afternoon was well-advanced, the drab overcast promising an early nightfall. The western sky began shading to deeper dusk. I started the truck, and turning east, drove back to the track that led to the stock-watering impoundment. A depression there would provide enough shelter to set up the Coleman cooking stove without being buffeted by the wind.

The raw day was melding into an equally raw evening and cooking out of doors hardly promised to be a great pleasure, but in short order a cheering pot of beef stew began bubbling on one burner while the coffee perked merrily on the other, dispelling, mentally at least, some of the damp chill.

I tested the bubbling stew, found it comfortable on my tongue, and spooned it hungrily from the pot, dipping slices of heavy rye bread into the dark gravy. After the stew I opened a can of peaches, finished them, filled the thermos with coffee, and poured the remainder of the steaming liquid into my cup. The coffee was cool enough to drink by the time the cooking utensils were washed and put away.

I stood outside in the lee of the truck sipping the coffee as evening descended over the prairie. When the darkness became complete, I entered the truck, and lighting the lantern, reviewed the several books stored in one of the drawers. The ethereal-toned night brought on a philosophic mood. A volume of Durant's *The Story of Civilization* answered that mood and my mind soon became immersed in the lives and philosophies of Diderot, d'Holbach, and Voltaire.

I read late into the night, engrossed in the thoughts of two and a half centuries ago until the worn arguments made me weary. Then, closing the book, I sought the comfort of my sleeping bag, extinguished the lantern, and surrendered to the dark. For a short time my mind mulled over the philosopher's endless search through tangled webs of maybes and possibilities, probing in shadowy, surreal worlds for answers to questions that remain unanswerable. Then I cleared my mind of their ponderings, and listening to the rush and the whirl outside, fell asleep to the reality of the wind.

A frigid dampness enveloped me in the morning. I lay curled deep in the friendly warmth of my sleeping bag, reluctant to face the dark cold. Finally, willing myself up, I arose and shivered quickly into my clothes. I started the truck, and as the engine warmed, poured a cup of coffee from the thermos and watched its steam form a misty circle on the windshield, then ate a hurried breakfast while staring through the mist into the predawn darkness.

A final sip of coffee finished breakfast. I turned on the headlights and carefully maneuvered out of the depression back onto the track, bumping along until reaching the east-west road. I turned west and drove toward the starless horizon. Off to my left the silhouetted hill forms of the breaks traced darker against the overcast background. I passed the two hills between which the dry wash ran and continued half a mile beyond, then turned off the road, facing south. It was still too dark to begin a stalk. I poured a second cup of coffee and sat in the warmth of the truck waiting for the early light to show in the east.

The night grudgingly began to give way. My eyes strained to make out the wash area but it lay hidden behind the predawn mantle. I began to grow impatient, the excitement of the approaching day and impending hunt welling up within me. Succumbing at last to my restlessness, I stepped outside and loaded my rifle. The dimming night still concealed the distant wash area but closer terrain features showed faintly. My restlessness grew. With the light still questionable in the east, I gave way to my impatience and began walking across the shadowed prairie.

The air was hushed. The biting wind of the preceding day had exhausted itself in the night. A peaceful quiet lay over the prairie. I continued forward slowly, straining to see into the gloom, trying to judge the ill-defined distance to the wash.

Suddenly, ahead of me, faintly silhouetted against the eastern sky, the barely perceptible forms of four antelope materialized. Vague shadows though they were, one thing was distressingly clear. They were alert. And they were facing directly toward me.

I froze, chagrined at my foolish impatience, and stood staring back at the vague shadows. They remained immobile, as though unsure of the obscure form in the distance. The light was still faint and the antelope were looking into a dark backdrop of a western overcast. My outline must be as indistinct to them as theirs was to me.

I lowered myself to the ground, trying to blend into the prairie. The antelope continued watching, alert but apparently not alarmed. I lay hugging the bunch grass hoping time would dispel whatever concern they might have. The scope offered dim definition, making it impossible to tell if the buck was among them. They continued to watch toward me as I willed myself deeper into the sage-scented ground. After several minutes they turned, and taking a few, seemingly unalarmed steps, disappeared from view. They must have been standing on the rim of the wash.

I stayed still, waiting for sufficient light to avoid another blunder. The skyline remained empty. If any movement was taking place it was well-concealed beneath the bank of the dry wash.

The darkness slowly cleared to reveal a somber, gray morning. When the light was sufficient to see the crosshairs clearly, I arose from the ground, cautiously scanning the unfolding horizon. No antelope were in view.

Hopefully the herd was still bedded beneath the rim of the wash. I carefully duplicated my approach of the preceding afternoon, but with a heightening sense of futility as more of the rim-hidden area came into view. My foreboding proved correct, for after crawling the final few yards, the ground showed empty.

I lay on the rim, viewing the deserted space, irritated by my blunder. Then, shaking off my disgust, I stood up and began searching for the antelope. Off to the north, the dry wash blended into the flat expanse beyond. I glassed the area thoroughly. Nothing. Ahead, to the east, the broken hill country continued, but since the fierce winds had subsided, that ground held little allure. To the south, a series of rolling hills fringed a large, saucer-shaped basin, most of which lay unobservable from my position. That direction seemed the most promising.

I dropped off the rim of the wash and proceeded rapidly south toward the crest of the nearest hill. The hill's ridgeline extended east and west. I glanced along it while moving hurriedly across the intervening prairie. Tracks imprinted amid many fresh droppings pointed up the slope. The antelope evidently had gone this way. If they were not unduly alarmed, they were likely feeding somewhere ahead.

I slowed near the crest of the hill and began a cautious ascent. The crest of a second hill began to appear. I paused and carefully scrutinized its entire length, then took a step forward, then another. The head and back of an antelope came into view. I sank to the ground.

I carefully wriggled to the crest and peered through a stunted sagebrush. A dozen does and fawns grazed contentedly on the opposite hillside. The buck was not in sight. The rest of the herd was likely on the other side of the hill. I cradled my rifle across the sagebrush and settled down to observe.

The antelope drifted toward the ridge of the far hill as they fed. The heads and backs of other animals occasionally appeared over the hill only to vanish again down the reverse slope.

Then a pair of black horns emerged, moving behind the crest. Back and forth they trended, showing larger, then smaller, disappearing, then reappearing. A rush of excitement surged through me. I nestled expectantly into my scope.

The head of the buck gradually appeared above the crest. He hesitated for a few seconds, scanning the hill. He moved again. Part of his neck came into view. I watched him through the scope, trying to will him into taking a few more steps to expose his chest, but he paused instead, watching in my general direction. A minute passed before he turned and slowly vanished behind the slope.

With the buck out of sight, I shifted my scope to the farthest doe, trying to estimate the range with the double crosshairs. Close to three hundred and fifty hundred yards to the doe, probably another fifty or sixty yards from her to the crest. And the buck was showing beyond that.

The does and fawns fed up the slope, and in ones and twos, disappeared over the crest. The buck continued his movement on the other side, his black horns seemingly floating detached above the barren crest. Occasionally ears showed. A few times he faced me with part of his head exposed. I held the crosshairs steady between his horns, but could never feel comfortable with the shot.

The last doe eventually disappeared behind the ridge, allowing me to wriggle over the crest to a point where it was possible to stand up unobserved. I arose and began a steady jog toward the other ridge, slowing to a cautious walk two-thirds of the way up. The slope of another hill came into view. I began to crawl forward. The entire area between the two low hills soon became visible. It was empty.

I squirmed quickly over the crest and several yards down the other side, then, sure of not being silhouetted against the skyline, stood up and began walking rapidly forward.

A startling rush erupted to my right. I turned and was astonished to see a group of antelope dashing madly across the slope in a tight cluster less than a hundred yards away. And running strong among them, showing large in both body and horns, was the buck.

They raced away, quartering to my right front. I raised my rifle. The scope filled with a jumble of bodies. I tried to isolate the buck for a clear shot but the maze of does and fawns made it impossible. Down the near slope then up the far one they ran while I tried to hold the crosshairs close to the buck in case he should break into the clear. The herd began to string out as it neared the far ridge. The buck settled in toward the rear and it seemed possible that he might present an open target, although the range had become marginal. But the herd rushed over the crest still too tightly grouped to risk a shot.

I broke into a run, sprinting after the disappearing animals. I reached the crest of the next hill blown and winded only to see the antelope racing across an expansive basin, well out of range. They coursed swiftly away without breaking stride, growing smaller in the distance until they reached the far ridges where one by one they vanished from sight into the hills.

I turned to look back at the recent scene of frantic activity. The long ridge I had crawled over curved away to the right, forming a large pocket that was not visible from my prone position atop the crest. The feeding antelope had drifted into that pocket during my crossing between the two ridges. Standing up and stepping forward brought me into full view of the animals. Another blunder.

The rolling hills into which the herd had fled appeared to be at least a mile away across the basin. I carefully searched the visible slopes through the binoculars. No antelope could be seen.

The dreary morning matched my mood. The chances of overtaking the frightened herd seemed slim. The rolling hills stretched to the horizon. How far into them the startled animals had run could only be surmised.

I decided to swing away from their line of flight and make a large loop in an attempt to approach the herd from a direction other than the one from which danger had threatened. I tucked the binoculars inside my jacket, slung the rifle over my shoulder, and began an angling trek across the deserted basin.

I drifted far to the southeast before turning southward to top a small rise, bringing into view an extensive expanse of prairie. The level ground extended south and to the west where it rose toward the series of hills into which the herd had fled. I scanned the open sage flat. A small group of antelope appeared to the south. I dropped to the ground and pulled the binoculars from my jacket. A dozen does and fawns fed slowly along, attended by a pair of respectable bucks.

I glassed expectantly, searching beyond the feeding antelope for others, hoping this might be part of the larger herd. The antelope fed leisurely, out of range but approachable. I lay for several minutes considering the bucks. A haunting vision of a stately horned patriarch competed with them. Finally I eased back off the rise, turned westward, and began walking below the crest, hidden from the small herd.

I followed a meandering course over the gentle prairie, dipping through shallow, rock-bottomed washes while detouring around the occasional deeper ones. The antelope off to the south faded beyond concern.

I wended my way toward a distant hill rising above the prairie flats, then climbed cautiously toward its top, pausing frequently near the crest to scan the unfolding vista. An extended plateau slowly came into view, stretching off to the west and south in a series of moderate, rolling hills interspersed with hidden gullies and washes. The horizon extended for miles. Somewhere, presumably, within those rolling hills, the larger herd lay sheltered.

The basin the antelope had fled across was visible a short distance to the north, its southern edge giving way to the northern rim of the plateau. After glassing the intervening distance carefully, I began a cautious stalk over the undulating terrain, pausing often to observe the long, gradual slopes while peering into sheltering draws and valleys.

The morning remained overcast with just a hint of mist in the still air. The pungent aroma of sage scented my passage as I roamed over the wide panorama, searching the distant ridges for some trace of the herd. My path wandered through the flats and contours, taking me ever deeper into the seemingly endless stretch of rolling prairie. I stopped often to glass to the south and to the west, occasionally succumbing to a protracted circular search to view the immense openness surrounding me. Only empty sage prairie flowing into grass-fringed hillsides could be seen in all that vast circumference. Not a sign of humanity disturbed the scene. For a brief, priceless moment, I caught the awesome sense of timeless space that must have surged through the first lone traveler in this land. An enthralling sensation, this solitary roaming of the prairie, with its stimulating sense of unfettered freedom.

I approached another long crest. All at once a flash of movement became visible on a southwestern ridge. I quickly dropped to a prone position and watched as a group of antelope began crossing over a small hill, moving rapidly in my general direction. The group swelled into a good-sized herd. A tremor of excitement coursed through me as they began to string out on the forward slope, for, topping the skyline close behind the last doe, was a large, stately horned buck.

There was no way of identifying the animals with certainty, but the size and composition of the group led me to believe that here, again, was the herd of early morning. What caused them to be rushing my way was not clear. One thing, however, was becoming rapidly clear. If they held their course, they were going to pass very close to me.

The lead does veered slightly as the herd traveled down the slope, funnelling the following animals into a narrow depression out of my view. The depression angled around me, but exactly where it led could not be seen from my position. I turned, quartering in the suspected direction, and lay, with my rifle ready, waiting for the antelope to reappear.

The seconds ticked into suspenseful minutes with only the empty prairie showing. The antelope remained hidden. When they did not reappear, I carefully stood up to find out if the added height would allow me to see farther into the depression. Nothing was visible. I took a few cautious steps forward and dropped quickly back to the ground.

The antelope were there!

The herd had stopped and gathered into a loose cluster in a small hollow less than a hundred yards away. The buck was in their midst. My quick view also disclosed two does moving up the gradient toward me. I squirmed around to bring my rifle to bear on the open flat the does seemed to be moving toward and waited.

My wait was of short duration, for soon one, and then the other doe, emerged into view. They trotted slowly, in tandem, across my front fifty yards away. The does traveled only a short distance before stopping to look back. I followed their gaze, and there, slowly emerging from the depression, presenting a tan and white image of form and grace, came the buck. He walked up onto the flat, and seeing the does, stopped and stared at them.

I quelled my raising excitement, positioned the crosshairs just behind the near shoulder, exhaled half a breath, and slowly squeezed the trigger. The buck spun a quarter turn at the shot and stood facing directly toward me. I quickly worked the bolt, then holding square in the middle of his chest, fired again. He collapsed instantly.

The two does bolted into flight at the report of the rifle but ran only forty or fifty yards before stopping and looking back at the fallen buck. After a moment they began to walk hesitantly toward him, appearing curious as to why he choose to lay down at that spot. The does remained unaware of my presence. The rest of the herd began filing out of the depression onto the flat. They also stopped to look curiously at the buck, but in no way took alarm. Before long the entire herd was feeding leisurely around him, totally unconcerned and seemingly oblivious to the fact, or even the concept, of his death.

The fascinating spectacle held me in place. I lay on the prairie absorbing the scene until my desire to examine the buck brought me to my feet. My sudden appearance galvanized the herd into immediate action. The startled animals were directly putting great expanses of distance between themselves and the astounding apparition without ever a backward glance to see if the buck was following.

Fifty steady paces brought me to the fallen animal. I marveled at his size and the beautiful, black symmetry of his horns. Certainly he ranked as one of my finest in some twenty seasons. The first shot went exactly where intended. Why the buck did not fall immediately remains a question.

I stood there in rapt admiration, savoring the moment and the sweet flavor of success, made doubly pleasurable in light of my earlier disappointments. The buck lay in regal repose, framed in fitting display amongst the misted-green sagebrush, while off to the north the vanishing herd raced over the gray-clouded prairie, its movement lending a singular vibrancy of life to an otherwise barren aspect. Soon the fleeing herd disappeared into the prairie folds, and the boundless horizons became empty.

The deserted prairie seemed to reach out beyond measure. None other, save myself, appeared to exist in all that vastness. I stood pondering for a moment the solitary grandeur of the scene. Then, succumbing to my contemplative mood, I sat down to linger awhile longer, to gaze out over the vast prairie, and to savor again the sweetly pungent aroma of the antelope and the sage.

Boone and Crockett Club

Dear Mr. Howard:

Re: Score Chart for trophy pronghorn

This File is completed, and the data for your trophy is entered in the records archives, as well as the current 19th Awards Entry Period.

Barring unforeseen circumstances, your trophy will be listed in the Boone and Crockett Club's 19th Big Game Awards book.

Congratulations on such a fine trophy and thank you for your interest and participation in the program.

Chapter 15

The Yukon

Kipling named them. Those restless spirits that summon us to adventure. The Red Gods, he called them. The whisper of the Trues.

It was those same restless spirits that summoned me in the hazy August of 1983, summoned me north to far-distant lands, there to go in search of a long-held vision.

We dream our varied dreams. We seek our inexplicable aspirations. Who can say why one will devote his seasons to a singular search for that majesty of an elk, while another will hunt with exclusion for that whitetail of whitetails? I never hunted to exclusion. All the game filled my seasons with equal measure. Yet sometimes in my dreams there did arise an image of a first among equals, a haunting vision of a snow-white ram with horns of burnished amber.

The great white rams live in the mountains of the far north, mountains in lands with adventurous names that stir the imagination. Alaska. The Yukon. The Northwest Territories. Who can say those names without a twinge of yearning? It was the Yukon that summoned me first. The others would summon me in their time.

The Yukon's hunting grounds are divided among twenty outfitters. If a nonresident would hunt the Yukon, he must hunt with one of them. I contacted Pete Jensen, whose hunting area covered forty-five hundred square miles north of Dawson, and made arrangements for a fourteen-day combination hunt for Dall sheep, grizzly bear, moose, and caribou.

I left Wisconsin at six-thirty on a fresh-awakening Sunday morning with an airplane ticket stamped Madison to Denver to Vancouver, British Columbia, to Whitehorse, Yukon Territory. The Great Plains and the Rocky Mountains passed in review as we soared westward to the Pacific Coast and then north over the rugged British Columbia wilderness.

We touched down in Whitehorse at four-thirty local time. I made my way to a downtown hotel, stowed my gear, and set out on a walking tour of the territorial capital.

Whitehorse is situated on a low plain fronting the Yukon River. Government buildings constitute most of the modern structures. Some of the older buildings date from the turn-of-the-century gold rush era. Rustic taverns offering colorfully named beers such as Grizzly harken back to a wild, adventurous time. That time finds itself frozen in an impressive sternwheel river boat resting in permanent retirement at the edge of town. The S.S. Klondike II, built in 1937 and restored as a national historic site, carried silver-lead ore, general merchandise, and passengers up and down the Yukon River for nearly two decades.

Noon of the following day saw me again airborne for the final leg of my flight, a three hundred mile route from Whitehorse to Mayo to Dawson where we arrived a little before two o'clock. Sharon Jensen, Pete's wife, met me at the airport. We drove into Dawson to pick up my license and tags before heading north on the Dempster Highway for the ninety-mile trip to Pete's base camp.

The Dempster Highway stretches four hundred and sixty miles north in singular relief across the pristine Yukon wilderness. People are scarce along the graveled dirt road. The majority of the twenty-five thousand residents of the Yukon tend to gather in and around Whitehorse and Dawson.

We arrived at the base camp in late afternoon. There I met Willie, my Indian guide, along with Bill and Jack, father and son hunters from Alberta, and their guides, Bill and Lawrence. The base camp consisted of several flat-roofed plywood structures grouped around a comfortable cook building. After supper I selected a bunk in one of the outbuildings and made preparations for the morning before drifting off to sleep.

A drizzling rain took some of the edge off the morning's excitement when we gathered for breakfast. Still, rainy weather notwithstanding, an impatient anxiousness hastened everyone through their bacon, eggs, toast, pancakes, and coffee.

Bill, Jack, and their guides soon set out to the east. Pete, Willie, and I loaded two saddle horses and three pack horses into a trailer and headed south along the Dempster. We came in time to a broad valley winding up and over a distant mountain pass. There we unloaded the horses and in the joy of the rain struggled to keep everything dry under tarps while the dripping pack animals stood patiently under their increasing loads. Late morning passed before Pete bid us good luck and started the truck to return to base camp. Willie led off into the haze and our little pack string struck out in single file toward the gray-looming mountains.

A sodden mist enveloped us as we plodded through the rain-dappled valley. We climbed steadily through an alpine meadow already showing faded fall colors of dusky greens, reds, and golds amid the dull browns of the ground brush. Stunted spruce grew in scattered order in the lower reaches, while grand mountains rose around and far ahead granite peaks reached jaggedly into the dirty-gray clouds. Low-hugging swirls of mist danced eerily about the stark mountaintops, then curled down to engulf the pass. Not a sound came from those lofty peaks. The swirling mists danced their muted dance to the silent music of the pinnacles, then whirled away in somber cadence. Raw wilderness brooding in the haze. A foreboding yet exhilarating sight. I shivered slightly from the excitement and the chilling dampness, then huddled deeper into my raingear and watched the three pack horses and Willie plod steadily toward the misty pass and the dark mountains beyond.

We followed no trail but held to the contours as we wove a sinuous path up the valley, splashing across a flat-bedded creek that tumbled down from the distant heights. The midday and then the afternoon hours passed in unvarying rhythm as the horses climbed steadily. The little creek gradually trickled away.

We crossed the flat at the top of the pass with dusk settling imperceptibly into the haze and looked down into a long, deep valley, its bottom hidden in the darkening. Willie turned toward a growth of stunted willow brush just over the pass and announced, "We will stay here for the night."

The pack horses quivered with pleasure with the release of their loads. We covered the panniers and gear with tarps. While Willie hobbled the horses and fed them some grain, I draped our largest tarp over some waist-high willows, cut out enough of the branches for a sleeping area, laid another tarp on the wet ground, and rolled out our sleeping bags. I shaved the wet bark from some standing dead willows, feathered them with my knife, built a little stick pyramid, and shortly had a coffee-sized fire smoking low in the damp air. The four sides of our makeshift shelter lay open to the night and the smoke from the wet willows drifted about with the slightest eddy. Willie drew water from a mountain rill and coffee soon added its aroma to that of the willow smoke. We sat hunched under the tarp sipping the hot coffee between bites of our sandwich supper. Rain pattered on the tarp while a light breeze sighed over the pass and night settled down on the mountains.

The horses were gone in the morning, but the rain had stayed faithfully with us. We boiled some coffee and ate a hasty breakfast, then Willie went in search of the horses. I broke camp and stood huddled in the rain waiting for his return. A few hours passed before the welcome neigh of a horse brought me out of my silent contemplation of the cloud-shrouded Ogilvie Range. We packed and saddled the horses, then set off into the misty valley below.

Again the steady rhythm as the miles passed behind. Spruce began to grow thicker as we dropped into the valley. Taller willows bordered the little creek that flowed full along our route, many showing the nipped-off signs of moose. The rain continued. I burrowed into the depths of my raingear and let the steady pelter and the rhythm of the horse work its hypnosis. At one point Willie brought me alert with a pointed arm to the right. An animal was standing in the distant haze watching our silent procession. A young bull moose, it turned out to be, when the binoculars were pulled out from under a couple of layers. He was still watching when we entered some thicker spruce along the creek and came to a place that suited Willie for a campsite.

We unpacked and unsaddled the horses. Willie led them to a small meadow while I organized the panniers and gear under tarps. Willie's return set us to work stringing a rope between two tall spruce over which we draped a white wall tent. Cut poles formed a frame to hold out the walls. A fly was suspended over the top of the tent for much needed extra rain protection. We smoothed down the inside, laid a ground tarp, organized our bedrolls and duffel, and for the first time in two days sat comfortably sheltered from the rain.

Night came mistily upon us. Willie fired up a two-burner Coleman stove that took some of the dampness out of the tent. A warm supper was not long in working its drowsing effect. Sleep came to the dreary accompaniment of the patter of rain.

Clouds hung low over the mountains in the morning. A persistent mist fogged the valley. The Coleman stove offered a few moments of welcome warmth while the coffee boiled, then the dampness stole through us again. I donned raingear and wrapped my rifle in a waterproof covering while Willie brought up the saddle horses. They stood moping under the dripping trees as we busied with damp blankets and damp saddles. After a final cinching, we mounted, and with Willie leading, set off up the valley.

There seemed little hope of spotting sheep, the mist and the clouds lay like a veil over the heights. We plodded along past the spot where the young moose had watched us the day before, but he too lay veiled somewhere behind the haze. Lofty mountains reached into the obscuring vapors, home to sheep, Willie assured me, but a home well-concealed that morning from our prying eyes.

A lesser valley branching up into the mountains held hopes of clearing and we turned our horses toward it. They clopped steadily upward until we came to a cluster of willows. There we tied them and continued on foot. The climb was steep. I followed behind Willie envying his wind and seemingly tireless legs. We pushed ever higher through the mist, Willie carrying a backpack and I my rifle. At last we came to a blessed halt, sat down on a promontory, and tried to penetrate the surrounding clouds with our binoculars. The clouds occasionally wisped clear, offering glimpses of farther slopes, but they soon closed again to lock us into a soupy haze. The horses lay hidden below, and any sheep, were they on those mountains, lay equally hidden in the gloom.

Rain visited us, light but steady, deepening the already dim aspect. Tiny rivulets trickled down our raingear, joining others on the rocky slope in their winding descent to the mountain rills below. A cloud settled down. We tucked our binoculars into our coats and sat on the mountain like a pair of insignificant boulders lost in an unfathomable sea. The overwhelming immensity wrapped us in silence.

We waited in the haze hoping for a break in the cloud, but it hovered persistently along the slope. When time served only to deepen the gloominess, we came down off the mountain in company with the rain, found our horses in the dripping willows, and worked our way down into the valley and back to our welcome tent standing dreary but dry inside the spruce.

We savored a momentary burst of heat from the stove while cooking supper, then felt the damp seep in again when we extinguished the flame, needing to conserve our limited fuel. The rain rippled against the tent while the dripping spruce pattered intermittently through the evening. When the darkness deepened, we sought the warmth of our sleeping bags. I listened in the night to the wearying rain and tried to hold on to the fleeting vision of a golden-horned ram reigning resplendent on a sun-dazzled mountaintop.

The following morning we rode downstream along the rushing creek that furnished our drinking water, searching fresh mountains for a break in the covering clouds. We forded the creek and climbed the horses ever higher until the rugged slopes suggested ascending on foot. Higher still we climbed on weary legs, into the clouds and rain, feeling helpless in the closing haze but hoping to be in position should the morning clear.

The morning did not clear, nor did the afternoon. We angled down off the mountain in the rain and plodded our soggy way toward camp, leaving any sheep that might be residing upon the heights shrouded in the impenetrable bleakness. Still we hunted, on the lookout for moose or caribou. Or, hope upon hope, a grizzly.

The valley held signs of moose—clumps of willows showed droppings and browse marks. Caribou, Willie informed me, were a maybe thing. Who could predict their movements? Grizzlies were known to roam that valley, although they too were a here today gone tomorrow wanderer. But sheep were surely in the mountains. Willie was confident. We would find them in time when the rain clouds had run their course.

We saw no game on our ride back to camp. Once there Willie tended to the horses and I made a few trips to the creek to replenish our water supply. Willie's return signaled our brief ration of evening heat while supper cooked on the Coleman stove. We finished eating as the last remnant of warmth faded from the tent with the dying afterglow of the burners. Then the chilling dampness seeped in and I sought the comfort of my sleeping bag, the last dry refuge after four days of mist and rain.

The morning of the fifth day promised no relief. Clouds still held steadfast on the mountains as though they had taken up permanent residence. We shivered into clammy clothes and welcomed the little flame of the stove and the inner warmth of the coffee, then set out once more into the mist and haze, the horses as droopy as our spirits.

The late morning came with an easing of diffused light through swirls of thinning overcast. Binoculars offered hopeful glimpses of more than just reflected clouds. We sought higher ground and Willie climbed on springy legs while my leaden limbs grew heavier with each hard-won yard. Higher we climbed, the diffused light offering shadowed views of distant slopes.

Spent legs had long been screaming for a halt before Willie finally sat down by a sheltering boulder and began glassing. I sat wearily beside him, needing a few minutes before my binoculars would hold steady.

The clouds still hovered but there were moments of clearing. The mountains across the valley continued to lay obscured but nearer mountains revealed their rocky slopes. We sat by the boulder and searched them carefully before climbing again to another vantage point where we searched other far slopes and then watched dark clouds roll up the valley and up the mountain to engulf us once more in a misty haze.

We waited in the clouds, caught up in the elusive nothingness, watching the figments part and blend then part again in wispy swirls that lost their definition against the shifting mass of gray and dark beyond. In time the grayness thinned and we sought our binoculars and searched again until higher clouds sent their chilling rain. Then we huddled tighter against the boulders and watched the brooding mountains standing watch in quiet resolve, aloof witnesses for the ages to the ebb and flow of the mutable skies, this day no more meaningful to them than the eternal others that have drifted by in the timeless cycles born before the mountains came to be.

We held to the heights during the day, coming down to the valley with light enough to see us back to camp. The game of the valley remained as obscure as the game of the mountains. We saw nothing that day.

Dawn of the sixth day. A Sunday morning rising up. I offered a silent prayer for clear skies but looked out upon a drear landscape. Someone else must have prayed harder for rain.

We witnessed their prayers answered as we set out in a light drizzle that held through the morning, a persistent, nagging wetness that chilled through dank clothes.

We rode farther down the valley, past mountain slopes that remained empty of telltale specks of white. We found new mountains to climb, new heights to search, new leg muscles to cramp, but we found nothing new in the stark emptiness of the rain-beclouded slopes or in the dreary valley locked in the mist below.

The valley mist rolled up to envelope us in the afternoon and we found ourselves lost once more in the stifling dimness of the gauzy haze. We waited on the slope for the haze to disperse but the dimness lingered wearily like a long-overstaying houseguest. It followed us down into the valley and hung with us on our ghostly ride through the wisping creekside willows, pushing its unwelcome presence upon us until we sought the refuge of our tent and felt it even there seeping close around us. The night came darkly in a penetrating, misty dampness.

The relentlessness of another gloomy day wearied our awakening the following morning. I slipped into clothes chilling with their dampness and listened to the inevitable patter from dripping trees. We ate breakfast in resigned silence then went out to saddle the horses and struck out through the valley once more. The mountains lay dark in the clouds.

We climbed again. We glassed again. We endured the rain again. We saw nothing again.

The morning passed in dreary repetition of the others, as did the drizzly hours following a clouded mountain lunch. Late afternoon brought us back to the valley where the horses waited patiently in a clump of willows. We turned the horses toward camp, still searching the slopes in a desultory fashion after a weary day of emptiness.

We came with the early evening to the little pasture where the horses were tethered, unsaddled them, covered the saddles with a tarp, then walked the faint footpath we had pressed into the earth to camp. Willie began preparing supper. I walked down to the creek for water. Spruce grew thick along that section of the creek. When the tent came into view on my return, I noticed Willie standing outside, staring toward the mountains across the creek. He turned when he heard me approach.

"Sheep."

"What?"

"Sheep. There are two sheep on that mountain. I think they are rams."

I set the water buckets down and turned my excited gaze toward the mountains.

"Where?"

"Do you see that peak?" he pointed.

I followed his outstretched arm.

"Yes."

"They are just below it to the left."

I stared intently at the mountain. It rose sharply from the valley floor, swooping upward into sheer granite facings. White scars traced down the lower slopes, snowslide runoffs etched deep through the centuries. Tall, chiseled sections jutted out near the top, showing like impregnable watchtowers guarding the pinnacled peak.

I searched between the watchtowers and the peak, and there, like two blurred patches of snow, tucked into a hidden bench, secure in their mountain fortress, stood the sheep.

I reached inside my coat for my binoculars and tried to focus through the gathering dusk on the distant forms. The sheep showed hazy white against the dark granite. I stared intently through the binoculars, looking, looking. There were horns. I was sure there were horns.

"They are rams. But I can't see them clearly."

"I will get the spotting scope."

With that Willie set off to retrieve the scope from his back-pack while I stared in growing excitement at the vision on the mountaintop.

The rams appeared to be feeding, but what that sheer rock face could offer in the way of food was not apparent from my perspective. I tried to envision a way to approach them, but it appeared hopeless from this side of the mountain.

Willie returned with his spotting scope and was soon com-menting in excited tones.

"They are good rams. One is a very good ram. Here, look."

I peered through the magnified haze at the distant peak. There was no sun upon the mountain, but my dazzling dreams of a stately, golden-horned ram still shone forth in splendor in the dancing mirage of the scope. The alabaster rams leaped out in bold relief against the dark granite peak. What magnificent creatures. How regal their bearing. And what a sublime setting for those lords of the pinnacles. Either ram was a dream ful-filled. The larger, a dream beyond dreaming.

"We will try tomorrow," said Willie. "It is a very good ram."

Morning of the eighth day. Misty in the dark before the dawn. Willie brought one of the horses up and we barebacked across the swollen creek and tethered it with some grain and set out to climb the long climb around to the back of the mountain. The rams lay concealed in the dark.

Light came faintly an hour into our climb. Our way curved us around and out of view of the bench the rams were last seen on. The grade was steep and we climbed slowly, letting the morning stiffness work itself out.

The dawn broke silent, the only sounds the crunch of our boots and the faint swish of our raingear. A penetrating mist dimmed the morning light. I climbed steadily, my senses focused on the rocky slope ahead, caught up in the mist and the labor of the ascent.

Suddenly Willie came to a halt and sank down onto the mountainside. I followed suit and looked toward him. His gaze drew my gaze upward.

A bear was crossing above us! A grizzly bear!

We crouched motionless. The bear moved across the mountainside in an easy, fluid motion, two hundred yards up the slope, its great body rippling in the morning mist. The same mist that must have rendered our labors up the mountain invisible. From time to time the bear halted in its passage to investigate something in the patches of mountain bush. I raised my rifle to get a closer look through the scope. The grizzly jumped into view.

Willie pressed the rifle barrel down. I looked at him, surprised. He shook his head and made a motion with his hand indicating we should circle behind the bear.

I nodded. Perhaps it would be better to get above the bear before considering a shot. Willie set off at an angle. I followed, crouched low behind him. We climbed warily, trying to pick a quiet path through the ground cover, tensing at each muffled sound, trusting to the mist to conceal our stooped circuit up the slope. I concentrated on the ground, placing my feet carefully to avoid a noisy misstep. Excitement began its flood of adrenaline, banishing all but the immediate. The ancient responses had begun.

I climbed, engrossed in thoughts of the bear and the great ram somewhere on the other side of the mountain. Was the ram still there? Would he be there if we delayed for the grizzly? A dream of dreams lay on the other side of the mountain. Might it be better to concentrate on that dream, or take the seeming certainty? A grizzly was a prize beyond measure, and one was there before me. Ram or grizzly? Or need I choose? Perhaps both? There would come a time to decide when we were above the bear.

Time seemed frozen in the mist. We continued ever higher, my breath coming harder, heart pounding, weary legs beginning to protest. Adrenaline coursed, driving me on.

Finally we halted. I turned to locate the bear and caught a fleeting glimpse of rippling motion disappearing over a small ridge. Then nothing but an empty mountain. I stared in astonishment, then turned to Willie.

"What happened?"

"We would have scared the rams if you had shot the bear."

Willie had made the decision for me.

I stood in stunned disbelief. Words failed me. I turned with a sinking feeling toward the small ridge but there was nothing to see except the stark mountainside. The grizzly was gone.

We rested awhile in forced silence, then resumed our circuit up and around the mountain. There remained still the rams.

The valley side of the mountain presented an imposing front. If the backside matched it, the rams were beyond our reach. As we labored up the mountain we angled around until the back of the peak came into view. The slope continued steep but manageable. We rested for a few minutes then set out once more up the rocky incline.

Higher we climbed, angling steeply, the peak slowly drawing closer. The morning was well-advanced. We could only hope the rams had found their fortress lair comfortable enough for another day.

Willie led, legs moving in easy rhythm, his compact, wiry frame drifting naturally up the loose rocks. I struggled to keep up in spite of being seven years his junior. But Willie was at home, bred to the mountains, heralding from a distant people in the British Columbia ranges, as comfortable in the heights as the great ram we now so eagerly sought.

The peak drew closer. We halted to rest. I sat on the rocks drawing in deep breaths of fresh oxygen. Willie sat beside me. All at once he tensed and whispered hoarsely:

"Don't move. There are sheep below."

I froze, eyes darting downward in search of the sheep. They leaped into view. Two rams, a ewe, and a lamb. Feeding on a grassy bench.

Willie eased his binoculars to his eyes.

"They are the rams," he whispered excitedly.

We dared not move. That we had escaped detection on that open slope seemed a miracle. The four sheep fed below us, bodies facing away, heads down. The two rams must have crossed over the peak and down to the bench while we were working to get above the grizzly. Where the ewe and lamb had come from remained unclear.

The sheep fed farther out onto the bench, removing any hope of retracing our steps to get back out of sight. The rams paused often in their feeding to survey the slopes around them. They had yet to look in our direction.

"Shoot," Willie whispered.

"It is too far."

"You must shoot. If they see us, they will be gone."

I had no idea what the range was, but it was excessive. Several times during the summer, in preparing for the hunt, I had fired at three hundred yards. The bench appeared to be at least twice that distance, maybe more.

"It is too far."

"You must try, or we will loose them for sure."

I decided to test the range through the scope. I came slowly to a sitting position, wrapped into my sling, and tried to center the large ram. The slope angled sharply. By the time I raised the rifle high enough to get the ram properly centered, my arms wobbled above my knees. Willie slid in front of me.

"Rest across my shoulder."

The ram settled in the scope. A stirring sight in the magnification. Full curl and a flaring quarter-curl plus. But oh so far away.

"They will see us soon," urged Willie.

I knew the rifle's trajectory out to five hundred yards. Beyond that was a prayer. I lifted the horizontal crosshair above the ram, tried to adjust for the uncertain range and the effect of the downward angle, steadied the image, and fired.

The sheep scattered. The ewe and the lamb ran across the bench while the two rams raced toward a distant, craggy mountain. I tried to pick up the rams in the scope but it was hopeless. They charged across a small valley, up a rock strewn slope, into a jumbled tangle of rocky spires.

"We will never get him now," Willie said dejectedly, watching the great ram pick his way up the jagged granite facing. "We will never get him now."

We sat in the gloomy morning watching the rams until they disappeared from sight. A heavy pall settled over us. The only thing missing was the rain. But the dark clouds choose merely to hover broodingly, as though the heavens knew our spirits were dampened enough.

"Will they stay on that mountain?"

"Maybe."

"Can we get around to the top of it?"

Willie studied in silence. The mountain loomed formidably in the distance. Impossible from the craggy side, especially with the rams looking down. The passage around would be measured in steep and rugged miles. The day was near half-done.

"We will try."

The downward slope hastened our descent from the mountain. We retraced our route of the morning hoping the rams, if they were watching from the craggy heights, would see potential danger passing away. In a lower ravine, shielded by a down-running ridge, we turned and began climbing toward the curved-away side of the ram's refuge.

The day continued overcast, rain clouds threatening as always. A deep dampness permeated the air, penetrating our clothes from the outside while our weary toil formed beads of sweat inside. Dampness remained inescapable. We pushed on, coming eventually around to the side of the craggy mountain.

An hour passed in weary climbing, then another, the mountain seemingly rising forever into the clouds. We labored up the steep slope, dreaming of the summit showing temptingly a few more wearisome steps ahead, only to find a false summit that rolled into another punishing slope with the true summit beckoning us ever higher. Up we climbed, even Willie pausing more often now, gathering energy for the final push to the top, only to struggle upward over another false summit rising into another heartbreaking slope.

There came at last the final summit. We reached it with an exhausting effort and looked out over a breathtaking view. The Ogilvie Mountains surrounded us with awesome grandeur, like massive volcanic islands adrift in a sea of clouds. The immenseness was overwhelming. We rested, gazing out over the peaks, then turned our thoughts to the rams.

We followed along the rim of the mountain toward the rugged facing the rams had disappeared into. The walking was almost effortless compared to the rigors of the climb. We reached the edge of the steep downslope and cautiously peered over. A daunting labyrinth of jagged spires and chaotic rock formations met our gaze. A veritable jungle of tangled granite. If the rams were still holding there, we would be sorely pressed to find them.

We hunted along the edge of the mountain, searching the labyrinth below, sitting often with binoculars, peering into the clefts and crevices for a telltale speck of white. The dark clouds hovered close.

Then a ram materialized. Fleetingly. Passing behind a rocky spire and disappearing in an instant. Too quick to tell which of the two rams it was. But thrilling in the realization that at least one of them was there. And if one, probably both. We searched intently, but not another glimpse of a ram did we see.

The steepness of the rock face left a lower section unobservable from the mountain rim. The ram appeared to be heading in that direction. We continued our intense scrutiny.

The rocky maze hid any continuing movement. Willie finally suggested we climb down far enough to observe the lower area. We began the descent.

The rock face was precipitous. I climbed down with my rifle slung across my back, needing both hands and feet in places. Loose rocks threatened to betray us with a careless step. Jagged spires rose up from below then passed above us as we felt our cautious way down through the labyrinth.

The lower area gradually came into view, but it revealed little more than we had seen from the rocky maze above. We searched diligently, but saw only empty grayness.

A light mist began. We stayed there in the rocks, searching, constantly searching, until the light for searching faded. The dark clouds began ushering in the evening. The mountain valley lay dim below.

We looked for a route off the mountain. The way down the rock face traced forebodingly. The way back up to the rim equally so. We decided to follow around until we came to the side by which we had ascended.

The mountainside continued steep and rugged, the passage painstaking. We worked slowly along until we came to an abrupt ledge that dropped down to and paralleled a rock slide trailing down the mountain. The rock slide appeared to offer an easy descent, but the climb down to it gave us pause. We studied the near perpendicular drop. Willie deemed it possible. He eased over the ledge and slid as much as climbed down it. I followed suit.

The rock slide began at the bottom. We held to the side of the ledge's granite wall and began our cautious descent, Willie leading. The loose rocks rolled like marbles beneath our feet and we clung to creviced handholds to slow our momentum. Below us the rock slide angled sharply to the right. We could not see beyond the turn. Willie stepped along, sending loose rocks cascading in front of him. I followed, clutching at handholds in crevices to keep myself in check.

Suddenly Willie sat down on the rocks, and grabbing along the granite wall, brought himself to a halt.

"Stop!" he commanded hoarsely.

I nearly slid into him before the friction of my body and my push against the wall halted me.

We held there, clinging to handholds. I looked past Willie. The area beyond the turn had come into view. A queasy feeling churned my stomach. The rock slide disappeared over a cliff.

The cliff dropped away to a valley, and somewhere below that valley was another valley where our tent lay hidden in the foggy haze that rolled slowly up the mountain. Rain came with the fog, a cold rain spitting sleet that rattled off the rocks, then settled hard among them, slicking the wet, shaley slide. The granite wall loomed unclimbable above us. A companion granite wall rose from the far side, equally unclimbable. We were in a box, a fearsomely slippery box, tilted at a fearsomely steep angle toward an abyss scant feet away.

Willie looked solemn when he turned to me.

"We are in trouble John."

There seemed little point in responding.

We sat in the rain and sleet watching tentacles of fog curl up the mountain. Lowering clouds hid the heights. A darkness gaped below.

"We must try to get back up," Willie whispered.

Rain pelted the loose rocks. The slippery slide rose treacherously.

"I will try first. Hold tight against the wall. Wait until I get all the way up."

Willie had first to get around me. I hugged the slick-sided granite wall. Willie wriggled by, clutching my clothes and crevices in the granite for handholds. Disturbed rocks bounded away into an eerie silence. When he passed me he continued upward on hands and knees, soon dropping flat to grasp a protrusion that checked a downward slide long enough to inch himself back up to the next crevice. Loose rocks tumbled down and I turned my head to avoid them. Slowly Willie pulled himself up the rock slide, slipping back occasionally only to catch himself with clutching fingers against the wall. Higher he struggled until he finally grasped a secure outcropping near the top of the slide and turned to motion me up.

I started, holding tight along the granite wall, pushing flat against the rain-slick slide rocks, trusting to friction to hold me long enough to release a tenuous handhold and feel desperately along the fractured granite for another, fingers numbing from the cold, pressing tense against the wall, groping for another crevice, searching blindly with boots to find some semblance of purchase in the slide rocks, pushing up against a toehold, feeling the slide rocks give way, pressing tighter until the sliding slowed while desperate fingers grabbed among the rocks, then inching higher again, letting the rush of tension drive me, sensing only the immediate rocks and the finger crevices and the scraping down until the boot found something to push against and the inching higher on my stomach and the heart-stopping sliding and the raw fear and the wild sense of relief when I at last clutched the outcropping Willie clung to and pulled myself up beside him.

We had still to get out of the box. Retracing our steps back up the wall seemed hopeless. The granite facing showed slick with rain. The mountain climbed precipitously above us. We looked to the other side. There seemed a chance. We had only to cross the slide.

"Once we start, we must not stop."

I knew.

"I will go first. Wait until I'm across."

With that Willie turned, and without hesitation, began running across the rock slide. Rivulets of rocks set in motion by his boots cascaded down, bouncing toward the cliff. Willie's momentum carried him surely along. A slip would have carried him just as surely down with the cascading rocks. He reached the other side.

I began running, feeling the rocks slide away beneath my feet, rapid steps, lifting up before the slide could capture me, racing with the racing of my heart toward the refuge of the granite wall. I clutched it in relief.

We found a passage up the wall and continued around the mountain, coming eventually to another rock slide. But no walls hemmed that one in and no cliffs interrupted its unbroken route to the bottom. We descended rapidly down the slide, our boots like miniature skis on the wet shale.

The dark valley led us to the mountainside above our camp-site valley, locked deep in a night fog. We climbed wearily down into it and came at length to the swollen creek, found the horse we had left tied there, and barebacked across to the welcome tent showing ghostly white in the dark gray of the fog. Sleep came without effort after a hasty meal.

A sound rattled me awake in the dark. A large animal sound. A shuffling. Something was rummaging around the tent. Cans rattled. The grizzly on the mountain flashed into my mind. Willie sat up.

"Load your rifle," he whispered.

The rummaging continued. We eased out of our sleeping bags and waited tensely. The shuffling sound came closer. We cautiously pulled back the tent flap. Fog obscured all. A ghostly form began to emerge. We watched in tenseness. An animal materialized. It was the horse.

Fog locked the valley in an impenetrable veil when we arose. We climbed no mountains that morning, for which I was supremely grateful.

The fog lingered, clearing some later in the afternoon when there remained little time left to hunt. The higher mountains lay cloaked in a darkening overcast.

Evening came and Willie went to tend the horses while I climbed a small hill a short distance from the tent to use my binoculars. The upper mountain slopes remained hidden but some of the lower slopes offered a possible game sighting. I scanned them but they continued empty.

I lowered my binoculars and gazed out over the wilderness. Below me scattered spruce led darkly down to the creek flowing full less than a hundred yards away. The mountains loomed starkly, wrapped in dark, swirling wreaths of clouds. Impermeable. Sublime. A brooding wild reigning imperious in its unyielding power. I pondered in silence.

Then a motion halfway between me and the creek caught my attention. I looked, and there came a wolf, trotting out from the denser spruce into a small opening. I outlined him in my binoculars. He appeared like a wraith, a gray ghost flowing effortlessly through the gloaming. The wolf stopped in the opening. He stood there, surrounded by the relentless wilderness, part of the raw energy of the wild, a hunter like me, needing to hunt more desperately than I, needing to survive. I watched him until he ghosted back into the spruce, then caught a final glimpse when he emerged for an instant far down the valley.

I told Willie of the encounter.

"Didn't you have your rifle?"

"Yes."

"Then you should have shot the wolf."

"There was no need."

"It could bother the horses."

"I don't think so. It kept on going."

"You should have shot the wolf."

Morning of the tenth day. We had passed into September. The dismal weather continued. We looked with hope toward the mountain of the ram. It lay shrouded in clouds.

There remained the chance of valley game while we waited for the higher country to clear. We saddled the horses and set out along the creek. Spruce and willows grew close near the rushing waters, giving way to gold-tinted mountain brush that climbed into the bare rock of the higher slopes. Clouds attended the granite heights. Small valleys angled into the higher country, choked with willows where the rains and snow melt flowed. We rode through a hushed silence, the creaking of our saddles the only muffled sound.

Noon came and we sat on a small promontory eating sandwiches beneath clouds that hung low and promised an afternoon of rain. We kept a constant watch.

Our vigilance was rewarded. Across the creek, high up on a bare rock slope, an animal appeared. It seemed small in the distance. We looked with our binoculars. The animal came into focus.

It was a grizzly!

The bear angled downslope toward us and disappeared into a dense growth of willows. We continued to watch, waiting for the bear to reappear, but it did not.

The willows grew down into a small valley, some of which remained hidden from our position. We left the horses and began a rapid climb to get above the willows. The rain clouds began their drizzle. We reached an abrupt drop-off that forced us into the willows, dark and eerie with the hulking presence we knew was somewhere in there. We proceeded with infinite caution, the wetness a blessing for a change, silencing our passage.

We finally broke clear and climbed far enough above the willows to see all of the valley, then sat down to wait. The minutes shaded into hours. The rains came and went. The horses stood patiently far below while we sat patiently above the willows. The mountainside showed stark around the dense growth. The afternoon passed. Dusk came and darkened the valley. The grizzly never reappeared.

The horses shied in a lower willow patch as we rode along the creek. We held them in check, then turned them and followed a more open route to camp. The horses remained skittish the rest of the way.

Rain again the next morning. Dark in the heights. We looked hopelessly toward the mountain where the great ram presumably lay cloaked in the clouds, then saddled the horses and rode along the creek to where the grizzly had eluded us.

We hunted through the morning without sighting any game. Early afternoon saw us scanning yet more of the lower open slopes. Far off, white dots took shape in the binoculars. Sheep. Eleven in all. Willie pulled the spotting scope from his backpack.

"They are rams. Two of them look like full curl."

We stayed low in the valley on the horses, able to keep out of sight along the creek. A ravine climbed into the mountain. We followed it. The rams stayed safely out of sight. The ravine soon became too rough for the horses. We tied them and continued upward on foot. From time to time Willie eased up far enough to keep track of the rams. After one of the times, Willie motioned. I cautiously climbed up until the sheep came into view.

They fed along the mountainside. Four in a tight cluster on the left, five loosely gathered close to their right, and two others sixty to seventy yards farther right. They were comfortably within range.

We studied the rams through the binoculars. They fed leisurely among the seemingly barren rocks, finding some sustenance where none appeared to exist, their white coats contrasting sharply with the grayish rocks of the mountainside, horns shaded dark in the overcast, cautious yet at ease on the open slope. A wonderful sight after all the weary days. There remained only one flaw in the picture. They were younger rams. Two maybe were full curl, that critical measurement that made them legal. The more we studied them the more we wavered. Were they or were they not? We remained unsure.

I watched them, trying to confirm full curl, wanting a ram very badly, time running out, the depressing weather unrelenting, the mountain heights locked in clouds, chances fading, hopelessness growing.

The rams continued to feed, drawing closer. I contemplated the largest ram in the scope, seeing a dream fulfilled, willing the horns beyond full, willing my mind to accept it, willing what I could not will to be.

I set my rifle down, pulled out my camera, and took a hopeful picture in the haze. Then we slid back out of sight, returned to the horses, followed down the ravine to the creek, and hunted farther into the valley. We saw no other game that day.

On the twelfth day, the sun shone. It peeked shyly through the clouds, a stranger in unfamiliar surroundings. It found us toiling hard, approaching the mountain of the ram. The weather had broken.

By midmorning we reached a large boulder at the start of the steep slope to the mountaintop. We rested in the shelter of the boulder. When we arose to begin the climb, we looked to see a ram posed far up near the summit. We dropped behind the boulder. Willie drew his binoculars from under his coat and cautiously peered around.

"It is the big ram. He has not seen us."

The range was beyond consideration. We stayed behind the boulder until the ram walked out of sight. Then we began the wearisome climb to the top.

The sun slipped in and out behind the broken clouds. We climbed in silence, pushing ourselves, knowing the ram was surely there. The unending slope grew shorter. We finally topped out, climbing cautiously the last few steps until the summit showed clear.

We rested a few minutes, then walked rapidly to the rim above where the ram had been standing. We began a thorough search, combing every visible inch, shifting to fresh perspectives, searching, searching. The morning passed into the afternoon. The sun smiled benevolently at times, aiding our search in the unaccustomed brightness. An overcast muted the sun's light as the afternoon faded, and somewhere behind the grayness the sun dipped behind the mountains, shading the slopes into shadow. We never saw the ram again.

We toiled up those wearisome slopes once more the following day, searching the heights all the way. We climbed again to the top of the mountain of the ram, and with some misgivings, probed among the labyrinth leading to the rock slide and the cliff. We found a more cautious way back. But we did not find the ram.

The following morning we broke camp before full light, loaded the three pack horses, saddled the other two, and began the long ride out of the valley. The overcast continued but it had not rained for two days, and it only misted a little that day, a veritable drought compared to the first eleven. We made it out before dark with the early start. Willie's family was waiting for him, camped in a large teepee close to Pete's base camp. He introduced me to his wife, a pleasant, shy woman with equally shy youngsters. I bid Willie goodbye there, in the comfort of his family.

I stayed one night in Dawson thinking to tour the famous Klondike gold rush town and possibly sample the Gaslight Follies and Diamond Tooth Gertie's, the only legal gambling hall in Canada. But I felt strangely depressed over the hunt and brooded instead along the river front. That was not my first unsuccessful hunt, nor would it be my last, but for some reason it affected me greatly. Perhaps I had dreamed too expectantly of great white rams. Perhaps I had dreamed too grandly of glory days, only to have all those glory days come crashing down.

Chapter 16

To Hunt These Hills Again

The disappointment over the Yukon hunt gradually dissipated and my thoughts turned once more to the great white rams of the north. I stayed in touch with Pete Jensen and before the year was out made plans to hunt with him again the following fall. Given the circumstances with the grizzly on my first hunt, Pete offered to waive his fee for a bear on the next one.

Early spring found me hard at a conditioning program of horseback riding and hill climbing. The rigors of the previous fall still remained fresh in my mind. During some of my climbing and walking, I began to notice a shortness of breath and discomfort in my chest. I put it down to a lazy winter and pushed a little harder to get back in shape.

My annual company-sponsored physical examination came up in April. When I mentioned my exercise problems, the doctor ordered a stress electrocardiogram. The treadmill was barely underway before the doctor had me sitting on a chair with a nitroglycerin tablet burning under my tongue. A three-day hospital stay was scheduled for further tests.

There is a fascination beyond the fear in observing a catheter tube snake its way up the artery from your groin through your body into your heart. The monitor the surgeon and I were watching offered riveting television as I lay strapped in a basket-shaped, movable table. The table tilted at intervals and a dye shot through my heart, tracing its colorful way through wriggling arteries in a rush of heat that threatened nausea. My heart pulsated in steady rhythm on the monitor. I watched in fascination, urging it on.

I did not take it as a good sign when three somber doctors later filed into my hospital room. Major blockage in my coronary arteries. Medication could alleviate the discomfort but my activities would be severely limited. Bypass surgery, quadruple from the looks of it, could correct the problem and likely return me to an active life. There were risks. Percentages were mentioned. I could think about the decision. I said there was nothing to think about. The surgeon handed me his card with a cryptic note inked on the back: *To St. Marys around noon Sun 5/13 – Surg 5/14 8 a.m.*

There is much to do the evening before surgery. Tests. More tests. A disinfectant shower. Then the attention of two cheerful young nurse's aids who chatted nonstop while they shaved every hair off my body. I do not recall what they chatted about. Then another disinfectant shower, followed by pokes and probes and needles and tubes. Then alone with one's thoughts in the darkness.

In the morning a gurney came and I lay on it watching the ceiling roll by before everything ceased to be.

"John.... John.... Are you awake John...? John.... John.... Everything went fine John.... Are you awake John...? Your wife and daughter are waiting.... I just need to check you over John. I'll only be a minute.... Nurse! Nurse! Come quick! We've got a bleeder! Get him back to surgery! Fast! Let's go! Let's go! Move it! Move it!"

"John.... John.... Are you awake John...? John.... Everything is okay John .... Your wife and daughter are here.... They'll be in shortly.... Everything is fine John."

The last day of September. Wyoming. There could be no Yukon that year.

Chuck was gone when I stopped at the ranch house. I drove back out the mile-long lane to the dusty county road and followed it north to a faint track that cut off west into the rolling prairie. The track led me ever deeper into the grand solitude that stretched to the horizon.

Antelope came into view. Curious. Not alarmed. Safe in the distance. I stopped and focused them in my binoculars. A small herd. A dozen or so. One good buck. They remained watching as I continued down the track. Then they resumed feeding.

The track wound through the short-grassed prairie, riding the contours of the hills, dipping eventually into a sheltered draw holding water behind a small earthen dam. Rusting hoops and rotting barrel staves lay scattered nearby, faded remnants of a still, left over from the prohibition era. A level spot deep in the draw provided a sheltered place to camp.

Sunshine warmed the prairie through the calm of late afternoon. I climbed out of the draw, sat on a high point, and glassed until the sun dipped low and evening came, then returned to the Blazer, lit the Coleman stove, and cooked supper as stars began filling the sky.

The weather remained pleasant. I took the foam-rubber mattress and my sleeping bag out of the bunk in the back of the truck and laid them on the ground. There was a need to be a part of the night. I lay there, watching the great immenseness of sky, stars seemingly so close, yet millions of light years away, massive in their billions, yet mere pinpricks in the fabric of space, their essence approaching eternity, reaching back into timelessness, back into the void, back into infinity and the unfathomable creative power beyond.

I awoke in the morning with the stars fading into an eastern glow. I made coffee, ate a can of peaches and a bread roll, shouldered a day pack and my rifle, climbed out of the draw, and began walking into the morning light toward the area the antelope had been feeding in the evening before. The day started with a light breeze.

The antelope were gone. I continued east through the rolling prairie until the breeze steadied from the west, then circled to quarter into it and probed the hills and draws.

Half an hour passed when four antelope appeared, a buck and three does, catching me in the open as they topped a far ridge. They watched me for a few seconds before braking away to my left and disappearing back over the ridge.

I followed at a rapid walk, slowing as the ridge began exposing the ground beyond. The antelope came into view, still running, circling into an extensive flat. I dropped to the ground.

The antelope slowed, came to a halt, looked back in my direction, and evidently not seeing me, began feeding.

I studied the ground. A dry wash cutting through the flat appeared to angle close enough to the feeding antelope to present a shot. I backed off the ridge and began walking rapidly behind it. The contour of the ridge shielded me to the far end of the wash. A short expanse of open prairie remained. I crept low across it into the wash and followed the twisting course in the direction of the antelope. In places the shallow bank forced me to stoop and crawl to stay out of sight. One short stretch had me on my belly before the wash dipped and gradually flattened out onto the prairie. I reached the dip and cautiously raised my head.

The antelope were staring at me.

They must have seen movement. They were curious, but they would not remain curious for long. I tried sighting through the scope from a prone position, but the intervening ground and sage prevented it. My attempt to assume a sitting position caused the antelope to bolt and run swiftly out of range. They eventually stopped and resumed feeding, keeping a cautious watch in my direction.

No chance of approaching closer and little likelihood of them coming in my direction with suspicion lurking. I held there for a short time, but they remained watchful. I backed away into the wash and retraced my route toward the rolling hills, leaving the quartet undisturbed in the distance.

Two hours elapsed before another group came into view, seven does, a small buck, and another medium-sized buck. They fed on the side of a gentle slope, unaware of the presence on the next ridge.

The antelope gradually drifted around the slope. When the last doe was out of sight, I arose and hurried over the ridge and across the wide valley, slowing along the slope as the curvature progressively revealed the continuing prairie. Soon my steps shortened, with searching pauses in between. Step. Pause. Step. Pause.

An antelope appeared. I slowly settled to the ground and began squirming forward. The rest of the herd came into view, feeding in a small cluster where the prairie flattened out from the slope. Close. The two bucks barely a hundred yards away.

I steadied into a prone position, centered the larger buck in the crosshairs, and fired. He ran a few yards with the rest of the herd before falling.

I dressed the buck, returned to the Blazer, and drove around the hills to the antelope. There still remained the task of getting the buck onto the roof of the truck. Heavy lifting had been put on hold. A couple of ropes looped over the roof drew the buck up in manageable stages.

Chuck's pickup was gone when I returned to the ranch after dropping the antelope off at the locker plant. I turned away from the ranch house and followed the south track across the prairie. The midday continued pleasant. The junipers and pines shimmered green in the hills to the west.

The canyon rim halted me long enough to shift into low gear. I nosed the Blazer over the rim and down the rutted slope to the dry creek bed. West along the creek bed, then back up the far side of the canyon to top out and follow along the rim to the water tank before dropping back into the creek bed where the junipers and the sheer bank funnelled me into the hills.

My campsite above the creek came into view on the north bank. I maneuvered the truck to angle straight up the steep incline, then spun up the slope into the little sheltered area, turned the truck to face south, and gazed out over the familiar evergreen-clad hills and listened long to the quiet.

The hunt at length called. I loaded my rifle, adjusted my day pack, and set out into the hills.

The quiet continued and my steps matched it. Pine needles helped silence my climb toward the higher ground. Flinty rocks began braking the silence near the crest of the cone-topped hill, grating softly under my boots with a muffled crunch. My breath came harder nearing the crest. I rested just under it, watching for a while into the lower pines and junipers before the farther hills pulled me on.

The afternoon waned as I probed the hills, still-hunting through the evergreens and watching from vantage points on the higher crests. Shadows began to lengthen as the sun arced toward the western ridge. The breeze of the morning had quieted and the hills lay in a hush.

I watched in the quiet from a rock seat just below the crest of a flinty-rock hill. Below me a rolling section of scattered pines topped out above the denser junipers growing close in the lower draws and washes. Clumps of bunch grass struggled through the gip rock that showed white among the evergreens. I tipped the brim of my hat lower to shield my eyes from the western sun and scanned the openings below.

The deer came as so many before him had come, a ghost of a movement filtering through the pines, stopping always behind a pine, a shadow in the other shadows, a figment, drifting in and out, setting my heart racing, triggering the primal responses, tensing with the strain of holding the rifle at ready too long, the scope at last transforming the ghost into reality, the settling of the crosshairs, the push and the roar and the falling and the primal elation and the waiting for the rush to subside. Then the forty paces to the buck. The wonder at the grandness. A four by five. A nice buck. A very nice buck indeed.

And a long way to camp. I dressed the buck, fastened my drag rope around the base of his antlers, looped it over my shoulders, and set out up the first hill. The rocks offered resistance. I rested often before reaching the top. The drag down came easier. When the pines started the deer slid easily over the needles like a whitetail on snow. Then another upward hill had me struggling. I began carrying my pack and rifle to a point ahead, then returned to pull the resisting weight in heart-thumping stages toward the top. I rested at the crest, welcoming the canteen in my pack. Then down into a pine-needled draw, almost racing there over the slippery needles to the next weary hill where the pack and the rifle were again first carried ahead. Progress up the hill became measured in yards before a rest brought strength enough to pull the buck the next several yards. Then down and up another hill. And on into the gathering dusk.

A final rise brought me at last to the high bank of the creek bed. I propped the buck there at a height to slide him onto the roof of the Blazer when I went out in the morning. I rested awhile, then cut a piece of tenderloin from the buck, enclosed it in a clean wrapping, put it in my pack, lowered myself down the bank to the creek bed, and followed it to camp.

Dusk came, the clear air cooling with the faint glimmer of the first stars. I gathered several armfuls of dead branches and started a fire. The dried wood crackled and flared before settling into a dancing flame. I fashioned a holder out of green branches and set the tenderloin to broil, then opened a can of stewed tomatoes and placed it at the edge of the fire. Soon the coffee pot was perking a merry accompaniment to the sizzle of the steak.

The dusk deepened. The hills loomed dark. The stars came upon the night. Only the sound of the fire and the faint murmur of a breeze disturbed the quiet.

There was still a need to test the mountains. An easy test, a hunt for grouse above a high meadow in the Medicine Bow Range I remembered tucked back deep where elk had once bugled me to sleep. I would camp in the mountain meadow a night or two then drift down through the North Platte Valley. Trout, I knew, would serve me for supper there. I would take the buck to the locker plant early in the morning before heading south to the mountains. The way to the mountains was long. But I had time. Yes, I still had time.

I sat by the flickering fire and watched the dusk settle into darkness. The silhouetted hills faded against the deepening sky. The night came hushed, the wind a faint murmur sighing a mournful refrain through the pines. The fire crackled. A resin knot caught and flared, then died to an ember. Dark descended. The wild closed round and a profound silence reigned. An affecting mood prevailed. Memories stirred. The haunting verse from *John Armstrong's Last Good Night* echoed in paraphrase through my mind.

I am only a little wounded. I am not slain. I laid me down for to bleed a while. Then I did rise. And I will come to hunt these hills again.

Quiet then, in the night, with the stars drifting down.

PART III

Chapter 17

Caniapiscau Caribou

It is still a thing of no small wonder to me to go to the wild places. To find myself in country so remote that rivers are the only roads. To stand on the banks of one of those rivers and view scenes essentially unchanged since its forming. To become immersed in the timelessness. To sense the grand remoteness as the wilderness settles deep. To feel the touch of isolation. To know that nothing lies beyond the river except evergreen waves of stunted spruce, the untrammeled tundra of the Barren Grounds, and the Arctic. And to know beyond that, there is nothing but the wind.

If you would go to the windswept wilds of northern Quebec you will find such a wilderness. And you will find such a wilderness river. It is called the Caniapiscau. This pristine waterway wends through a remote country of black spruce and tundra dotted with lakes and streams. A landscape uniquely captivating in its starkness. No permanent settlements disturb the river's tranquil banks and for most of the year the country it traverses is locked in the frozen grip of the northern winter. But in the brief season of open water, floatplanes bring visiting fishermen to the river. And in the waning days of summer there comes to the Caniapiscau those of a kindred spirit, the caribou hunters.

When the Quebec government first issued permits to hunt caribou in the 1960's, the annual migration took the animals along the George River, a parallel watercourse one hundred and fifty miles east of the Caniapiscau. The government estimated the herd at fifty thousand. The modest hunting pressure of the sixties had no more effect upon these numbers than did other natural predation. In fact, the herd grew, until a quarter of a century later it numbered seven hundred fifty thousand. The largest caribou herd in the world.

Perhaps it was those burgeoning numbers that caused the main migration patterns of the sixties and seventies to shift away from the George River, for in the early 1980's, the caribou started migrating farther west. Since the successful hunting of caribou in those northern regions is dependent upon intercepting the annual migration, the hunters began shifting their camps westward. In time, they came to the Caniapiscau. And in time, so did I.

In the summer of 1989, I journeyed north through a glistening Wisconsin August, dreaming dreams of wilderness rivers and vast caribou migrations. My route took me through the Fox River valley, then into Michigan's Upper Peninsula, an area memorialized in Robert Traver's three classic books on trout fishing. I camped for the night north of Engadine.

The following morning I crossed into Canada at Sault Ste. Marie and followed along the North Channel of Lake Huron through the copper mining district of Sudbury. Once past Sudbury, I skirted the northern shore of Lake Nipissing before swinging southeast to follow the scenic valley of the Ottawa River.

I camped fifty miles west of Ottawa that night and continued into Canada's capital the following morning, arriving in time to witness the time-honored ritual of the Changing of the Guard.

The outskirts of Montreal came into view a few hours after leaving Ottawa and I found my way to the local office of Jack Hume, my outfitter. A sign informed me to return at four o'clock the following morning. Downtown Montreal tempted, but I had recently enjoyed the better part of a week there and knew four o'clock would come early enough.

In the morning I arose to the sound of rain, ate a hasty breakfast, then rummaged through my duffel bag for some light raingear. A small group of hunters had already gathered at Hume's office trailer when I arrived in the predawn darkness. The subdued murmur of their conversations radiated an electric feel of excitement that the light drizzle failed to dampen.

Two of Hume's representatives were busy sorting and weighing the seventy pounds of baggage allowed each hunter. A tardy group of Quebecers delayed us half an hour. They showed up a little before six-thirty, and shortly thereafter our four-prop commercial charter lifted into the cloudy skies. A heavy overcast blocked all view of the countryside for most of the eight hundred miles north. The skies opened briefly as we began our descent to reveal a montage of rolling hills dotted with sparkling lakes and waterways.

After a three-hour flight we landed in Schefferville, a once thriving mining community of several thousand reduced to several hundred when the mines closed. The boarded-up houses, abandoned vehicles, and scattered debris gave the town a desolate, forlorn appearance. No roads lead to Schefferville. A weekly train from Sept-Iles, three hundred and fifty miles to the south, or an airplane, offer the only access.

A Hume representative met us at the airport and transported hunters and equipment to Hume's headquarters on the shore of a lake outside of town. There I purchased my fishing and two caribou licenses and was introduced to Wayne and Charlie, from Massachusetts; a second Wayne and Mike, two young Quebecers; and Dave and Larry, two bowhunters from Michigan. We were the first group going into the main camp that season.

We lifted off at noon, squeezed into jump seats amid as much baggage as the heavy-ladened Otter could handle. We droned north, the throbbing engine noise stifling any attempts at conversation. The passing terrain appeared bleak and lifeless in the gray, overcast afternoon. Open barrens, with pockets of stunted spruce, blended into low, rolling hills. Lakes and waterways covered the landscape in profusion. Countless trails laced the ground, presumably those of caribou, but the miles throbbed by without the appearance of a single animal.

Gradually, off to the left, a large, winding river took shape. The Caniapiscau. The pilot made a sharp bank, and forty-five minutes after takeoff, we set down on the smooth surface of the river.

On a long ridge fronting the east bank of the Caniapiscau, tucked in among the spruce, a cluster of low, wood-framed buildings appeared. The pilot taxied past them to a level stretch of riverbank where a number of square-sterned freighter canoes lay beached. Our guides were waiting. In a short time our gear was hauled to the bunkhouse from where we watched the Otter lift off and disappear into the gray sky.

We set about organizing our gear, then assembled for a belated lunch in the cook building. The camp was situated around the homespun wooden structure. Its front windows offered a panoramic view of the Caniapiscau. A food-storage cellar along with a couple of small cabins and tents for the cook and guides were sited close by. The bunkhouse nestled in the spruce a short walk to the south.

After lunch we paired off with our guides and set out to hunt. My guide introduced himself as Howard, a name we smilingly agreed would be easy for me to remember. With little further ceremony, we pushed off in a freighter canoe and quickly became immersed in a glorious, wild venue. I glanced curiously at my watch. Two-thirty. A mere eight hours since leaving the bustling metropolis of Montreal nearly a thousand miles to the south. It seemed half a world away.

We followed north with the current between low hills covered with black spruce and juniper. Stands of birch glistened white against the green background. Wide expanses of light-colored sand jutted into the river from the eastern bank. A consequence, according to Howard, of unusually low water levels.

Camp was two miles behind us when Howard swung the canoe toward the west bank. We touched ashore at the base of a steep hillside amid a jumble of large boulders. After beaching the canoe, we took positions commanding a view of the eastern bank, our outlines broken by the rocks.

Howard's strategy soon unfolded. The migrating caribou, when and if they came, would come from the east. When the caribou reached the river, they would swim across. Our vantage point allowed us to observe a two-mile stretch of the river. If an acceptable bull appeared, we would move along the western bank to intercept it. We had but to wait.

A funnel-shaped section of dark ground directly across the river stood out against the lighter-toned sand. Howard informed me that several caribou trails through the spruce came together there. His pronouncement resulted in my frequent glassing of the area.

Half an hour passed. I scanned the darkened section yet another time. Motion drew my eyes to the spruce. An animal emerged from the trees and walked onto the sandbar. Close behind, in single file, came five others.

"Caribou!" I whispered excitedly.

We focused our binoculars on the group.

"Three cows and three calves," proclaimed Howard.

The caribou walked steadily down to the river. They reached the water, entered it without hesitation, and began to swim across. The half-grown calves swam easily behind their mothers, their noses almost touching the upturned tails of the small-antlered females. The caribou touched ashore two hundred yards above us, scrambled over the rocky bank, and were rapidly lost to sight in the sheltering conifers.

The thrilling sight of game intensified my search of the opposite treeline, but no other animals appeared. The excitement slowly subsided and I settled into a less intense watchfulness.

An hour passed before the sight of four caribou walking out from the trees half a mile down river again attracted my attention.

"Two cows and two calves," announced Howard, as he lowered his binoculars. We watched them swim in single file toward the west bank. Ten minutes later, another cow and calf came onto the sandbar and crossed the river, landing close to where the first group had entered the timber.

The activity spurred a renewed glassing of the opposite treeline, but no other caribou came onto the sandbar. Once again the excitement subsided.

We sat hidden among the rocks, merged into a oneness with our surroundings. An occasional misty shower blew in and then away on the swirling clouds. We huddled in the lee to break the wind and to shelter from the rain. The broad river flowed dark and silent before us. The overcast skies lent a somber feeling to the stark hills. All the landscape lay clothed in dull, muted colors. Even the greenish sheen of the spruce failed to brighten the bleak shadows of gray. The austere scene brought a powerful and intensely exhilarating sense of primal wilderness.

Another hour passed. Then a single caribou appeared. I raised my binoculars, hoping for a bull, but the magnification revealed the small, velvet-encased antlers of a cow. The cow plodded across the sandbar to the water's edge. She hesitated a moment before walking into the river to begin her solitary swim to the other side.

A few minutes later four more cows emerged, followed by three cows and a calf. The two groups joined as they walked toward the river. But instead of entering the water as had the cow before them, the caribou turned downstream and began to walk along the edge of the river. The caribou reached a point opposite us where they stopped, and, as though acting upon a single command, laid down together.

The caribou lay on the sand for fifteen minutes, during which time a cow and calf appeared. Shortly after their appearance, another seeming command brought the resting caribou in unison to their feet. They walked down to the river, entered it, and swam effortlessly toward us on a course that would bring them close to our position. I maneuvered behind a screening of boulders to within fifty yards of their landing place and took their picture as they bounded out of the water. The caribou remained unaware of my presence. They stood for a few minutes before climbing out of sight up the hill behind us.

I returned to where Howard was waiting and he advised me that it was time to return to camp. My reluctance to leave while daylight remained was answered with the assurance that the next day would bring more than enough caribou for the few we might miss that evening. We were, according to Howard, experiencing the beginning of the migration, scattered cows and calves. The migration would build tomorrow, bringing with it the bulls. With that promising thought, we returned to camp.

The other hunters, who had gone out in pairs with a single guide, reported similar activity. A mixed number of cows and calves, but no bulls.

We were discussing our afternoon's experiences in front of the cook building before going in to eat, when someone excitedly exclaimed, "Hey, look! Down the riverbank. Two bulls!"

We turned as one. And there, two hundred yards south of camp, walking unconcernedly toward us along the edge of the river, came two heavy-antlered caribou bulls.

We stared in amazement, immobilized by the unexpected sight. Time seemed frozen, yet the caribou continued toward us. At last, shaking off my amazement, I began running toward the bunkhouse where my rifle stood stacked behind my cot. Wayne followed. The others waited.

Wayne and I grabbed our rifles, hurriedly stuffed cartridges into the magazines, and began running south along the top of the ridge that paralleled the river. The heavily forested ridge, upon which the camp was situated, rose thirty to forty feet above the Caniapiscau. A path used to bring supplies from the landing area had been cut through the forest to a point where the ridge sloped down to the riverbank. Wayne and I ran along the path toward the caribou, shielded from their view by the dense spruce.

Halfway along the length of the path, at an offshoot trail that led down the steep hillside, we stopped and held a brief council. We decided that by dropping down to the river at that point, we should be very close to where the caribou were last seen. I began a cautious stalk down the rutted footpath with Wayne close behind. We agreed that if the caribou were within range, I would take whichever one was on the right, while Wayne would take the one on the left.

We inched down the sandy path, expecting at any moment to see the caribou as more and more of the riverbank came into view. We moved in tense silence, focusing below, only to be startled by the sound of running feet above us. Looking up, we saw Ernie, one of the guides, appear on the path. Seeing us he stopped, and motioning for us to follow, called out, "Come quick! They're going the other way."

With that Ernie again began running along the pathway. We sprinted up the hillside to follow him. Ernie, well on his way before we topped the hill, took the lead by several yards. Wayne dashed after him. I followed tight on Wayne's heels, racing excitedly over the hard-packed surface.

The trees began to thin as we neared the end of the descending path. The wide expanse of the sandbar, with the river showing dark beyond, came into view. We cleared the last of the trees, breathing hard. And there before us, heading directly toward the river, ran the two bulls. The range was reasonable, but their straight-away position presented the worst possible angle. We hesitated but an instant, then resumed our chase after the rapidly departing caribou, hoping they might turn before entering the river.

The soft sand clutched greedily at our feet. We struggled to stay close. The bulls raced on. My breath became labored, my legs weary. Yet, whether illusory or not, the running animals still seemed within range.

The caribou dashed across the sandbar. As they neared the river, we came to a halt. I dropped into a sitting position, wrapped tight into my sling, and tried to settle the bulls in my scope. My labored breathing and pounding heart sent the scope weaving in a hopeless arc. I sucked great gulps of air into my lungs, fought to control my breathing, then found the crosshairs holding reasonably steady against the caribou. I waited for them to turn.

But they did not turn. They never deviated from their course. The grand bulls ran straight into the water, splashed through the shallows, and were soon swimming strong across the river. I longingly contemplated their wide-beamed antlers bobbing in the scope.

The two caribou continued their straightaway crossing of the river, only their backs, heads, and towering antlers show-ing above the water, appearing like disembodied creatures from a child's fantasy tale. They closed on the western bank. The bulls touched bottom and plunged toward the sandbar. They gained the shallows, splashed through the water, reached the firmer sur-face, and began racing toward the spruce forest. Across the white expanse the grand bulls flew, antlers rising impressively atop their rocking-gaited forms, into the evening swirl of mist and haze. And then, as though they had been but a mirage, the cari-bou vanished into the green folds of the spruce-shrouded hills.

During dinner that evening a few of the hunters speculated that we might be eating in the best stand on the river, since the cookhouse was the only place from which anyone had seen a bull. Wayne, the young Quebecer who had been a spectator during the earlier action, took the discussion to heart. He declared that he would be on the riverbank by first light, just in case another pair of bulls paid a similar visit.

Shortly after we settled into our cots, a violent rain storm swept through camp. Sheets of water driven by a howling wind savagely pounded the plywood sides and tin roof of our shelter. I dug deeper into my sleeping bag as the angry elements hammered our little wilderness outpost. The wind raged through the night.

Calm returned in the morning. We arose at five o'clock to discover that Wayne, true to his dinner-time declaration, had already tucked himself behind some spruce trees along the river. We were in the cook building drinking our first cup of coffee when Mike, standing by the window, announced, "There go some caribou."

We crowded around him to watch a group of eight cows and calves start across the river half a mile south. They were hardly halfway across when another group of eight came out of the spruce and began walking north along the river toward camp. We watched with heightened interest, for one of the second group was a bull, and should he continue on his present course, Wayne presumedly would have an easy shot.

The caribou plodded steadfastly northward. We had no idea where Wayne lay hidden, just somewhere in the spruce along the river. The bull drew within range of the cook building. We waited expectantly. The caribou trudged on, coming closer.

A shot shattered the silence, spinning the bull around. He stood for an instant, then collapsed upon the sand.

We were not long in joining Wayne beside the fallen bull. While we were congratulating the young hunter, another group of twelve came toward us. They in time noticed the strange assemblage and prudently retraced their steps.

During breakfast a few of the other hunters voiced serious thought to remaining in camp for their day's hunt. But when the time came to load the canoes, none could resist the lure of the river.

Howard and I returned to our stand of the previous day. Scarcely half an hour passed before a cow, followed by two calves, appeared across the river. The trio walked across the open sandbar, entered the river, and swam to the western bank.

The morning opened gray and overcast with scattered light rain squalls blowing in on a strong north wind. The bleak landscape occasionally became enlivened by the further appearance of small groups of caribou marching ever onward in their migration ritual. Two cows with their calves. Half an hour later, another cow and calf, followed by a mixed group of six. And a few minutes after them, a single cow with her calf. Then a long period of staring at the empty riverbank.

At nine o'clock a surge of excitement aroused us. Seven caribou walked onto the sandbar, two of which carried the outsized antlers of bulls, the first seen from our stand. Our excitement was short-lived, for the binoculars revealed the spindly antlers of immature bulls, teasing shadows of the impressive antlers adorning the bulls of the previous evening. The small herd followed the now familiar course across the river and vanished into the western hills.

A lengthy period of inactivity followed, the inevitable bane of the hunter who chooses to wait. The temptation grew to cross the river and probe through the hills on the other side. Howard reminded me that the caribou were migrating through the area. A stationary hunter on the river would see far more animals than a moving hunter in the heavy spruce. His logic was obvious. I settled back into watchful waiting.

At noon Howard broke out the lunch box. We crouched behind the shelter of the large boulders to break the force of the north wind, ate our sandwiches, and welcomed the warmth of the strong, hot coffee. We talked of the restless wanderings of the caribou and their incredible numbers. Howard told of times when they were so thick in the river that thousands were backed up on the banks waiting a turn to cross. A scene beyond the scope of my imagination.

We put the lunch box away and resumed our patient vigil. Before long a large number of caribou began filing out of the far treeline. Cows and calves came first. A small bull appeared next, followed closely by more cows and calves. Fifteen in all.

And then, sweeping antlers towering over the rest, a mature bull strode out from the spruce to follow behind the others. Surely he matched the two bulls of the preceding evening. Howard, looking through his binoculars, pronounced him their equal.

The caribou walked across the sandbar toward the river. The lead cows seemed as though they were going to enter the water across from us. But just before reaching the river the cows turned and continued walking downstream. The bull followed after them.

The caribou continued north. It appeared that they intended to cross where a large sandbar jutted out from the western bank. Several earlier groups had crossed there. We began making our way toward it.

The sandy bank on our side lay strewn with a jumble of rocks and large boulders. A steep hillside, thickly covered with black spruce, rose sharply behind us. We moved unobserved between the cover of the boulders and the spruce background.

The restless herd plodded on, each member in cadenced rhythm. Had we needed to overtake them, we likely would have failed. Their deceptive gait steadily opened the distance between us as we stumbled over the rock-strewn ground.

The caribou arrived opposite the sandbar, stopped, and began milling around. We secured ourselves behind a large boulder directly across from them. The caribou continued milling. Two of the cows made a tentative start to enter the river, but backed away. Indecision reigned. I willed them forward, for if the herd resumed its march down the eastern bank, my chances would go marching away with them.

Finally the large bull took the lead and entered the water, followed by the small bull and four cows. The rest of the herd, in spite of the example of the others, would not enter the water. After watching their former companions for a few minutes, the remaining caribou turned and began walking downstream along the eastern bank.

The six caribou in the river swam single file, the small bull and the cows strung out behind the large bull. They drifted slightly with the current, but their course led steadily toward the jutting sandbar on our side. I marveled at their grace and the grandness of the approaching bull. On they came. I waited, caught up in mixed emotions at the inevitableness of the outcome. Better to have seen the bull in the timber or across a stretch of tundra and to have challenged him in a stalk. But this was the way of the river. So said Howard. I had come to hunt the Caniapiscau, and I seemed bound to hunt it the river's way.

The caribou neared the bank. Then, like Poseidon rising from the deep, the grand bull came forth from the water, splashed through the shallows, and clattered across the rocky ground scarcely thirty yards away. He filled my scope. The rifle recoiled. And the great stag fell to the ground.

I held for a moment, still awash in mixed emotions, then moved from behind the boulder and walked to the fallen bull. Against the pale background of the sand his brown-hued antlers loomed large, their regal form enhanced by the velvet sheath still encasing them. He was a splendid animal.

I stood in admiring contemplation, caught up in a wild display. Around me, as though seeking to counter the inevitable finality of the moment, nature staged an animated scene of vibrant, continuing life. The small bull and the four cows quickly scrambled out of the river and fled past me, intent on reaching the safety of the forest. Across the river, the other cows and calves trotted northward, the protective mothers gaining security for their precious charges in the ever-widening buffer of space. Nearby, in a sudden, startling rush, a cow with twins trailing close behind dashed toward the shelter of the spruce. How they came to be there baffled me. Far off on the eastern bank, another dozen cows and calves emerged from the tree-line, continuing the vivid pageant. Then, as though to relieve the muted stillness of the silent animal cast, a family chorus of wild-throated geese came strongly on the north wind, fledgling wings among them aloft on a trial of the heights.

The grand display lay framed in the panorama of a glorious wilderness setting. The leaden sky, painted by the wind with swirls of gray, showed wispy clouds scudding in confused array above green-clad hills. Pale stripes of sand flanked the verdant hills, stretching along the sky-tinged water like narrow ribbons down the wide, meandrous valley.

And through the valley, in brooding, somber majesty, flowed the mighty Caniapiscau, silent witness to the ageless cycle of birth and death, renewal replacing the fallen, as natural as the rhythm of the seasons.

Howard interrupted my musings by beaching the canoe close by, reminding me of the task at hand. We turned to skinning and quartering the bull. The north wind blew a minor gale, leaving us hard-pressed to keep the meat free of swirling sand. We managed to devise a makeshift wind-screen from some handy canvas, and in quick order had the bull quartered and the meat along with the antlers stowed in the canoe. We pushed off for a choppy ride on the wind-blown river back to camp. There we made short work of hanging the quarters in a screened-in meat shelter and were soon back on the river.

Seven caribou crossed ahead of us on our return journey to the stand. Two bulls showed enticingly among them, the larger a very nice one. They splashed ashore long before we got close. Four cows stood nervously on the eastern bank watching our approach before spooking into the timber as we passed.

By two-thirty we were again nestled into our morning's stand. We had hardly settled down before four cows and a calf appeared, crossing below us. Ten minutes later we came alert when four bulls walked onto the eastern sandbar. One stood out, certainly the equal of the bull taken earlier. We waited until they entered the river, then moved to intercept them. The bulls swam steadily toward us, their antlers towering impressively above the water. They reached the shallows and splashed ashore barely twenty yards away. I hesitated. Wavering. Unsure.

The bulls decided it for me as I watched them pass in grand procession and disappear into the hills.

We watched four small groups of cows and calves cross the river during the next hour and a half, then came alert as a group of seventeen stepped out from the far trees. Two large bulls showed prominently. We studied them through our binoculars. One bull carried tremendously long main beams but they were completely devoid of points. The second bull's antlers were well-developed, a temptation were its equal not already back at camp.

The seventeen caribou crossed the river to the south and began walking along the bank toward our position. The north wind blew strongly from behind us. I rested my rifle across a rock and watched the bulls through the scope, wondering how close they would come before catching our scent. At one hundred yards the entire herd suddenly became alert. The caribou began milling around. The blustering wind apparently confused the scent. They tested the air. Another gust decided it for them. The herd abruptly turned and beat a hasty retreat.

A short while later two cows appeared, trailed by a pale white calf. Its peculiar appearance brought to mind the sacred white buffalo of the Plains' Indians. Howard said that while white calves were uncommon, he nevertheless had seen a number of them over the years. He believed the calves lost their shading as they matured.

Another hour passed, interrupted frequently by small groups of cows and calves. Only one small bull put in an appearance by the time the lengthening shadows called us back to camp. Halfway there the largest herd of the day funnelled onto the eastern bank, twenty-two cows and calves, bringing my caribou count for the day to two hundred and thirty-three, of which fourteen had been antlered bulls.

The other hunters reported similar sightings. Five bulls had been taken.

The following morning brought another overcast sky. We gathered in the cook building and huddled around our coffee while the gray light formed in the east. The fierce north wind had subsided and the Caniapiscau flowed smooth. We watched the first caribou herd of the day, twelve cows and calves, leave a widening wake in the unrippled water as they crossed to the western bank.

A second herd of forty-one caribou, attended by a most impressive bull, appeared during breakfast far down the river, walking in our direction. Charlie, who had not filled a tag the preceding day, immediately dashed toward the bunkhouse to retrieve his rifle. We gathered around the window, eating snatches of breakfast, and watched the procession approach.

Charlie disappeared down the ridge trail. The caribou drew closer. They reached the canoe-beaching area, stopped, and began milling around. The bull stood enticingly. We waited for Charlie's shot. Several of the cows stepped tentatively into the water. The others continued milling. The suspense dragged on. Then one of the guides appeared around the bend from camp, unaware of Charlie and the caribou. At the sight of the guide, the herd began running back along the river. We listened expectantly, but no shot sounded. The caribou rapidly fled out of range.

When Charlie returned he related a disappointing tale of cows constantly blocking a shot at the bull.

After breakfast Howard and I returned to our familiar stand along the river, Howard's favorite. Each guide had similar preferred stands that lay widely spaced, none being in sight or sound of the others. Once away from camp there came the pleasant illusion of being the only hunter in that wild and lonely land.

We no sooner arrived at the stand when eight cows and calves put in an appearance on the eastern bank. They walked straight to the river only to turn at its edge and continue northward, eventually crossing at the sandbar where my bull had fallen the preceding day.

A quiet hour drifted by before another group of twenty cows and calves filed out of the eastern treeline. The caribou approached the river, but instead of crossing, turned and followed north in the footprints of the others. A few minutes later a single cow and her calf appeared, to march along on the same journey. Five minutes later thirty-seven cows and calves emerged in single file from the treeline to follow the north-bound tracks. Close behind them another group appeared. I counted sixty-two through my binoculars, including three small bulls. Next came a tight group of five cows with two of their offspring, followed by ten more cows and calves. A few minutes later, surging forth like a wave to add to the flood of life along the river, sixty more caribou poured onto the sandbar. Nearly two hundred caribou were stretched along the eastern bank. A vibrant display.

The last herd, which included four medium-sized bulls, walked down to the river. Instead of turning north as the other caribou had done, they continued into the shallows and started swimming toward our stand.

The caribou swam directly to us as though guided by a beacon. They reached the shallows in front of our stand, splashed out, and began clattering over and around the rocks in which we lay hidden. For a few minutes Howard and I literally became engulfed within the center of the herd. Several of the caribou passed close enough to touch without giving any indication they were aware of our presence. Their hoofs clicked sharply on the rocks and they wheezed and rumbled and grunted with the exertion of climbing the steep hill behind us. The smaller calves had trouble keeping up with their mothers on the steep slope. They repeatedly slipped and fell back, then scrambled frantically trying to catch up. The cows paid no attention to the troubles of their offspring, forging their way upward as though they were alone. Apparently the cow's job was to lead and the calf's job was to follow. The cow was doing her part and she left it up to the calf to do his. What the consequences of a calf's failure would be we were given no opportunity to observe, for they all scrambled successfully up the hill. The clambering gradually subsided. The hill became quiet. We found ourselves once more with only the soft murmur of the wind and the brooding silence of the river.

The stirring experience of being so intimately caught up in the herd held me enthralled long after the last scrambling calf had disappeared. When I again turned to observe the caribou across the river, only a final few showed far downstream, swimming toward the western bank in the wake of the others. The wide expanse of sand that so short a time before had been filled with life and motion stood barren and still. The sudden emptiness seemed startling.

We resumed watching the far treeline. Fifteen minutes after the herd passed over us, a group of fourteen, including two small bulls, emerged. They followed across the sand in the direction of the preceding bands, presumably heading for the northern crossing.

I watched the caribou through my binoculars, keying in on the two bulls while hoping to see a larger one follow out of the trees. No others appeared. I lowered my binoculars and began scanning the rest of the treeline with unaided eyes. My gaze swept along the spruce edging. An animal materialized out of it, running across the sandbar, coming from the north and moving swiftly toward the caribou. I called Howard's attention to it and raised my binoculars.

"Wolf!" we echoed simultaneously.

The caribou appeared unaware of the wolf's presence in spite of its right angle approach from their front. Apparently some undulations in the sand allowed it to remain out of sight.

The wolf broke its smooth stride with frequent leaps while it ran, seemingly jumping above the low sand ridges to keep the caribou in sight. Each calculated leap saw the wolf adjust its approach when the fleeting glimpse revealed the course of its heedless quarry. The caribou ambled on, oblivious to any danger.

I watched the unfolding woodland drama with incredulous fascination. I seemed on the verge of witnessing a wolf kill, for the caribou were about to be hemmed in between the wolf and the river. There appeared to be no escape.

The wolf apparently ran out of screening sand ridges as the distance closed, for the caribou suddenly bolted. Through my binoculars it appeared that the wolf was within a quick rush of its quarry, but the magnification distorted the distance. A greater gap existed.

The caribou dashed toward the river with their dreaded adversary close upon them. The wolf adjusted, closing fast. The frightened band reached the water's edge, turned, and spurted north along the bank. The wolf became blocked from our view by the caribou as the band raced frantically northward. Then, unseen but obviously in very close proximity, the wolf's attack caused the herd to split. In the confused melee a single cow and her calf became separated from the group. The pair, reversing themselves, began racing furiously back toward the south.

The wolf passed by the larger group and angled in pursuit of the cow and calf. The cow ran desperately, holding several yards in front of the wolf. The calf, matching its guardian stride for stride, stayed tight on the heels of the cow. Were it not such a perilous race the scene might have appeared ludicrous, for the smaller animal of the three was the one in deadly pursuit. We watched the contest in hushed silence, waiting for the inevitable closing of the gap and the death of the calf. No other outcome seemed possible.

The cow began to turn toward the spruce as she raced southward, possibly with the hope of loosing her pursuer in the evergreen thickets. The calf followed in desperate trust. The wolf seemed to sense an unexpected advantage. Instead of following directly in the tracks of the caribou, the wolf turned on an intercepting angle and rapidly closed on the left flank of the calf. A mere leap separated the wolf and the calf.

Suddenly the cow reversed her direction and began racing back to the north. The calf amazingly maintained its position tight on the heels of the cow. But the wolf overshot the turn. It scrambled in confusion trying to recover. By the time it did, the cow and calf had opened a considerable gap between them.

The chase swung back across our front with the issue that had seemed a forgone conclusion suddenly in doubt. Across the sand they flew, the caribou pounding on with their ground-covering gait, the wolf running full stride behind them. No intercepting angles favored the wolf this time. The gap between pursuer and pursued began to widen. The wolf, seeming to sense the futility of its pursuit, slowed to a trot, then finally stopped and stood in presumed dispirited contemplation, watching the caribou grow smaller and smaller in the distance.

The wolf lingered in the area, chasing another herd of forty back into the spruce before it wandered across the sandbar and disappeared into the evergreens.

The departure of the wolf signaled the return of the caribou. A band of forty soon appeared, possibly the same band the wolf had chased earlier. Five minutes later a group of ten came onto the sand, including one small bull. Both herds ambled down river toward the north crossing.

A few minutes later a large group of cows and calves began to filter out of the treeline. A good-sized bull emerged behind them, followed by another.

"Two nice ones," I ventured.

"Don't look all that much bigger than your other one," Howard responded.

The herd marched down to the river. We expected them to turn north and follow the other caribou, but they continued into the water and began swimming toward us.

I grasped my rifle, for in spite of Howard's assessment, the towering antlers above the maze of brown backs in the water looked most impressive. The caribou floated slightly downstream as they crossed the river. I shifted with them, concealed by the boulders. The lead cow touched land twenty yards away and scrambled over the rocks with her calf close on her heels. Other cows and calves followed, their hoofs clicking almost musically. Behind them came the bulls. They rose dripping out of the shallows, following in the tracks of the lead cow. I pondered over the bulls in my scope, undecided, wavering. Then decided that my indecision was in fact a decision and watched in admiration as the grand bulls entered the spruce, maneuvering their huge antlers through the branches as they noisily climbed the steep hillside.

With the clattering still in my ears, I turned back to the far bank. Twenty more caribou were already on the sandbar, including three fair bulls. They were joined by four cows, each attended by a calf.

A steady procession followed. First two good bulls, drawing serious consideration. Next, ten cows and calves, trailed by another group of seven. Then four more bulls, three looking very good. Behind them came a mixed group of fifteen, after which a large herd of thirty-eight spilled onto the sand with two fair bulls in attendance, followed by a smaller band of seventeen cows and calves. And still they came. A seemingly inexhaustible fountain of life pouring out from the hills.

A pleasant two hours went by as we enjoyed the passing parade. The overcast sky sent an occasional misty shower, though never of sufficient duration to dampen the pleasure of the morning's procession. Several good bulls stood out over the preponderance of cows and calves. A few had us studying long through our binoculars.

During a lull in the activity across from us, I turned my binoculars to the far southern portion of the river. Movement attracted me. A large herd drifted out from the spruce onto the white sand. They were at least a mile away, but even at that distance one of the bulls appeared huge. He not only towered over the small-antlered cows, but also dominated a couple of respectable looking bulls. I called Howard's attention to the bull. He agreed it must be an exceptional one.

"Never get to 'em, though. If they cross up there, they'll be gone long before we even get close."

"No harm in trying. They might decide to walk down the bank."

"Possibly. We can give it a try."

We quickly pushed off the canoe, pointed the bow south, and keeping tight against the western bank to minimize the current, began our slow progress toward the herd.

The caribou were crossing a wide expanse of sand on the eastern bank, heading for the river. We continued along the western bank, our outline broken against the backdrop of the wooded hillside. The tumble of boulders at the base of the steep hills extended into the river for most of the way. Our hope was to gain an accessible stretch of bank along which we could stalk the caribou when they reached the western side.

We forged slowly upstream. The herd crossed the sandbar and drew near to the river. I willed them to turn northward, but the caribou walked straight to the water's edge. They entered the river without even an expectation of a northward turn and began swimming across. The herd closed steadily on the western bank far ahead of us. I began to sense that our effort was going to fall short. Still we pressed on, hoping the caribou might remain on the bank or turn northward. But that they did not do. The caribou landed, and continuing straight ahead, disappeared into the western hills.

We turned around and with the agreeable help of the current began our return journey. A group of thirty-five crossed the river below us as we neared our stand, with one very good looking bull looming impressive through the binoculars. We were barely settled before a large herd of fifty-six spilled onto the eastern bank and strung out in a long file as they paraded in front of us on their march toward the northern crossing. Next came thirteen more, with two good bulls in their midst. Then another mixed band of twelve, followed shortly by seven cows trailing five calves in their wake. And so the flood tide continued.

We interrupted our observations at noon for lunch. The overcast skies dissolved into scattered cloud fragments while we were eating, and for the first time since my arrival sunlight graced the landscape. The valley assumed a delightfully bright aspect. Unfortunately Howard and I were not alone in enjoying the radiant warmth. The heretofore dormant blackflies and mosquitoes abruptly joined us with their unwelcome intrusions.

We noted during the morning that most of the caribou crossed well downstream from us. That, along with the persistent blackflies and mosquitoes, prompted Howard to suggest a change of stands. A large rock outcropping, near where my caribou had been taken the day before, not only provided a fine vantage point, but also offered a clearing exposed to the insect-scattering wind. We were not long in seeking its welcome breezes.

Small bands of cows and calves continued to emerge from the eastern woodland to roam north along the sandy bank until they eventually turned to cross the river, many just below our new stand. We watched the passing bands under a cloud-dispersed sky. The misty, damp morning had transformed itself into a sun-filled, reposeful afternoon. We removed our raingear and soaked up the cheerful rays.

Nearly an hour passed. I was lazily counting yet another group of caribou drifting onto the sandbar when a remarkable sight aroused me from my listlessness. Behind the last of twenty-two cows and calves, a grand procession of eight bulls issued forth in single file from the spruce. They were all heavily antlered, none appearing smaller than my bull of the preceding day, with two noticeably larger.

The herd came out of the treeline halfway between our current and former stands. The cows and calves continued in the lead, followed by the bulls, while a few calfless cows trailed along in the rear. The herd crossed the sandbar, angling slightly north, and appeared to be heading straight to the river. But like so many groups before them, the caribou turned just short of entering the water and continued north along the bank.

Magnificence held sway as the bulls marched in stately procession along the river. No haste marred their regal bearing, nor did they stand upon hierarchical order. The bulls advanced in a loose file, sometimes bunching, at other times stringing out among the cows and calves. The herd held center stage, for as if in deference to the courtly assemblage, no other caribou appeared. Bright sunlight flooded the scene, dancing off the sparkling blue water and highlighting the evergreen background. Nature resplendent.

The sun disappeared behind a closing overcast as the herd approached the heavily used crossing. A gust of wind chilled slightly without the compensating warmth. A hint of rain threatened. We thought briefly of raingear but deferred, too deeply engrossed in the scene across the way.

The lead cow came to the edge of the river and halted. The rest of the herd, closing like an accordion, bunched up behind her. There seemed to be some uncertainty on the part of the cow. The rest of the caribou, including the bulls, appeared to be waiting for her decision. We watched anxiously, for if the herd choose to continue north, our chances of intercepting it would disappear.

The caribou stood in close array along the edge of the river for several minutes. A few of the calves occasionally broke rank in their youthful exuberance. Finally the lead cow began to wade into the shallows, and like a logjam breaking, the rest of the herd surged forward and was soon swimming in a loose, oblong formation toward the western bank.

Once the caribou committed to the water, we moved rapidly to intercept them. Howard and I were securely hidden behind a pair of shielding boulders by the time the herd reached midriver. I watched the great bulls swimming steadily toward me, waiting like a patient bowhunter while an unsuspecting buck draws closer to his tree stand. The inevitableness of the outcome muted the adrenaline flow a little. But, as Howard pointed out, there was no other practical way to hunt the passing herds of the Caniapiscau. One waited either in the spruce or along the river. Best to wait where the shot would be clear and clean.

The caribou closed on the near bank. I eased the safety forward. The lead cows reached the shallows and waded noisily out of the water. They began walking diagonally away across the wide tract of sand with their calves following. Close behind came the bulls. They emerged splashing and jostling from the water, tightly bunched. I struggled through the scope to find the largest among the shifting jumble of antlers.

The bulls began to string out when they reached the firmer sand. I isolated the largest one in my scope, swung steadily with the crosshairs holding just behind his shoulder, and fired. The grand bull collapsed. The rest of the herd took alarm and raced across the sandbar toward the protection of the timbered hills.

I stood up and walked the twenty-five paces to the fallen bull. I gazed long in admiration at his sweeping, wide-spread antlers, the crowning glory that had been both his pride and his downfall. He was most imposing. Certainly he held senior to the bull taken previously.

Howard went to bring up the canoe and we set to work skinning and quartering the bull. Other caribou continued to appear along the river while we worked. I counted well over a hundred staged at various points up and down the sandbar. They seemed undisturbed by our presence, although none ventured close. We finished our task, loaded the meat and antlers in the canoe, then glancing south at the rain-threatening sky, donned our raingear and pushed off into the river to return to camp.

We intercepted a mixed group of thirty-seven caribou in midriver as we were returning. Ten bulls swam among them, two adorned with antlers rivaling the set lashed securely behind me. That parting group brought my caribou count for the day to one thousand three. A glance at my watch showed the time at two o'clock. We had been on the river eight hours.

Mike and Wayne greeted us upon our arrival at camp, eager to display two nice bulls taken that morning. Dave and Larry arrived a little after us, each having taken their second bulls with the bow. Dave beamed proudly over a forty-point set of antlers with double shovels. Wayne and Charlie arrived at six-thirty, happily displaying four sets of antlers. Nine bulls for the day, bringing the total to fourteen in only two full days of hunting and filling all the hunter's tags.

The following morning Howard and I loaded the canoe and set off under a sunlit sky on a five-mile journey down river to an area known as the Falls, a favored fishing site. The Falls turned out to be a narrow cataract that emptied into a deep, inviting pool. I could imagine the raging torrent had the river been at its normal level. The fish were cooperative. I landed several nice brook trout along with an eight-pound lake trout.

At noon we gathered several armfuls of dead spruce and built a fire over which we cooked butterfly cuts of tenderloin from my first caribou accompanied with succulent trout fillets. The combination of wild river, azure sky, and verdant forest added a wilderness garnish to a meal that rivaled any feast for the gods. A small band of caribou, attended by a single bull, crossed above us while we ate.

We returned to camp in midafternoon. A continuing restlessness sent me on a hike into the hills. I found miles and miles of rolling, spruce-covered terrain, heavily laced with crisscrossing caribou trails. A wild, seemingly desolate land, but an incredible pleasure to be roaming after the confining days of stand hunting. I reveled in the freedom, reluctantly turning campward when the setting sun signaled the close of day. I saw no caribou in the hills.

That night the northern skies favored us with an exquisite display, a full eclipse of the moon in concert with the northern lights. As the earth's shadow slowly covered the orange-glowing sphere above the western horizon, the aurora borealis flared into searching fingers of light in the north. Dazzling and throbbing and wild and wane. How wonderstruck early man must have been to watch the moon disappear in the midst of that awesome celestial dance. How wonderstruck were we.

Heavy fog obscured the river and surrounding hills the following morning. The sun burned through after a few hours, sending me on another restless trek. I hiked several miles to the south, following the river before turning east to again climb into the hills. The terrain remained unvaried. I followed caribou trails through the spruce, looping north and picking up an occasional west-running trail until the river came into view. The full morning's circuit revealed only a dozen caribou. Howard and I paid a repeat visit to the Falls in the afternoon. The trout sulked in an uncooperative mood.

Friday morning. The sun promised a pleasant last day in camp. I again hiked into the hills, following the river two miles north to explore the area across from our stand. I meandered unhurriedly through the spruce expecting to see a fair number of caribou but spotted only four small bands totaling fifteen cows and calves. The heavy migration had passed through, building on Monday, peaking on Tuesday, and subsiding throughout Wednesday. A mere remnant remained.

A turbulent storm front pounded us Saturday morning. The wind-driven downpour subsided at noon, only to resume at one o'clock and continue through the early afternoon. The guides informed us that if the floatplane could not get out of Schefferville by four o'clock, it would not come that day.

The camp fidgeted impatiently in the enforced idleness. The hunters and guides eventually drifted off to their respective bunks to sleep out the rain. I finished the last of my books, then, feeling restless, donned my raingear and hiked south along the river. I spotted one lonely cow with a calf and hid in some rocks to watch them plod soggily past at twenty-five yards.

The rain let up shortly after four-fifteen on my way back to camp. Half an hour later, the low, throbbing drone of an airplane signaled the emergence from the haze of a single-engine Beaver. The Beaver turned out to be a supply plane bringing in food and baggage for the next group of hunters. The Beaver was quickly unloaded and reloaded with seventy-five-pound boxes containing the meat from our caribou, and scarcely thirty minutes after landing, the floatplane rose skyward and was rapidly lost in the misty haze.

Ten minutes later we again heard the sound of an airplane engine. An Otter materialized out of the southern haze and landed smoothly on the river. Five hunters were aboard. We stood on little conversational ceremony as all hands turned to hurriedly unload the floatplane while keeping a weather eye on the darkening storm clouds pressing down from the north. Within twenty minutes, with the hunters from our party and their gear stowed aboard, the Otter lifted off into a leaden sky. The pilot banked south and I looked down for a final view of the camp. A twinge of envy trickled through me for the newly arrived hunters and their week ahead.

The camp slowly faded into the mist. I turned my gaze forward, settled into the copilot's seat, and watched in fascination as we wove through the darkening clouds.

The low ceiling held us at five hundred feet. Looking ahead I could vaguely discern areas where the crests of higher hills merged into the clouds. A challenge in a floatplane not equipped for blind flying. On we droned, searching for breaks in the lowering overcast. The breaks closed in. We found ourselves bumping through wispy sprays of dirty-gray mist with raindrops beading, then streaking, across the windshield. The pilot eased the floatplane down to four hundred feet, broke into the clear, and continued to weave through valley-like openings where strong winds fragmented the lower-lying clouds. We cleared a range of hills through a gauzy corridor in the overcast. Then, still bumping into vapory mists, the pilot throttled down to three hundred feet and began bearing from one small lake to another, presumably a precaution in case the overcast closed us in entirely. The diminishing evening light intensified the gloom of the cloud cover. We wended our way south, hanging suspended below the ceiling in a narrow trough of closing sky. At last, ahead through the gloom, a large lake took form. The welcome lights of the Schefferville landing twinkled at its far end. The pilot approached straight in, seemingly on a level with the lake without having to descend lower, and touched down softly on the gently lapping surface. There were no other floatplanes that evening.

I stayed at Schefferville's only hotel that night, a quietly busy place of weather-delayed hunters with a nice restaurant and bar. We left Schefferville at ten o'clock the following morning to the accompaniment of a familiar light rain and arrived in Montreal at one-thirty to a sunshiny August sky. And thence homeward, the magic land of the caribou reluctantly fading into a dreamlike world.

The great waterways of the north drew me into that country again. In August of 1995, I returned to northern Quebec to hunt caribou along the Pons River, the next major watershed west of the Caniapiscau. No heavy migration across the river favored me that year. I hunted primarily in the hills, seeing small, scattered groups of cows and calves, with very few bulls. One bull fell to my rifle in the hills southeast of camp, and another respectable bull fell along the river farther south. Rain remained a constant companion.

The following August brought me back to the familiar camp along the Caniapiscau. We missed a wave of the migration by a week. The six hunters ahead of us all filled. Our group of six managed only fifty percent and were fortunate at that. In six days of hunting I saw twelve caribou and two black bears. I filled my second tag with two hours left on the last day, a respectable bull nonetheless, as was the other.

Timing reigns supreme with the caribou of the Caniapiscau. When the great herds are on the move, the spectacle is wondrous to behold. When they are not, the hunter's days grow long. Still, there is always the grand isolation of the spruce-clad hills and the brooding majesty of the wild rivers to fill the hours. And when the silent dark comes, there remains the never-fading memory of a night when the skies danced a mystic dance, fair arrayed in all their celestial splendor, while the moon passed in shadow beyond the earth.

18

The Brooks Range

I have soared with clouds on golden wings,
And chased silver rainbows through the sky,
And climbed a thousand glittering heights,
And woven oh such glory days have I.

Drawn irresistibly to the farthest north, I came in time to the Brooks Range. There are no mountains beyond it. There is only the Arctic Ocean and the frozen barrens of the polar ice cap. But in those desolate mountain heights the elusive white sheep dwell in their northernmost refuge. And there I journeyed in their quest.

Wednesday. The fifteenth day of August 1990. An hour before midnight. Thirty-five hundred miles from home and thirty-five thousand feet above Alaska. Lightening flashes in the clouds below highlighted bands of rose and white that layered down into a dusky gray. It was not full dark. An evening-shaded gloam revealed the ground between the lightening-charged cloud formations. We descended through the eerily flashing heavens toward the glimmer of lights that became Fairbanks.

There was little time to sleep. Up at five-thirty, shower and shave, and back at the airport by six-thirty. A heavy fog hung low over the morning, delaying my flight.

By nine o'clock the fog cleared enough to permit takeoff, still a haze limited visibility to two miles. The jumbo jet of the day before with its hundred-plus passengers gave way to a single-prop Piper Cherokee-six, carrying its pilot, along with a young woman, a younger boy, and me. We shared the airplane with a cargo of crackers, eggs, and vinegar.

Mountains passed beneath us with scattered clouds hanging low in the valleys. Serrated rock formations rose up in places like wilderness replicas of Stonehenge. The remains of a crashed airplane showed starkly off to the left, a forlorn memorial on the top of a mountain. The pilot walked away, so our pilot informed us. He made it out to Fairbanks where he and a friend decided to fly back in a Piper Cub to look at the wreckage. The Piper Cub crashed, killing them both.

When you cross the Arctic Circle, you cross into the true north. There are lines clearly drawn on the maps to show that demarcation, but no line traced across the barren ground beneath us to mark our passage into that land of the midnight sun. Somewhere below, we passed that invisible meridian, and before long a dirt runway at the edge of a small village came into view. We landed at ten o'clock and taxied up to a sign that welcomed us to:

FORT YUKON
(GWITCHYAA ZHEE)-POPULATION: 637
LOWEST TEMP: -78° HIGHEST TEMP: +105°
LOCATED 8 MILES NORTH OF THE ARCTIC CIRCLE

I transferred my gear into a waiting pickup that took me to the log cabin home of Roger Dowding, the bush pilot who would be flying me to the sheep camp. There I met a fellow hunter named Jim, booked to share the same camp. Roger was sleeping after a long day and night of flying. We would leave for camp when he got up, whenever that might be.

Fort Yukon lies along the junction of the Porcupine and Yukon rivers, where the mighty Yukon reaches its northernmost point on its two thousand mile journey to the Bering Sea. Weathered, single-story wood homes and buildings front the graveled dirt streets. The largest building, a two-story, white-boarded hotel called the Sourdough Inn, offered rustic rooms and advertised burgers for five dollars in its equally rustic eating area.

Roger was still sleeping after my walking tour of the village, but there were stirrings. In midafternoon he emerged, introduced himself, and asked if we were ready to go. We were. At four-twenty Roger's Cessna lifted off the dirt runway and pointed north with me in the copilot's seat and Jim seated on the baggage behind. Roger offered us earphones and we soared over the flat tundra to the musical accompaniment of Enya on the tape deck.

The Brooks Range gradually rose in the distance and we were soon drifting through valleys with the rounded mountaintops rising above us. In places the valleys closed and deepened and the little Cessna wove through narrowing corridors, lifting almost imperceptibly at times to barely clear a connecting ridge before drifting down again between the closing, looming peaks. The haunting Celtic strains of Enya wafted through the earphones, a dreamlike, other-worldly accompaniment to our floating passage through the narrow-troughed colonnades.

A broader valley opened ahead with a fork of the Canning River tracing through it. Roger circled a flat stretch of ground close to a jagged-peaked mountain and brought the Cessna gently down. It was six o'clock. Our guides were not there, nor was anything else. A bare mountainside confronted us. We unloaded our gear and Roger took off for what he called the North Camp.

The sound of the airplane faded in the distance. Jim and I listened in silence, surrounded by an even more profound silence, caught up in the awe-inspiring mountain wilderness. The weather continued clear. We sat on our duffel bags basking in the pleasant day amid the grand isolation of the Brooks Range.

Time passed. We began to contemplate a night on the mountain. At long last the sound of an airplane drifted up from the valley. Roger made a circle and landed beside us. Wrong spot. We were moving twenty-two miles north. We loaded our gear and were quickly airborne.

Roger told us that on his way to the North Camp he saw a landed airplane and two men setting up a tent. Something about their behavior struck him as odd. On his way back, Roger noticed the men half a mile from where they had been, skinning a grizzly bear. Grizzly season was still two weeks off. He flew back to record their airplane number. One of the men saluted him with a one-finger salute. No doubt his second foolish act of the day.

We followed through the mountains to where a small tent camp took shape along the Canning. A narrow gravel bar split the river, offering a short landing strip surrounded by swift-flowing waters. Roger circled once before gingerly bumping down onto the bar. Our guides, Joe Hendricks and his son Joe, were waiting. We carried our gear across a shallow ford into camp and turned to watch the little Cessna bounce along the gravel bar and soar away over the mountains.

Camp consisted of three nylon tents, one for Joe, one for his son, and the other for Jim and me. A circle of stones with kindling pyramided in it promised a cheery evening fire. We organized ourselves for the morning, then sat around the fire eating and watching the dusk that served for night deepen. Eleven o'clock came with still enough light to read by, had one chosen to. I made my weary way into my sleeping bag and fell asleep to dreams of airy mountain valleys filled with haunting Celtic strains.

Friday morning. Three o'clock. We got up. It was time to hunt.

The same dusky light of evening illuminated the morning behind a yielding gray veil. We made coffee, ate breakfast, shouldered our packs and rifles, climbed the bank above camp, and followed south along the river.

The taller willows surrounding our camp gave way to a tundra-like carpet of course brown ground cover dotted with ankle-high green bushes. Rocks poked up from the irregular surface. The river flowed silent to our right. The mountains rose into a gray haze to our left. We hiked easily over the rolling flat. The morning opened comfortably brisk.

We split up two miles from camp. Jim and the younger Joe headed due east into the mountains while the senior Joe and I angled up a steep slope toward the mountains to the southeast.

We climbed slowly, the easy walking of the rolling flat giving way to the muscle-testing incline of the slope. The ground cover of the valley continued up the mountainside. We tread silently over it through the dusky dawning.

The steepness increased. The lower ground cover began disappearing among the rocks. We came eventually to a ridge that fronted a deep-cut valley. Another irregular ridge showed across the valley with a prominent flat-topped rock formation rising from it like a watchtower. Beyond the watchtower, a wider valley carried into a higher ridge that lay partially obscured by a haze flooded with reflective light from the rising sun. The mountains beyond the wider valley were lost in the prismatic glare. But we were not similarly lost to the vigilance of a young ram watching us from out of the haze. We saw him when he broke over the far ridge.

The presence of the young ram brought us to a halt. We sat down and began glassing. The obscuring haze was difficult to penetrate. Eight ewes and lambs finally came into focus off to the south. They fed without concern, unaware of us and evidently unalarmed by the movement of the young ram. Ten more ewes and lambs fed across the river to the west. Another small band of five fed not far from them. Our glassing continued for the better part of an hour. Other than those three groups, the slopes remained empty.

We resumed our ascent, climbing toward the crest of the ridge. Just below the crest, we angled around to the flat-topped watchtower ridge. A rock-rugged mountaintop continued past the watchtower, a barren moonscape with a serrated ridgeline that cut into the sky. We picked our way carefully over the rugged ground, detouring around sharp-thrusting granite rocks that resembled massive stone cutting tools discarded by a long-lost race of ancient giants.

Another steep valley began on the far side of the serrated ridge. We sat down to glass. A grand mountain panorama spread out in all directions. Ridges and peaks rolled endlessly away to the horizon. The river traced like a tiny cerulean ribbon through the winding valley far below. Patches of blue began framing some of the peaks as the hazy overcast started to clear. The day promised to become as grand as the view.

We turned our gaze from the mountain scene to the valley and immediately picked up three young rams half a mile away on the steep slope. They did not see us. Farther up the valley from where the rams fed, a ewe and a lamb appeared faintly through the binoculars. The sheep showed more clearly since the haze had dissipated, their white coats contrasting starkly with the dark mountain background.

A further hour of glassing held us. When no more sheep came into view, we crossed another ridge, topping out above a deep, steep-sided canyon with a trickle of a mountain rill twisting through the narrow, rock-strewn bottom. Three rams fed far down the opposite side. We watched them through our binoculars, young ones like the others.

We turned from the rams when a ewe came into view two hundred yards below. She spotted us and rapidly retraced her steps. We soon saw her running over a far crest. The young rams continued to feed, unalarmed by the actions of the ewe. We settled down to glass.

Forty-five minutes passed. The rams continued to feed along the steep slope. They eventually laid down, keeping a watch over the canyon. We continued to search for other rams along the rugged, pocketed mountainside. Another half-hour passed with our careful scrutiny, but the three young rams remained the only sign of life along the opposite side. In time they arose and drifted over the far crest, and the mountains became empty.

Our position high above the canyon floor gave us only a partial view of the south side as it twisted up toward the eastern peaks. The north side lay concealed except for the immediate portion below us. We could better view both sides from the bottom. The canyon also offered a natural corridor into the higher country. Joe led as we began the climb down. The way was exceedingly steep. In places I faced inward and clung to the mountainside in order to negotiate difficult passages. It was an hour shy of noon when the rocky canyon floor at last ended our steep descent. We were already eight hours into our day.

Joe decided on an hour's nap and we lay down on a grassy bench alongside the little mountain rill. We brought no food but the clear-flowing rill offered a refreshing drink. I rested on the grassy bench yet remained too keyed up to fall asleep in spite of having gotten only four hours rest each of the previous two nights. Sheep were being sighted. And rams. Young ones it was true. But higher country showed promisingly ahead with the hope of larger rams in the mountain fastness. And the day basked in sunshine.

At noon we began our climb up the floor of the canyon. In places the rock-strewn ground was wide enough to accommodate a single-lane road, in others the deep vee held only enough width for the narrow rill, making walking on the rocky side slopes awkward and dispelling any hope of dry boots. The floor of the canyon continued upward through a striking corridor of moss-covered granite slopes that angled steeply into the blue sky. The little rill tumbled over the rocks, creating tiny waterfalls that cascaded down like miniature Niagaras. Rock climbing became the order of the day through some stretches.

The canyon wove a serpentine route through the mountains. Every several steps created a new vista. We proceeded slowly, stopping often to observe the newly revealed slopes on each side.

Then a ram appeared, a good ram, on the south slope, moving away from us, although not in an alarmed state. He quickly lost himself in the bouldered mountainside. We hurried up the canyon, stumbling over the jumbled rocks and splashing through the rill. We followed half a mile, searching every vestige of the south slope, but the ram had disappeared.

"He's probably laying down in the shade of some boulder," Joe offered. "We'll wait here until he gets up."

An hour passed. Then another. Followed by a third. The sun arced over the canyon, its light shading down the far slope and back up the opposite side. The little rill sparkled when the sunlight reached it, splashing blue and foamy white through its gray granite bed. Greenery struggled up in places, the life force of the plants finding hold wherever a trace of soil and moisture combined. The mountains towered in utter silence. We waited in the quiet, listening to the faint trickle of the rill. The ram did not reappear.

"He must have crossed over without us seeing him," Joe surmised. He looked toward the west-arcing sun. "We should think about starting back. We're going to be a long time reaching camp as it is. If we backtrack down the canyon, we can come out along the river. Or we can climb up here and hunt the ridges down. You got a choice?"

"Which gives us the best chance at a ram?"

"Well, the best chance would be up the canyon. But that's the long, roundabout way. And the roughest."

I looked temptingly at the downhill route. Two short nights of sleep were beginning to catch up with me. My leg muscles ached from the unaccustomed climbing. My stomach grumbled. Twelve hours since breakfast, and supper might be a midnight dream if we continued into the higher country. I looked again toward the rugged heights. The mountains would still be there in the morning. Yet, I could not let them wait.

"Let's go up the canyon."

We refreshed ourselves with water from the rill and resumed our climb.

Barely twenty minutes passed before a bend revealed an indented section of the south mountainside. A medium-sized ram came into view. We glassed him for several minutes thinking he might be a companion to the larger ram. But he moved away alone.

We continued upward, Joe in the lead. Another bend slowed us as we cautiously angled around. Suddenly Joe froze. I followed suit. Joe carefully sidled back.

"Two rams," he whispered. "One is a very good one." He made a deep circular motion with his hand indicating a full curl and then some. Excitement began welling up even though I had yet to see the rams.

We started to ease forward, then froze again. A small ram came into view, running down the mountain from the side where the rams had been spotted. He crossed the rill and ran parallel along the rocky slope behind us. We made ourselves one with the mountainside. Shale disturbed by the hoofs of the small ram trickled down the slope directly to our rear. We dared not move. I plastered myself against the mountain. The sound of the ram continued noisily behind us before gradually fading away. I remained motionless. Joe finally relieved the tension.

"He's out of sight."

A ridge tracing down the mountain to our right created the bend around which Joe had seen the rams. We began the steep climb to its crest. I halted just below the top, waited until my breathing settled, then carefully raised my head to look over.

I stared in awe. A majestic ram was there, alone, walking slowly up the open slope, head carried high in haughty dignity, a princely vision of argent white against the dark-toned mountain. Sunlight flooded the scene, glinting off great curling horns of burnished amber flaring beyond full. The ram climbed with courtly measure, framed by the azure sky, a stately lord in his realm, regal beyond imagining. I caught my breath at the sight.

Then I caught myself. The ram was moving toward the start of another parallel ridge a hundred and fifty yards away. Several more steps would put him behind the ridge and out of sight. I wriggled higher up toward the crest until my rifle lay steady over my crumpled hat. The ram came into the scope, walking slowly. I tried to quell my nervous excitement. The ram walked on. The crosshairs followed, settling low on the front of his chest. My breathing eased. I held it still and began squeezing the trigger. A few steps separated the ram from the ridge. Then a single step before he would disappear behind it. The rifle recoiled. The ram lunged ahead, then turned downhill and fell. He struggled slightly. I fired again. The struggles ceased. The ram slowly relaxed, stayed in place a few seconds, then rolled and tumbled down the mountainside, coming to rest a few paces from the sparkling rill. Silence closed in again.

I lay on the ridge, staring at the fallen ram, lost in a state of subdued elation. A dream long in the dreaming had come into fulfillment there upon the mountain.

Joe offered congratulations, after which we crossed the ridge and made our way down to the ram. Joe knelt beside him.

"That was a good shot. A lot of hunters would have shot over. They read too many stories and sight in for too far away."

We took some pictures, dressed the ram, and began the caping. While we were busy at our task, Jim and Joe came around the ridge from which I had shot. Their surprise at seeing us equaled our surprise at seeing them. They had spotted the ram from far up in the mountains at ten-thirty and had been stalking him ever since. They had never seen us nor heard my two shots. I looked at my watch. It was almost four-thirty. A sore disappointment for them after nearly six hours of rugged work.

An hour and a half elapsed while the cape was carefully skinned and the meat deboned. Two ewes appeared in the mountains above and watched the proceedings for a few minutes before wandering out of sight. As we were preparing to leave, I went down to the rill to get a drink, then turned for a final look into the mountains. Far away, toward the head of the rill, in a small pocket, four white dots hinted at sheep. The binoculars confirmed my suspicions. They were sheep. And two looked like good rams.

The spotting scope was hastily set up. Two rams and two ewes. And the rams were indeed very nice ones. The hunters, though, were not the only ones observing. The sheep were looking back at us.

Joe asked if I would climb up a side mountain with the hope of holding the ram's attention while Jim and Joe made a stalk. My weary leg muscles protested, yet up the steep slope I climbed, far too slow, no doubt, to cause the distant sheep any concern.

The ruse worked. While the sheep keyed in on my movement, Jim and Joe set off under cover of the twists and turns of the little rill. I enjoyed a fine, front row seat for the stalk. The hunters closed to within three hundred yards or so before cover ran out. Several shots echoed round the mountains. I watched through my binoculars as the sheep scrambled for the heights. Neither of the rams gave any indication of being hit.

The disappointed hunters trudged slowly back. I paralleled them down the mountain. Joe was waiting alongside the rill. He and the younger Joe split the meat between their backpacks while I secured the ram's head, horns, cape, and my rifle on mine. We began our descent.

There is an illusion that going down the mountain is easier than going up. Gravity favors you, but that is all. We picked a careful passage through the jumbled boulders. The heavy loads jarred our knees and affected our balance, threatening stumbles that could have proven serious. We began angling up the side of the canyon to get away from the rock-strewn rill. The going became less rugged although the awkward load on my back continued digging deeper and growing heavier with each labored step. The dusky shadings of the Arctic night followed us down the mountain.

We came with the deeper dusk to the river flat and turned north along its relative level toward our hidden camp. The welcome tents at last emerged in the distance like friendly beacons in the night. We left our loads for the morning, ate a hasty supper, and slipped exhausted into our sleeping bags. It was half an hour past midnight, nearly twenty-two hours since arising.

Saturday morning. Seven o'clock. Dark clouds hung low over the mountains. A dim, rain-threatening dawn. The camp slumbered and I turned over to slumber with it.

Rain pattered me gently awake again at eleven o'clock. The camp was stirring but there would be no hunting that day, the mountains lay locked in impenetrable clouds. We finished caping out the ram, found a deep, cold-running pool in the river, and set the cape in it to soak clean. We played some cards and read a little and watched the day fade into the rainy dusk of night.

The rain continued through the night and into the following morning. Jim chafed at the enforced idleness. My caribou permit also made me a bit anxious for the weather to clear, but occasional trips to the river to check on the ram tended to sooth my anxiousness.

The weather began braking around midafternoon. By six o'clock we were able to enjoy an open-fire cookout featuring succulent mountain ram tenderloins. Exquisite.

A few hours after supper, Jim and the younger Joe shouldered backpacks and headed into the mountains. They disappeared up a canyon where the spotting scope had revealed six rams when the rain cleared.

After Jim and Joe left, two peregrine falcons swooped in to grace the cloudy evening. Hunters also, seeking their flying prey in the valley of the Canning. They found none while we watched, eventually drifting farther up the valley until they, like the other hunters in the canyon, became lost to sight.

Clouds rolled through the valley again. The following morning found the mountains socked in. Jim and Joe had not returned. By midmorning the valley had cleared slightly, but caribou hunting still remained a hopeful wish.

Early afternoon saw the mountain hunters back in camp with a chilling tale of an Arctic fog bank that locked them in a frost-ladened mist through a miserable, bitter night. Visibility became measured in feet. They dared not chance a descent. Sleep eluded them in the piercing cold. They were not long in seeking the comforting warmth of their sleeping bags.

A little sunshine brightened the late afternoon. Still chilly, yet very pleasant. I glassed for caribou but saw only the dark waters of the Canning moving through the mountain valley.

Tuesday. Low clouds and fog early that cleared by nine o'clock. Jim and Joe waded across the river to hunt the mountains to the west. I hunted south back to the mouth of the canyon where my ram had been taken. No caribou were in evidence but two rams were observed in the heights when I returned to camp.

Joe considered a move to his south campsite for a better chance at caribou. Roger was due in and we could fly there with him. Roger's later arrival, however, dashed those hopes. He had not seen a single animal in the twenty-two miles along the river between the two campsites.

An animal other than a caribou did excite us with its presence later that evening. A grizzly bear, moving toward us on the far side of the river, ambling slowly in the open, foraging along the river, stopping to investigate some possible delicacy, then strolling on, oblivious to our prying presence as we watched him grow larger in the spotting scope. The wind held in our favor and a stalk seemed a definite possibility. But the season of his hunting remained days away. We were content to observe the grand beast instead until he turned into a willow thicket across from camp and vanished into the mountains.

The hunters returned late that evening, crossing the cold trail of the grizzly before fording the river. They saw neither bear nor sheep.

The next dawning revealed half an inch of frost glistening on the low ground in the morning sun. Jim and Joe climbed early into the mountains to the northeast where a band of rams had been observed.

With my caribou hunt a seeming nonevent, I gathered some fishing tackle and headed south along the Canning. The day remained clear and the pleasure of wandering the mountain valley was enhanced by the occasional grayling that came to my fly. Iridescent beauties, those Arctic river dwellers, flashing blue and bronze and silver beneath their long, flowing dorsal fin. They occupied me well into the afternoon before I finally turned campward, unslinging my rifle when stretches of dense willows required a cautious passage. Grizzlies, I knew, also wandered that valley.

Joe was watching two rams high up in the mountains when I came into camp. They were barely discernable through the thirty-two power spotting scope, and invisible to the naked eye. A possibility for Jim and Joe should they draw a blank that day.

That day, however, had brought success for the persistent hunters. They arrived back in camp half an hour before midnight with a ram that could pass for a twin of mine. They had been sixteen hours in the mountains.

Thursday. Another beautiful day. Two rams made an appearance on the west side of the river. The grayling held my attention for much of the day.

The following morning dawned clear although a front began developing in the northwest. Jim and I packed duffel bags and waited around camp for Roger's Cessna. It arrived a little before five o'clock and we were soon bumping down the narrow gravel bar in the middle of the river mentally urging the little airplane up as the river and the mountains sped toward us. The lofting Celtic melodies of Enya again accompanied our flight through the weaving valleys and out onto the barrens. We touched down at Fort Yukon an hour and a half later and stayed the night at Roger's before catching a noon flight to Fairbanks the next day.

Jim and I parted company in Fairbanks. My connecting flight had already left and I spent the next few days and nights flying standby to whatever airport got me closer to home, catching catnaps on hard airport benches. Still my hours on those hard benches did not pass all that unpleasantly. There was a backpack with a soft, fleecy pillow of mountain ram cape upon which to rest my weary head, and a cradle of burnished-amber horns to inspire my untroubled dreams. And in those dreams, in those no longer wistful dreams, great white rams looked regally down from mountain heights while I soared through valleys on gold-touched wings, listening to faraway murmurs of haunting Celtic strains, and to echoes of the siren's call of the beckoning, north-borne wind.

Chapter 19

The Blizzard Bucks

During the millenniums of the never-ending winter, a massive glacier covered half of North America under a mile-thick mantle of ice. Eighteen thousand years before our time, the earth shifted once more in its orbital cycle, and the strengthened rays of the sun began to exert their influence on the ice flow. The great cold began to loosen its grip on the north. But it yielded grudgingly. Another eight thousand years elapsed before the last traces of the Wisconsin glacier finally scraped out of the land that gave it its name.

The blessed days of warming returned. Spruce and birch began to take root around the glacier-carved lakes and wetlands that dotted the tundra-like terrain. Mammoths, bison, and caribou ranged this newly temperate region, and nomadic hunters followed wherever the far-ranging herds led. The warming climate soon spawned mixed conifers and hardwoods. Small bands of archaic people began to call these woodlands home. In time the Ojibwa came to settle this land, living free among the abundance of fish and game they found. They called the wetland-rich area Chequamegon, the place of shallow waters.

Eight hundred sixty thousand acres of these pristine Wisconsin woods, lakes, and wetlands have been set aside in the Chequamegon National Forest. Wildlife abounds within this vast expanse. Over two hundred and thirty species of birds keep company with a variety of woodland animals, including the scarce pine martin and timber wolf. A wandering moose now and then finds its rare way through the forest, and a small band of elk again track through the deep glades after a hundred and thirty year absence. White-tailed deer flourish in cutovers and edgings, and the wary black bear thrills the deep-forest rambler with an occasional startling glimpse. Hunters also wander the Chequamegon, as they have for ten thousand years. They come in the brilliant-leafed days of autumn and the frost-tinged days of winter, to roam free like the Ojibwa in search of game in these splendid, glaciered lands.

Most of my deer hunting in Wisconsin occurred in and around the woods and the waters of the Chequamegon. This vast national forest is tiered into three separate blocks that extend north and south over one hundred and fifteen miles through six northern counties. It was in the lower block west of Medford that I shot my first deer. The following year found me sixty miles north hunting in the central block east of Park Falls, the self-proclaimed Ruffed Grouse Capital of the World. For the next fifteen years my hunting grounds shifted to an area adjacent to the central block that we called the Ridge. Often in my still-hunting west from the Ridge, I crossed the seamless boundary into the Chequamegon. A great windstorm devastated the Ridge area in 1977, and new hunting grounds were sought.

We were four at the time: Myself, Fred Klett, Dick Holmes, and Carl Thompson. Carl knew of country to the west around Mikana near Red Cedar Lake. We hunted the Mikana forests for a few seasons until Fred bought a cabin in Waushara County, in the central part of the state. Deer were prevalent in the area and two nice bucks fell to my rifle there. My son, Mike, shot his first whitetail a few miles northwest of Fred's cabin. But the settled aspect of the country, restricting one's wanderings between No Trespassing signs and bringing a heavier influx of hunters, eventually turned me north once more.

I hunted the Indian Trail country of Mikana on my own for a few seasons, then returned to the northern Chequamegon and found no cause to leave it again.

It was never just the shooting of the deer. It was the wilderness experience within which the hunt took place that gave the shooting of the deer meaning. Fine whitetails wandered regularly through my back yard and the thick river woodland that bordered it. They could easily have been shot with rifle or bow from my deck. But wherein lies the touch of the wilderness? Wherein lies the quest?

I am drawn to the wild places of the northern forest, and the solitary roaming of the cedar swamps and the aspen edges and the deep timber and the hardwood ridges, where the early snows cloak the forest in a grandness of pristine white, and ravens on whispering wings are the only distracting sounds in the hallowed quiet. And where, in the awesome presence of the timeless rhythms, one touches deep into the primal wonder.

I roamed free then, camping in my Blazer in the Chequamegon wherever a faint track took me deeper into the forest solitude. An occasional night of below-zero temperatures made rising from my down sleeping bag a dark-morning challenge, but the wilderness began only a step away, and the priceless days of a lone hunter's freedom lay before me, with no one's ways to follow but my own.

There did come three seasons when my solitary wanderings were interrupted. An invitation came to hunt private property in the far north. Large bucks were said to favor the area. In fact, Rob had purchased the substantial acreage for that reason. Deer were plentiful on his home property in southern Wisconsin, but bucks with above-average antlers continued to elude him there.

The prospects were intriguing. The location finally decided it for me. The property butted up against the Chequamegon.

-1-

The northern block of the Chequamegon touches almost to the shores of Lake Superior. The Canadian winds blow cold across the lake in the months that harken back to glacial times. I followed west on a graveled, snow-covered forest road through the Chequamegon. A lane turned off to the north and I crossed the forest boundary following truck tracks through the snow that dipped steeply down and then up again through a spring seep that fed an ice-covered lake to the right. A small island rose from the lake, showing dark evergreen from atop the hill where Rob was waiting beside a wood-framed shed that would serve as sleeping quarters. It was late November, the day before the 1989 gun season.

We split up to scout our separate ways. The country was new to both of us, the property having been recently acquired.

A typical northern forest surrounded the lake, a virtual extension of the Chequamegon. Trout Brook bordered the east, flowing north between ridges that rose sharply along much of its length. Swales and swamps separated the higher ground, and to the north a prominent hill gave a distant view toward Lake Superior. Deer tracks meandered through the swales and hardwoods, some of intriguing dimension. A draw funnelling down to the brook suggested a deer crossing. Tracks confirmed it. Prospects looked encouraging.

Opening morning. Still one of the most magical of times. And as always, somewhere in the distance, the faint echo of the first shot in the still-darkened forest.

The day dawned pleasant with a covering of snow opening up the thick woods. I passed the early hours watching an area where tracks, droppings, and a series of buck rubs held promise, then followed south around the lake into a section of thick evergreens. More tracks, droppings, and two beds indicated the earlier presence of deer in the area, but they lingered there no longer.

Hardwoods started after the evergreens and I continued still-hunting through the brushy growth that swished against my clothes in the denser stands, dissonant notes in harsh concert with the muffled crunch of my boots in the snow. I paused often, searching the limit of visibility, for there would be no close encounters with the alerting sounds.

Midday passed and I paused and passed through the stark winter woods where soldier-straight trees stood close-rank guard in the snow. A sky of steely gray framed the winter scene.

My passage through the forest halted me often on little prominences that gave an elevated view into the surrounding cover. The afternoon continued in silent watch and distressingly not so silent movement between vantage points. The evening hour brought me along the edge of a small, tracked-up opening off the south end of the lake. There came always the expectation of deer movement in that bewitching final hour. But dark came with tracks and droppings still the only thing of deer seen during the day. Rob reported a similar lack of success.

Our success did not improve over the next two days. Fresh tracks confirmed the movement of deer through the area, but never during a time when either of us was in a position to observe them.

A crust lay on the snow the morning of the fourth day. A brittle, crackling crust that telegraphed footsteps far beyond the possibility of vision. There would be no still-hunting that morning.

I crunched around the west end of the lake in the dark before the dawn. The snow gave a faint reflective lighting to my noisy movement through the hardwoods. I passed the little clearing and the swale running east from it into a thicket of conifers. Beyond that lay the draw through the ridges lining the brook. Fresh tracks were observed there during all three days of hunting. I had watched the area several times, but the tracks seemed to appear only after the night. I turned toward the hardwoods above the draw, breaking a noisy trail through the crusty snow. A vantage point at length halted me and I leaned against a maple and listened to the grateful silence as the dark began to fade from the deep forest.

The steel-gray sky held back the light. When it came, it came slowly into a dullness that masked dim-standing trees and the screening brush that blended so well with the winter coat of the deer. The dawning filtered softly through the forest in company with a silence that reigned supreme.

The coming of the light banishes all but the intenseness of expectation. It is the best of the day. Should it ever come to only one hour to hunt, that hour must be the first.

I stood by the maple, holding still and silent in the little scraping of dark earth I had cleared through the snow. A precaution should a turn be necessary.

The promising first hour passed. Half an hour more drifted by in silent waiting. My rifle leaned against the maple, a momentary rest for my arms. I shifted slowly to my left leg, leaning against the tree, relieving some of the muscle strain, trying to be a part of the tree, trying to be a part of the forest.

Crunch. Crunch. Crunch.

Behind me! Movement through the crusty snow!

Crunch. Crunch. Crunch. Crunch.

Coming toward me!

Crunch. Crunch.

My left hand curled around the rifle barrel. A pause in the movement. I froze.

Crunch. Crunch. Crunch.

The rifle came away from the tree, sliding slowly up, screened by my body.

Crunch. Crunch. Crunch. Crunch. Crunch.

Right hand around the pistol grip, left hand to the fore-arm, safety eased forward, gloved hand muffling the faint metallic click.

Crunch. Crunch. A pause.

I strained my peripheral vision, trying to detect movement without moving my head, unable to determine from the sound which side the expected deer would appear on.

Crunch. Crunch. Crunch. Crunch.

I held. Tension rising. Wanting to turn. Desperately wanting to see. Fighting the impulse. Fighting the impatience.

Crunch. Crunch. Crunch.

To my right! There to my right! Twenty yards away! A deer! A buck! A large-antlered buck!

The deer crunched a few more steps, then stopped and turned his gaze in discovery of a foreign object against the maple. He looked but an instant, then bolted to his right.

I swung like a shotgunner tracking an exploding grouse, twisting half-around, mounting the stock to my shoulder, capturing movement in the scope, swinging with the movement, barely feeling the push as the rifle recoiled, chambering another round as the great buck tumbled into the crusty snow and lay still in the intense stillness of the morning.

I held my rifle at ready for a minute, covering the deer while waiting for the tension to subside, then crunched the thirty paces to where the buck lay. A very fine eight-point.

I stood awhile in admiration, then dressed the deer, looped my drag rope around his antlers, and dragged him over the blowdowns to the lane, where we later picked him up with the truck.

That was the only buck either of us saw that season. I gave the deer to Rob in appreciation for the hunt, and also to help him start an antler collection of bucks taken on his new property.

-2-

A trailer stood atop the hill above the lake the following year, expanded quarters from the small shed we bunked in the season before.

The deep cold from the north had yet to come down that November. The little lake below the hill remained open and a good-sized flock of migrating Canada geese was claiming it as a temporary home. Their raucous honking clamored boisterously through the forest.

The warmer weather quieted the opening morning, allowing silent passage through the hushed woodlands but for the riotous din of the geese. They seemed reluctant to leave the lake and their constant chatter echoed distractingly in the morning calm. I made my way amid the disruption to a watching point above the draw the buck of the preceding year had been moving toward. Fresh tracks again indicated deer using the area, but the forest remained empty as the dawning slowly blended into a comfortably pleasant day.

I continued my vigil well into the morning. The weather induced an almost lazy reluctance to move. Eventually the lack of game activity sent me still-hunting toward the north.

I followed the ridge above the brook until it merged into a lower swale. The more open aspect of the swale held me for an hour watching for movement through the thinned trees. When the swale continued as empty as the area above the draw, I still-hunted north through a boggy willow swamp. Tracks showed there, but the thick willows offered scant hope of seeing a deer.

A large, open hill rose beyond the swamp. I trudged up it in the continuing presence of deer tracks. On the far side of the hill, denser woods opened into a several acre stand of maple with a surprising lack of underbrush. The brook ran along the east side. I watched the maples and the dense edging on the other side of the brook into the afternoon before retracing my route up and over the hill, through the swamp and swale, and back along the ridge to the lake and a small opening on its south side. Tracks remained the only thing of deer to be seen.

The pleasant evening kept me at the little opening long after the closing hour passed. A large boulder offered a dusk-shadowed place to stand. The clamoring geese fell silent. The night solitude settled down. I could not bring myself to leave the hushed, dark-enchanted woods. I listened to the intenseness of the deep beyond the dark and the faint cracks and crackles of frost-snapping branches, some of those faint cracks perhaps betraying the stealthy steps of the brown ghosts of the forest as they printed their tantalizing tracks in the night.

The following morning I returned to the draw. There is an irresistible pull back to the places where success has visited us, hoping always that the lightening that struck there once will come thundering down again.

Deer had been invisible to both of us the day before, and they remained invisible from my stand that morning. The noisy geese after awhile prompted me to move. I turned toward the south and crossed into the Chequamegon.

A faint trail carried me deeper into the forest. The morning became hushed as the sound of the geese faded away. The silence barely registered before another sound startled me. A ruffed grouse thundered out from an aspen thicket close on my right, followed by a second, and then a third. I dreamed a hopeless bird hunter's dream of a triple on grouse as my rifle tracked their forms through the leafless aspens.

A fainter offshoot trail turned me west across a spring seep and up a gradual incline that steepened before leveling out on a rock-faced promontory overlooking a mixed stand of hardwoods and conifers. I eased carefully to an overlook and began to study the ground below. Gradually, in a small thicket close by, an indistinct form began to take shape. A deer lay bedded, screened by the thick brush. A doe. Soon part of another deer took form. A second doe, bedded next to the first.

I continued my scrutiny, searching in sections, resisting the impulse to scan broadly, concentrating on each small area before shifting my eyes to another, trying to discern an antler, or a flicker, or an out-of-place shape.

A sudden sense of movement to my right turned my gaze expectantly. Two deer. Drifting near the bedded does. But no need to strain my eyes looking through the brush for antlers. They were close enough to reveal the absence of even a spike. A doe and her fawn of the year. They halted a short distance from the other two deer and bedded down, almost disappearing into the brown background as though an artist had painted them over in a touched-up forest landscape.

A bonus permit in my pocket allowed the taking of does, but the hunt was still young and the thought of disturbing the ground while a buck possibly lay bedded there removed further temptation.

I spent an hour, then another, burning every feature of the ground into my mind. The first two does rose and wandered off during the second hour, followed shortly by the other doe and her fawn. Bucks there may have been in the deeper thickets, but they neither rose nor otherwise revealed themselves. My eyes finally grew weary peering into the same empty ground. I turned away from the bedding area and resumed still-hunting along the faint trail.

By evening I had circled through a section of the Chequamegon back onto the stand above the draw. The geese serenaded me for a time with their raucous honking before they lapsed into silence with the deepening dusk.

Rob greeted me at the trailer and in a reflection of my day reported no bucks. Nor could either of us report a buck for the rest of the season. They surely roamed the ridges and the swamps. But the great bucks of the north seemed always to roam an extra step beyond our vision, and our tracks mingling with theirs remained our closest encounters.

-3-

The trailer swayed gently in a gathering north wind the evening before opening day the following year. I poked my head outside just before retiring and watched a few dancing snowflakes skip around the lee of the trailer and settle fitfully to the ground.

The wind rocked harder through the night, and the dark before the morning revealed a full-blown blizzard well under way. The Canadian wind roared down from the north, racing across the open expanse of Lake Superior, gaining momentum with its unrestricted passage, crashing into the great forest of the north, driving a heavy blanket of snow in horizontal streaks through the bending, cracking trees of the Chequamegon.

We viewed the storm with questions about whether deer would be moving in that gale or hunkered down in some sensible shelter. Rob believed they would be bedded and was inclined to wait out the storm. But it was opening morning, and I could not spend it inside a trailer. I zippered my rifle into its case, shouldered a day pack, and set out into the face of the blizzard, heading north.

The wind pushed against me. The driving snow began to plaster my front. I trudged on in the dark heading toward a small swale bordered by a slight elevation along its south edge. A giant pine grew there, offering a chance for occasional shelter behind its trunk while I watched into the trailed thickets.

Dawn opened with me beside the great pine, its lower branches shielding above my head. I stood leaning tight against the side of the tree while the driving, plastering snow transformed me into a whitened extension of the whitened trunk. The piercing wind began draining some of the warmth from the exertion of my walk. I sidled partially around to the lee of the trunk and tried to keep a watchful eye on the swale. The driving snow hampered my vision. The blizzard stormed on.

I huddled against the pine, immersed in the storm, caught up in the power of the untamed forces, existing within them, a part of them, sensing a deep primal pleasure in my intimate involvement with the elements.

The great pine helped deflect the main force of the blizzard and I found occasional relief behind its sheltering trunk. Even so, the piercing wind chill in time compelled me to move. I cradled my cased rifle in my arms and struck out north, still-hunting in a less than still manner. There seemed little need to be concerned about a silent passage with the raging wind roaring through the crackling trees.

Drifts of snow began to hamper me slightly through the lower swamp. The covered willows dropped their additional layers on the layer already covering my coat as I brushed cautiously through. Beyond the swamp the open hill had me bending against the full force of the wind until my hurried passage over it brought me into partial shelter watching the open stand of maples and the brushy covering along the east side of the brook. No tracks had been evident in the growing accumulation of snow.

The snow rose steadily with the passing hours. The piercing wind again compelled me to move. My weary steps grew labored pushing through the deeper drifts. I retraced my route over the hill where my tracks of a few hours before were obliterated. The swamp showed as a wall of white with the dense willows heavy with snow. Trickles of icy flakes brushed down my neck during my passage through, but at least the wind bit less aggressively against my back.

Midday came but none of the wild elements of the forest rested with the passing into afternoon. The blizzard raged on in all its frenzied fury.

The swale came into view on the far side of the swamp. I pushed along its west edge. A movement to the left halted me. I stared into the shifting patterns of the blowing snow and saw a deer walking through the swale. It was quickly lost to sight in the brush. I hurried around to the little elevation by the great pine. The deer again came into view. A doe. Walking at a steady pace. Unalarmed and seemingly unaffected by the raging elements around her.

A permit allowing the taking of either a buck or a doe was attached to my license. The weather argued for the acceptance of any deer. I began to unzip my case. The snow billowed. I withdrew the rifle as another gust of wind sent the driving flakes in a swirl behind which the doe vanished and then remained vanished as the swirl cleared away to reveal only snow-clad brush. I watched intently, but the deer had disappeared into the storm.

I cased my rifle, set it against the lee of the pine, then leaned against the trunk and turned toward the swale. The wind sorely punished my face. I watched into the storm until the biting blast drove me behind the tree long enough to ease the freezing of my cheeks. When I resumed my position alongside the pine, the aching returned.

The doe had come from the direction of the brook and turned toward the willow swamp. I decided to watch by the pine until the wind chill forced me to move.

Half an hour passed. I tucked for the third time behind the pine for momentary relief. The wind and snow continued their frantic dance.

I eased back to the side of the pine and suddenly felt the seeping cold vanish as the adrenaline-inducing form of a deer took definition through the swirling snow. The swirls cleared for an instant to reveal the deer in full.

It was a buck! A very large buck! Passing in front of me from left to right toward the brook. Opposite the way the doe had come. Closer than the doe. Barely thirty yards. Unaware of my plastered presence against the pine. Unaware as I reached around the trunk for the case and slid the rifle from it in haste as the deer continued away to my right in a steady walk.

The wind hampered my attempt to hold the scope on the deer. Brush and whirling snow hid the brown form as I struggled in growing frustration to settle the crosshairs. A line of trees shielded the deer. I shifted around to the front of the pine. The buck continued straight away, his angle taking him hopelessly deeper into the brush and the storm. The wind rocked me relentlessly. I rested the rifle against the pine. The deer became lost behind a growth of whitened brush. Then he reappeared, a vague shadow in the blowing snow, fading away. The storm was about to envelope him completely when the buck turned right toward the ridge above the brook, took a few steps, then broke into a startled run as the rifle recoiled. He dashed a few headlong yards before stumbling and falling, coming to rest in a drift of snow while the blizzard roared over him mounding fresh flakes upon his dark winter coat. A marker of antlers rose high above the drift.

I struggled through the snow to the deer. He was a splendid eight-point, possibly the largest-bodied whitetail I had ever taken, with an impressively wide-spreading rack. I dressed the buck, then plowed back to the pine, deciding to leave the heavy task of dragging him out until the blizzard subsided. The buck would keep as well in the snow by the swale as at the trailer.

The storm continued but the pine offered some shelter. The excitement and exertion had warmed me. Deer were moving and there were nearly four hours before dark. But no other deer moved through my little stormy world the rest of the afternoon, at least none that I could see.

The blizzard raged through the night. It was still roaring down from the north when I looked out in the predawn darkness upon a blustery forest buried deep in white. Yet, the dawning called.

A bonus permit enabled me to continue hunting after filling my buck tag. Hunters in the same party could also fill each other's tags—with the agreement of the tag holder, of course—a Wisconsin hunting tradition tracing back over a hundred years. We decided to hunt in concert for Rob's buck in keeping with that time-honored tradition.

I stepped out of the trailer into knee-high snow and turned my steps toward the swale. When I reached it, I looked for the buck. He lay completely buried under the snow, even his upturned antlers, spreading a few inches shy of two feet, remained invisible. I left him in frozen repose and watched by the pine until the inevitable wind chill sent me moving.

The wind continued full but the snow fell with less volume. Nearly twenty-four inches had accumulated in places. Movement through the deeper, wind-blown drifts became slow and labored. The exertion quickly banished the chill. I plowed north into the wind, covering much of the same ground as the preceding day and swinging through new areas that showed an occasional furrowed track. I followed one track a short distance into a deep swamp but soon gave up in the cascading labyrinth of willows and falling snow.

Time passed more rapidly than my slow passage through the whitened winter wonderland. By afternoon the snow had let up although the wind continued to pound out of the north, sending cloudy swirls in an icy dance through the glaciered forest.

I came with the coming of the final two hours to the swale and to the company of the great pine. Winter held its absolute rule over the forest. The wind continued bitter out of the north. Within half an hour it had stolen away the warmth from my exertions. I huddled against the pine seeking some measure of comfort from its protecting closeness. The deepening-gray skies hung low, hidden at times by snowy swirls and blowing snow from the swaying trees. Evening began to descend.

Then, out of the swirls and the gloaming, a deer emerged from the thicket along the brook, following the same general line as the doe the day before. But it was not the doe. Heavy antlers adorned the deer's head. The buck angled right past the brook on a line toward the ridge where the buck of the day before lay. I fought the same wind in an almost eerie repetition of my frenzied moves of the afternoon before. It seemed a dream repeating itself. The wind blew. I struggled to capture the deer in the scope. He pushed on through the brush and swirls. I finally captured him in a desperate push against the tree to steady myself, and fired.

The buck broke into a run, dashing up the slope behind a screening of brush and maples that defeated my attempts for a second shot. I hurried as fast as the drifted snow allowed to his furrowed tracks, followed them a few steps, and saw with satisfaction the telltale red brightening his route. I pushed on a few more steps and came upon the buried buck of the day before, which the wounded buck had jumped over in his flight. Then up the slight incline into a snow-clad mixture of flocked conifers and hardwoods.

The wind blew strong against my back. The buck's tracks trended south. The white snow exaggerated the spreading spots of blood. I pushed on in his furrowed track, letting the deer break the trail, nervous with the wind gusting ahead of me, hoping the force of it would dissipate my scent, wanting to get a line before attempting a circle ahead of his route.

I followed slowly, as much from necessity as from caution. The deep snow took a toll of energy. But the buck was fighting it too. His trail wove through dense-brushed maples and around snow-clad pines. The blood spots indicated a hit in the right front. If the wound was slowing him, it was not apparent. I pushed as fast as possible in his wake, weaving through the trees, hoping he would steady on a course, feeling the wind driving hard behind me, watching intently.

The buck exploded from his bed. He bounded away, white flag bouncing through the evergreens as the rifle came to my shoulder and the scope isolated the fleeing buck for an instant when I fired after the disappearing form in a desperate attempt as the trees swallowed him.

I pushed ahead to the bed. The bloodied indent confirmed a hit in the right front. But it gave no indication of how severe. I followed his frantic jumps, sensing a miss with my last shot as each continuing bound plowed through the deep drifts. The buck soon settled into a steady gait. I followed with a sense of growing hopelessness. The buck did not appear to be severely wounded, he was pacing relentlessly, knowing danger was on his trail, wind in his favor, daylight fading, security assured with the coming dark.

There seemed little point in attempting to circle ahead of the deer with daylight soon to be gone. I resolved to follow as long as light remained and resume trailing in the morning. Still I moved cautiously, straining to watch far ahead into the brush in the direction of his tracks.

The north wind moaned relentlessly through the trees. Even with my exertions a chill came from time to time as I halted in the furrowed trail to scrutinize the brush. Evening began its darkening. The deep gloaming intensified the seeping cold. The dark forest began to loose definition against the gray sky. The winter pierced deep.

I pushed on, coming to an abrupt slope that angled down into a deep-cut draw. A small rill carrying runoff from the lake lay hidden beneath the snow and ice at its bottom. The deer's tracks led down into the draw. I eased carefully toward the edge of the slope and came to a sudden halt, riveted like a statue in half-step.

The buck was bedded there! Twenty-five yards away! Antlered head up and alert. Looking toward the rill. Body in a straight line facing away from me. Motionless in the snow.

I moved with infinite caution, bringing the rifle to my shoulder. The wind pushed hard behind me. The deer paid no heed. I tried to settle the crosshairs on the buck's spine above his lungs. The wind rocked. The trigger squeezed. And the antlered head lowered slowly into the snow.

I stood awhile looking down at the deer. The dusk had yet to hide the bottom of the draw. Brush and willows guarded the hidden rill and climbed part way up the winter-white slope. The dense forest stood stark in the gathering gloom. The wind drove a chill through me, stealing away the rush of warming excitement. Still I waited a little longer, letting the primal feelings ebb, then stepped over the edge and followed the furrowed trail down to the deer.

He was another splendid eight-point. Not as wide beamed as the first, but close. I knelt to examine the buck. My first shot hit below the right shoulder without penetrating the vital area. No evidence existed of the second shot. I dressed him, climbed out of the draw, and followed around the lake to the hill the trailer sat upon. The wind moaned wearily through the night.

We retrieved both deer the following morning, laying them side by side in the snow where Rob took a picture of me with them, and in turn asked me to take a picture of him with the bucks. Both sets of antlers were added to the set taken the first year for display in the cabin Rob was planning to build on the hill overlooking the lake.

In the afternoon I backtracked the second buck and found where he had bedded in the open stand of maples sometime during the day after I quit watching it. He left that bed and followed along the brushy brook to where he came into view in the afternoon. Both bucks were headed toward the ridge above the brook, but to where beyond that was impossible to know.

We had a challenge getting out the next day. The lane lay deeply drifted. I forced a track with my Blazer down and up the steep hill through the spring seep, backing and then surging forward over and over until the level on the top was reached. We fastened a tow chain to Rob's truck, and with my Blazer's four wheels churning, the chain straining, and Rob's truck's two rear wheels spinning, reached the top of the hill, where the Blazer then broke a trail out to a plowed road.

I journeyed back to the snow-clad North Woods for the final weekend but saw nothing more of deer except their tracks. Rob finished the season on his home property in the south where he took a nice doe. Rob elected to hunt on his southern property the following year. He sold his northern property the next summer.

I returned to the Chequamegon, camping in my Blazer, roaming unhindered, accepting the deer-empty days as part of the trade-off for the spell of the North Woods, and glorying in those red-letter days when the path of the weary hunter at last crosses the path of the wary buck.

Deer there are in those hallowed northlands, although not in the concentrations to be found in the agricultural lands to the south. Nor do the unbroken expanses of the great forest typically offer as many sightings. But one still clings stubbornly to the solitary roaming of the north country, testing the ways of the wild, bending as one must to the whims of the weather, needing the wilderness quest to give the shooting meaning, and dreaming always of a stormy opening weekend, when a great blizzard briefly parted its swirling snows for a pair of wondrous moments in memory.

Chapter 20

In The Land Of The Ojibwa

In the beginning there was only Kitche Manido, the Great Spirit. Nothing else existed. Kitche Manido created the four basic elements—water, rock, wind, and fire. From them Kitche Manido formed the stars and the sun and the moon and the earth. Then Kitche Manido caused the plants and the trees to grow upon the earth and created birds to fly in the air and animals to roam upon the land and fish to swim in the waters. And in the forming, Kitche Manido imbued every part of creation with a spirit and a purpose in the Circle of Life.

Last of all Kitche Manido created the Anishinabe, original man.

After a time a great flood came upon the earth. All the animals in their turn dove into the flood seeking land, but the spirit waters held the land deep. Near the last the humble muskrat dove in its turn and emerged clutching in its paws a particle of soil. From this the earth was re-created.

In those days the Anishinabe lived by the Great Salt Sea in the east. Then a vision of a megis, a cowrie shell, led them westward to the Great Lakes. They found fish to catch and game to hunt and sugar maples to tap and wild rice to harvest. And they dwelled upon these promising lands. They dwell upon them still. And still among themselves they are the Anishinabe, original man. Among the others, they are the Ojibwa.

-1-

The land of the Ojibwa extends far into the Ontario wilderness. I cast my gaze north toward those pristine woods and waters. Spring of 1993 found me northeast of Sault Ste. Marie, or Bowating as the original Ojibwa inhabitants called it, where a fine black bear ultimately rewarded nine arduous days of hunting. The first days of autumn found me again in Ontario, this time on a land and air route toward the far northern Ojibwa village of Webequie, there to search beyond its island confines for the illusive moose.

Highway 17 angles northwest out of Thunder Bay. Along its route you cross an imperceptible ridge and pass into the Arctic Watershed. All waters beyond that ridge flow north into the Arctic Ocean. Highway 599 turns north from 17 on a long wilderness trek to Pickle Lake. Beyond Pickle Lake you must fly, or canoe and portage, to Webequie, except during an eight-week period in February and March when a three hundred mile ice road is plowed in a twisting route across the frozen lakes. Supply trucks make a three-day trip to Webequie over this tortuous route, crawling cautiously along to prevent the ice from buckling.

Webequie is situated on a large island set in the midst of a lake-rich wilderness. The village of six hundred and fifty occupies the north end of the island. A dirt runway covers a few cleared acres at the southern end. We circled the runway once before landing, waiting for a grader to finish smoothing the roughened surface.

I transferred my gear into a cramped, two-seater floatplane and was soon airborne again for a twenty-minute flight into an outlying lake. There I met two Ojibwas, Ronald and Marlin.

Ronald, my guide, was the older, several years my senior. He spoke no English. Marlin, a young man in his twenties from a neighboring village, served as interpreter.

My gear was shortly organized in a corner of a small, dirt-floored log cabin with a metal-drum stove centered between a built-in bunk and a cooking counter. The guides had pitched a makeshift tent between the cabin and the lake for themselves. Drinking water came from the lake. A deep hole for food storage was dug behind the cabin. Meats and other perishables were wrapped in plastic bags, buried in the cool earth, and dug up as needed.

Noon had passed by the time everyone was ready. We loaded a twenty-foot freighter canoe and set out into a maze of lakes and connecting waterways. A warming sun highlighted our passage along the green-shielded shorelines.

The sun's warmth faded with the afternoon. A cold front began clouding the sky, making raingear a welcome windbreak from the chilling air. We scouted areas familiar to Ronald, finding one set of large tracks that he proclaimed to be those of a bull before completing a large circle back to camp. The sky continued gray and Ronald indicated we would not hunt that evening because of threatening rain.

The rain came an hour later, a light drizzle that intensified into a heavy downpour. I suggested to Ronald and Marlin that they might be more comfortable sleeping in the cabin, but they demurred and after supper slogged through the rain to their tented shelter. Perhaps the mice reportedly sharing the cabin dissuaded them.

The rain continued through the night and into the morning. Ronald arrived at seven-thirty and built a fire that soon had me standing by the open door in a tee-shirt. A light rain continued to fall. The woods dripped. A gloomy, soggy day.

We got underway at ten o'clock with me in the bow of the canoe, Ronald handling a fifteen-horsepower Johnson outboard motor, and Marlin in the middle with a shotgun. The rain subsided but the skies continued an oppressive gray with a dampness that chilled deep as we sped across open water between our probings into sheltered bays.

Marlin's shotgun regularly shattered the silence as the bays revealed resting flocks of ducks and geese. Scattered flights raced south in the gusty, lowering sky, a number of them launched by Marlin's repeated shooting. A drake and two hen mallards, a black duck, and two Canada geese eventually added their weight to the canoe. Ronald and Marlin seemed immensely pleased, but the incessant shooting began to wear on me.

We stopped in midafternoon for a shore lunch of fresh caught walleyes, beans, bread, and coffee. The warming fire and the warming coffee helped displace the chilling damp.

After lunch we crossed to another bay where I was stationed by the canoe while Ronald and Marlin set off into the woods carrying rifles and shotguns. Time passed. Six shots echoed through the forest. Honking geese clamored overhead. Ronald appeared an hour later, followed in fifteen minutes by Marlin. They had no geese. We returned to camp.

The skies began to clear an hour before sunset, but unlike the evening, my mood was anything but sunny. I questioned Ronald through Marlin about the duck and goose shooting while we were supposedly moose hunting. We were scouting, I was told. Beyond that I could get no satisfactory answer.

An early rising the next morning. Clear skies promised a perfect day. We scouted again in a repeat of the morning before.

Rocky shorelines dense with birch and spruce bent into hidden bays where smooth shores revealed only our imprints as we searched yet another bay and another for elusive sign. Geese erupted noisily out of several of the bays, but the shotguns remained silent.

A narrow isthmus blocked our way at one point. Ronald and Marlin portaged the canoe while I carried its contents across the sparsely timbered isthmus to a winding river. Tracks of a large moose showed prominently there. We drifted silently with the river in intense scrutiny but saw nothing as the river widened into another lake.

We crossed the lake to a small island. A picturesque bay indenting into the island made an idyllic setting for a shore lunch of northern pike, beans, bread, and tea. The afternoon continued glorious. Wisps of broken clouds danced across the blue heavens, encouraged by a westerly wind that settled into an intermittent breeze.

By four o'clock we were back at camp where coffee provided welcome warmth before the evening's hunt. Other than the tracks by the river, we had seen no sign of moose.

At five o'clock we headed south into a new area. Marlin fashioned a moose call during our stop at the cabin and said we would call that evening. We came in time to an elongated bay where the motor fell silent. We quietly paddled through reed beds for half a mile before beaching the canoe.

I remained along the shore while Ronald and Marlin set off with their rifles and shotguns. Ronald stopped in sight near the bay while Marlin disappeared into the woods. The silence was soon broken by six shotgun blasts. Geese roared lustily down the bay. Two shots from Ronald dropped one of them. He returned and we paddled out to retrieve the goose. Three more shots from the direction of Marlin. We paddled up the bay, scraping noisily through shallow stretches, and retrieved Marlin along with two geese and a drake pintail, then splashed around the bay looking for wounded geese. We found none.

Again we beached the canoe. Ronald headed south with his rifle and shotgun. Marlin and I sat down in the marsh grass by the bay.

"We are waiting for the moose," he informed me. I sat incredulous for the half-hour that remained before dark. Only a moose struck deaf would venture near that bay. At least Marlin did not add to the pretense by using his call.

I had a less than satisfactory conversation with Ronald through Marlin when we returned to the cabin. Marlin's English was passable but doubts remained about whether Ronald and I were truly communicating. I gathered that I was being exposed to some local culture along with my moose hunt. I tried to convey that I could do with a little less culture and a little more moose hunt.

At least the night was satisfactory. A brilliant half-moon nestled in the star-studded heavens. I stood outside long after Ronald and Marlin disappeared into their tent, glorying in the wilderness. I listened for a loon, but only silence filled the night.

Marlin brought his shotgun down to the canoe in the morning, then saw me and returned it to his tent. The sun was well up by the time we got underway. Our route took us south to a small bay where a feeder stream emerged from the forest. We left the canoe and followed up the stream on foot. The confined stream gradually opened into a broad waterway with extended marshes flanking both sides. Moose tracks showed enticingly along the way. Beyond the marshes the forest closed in again and we looped through the dense woodland to emerge on another large bay. No tracks were in evidence. We followed along the lakeshore to the feeder stream and our canoe.

We pushed off into the lake. A wind had come up, chilling our passage to the bay of the previous evening's goose shoot. We beached the canoe at the entrance to the bay and scouted the surrounding woods. Not surprisingly, no moose tracks were found. We returned to the canoe and paddled toward the head of the bay. The wind buffeted us, testing our energies at the paddles.

The sheltered head of the bay brought welcome relief from the wind. We pulled the canoe onto shore and ate lunch. A light rain started. We donned raingear and headed into the woods. Ronald led, keeping a steady pace through deep stands of spruce and boggy swamps. A burned-over area held initial promise, but the fire had been too recent for the emerging growth to yet entice moose. The soot from the burned trees blackened our raingear. Blowdowns impeded our progress. Ronald kept a steady pace through our three-hour circle back to the bay. Not a sign of a moose in our less than stealthy passage through the bush.

We boiled a kettle of tea in the rain, then paddled through the bay to the lake and were back in camp by two-thirty.

Two hours passed. The light rain continued. We sat in idleness. Finally I suggested we head back out. Marlin then informed me that they had to make a supply run to a distant camp and did not expect to be back until eight or nine o'clock. The pleasant prospect of a solo hunt intrigued me, but without a canoe my hunt would be confined to the sign-empty area around camp. I said I would go with them, hoping for a sighting along the way. There was none. We were back in camp by six o'clock. We did not hunt that evening.

A heavy fog shrouded my early arising the next morning. I made pancakes for breakfast. Marlin complained of a toothache. I gave him some Tylenol. The fog cleared by nine o'clock and we struck out to the north. Weaving waterways guided our passage through the clearing morning. A glorious day opened. I faced into the wind and watched the grand panorama pass in review. There was still the wonder of the country and the pleasure of being immersed in its unbridled wilds.

We crossed a large lake where a rock-filled channel on the far side required a lighter canoe. I enjoyed a diverting walk while Ronald and Marlin poled the canoe through the rocks. We paddled a short distance beyond the channel passage to where a well-tracked-up pathway revealed the thrilling sight of fresh rub marks on four separate saplings. We tread silently over a profusion of prints until another bay opened ahead. Marlin called once. Five minutes passed. "No moose," said Marlin. We left.

Back to the canoe and off across the lake to another bay where a cut portage connected to a second bay. Tracks abounded. Ronald sat down on a log. Marlin moved away and called repeatedly. A few minutes passed. Marlin moved another hundred yards. More calling. "No moose," he said, and we returned to the canoe. The time was noon.

A long boat ride took us through a magnificent, sun-filled afternoon. Scattered clouds showcased their whiteness in the brilliant blue sky. We wove a circuitous route through the emerald-green landscape to another sparkling bay and ate lunch in another idyllic setting. The venue was sublime.

After lunch we paddled up the bay and carefully examined a marshy point of land. There was no sign. We paddled across the bay and secured the canoe out of sight. Ronald stayed with the canoe while Marlin and I found a comfortable spot to watch the signless point across the bay.

The afternoon wore on. Three mallards set down on cupped wings and busied themselves in the marshy shallows tipping for pond seeds. A bumblebee buzzed within reach, spreading pollen as it darted from wild flower to wild flower. Two bald eagles soared majestically overhead, circling in lazy drifts high above the spruce. Six or eight small birds suddenly swooped into the marsh grass fifty yards away, too fast to count or identify. Then a whooshing sound alerted me to a hawk, pressing close to the marsh grass above the hidden birds. They did not flush. The hawk eventually soared away. I never did see the little birds leave.

Two hours passed. Marlin returned to the canoe for his call. Twice the grunting tone broke the stillness. At five-thirty, with the prime of evening close upon us, we left and returned to camp.

We would not hunt the following day. It seemed the reason had something to do with Ronald's religious beliefs. I said I would hunt on my own, but the canoe was not at my disposal. The evening passed in watching Ronald and Marlin straighten their fish net.

I lay awake in the night listening to a strong wind blowing. Rain drops pelted the roof of the cabin. The wind and rain began to clamor. The angry elements stormed on in a kindred mood.

Heavy rain at dawn. I arose, dressed, made breakfast, then stood by the open door sipping coffee while I watched the morning pass in the rain. Ronald and Marlin slept in. The rain stopped around nine-thirty. Marlin came into the cabin after the rain and lit a fire which nearly drove me out. Ronald came in half an hour later and fried some pork chops and chicken in a pan full of lard for their breakfast.

I talked again with Marlin questioning whether he would hunt. Ronald could stay in camp in respect of his convictions. Marlin deferred to the older man, but after some discussion, he said we would go out that afternoon.

At one-thirty we pushed off and made a circle into a bay behind camp. The canoe was beached and we hiked through the woods for forty-five minutes to another bay. Along the way we stopped once and Marlin called. When the bay was reached, he called again. It started to rain. We waited ten minutes and retraced our route to the canoe and back to camp, arriving at three-forty-five. We hunted no more that day.

I awoke in the dark to the rush of a heavy wind. I lay in my sleeping bag listening to the elements surge outside. A rustling of some creature in the corner where the food was stored intruded on the night. Too rambunctious to be a mouse, and too comfortable in my sleeping bag to get up to see what it was. The rustling continued. I yelled. It quieted for a while. I turned over and went back to sleep.

Six-thirty. I got up and looked out upon a striking scene. The forest lay cloaked in a light mantle of snow. The wind had ceased and the morning broke in fresh-whitened silence.

Ronald came into the cabin at seven o'clock and lit a fire. We ate bannock for breakfast. The bannock had been fried in lard the night before. A heavy film of white fat coated the surface. Ronald ate it with relish. I broke the bannock open and ate the flour inside.

Marlin came in at eight-thirty. His tooth still bothered. I gave him some more Tylenol. He had seen marten tracks in the snow. Perhaps my cabin mate.

An hour after Marlin's arrival, we set off in the canoe through a frost-tinged wonderland for my final day. We stopped first at the spot where their fish net had been placed the evening before and hauled it into the canoe. Twenty good-sized suckers and whitefish struggled in the net along with two northern pike, one of respectable size. Three walleyes also flopped about and were released into the bottom of the canoe for lunch. The net with the rest of the fish was returned to the lake for later retrieval.

The wind returned, blowing scattered snow squalls across the lake and cutting through our clothes. We pounded over the water in a frigid crossing, arriving at an inlet and connecting stream where we warmed some during a hundred-yard portage around a beaver dam. At the end of the portage we came to a mile-wide lake stretching three miles to the north. We loaded the canoe and paddled along the south shore until a small, high-banked stream turned us into its shelter. Marlin called once. Five minutes passed. We left.

The motor hummed dully as we crossed to the far end of the lake. There we beached the canoe and a fire soon banished some of the chill while we filleted the walleyes and set the coffee pot to boil. Two hours elapsed over lunch. Three o'clock passed before we got underway.

Halfway down the lake, Ronald turned toward shore. A hill rose sharply to the east. The route over it through a profusion of blowdowns gave my legs a good workout. A near hour of walking brought us to another lake. While Marlin sent the first of several calls over its surface, Ronald found a comfortable place to lay down and went to sleep. No response to Marlin's calls except for the haunting refrain of a loon that swam into view seventy-five yards away. Over and over the loon sent its spectral cry through the windswept wilds. A grand and glorious refrain, the absolute embodiment of all that is wild and free and mystical.

Ronald awakened in half an hour and we returned to the canoe and camp with a good hour and a half of prime evening remaining. Ronald and Marlin trooped to the cabin to prepare their meal while I stood alongside the lake and watched streaks of white form against the deepening, purple clouds.

The evening came in hushed shadings. Wind-rippled waters lapped in gentle rhythm against the lakeshore rocks. There were no loons to offer a wilderness aria, but the soaring refrain from the earlier loon still echoed in my memory. The night did not hurry, nor did I hurry from the night.

The marten, or whatever it was, rattled about the cabin during the dark hours, keeping me half-awake. I tried to scare it off without success. The commotion disturbed me yet another time at six o'clock. I got up, lit a candle and a fire, ate breakfast, packed my duffel bag, and waited for the floatplane. It arrived at eight-thirty and set me down in Pickle Lake an hour and twenty minutes later.

When I returned home, I made arrangements to withhold payment for the supposed hunt and contacted those in charge. A reply came shortly.

October 16, 1993

Dear John,

Our sincere regrets over your experience of moose hunting. We thought we had everything in place to provide a quality moose hunt but your comments have proven we have some serious work to do before the next moose season.

Please understand our intent was to provide you with a well-organized, well-guided moose hunt.

We, the Chief and Council, would like to invite you back to take part in the 1994 moose hunt. All expenses from Pickle Lake north will be taken care of including flights, guides, meals, and accommodations. We will supply you with a moose tag. All you have to do is purchase your hunting license and get to Pickle Lake.

We hope this gesture will convince you that we are serious and would like to rectify problems we encounter.

We look forward to your reply.

-2-

A change in flight plans took me to Nakina instead of Pickle Lake the following year. The route turned northeast from Thunder Bay on Highway 11 through scenery that was both familiar and new. Two days of steady driving brought me from my home to road's end at a small terminal building beside a dirt airstrip. I camped for the night awaiting a morning flight.

You know you are in good country when Bearskin Airlines is stenciled across the fuselage of your airplane and the pilot informs you he will be stopping in Lansdowne House, Webequie, Summer Beaver, and Muskrat Dam.

We taxied down the dirt runway and lifted off at ten-fifteen, rising over a hazy wilderness of endless green and blue. After a brief touchdown at Lansdowne House to deliver supplies, the familiar runway at Webequie came into view. We landed at fifteen minutes after noon and my gear was transferred to the floatplane dock to await my flight into camp.

The floatplane arrived a little before two o'clock, and shortly thereafter, we were airborne. The pilot had trouble with his directions and he wove and circled over a confusing montage of lakes while we both searched for some indication of a camp. At last a small cabin appeared. Two figures emerged from it. Down onto the lake, the pontoons skimming the water until they grabbed and settled.

Two Ojibwa brothers, Stephen and Johnson, greeted me. Stephen spoke halting English while Johnson's English was on a par with my near nonexistent Ojibwa. Johnson and I smiled at each other a lot.

The cabin was situated on the brother's trap line. They showed me to a small tent pitched a short distance from the cabin and indicated that would be my quarters. I arranged my sleeping bag and duffel, gathered my raingear and rifle, and barely four and a half hours after leaving Nakina, found myself setting off once more into the glorious northern wilds.

We were two in the canoe, Stephen and I, and we presently immersed ourselves in a network of interconnecting lakes. Pines, spruce, poplar, and birch spread unbroken along the shores except for an extensive area that showed the stark effects of a recent fire. A small copse of unaffected trees glinted gold and green and red amid the scorched desolation, a reminder of what once was and a beacon of hope for what would be again. Second growth was already well underway, tempting browse for the antlered denizens that roamed these forests. The sun attended us brilliantly.

Several bays revealed only a single set of tracks, whether bull or cow I could not say. Stephen simply shook his head. A narrow stream meandering through bogs and meadowed openings drew us deeper into sheltered glades. We paddled up the stream until boggy shallows halted us. A quiet, secretive mood filtered through the hidden glades as the shadows began to suggest the moment when day-shy creatures began their emergence into the night.

We waited for the twilight, then began a stealthy passage back down the stream, searching around each new twisting as it revealed a fresh perspective. The lake came into view without a hoped-for glimpse of a moose. A full moon shone upon us by the time we reached camp. After a late supper of pork chops, boiled potatoes, and coffee, I settled into the tent where my sleeping bag soon banished the chill that came with the night.

Stephen and I were underway well before first light the following morning. The full moon guided us upon a mystical passage over dark waters that parted seamlessly before the canoe. The brisk air nipped enough to sense the north and I watched the mysterious forest cast eerie moon shadows that turned the shoreline waters a sheeny black, their wavering silhouettes reaching out for the light, reaching out for the morning, reaching out for the dawn and the hopes that come alive with it.

When enough light shaded through the forest, we paddled up the marsh stream of the preceding afternoon. The dawning offered promise but the tempting country remained as empty in the morning as it had been the evening before.

Another stream drew us until a beaver dam halted our progress. We secured the canoe and scouted for tracks. None appeared.

We searched along the shores, drifting from lake to lake as each far shoreline revealed a connecting way to another lake and still broader passages between them.

Heavy rain began around midmorning and Stephen made a hurried crossing to an old trapper's shelter that he told me Johnson had built. Patchwork canvas overhead guarded part of the dirt-floored area and we found welcome refuge from the downpour. We found little refuge from the wind, however. A gaping hole in one side of the canvas wall revealed where a black bear had gained entrance to the shelter, and a second gaping hole on the opposite side revealed where it had exited. In its heedless passage through the shelter, the bear ignored the doorway left open in an attempt to prevent such damage.

While we waited out the rain, Stephen rummaged through the debris left from the bear's intrusion and found a battered pan. The pan had seen better days but Stephen looked upon it as a treasure. He had forgotten to bring the coffee pot with him that morning.

The rain subsided but the cold front accompanying it kept my raingear in service as a windbreaker. The gray skies hovered above as we continued probing shorelines and bays. The fresh tracks of a cow and calf crossed a muddy stretch of shoreline, and a sandy point revealed several older tracks, but of bulls we found no recent sign.

Noon approached and the sun emerged from the passing rain clouds to bask the earth in drying warmth. Stephen pulled into a pleasant little cove where we enjoyed a lunch of fresh walleyes, beans, bread, and jam. The boiling coffee in the battered pan bubbled in merry accompaniment to the woodland music of a gurgling stream beside us.

After lunch we crossed to a promontory that overlooked an extensive burn area with its emerging second growth. Willows grew in profusion. A number of survivor trees scattered throughout the burn area showed off their autumn finery. Blackflies buzzed about, but not in sufficient numbers to bother.

We watched into midafternoon, then probed again along the shores, coming in time to a well-tracked-up sandy cove. We did not disturb it, but continued on. Intermittent rain followed our passage. One prolonged downpour forced us into another convenient trapper's shelter and we passed the time in halting attempts at conversation. I tried to pick up some basic Ojibwa words and drew a smile with my attempt at "Shoot big moose."

The rain finally let up and the battered pan came into service to bail out the canoe. We made our soggy way back to camp in a graying drizzle, but the darkening clouds began to show signs of breaking up as I tramped to my tent after supper. Rain had managed to trickle through the tent but my sleeping bag escaped the dampness and the heavy canvas duffel bag protected a change of dry clothes.

On our way by six o'clock the following morning. Dark with the night, and overcast. Johnson handled the stern while Stephen saw us off. I gathered their plan was to alternate days with me, allowing the other a chance to rest and catch up on camp chores.

We repeated the previous morning, looking for fresh tracks made during the night. The day continued gray and overcast, with a sharp cold that made the wind-sheltered bays a welcome refuge. Moose no doubt moved through the night, but by noon we had yet to discover where.

The first afternoon hour passed as we worked our way up a narrowing, rocky channel where we beached the canoe below a step-sloped waterfall. The rushing waters cascaded boisterously down and around jumbled boulders into a pool that yielded a walleye at nearly every cast. We filleted enough fish for lunch and topped them off with peanut butter and jelly sandwiches for desert. A patch of blue formed in the sky while we sipped coffee after lunch. The chill of the morning tempered and we lingered in the idyllic setting, soaking up warmth from the fire and the softening air.

It was two-thirty before we got underway. The rocky channel gradually widened into a deeper flow that broadened into a shallow bay. Thick reeds grew head-high around the edges and we paddled through them to emerge in an opening that continued to a stretch of shoreline backed by dense pines and birch. We beached the canoe and within a few yards of our landing place came upon a stirring sight. A set of large tracks crossed the light-colored sand, their mounded edges still dark and damp in the afternoon sun. We looked at each other and smiled.

We pushed off the canoe and paddled around a point that hid us from the bay, then slid the canoe into some reeds and stepped to shore. Johnson found a birch tree that suited his purpose and peeled a patch of bark from it. He rolled the birch bark into a cone and put it into the canoe. Then the waiting began.

The hours passed. We sat on the shore in silence. No need to converse, even had we been able to. Knowing without saying what the waiting was for. Accepting it. Letting the day drift. Letting patience take control. Waiting for the shadows. Steeling for the test that would come with the dusk. Trusting to the tracks. Trusting to our sense of them. Trusting to the coming moment. Trusting that the moment would come.

Evening descended. The sun dropped behind the trees and we eased the canoe out of the reeds and hugged the shadowed western shore. We paddled in silence, blending with the hush of evening. Reeds parted and closed softly behind us, our passing no more than the whisper of a murmuring breeze. Shadows darkened along the shore. Light dimmed over the silent waters. The evening came full upon us.

Then a murmur beyond the breeze held our paddles in mid-stroke. A subdued swishing. To our right front. We stopped and listened. The reeds blocked our view. Again the swishing, faint yet distinct in the stillness. I set my paddle silently down. It came then the time for Johnson.

He eased the canoe forward as I feathered a round into the chamber. I strained to see through the reeds. Twilight filled the spaces down into the dusk. Silence beyond the silence. Gliding with the silence. Our movement imperceptible but for the parting reeds. Ahead to a thinning in the reeds. Staring. Staring. Dusk drawing closing shadows into darkness. No noise to guide my eyes. Casting right toward the last sound. Straining. Straining.

A gentle rock of the canoe. I turned to Johnson. He stared straight ahead. I looked, and out of a shadow on the shore, against the lightness of the dying marsh grass, a darker shadow emerged. The dark shadow became an object outlining antlers faint against the light brown grass. Then into the shadows again. I could not find the dark shadow in the scope.

The canoe whispered forward, closing on the shadows, one of the shadows moving, but always into deeper shadows that blended into oneness.

A muffled grunt coughed through the birch-bark cone. The dark shadow stopped. Again a muffled grunt. No movement from the dark shadow.

Forward into the gloaming, the scope drawing desperately on the fading vestiges of light, trying to fathom a shape, an antlered form in the gathering dusk.

Another muffled grunt. Silence from the shadows. On through the reeds, straining to define the form. Sensing it more than seeing it. Wishing it then to move, but Johnson holding it in place with yet another muffled grunt.

A pause and then ahead, gliding through the darkening, staring, staring, my world reduced to a phantom form wrapped in dimness. Searching as our gliding slows and the coughing grunt holds still the dark shadow.

Deep into the dusk, closing on the shadow, closing until the gathered light in the scope finds form among the formless shadows and the parting reeds reveals the form staring hard toward the ill-defined motion edging toward it through the deepening traces.

Then thunder and lightning peal and flash through the gloaming.

Whoomp! The sound of a bullet striking. Bolt up, back, forward, down. Again the peal and the flash. Whoomp! Again the loading. Again the silence shattered. Again the whoomp!

Then movement by the dark shadow. To the right. Slow. Deliberate.

Willows blocking the walking shadow. Magazine empty. Another cartridge finding its way in haste from the belt carrier to the chamber. Defining the moving form through the willows. Hearing the sharpness of the report and the dull whoomp echoing back. And watching in growing dismay as the dark shadow walks on.

Right hand reaching again in haste for another cartridge. Nervousness threatening. Fingers fumbling the cartridge into the chamber. Rifle up. Capturing the front of the moving form in the scope. Stilling the nervousness while the trigger squeezes. Whoomp!

And still the dark shadow walks on.

Another round grasped with tension mounting. Looking down for an instant to insert the cartridge and looking up to see the dark shadow slowing then holding in the other shadows while the scope searches and at last captures the dark shadow as it settles slowly into the waiting shadows of the ground. Feeling the rising flood of relief and elation. Then letting the flood surge through me while the calm of the coming night washes full around.

I held the rifle on the dim form until Johnson stepped out of the canoe, then got out and walked to the fallen animal. The great beast lay still upon the earth. We stood a moment in contemplation. The forest fell into absolute silence. I would have remained longer in the silence, but Johnson reached for his knife and the magic slowly dissolved. We came down into the mundane.

The darkening prevented a careful examination of the moose as we worked to dress it without any light. Camp lay two hours away and Johnson indicated that we would leave the quartering and packing for the next day. We returned to the canoe and began a spellbound circuit through the night. A full moon rose, transforming the lakes and forest into a magically enchanted land. The weird play of moonlight in the dark soon confused my directions and even Johnson halted at times to puzzle out his route. On a few occasions I thought we would be spending the night on one of the moonlit islands, and I began to look forward to what would perfectly cap a day already growing matchless in memory. But Johnson pushed onward and we at last passed a large boulder rising from the water that I recognized. Not long thereafter a lonely light flickered far off in the dark. Stephen was guiding his brother home. We had been gone seventeen hours.

Up at seven o'clock the next morning. Pancakes served for a quick breakfast. Johnson stayed in camp while Stephen and

I retraced the long route of the night before. Nothing looked the same in the daylight, and as we wove through the multi-channeled waterways and lakes, I marveled that Johnson had been able to give his brother precise directions to the moose.

The daylight allowed me to examine the animal more closely. All five shots appeared to have been solid hits. The vitality of those great beasts is humbling to behold. I was using my .338 Winchester Magnum. Of five other moose taken with those same two hundred and fifty grain Nosler bullets, only two fell to a single shot, although none of the others required as many as the bull of that evening. It is worthy of note, given the relative power of the two calibers, that three moose taken with my .270 Winchester succumbed to a single shot each.

My help with the quartering was limited to holding a leg while Stephen, with only a regular belt knife, had the moose ready for transport in less than half an hour. We left nothing behind except hide and entrails. Everything else is consumed by the Ojibwa, including the nose, which Stephen told me was a delicacy. I kept a small portion of the meat for myself and the rest went to the village.

Walleyes and northerns and roaming that grand country filled my days before the time came to leave. Stephen, Johnson, and I stood on the lakeshore as the faint sound of the floatplane coming to get me drifted out of the east. Stephen asked if I'd had a good hunt and I told him I had. Would I come again, he wondered? I said I would. Next year, he questioned? No, I replied, I had other plans. When, he pressed? Two years, I promised. I would come in two years. He smiled and said that would be good, and we turned to watch the floatplane skim down upon the lake.

The flight to Webequie went smoothly although the little floatplane lifted slowly with a full load of moose meat cramped in with me and my gear. I had a layover in Webequie before my flight to Summer Beaver and Nakina, which gave me time to respond to a postscript that had been attached to the October sixteenth letter. It read:

NOTE: If at the end of the second hunt, you feel you have received services contracted for in the first hunt, payment could be made for the second hunt—your choice entirely!

I paid for the hunt.

-3-

I returned to that enchanted country two years later in keeping with my promise to Stephen. But the brothers settled into a routine of alternating days with me, and it was Johnson who shared the thrill of another fine moose taken at two-fifteen on a sunny afternoon.

Truly, it is the country that draws me as much as the game. The pristine forests and waterways of that remote northland would draw me more frequently were it not that other lands also compel me.

Two more years passed before my wanderings again brought me to the brother's trap line. Constant rain turned that hunt into one of constant frustration. I made plans to go into camp with Stephen by canoe, a six-hour journey with a portage around a challenging stretch of water called the Big Rapids, where the canoe has to be lined up by hand part of the way. The untamed Winisk River flows magnificently there. But the unrelenting wind and rain made the passage questionable. Two days were spent in a cabin in Webequie waiting out the weather. Finally, on the third day, it cleared enough for a floatplane to get me in.

The floatplane would have barely had time to return to Webequie before the heavy rains came again. I wore double raingear to try to ward off the incessant drenching. I fear I tried the brother's patience with my need to be out from dawn to dark regardless of the weather. The days passed without a single sighting.

On the last morning, Johnson and I started out in the dark, but Johnson turned the canoe around in half an hour and I could not fault him. The heavens poured. We sat the rest of the morning and most of the afternoon in camp, my thoughts as dismal as the weather. Then, with less than two hours remaining, Stephen offered me his heavy stormproof coat and Johnson and I set off into the rainy wilds.

There are incredibly magic moments that sometimes come when hope has faded into resignation. One came in the darkening of that rain-swept last evening when a bull moose materialized like an otherworld creature out of the gloaming.

I stood beside the lake, a few steps in front of my tent, and watched a rain squall patter its drops across the waters. The ripples calmed again with its passing. A heavy overcast hung like a blanket just above the trees, dark and foreboding except for wisps of gauzy gray that floated like airy tunnels through the black. I wondered if there were tunnels enough for the floatplane to get through. Then the faint throb of an engine pulsed through the vaporous corridors. A fleeting glimpse revealed a floatplane weaving through the darkened heavens, floating tiny and fragile through shifting wisps of dirty clouds, appearing then disappearing, its pontoons barely skimming the higher treetops beneath the clinging blanket of black.

It would be an interesting flight out.

Stephen came beside me and we watched the floatplane bank low.

"You will come again?"

"Yes."

"Next year?"

"No. I cannot. I have other plans."

"When?"

"Two years. I will come again in two years."

And I did.

Southern Nights

*There are muses
In the mountains and the plains,
And the southlands
Conjure up their own special enchantment.*

The snowbound days after New Year's tends to find big game seasons closed in the north. Smaller game still offer reasons to roam the winter woodlots, but those who dream of larger game find their thoughts turning southward.

January of 1994 saw me driving through a moderating climate toward Alabama. A nearly four-month deer season in that state continued until the first of February, and a limit of one deer a day offered tempting visions to a hunter accustomed to a home state limit of one or two deer a year.

My inclination to seek the north followed me even into Alabama, for I turned in that direction toward the hills above Princeton where I made arrangements to hunt on twelve thousand acres that abutted Tennessee.

Deer no doubt were plentiful there. One resident hunter I talked with had taken twenty-three so far that season. But the wary survivors of the season's first three months held deeply in the brush and the night.

Fog hid the morning the first two days. A heavy rain continued throughout the other days of my hunt. Three does moved out on a downward slope late the second day, but bucks remained well beyond my vision.

The hills, however, were a delight as well as a surprise. The country approached mountain status. One long ridge took me inadvertently into Tennessee, a discovery made when a small survey marker designating the state boundary caught my attention on the way back. There was little difference in still-hunting whitetails there than in Wisconsin, except for the absence of snow and the steepness of the terrain. The deer remained as elusive.

When next I headed toward Alabama in December of that same year, I traveled deeper into the south, arriving by airplane in Montgomery and continuing by rental car to Enterprise. My friend George met me there, having driven up from Florida to hunt deer with hounds with his Alabama cousins and offering me an opportunity to join in.

Hunting deer with hounds is part of the southern heritage. Classic authors like William Elliott and Archibald Rutledge have recorded the centuries-old tradition. Elliott and Rutledge were Carolina men, but their stirring accounts will invoke the passions of any southern houndsman.

My introduction to the tradition came the morning after my arrival when I made the acquaintance of several of George's cousins and their eager hounds. Of the hounds, Walkers predominated, a breed familiar from my coon hunting days in Wisconsin. Julys were a new breed to me, but the blueticks, redbones, and black-and-tans bore recognizable markings familiar from the many coon dog trials my friend Fred and I attended in Wisconsin during the fall. Fred's father had bred and trained coon hounds. Fred's expert knowledge acquired as a result garnered us more than a few winnings in first-line and first-tree stakes at the trials.

The morning assemblage of hunters turned out to be a gathering of the clan—as much a social outing as a hunt. Besides the cousins, there were friends of the cousins, and friends of the cousin's friends, and in all likelihood cousins of those friends. We presented a goodly lot in numbers. Knots of hunters large and small stood in groups and caught up on the latest doings of Billy Charles's Walker dog and David's squealy mouthed bitch, reputed to never quit once on the trail and identifiable by a distinctive voice that gave the hound her name.

The hunters were organized in near military fashion. George, a retired army colonel, no doubt could have brought more order to the proceedings, but he knew that even a general was outranked by the houndsmen setting up the morning's hunt. We stood compliant and fell in line with the other standers to march in single file along the edge of an extended woods bordering a large, fallow field. A similar woods stretched along the far side of the field. One by one we dropped off at hundred-yard intervals until our skirmish line presented a hopefully unpassable barrier to any deer driven our way. Shotguns were the only weapons permitted, with buckshot the only charge allowed.

The morning began sunny and pleasant. The hounds were taken to the other side of the heavy woods opposite the open field. We waited in the morning silence, eyes fastened across the field, ears tuned for the opening chorus of the symphony of the hounds.

Long before the first note reached us, a doe broke from the far woods and loped nonchalantly along its edge. Does were legal during that week between Christmas and New Year's, but the range would have presented a challenge even for a rifle. With a load of twelve-gauge, double-ought buckshot, the distance was impossible. The doe continued along the edge, turned, and disappeared back into the woods.

The faint cry of a hound wafted over the field shortly after the doe's disappearance. A second followed. Both hounds soon emerged from the woods on the trail of the doe. We watched them puzzle out the scent, then follow along the doe's trail and disappear into the woods. Their frantic barking gradually faded into silence.

Fifteen minutes passed. Startlingly, from my right, in the woods behind me, a shot rang out. I turned but could see nothing in the dense cover. Silence returned.

The morning continued without any further activity. In time the skirmish line began to close toward me. I turned and followed the other standers back to our gathering point. No deer were taken. The shot behind me had been at a buck, but it escaped.

There came a lengthy time for more congenial visiting while the houndsmen rounded up their dogs. At last the assemblage crowded into pickups and set off in convoy to the next area where the standers were again organized while the houndsmen continued around to a release point.

George and I followed into heavy woods bordering a small stream. George crossed the stream and continued out of sight. I halted alongside a tree that gave a fair view down to the bank of the stream. We were well into midmorning. The weather remained pleasant, reminiscent of an early spring day in Wisconsin. The little stream sparkled in the sunlight. Birds flittered about. A deep silence prevailed. I settled alongside the tree, watching carefully into the surrounding woods.

The gentle silence was rudely shattered by the rousing, electrifying cry of the hounds. They bayed as though hot on a trail, and they seemed to be driving along the stream. A prickly sensation trickled through me. I watched intently, shotgun at ready.

The high-pitched yelping drew closer. Movement through the brush alerted me. I tensed. A hound came into view, then another, and another, worrying over a trail, running past me in hypnotized disregard of my presence. Their baying gradually faded into the distance.

George came through the woods toward me. We concluded the deer must have passed through before we were in position along the stream. None of the hunters reported a sighting.

Back once more to stand around in waiting while the hounds were gathered. Midday came and went before we were off again in the pickups, heading south toward Chancellor and land owned by Bennie, one of George's cousins.

We eventually turned off the blacktop highway onto a graveled country road that in turn passed us onto a narrow dirt lane where the pickups kicked dust swirls into the cloudless sky. A rutted drive turned us left again then right before another left brought us to the end of the drive and a small cluster of buildings. Open fields surrounded the buildings. An extensive woods lay off to the south.

We trooped into the woods. I was stationed on a small rise giving a good view along the edge of the timber and partially into it. All the other standers were soon out of sight except for one who climbed into a tree stand a few hundred yards down the edge of the woods.

Again the waiting as the afternoon sun slowly passed. The sound of hounds came faintly on a light breeze, then faded away. Shots broke the stillness, but far from where I waited and watched. The quiet held and I held in place until the other standers filed out of the woods. I followed them across the open field toward the buildings. Two hunters were in happy possession of a six-point buck and a doe.

We gathered around the buildings. While George helped with the deer, I was given a short tour of one of the sheds where a sheet of plywood lifted off the top of an old bathtub revealed an impressive display of several large rattlesnakes, future contestants, so I understood, in the Covington County Rattlesnake Rodeo.

I gave that bathtub the same wide berth I gave my friend Dick's truck whenever he was hunting rattlesnakes on the Mississippi River bluffs in southwestern Wisconsin. Dick was fond of the snakes. He captured them alive and carried them around in gunny sacks in his truck. More than one unsuspecting passenger made a hasty exit when they discovered why the gunny sack under their feet was moving.

The deer were still being processed when I wandered back to the barn. There were enough willing hands offering help so I turned toward a bonfire that Bennie was getting underway to ward off the evening chill. A convenient log offered a seat across from Bennie. After brief acknowledgements, we sat without further conversation while a couple of youngsters came over to stand in respectful silence behind us. Dusk was settling and two women came out of one of the houses to gather up some smaller children. The hunters worked on the deer, sipping beer and reliving the day's hunt. The fire crackled and I welcomed its warmth.

Bennie stirred up the flames, then drew some added warmth from a clear mixture in a Mason jar and glanced over at me.

"You come with George, did ya?"

"Yeah."

"Where ya from?"

"Wisconsin."

"A Yankee, huh?"

"I guess."

The fire began to die down and Bennie told one of the youngsters to fetch some more wood. They both scurried off and soon were gleefully throwing branches on the fire. Bennie spoke again.

"You ain't one of them Damn Yankees, are ya?"

I looked to see if he was smiling. He stared straight into the fire.

"That depends on what you're talking about."

He took a sip from the Mason jar.

"You know the difference between a Yankee and a Damn Yankee, don't ya?"

"Can't say that I do."

"Haah."

One of the youngsters threw another branch on the fire. Sparks flared into the darkening.

"A Yankee's a Northerner who comes down for a while and then goes back home. A Damn Yankee is a Northerner that comes down and stays."

He took another sip.

"You goin' back home?"

"I'm planning on it."

A wry smile teased across his face. He held out the Mason jar.

"Well then, here, try a pull on this."

There was fire in that Mason jar. I put it out with a chaser of beer and watched the other fire flicker off the shadows of the hunters as they came into the circle of its light. The deer were done and we sat in the cooling of the night and talked of deer and dogs and rattlesnakes and hunts past and hunts yet to come until the coming hunt in the morning bid us turn in. We let the fire die into embers as a lonely hound chorused mournfully into the night. The moon stood sentinel above.

On the following day we repeated the day before. Hounds ran and deer ran before them, but none that George or I saw. We could only offer congratulations to the successful hunters and hope our fortunes would change at the hunt club George belonged to when the next morning found us forty miles northwest of Enterprise in Luverne.

George's hunt club was open only to members, and guests of members who passed a modest stipend to Buttons, the club president, for the privilege of joining the group for the day. The club leased hunting rights on a number of private properties between Luverne and Brantley, nine miles to the south.

We gathered at the clubhouse in the early dawn. Buttons was in charge and organized the proceedings. A property was selected for the first drive of the morning and the familiar convoy of pickups carried the hunters and the hounds to their respective stations.

The standers spread out along a narrow lane that bordered a dense woods to the north and a mixture of new-growth pines and brushland to the south. The hounds were to drive the woods. A shot, if one came, would require quick reflexes to track a bounding deer through the thick cover or while bolting across the lane into the pine scrubs.

A young lad on his first deer hunt took position on my right. I dipped around a slight curve to put some precautionary trees between us. The lad's father was on his other side.

The waiting began. Pleasant in the pleasant morning, anticipation fresh with the opening of a new day. The sun broke over the eastern treeline and the soft morning noises of the woods announced the wild's awakening. Time passed languorously. I waited in patience for the sound of the hounds.

A shot came first. Off to my left. Followed by another. I turned in that direction and stared down the lane. The next stander in that direction also stared to his left. Nothing appeared. The hounds remained silent.

Then their voices came faintly from the woods. I watched expectantly, staring down the lane and into the thick cover in front of me. The faint baying of the hounds drew near. A shot rang out to my right. I turned and saw the young lad, with shotgun raised, peering into the woods. The hounds came closer, briefly flashing through the woods before vanishing into the thick cover. Then a frenzied baying as I watched the young lad and his father walk together into the woods.

The lad had shot a doe. His first deer, and a proud one for both him and his father. The earlier shots had also been at a doe. Successful ones, I discovered, as the standers came toward me with the deer in tow.

Those two deer answered for the first drive, and also for the second, for not another shot broke the morning silence. Nor did the sound of the hounds during the second drive. Where they went seemed to remain a mystery.

Not all the hounds were released on every drive. Their retrieval sometimes took days if they got hot on the trail of a deer that led them cross-country. They eventually were recovered, although at times it seemed that the hunt for the hounds consumed far more of the day's hours than did the hunt for the deer. But for the true houndsman, the deer are secondary. It is the glorious music of the chase that stirs their soul and some deign not even to carry a weapon, preferring to take their stand on some distant listening post and follow the chase through the fields of their minds.

I stood with three such men on the next drive, Buttons and two others. Buttons was a lifelong resident of the area and seemed to know every hill, dale, and woodlot in the county. He had directed the stationing of the standers and given instructions on where to release the hounds. He stood then like the commander who has organized his order of battle, confident in the outcome if all performed as expected, but helpless to affect the outcome once the battle was joined.

The opening salvo came with the far-off baying of a hound. Buttons closed his eyes.

"That's Lonell's young redbone. Don't mean nothin'. He's just barkin' free."

We listened to the faint excitement of the young dog. Buttons smiled when a second, lower-pitched note joined in.

"That's Duke. Hear 'em now? He's on a trail."

Soon another hound added its voice to the rising chorus.

"That's old Bugler. We're good now. He won't open 'less he's runnin' hot. They got that deer in Morgen's Woods, down by the spring seep from the sound of it. That Mac boy's along the line fence there if he's where he's suppose to be. We'll see soon."

"Hear 'em hot now? Bugler's trailin' close. That Duke's hangin' near. The young dog's runnin' good."

"That deer's by the line fence now. Where's that Mac boy? The deer's over the fence. Hear that Duke puzzlin'? Now they got 'em. Bugler's on. Where was that Mac boy?"

"The deer's edgin' the line fence. Hear the dogs turn? He's by Darner's Creek now, hunkerin' in the brush and scentin' through the water. Terry's there. If he's near the creek we'll hear 'em shoot soon."

"No, he's gone by. Hear old Bugler? The water won't throw 'em. Terry must 'a lost 'em in the thick. But Duke's got 'em now. And hear the young dog! He's runnin' with 'em good!"

"The deer's turnin' by the pines. The Preacher might see 'em. But its thick there. Bugler's runnin' hot. And hear the young dog? He's pullin' tight with Duke."

"The deer's past the Preacher now. He's runnin' easy through Buford's. If he takes the south woods, Farrell should see 'em."

"There! You heard it! That's Farrell! We'll hear soon from the dogs if he hit. Yes! Yes! Hear 'em millin'? That deer's done. We'll wait 'till they bring 'em out."

And indeed the deer was done. And it was Farrell who came proudly with a fine eight-point, the best deer taken that day.

A spike and another doe finished out the day's drives. I listened from other stands to the music and the shots, but the chase always turned away from where I stood.

We gathered at the clubhouse that evening. The deer were soon processed amid the good banter and gentle chiding of those who saw opportunities pass without being able to shoot, or dare they admit it, took a shot and missed. Each successful hunter received one hindquarter. The rest of the venison was divided into equal portions with a numbered tag attached. A hat containing matching numbers was passed and each who desired some venison drew a number and claimed their like-numbered portion. Then modest libations were proffered, and for those who partook, and for those who did not, there passed another pleasant southern night.

George and I hunted a second day with the club, a blank one as it turned out, before he left to return to Florida. I accepted Buttons's invitation to hunt a third day. The hounds ran well that day, as did the deer before them, but they ran always beyond me. I drove back to Montgomery the following morning and caught a flight home in time for New Year's.

For admirers of hunting dogs, and those who enjoy the easy comaraderie of group hunting, the grand tradition of deer and hounds offers one of the great pleasures of a southern hunt. There is enchantment in the southlands, especially when the winds of winter are blowing through the north. And even when they are not. For who can quell the tingling shiver that comes when the chill of a December dawn is banished by the cry of hounds in hot pursuit, pealing like haunting bugles over the misted woods, rising on the wind, and coming—oh so surely—coming your way.

Chapter 22

On The Barren Grounds

The Land of the Little Sticks, they called those barren grounds, that stark treeless region of the Northwest Territories stretching from the last line of stunted timber to the Arctic Ocean, where firewood was nonexistent and small bundles of precious kindling were carried on the dog sleds to provide a stingy fire at day's end. Tea was the sole object of the fire. There was no hope of sustained heat from the meager blaze in the sub-zero cold that ruled the bitter nights and days. Men found rare cause to venture into that merciless land in the desolate months of winter. Yet some did come. Intrepid hunters like Warburton Pike and Casper Whitney, among others, in pursuit of caribou and musk-ox. And a hundred years after them I came to the Barren Grounds on a similar quest. But I came in the softer days of autumn to camps ready made, where floatplanes and motorboats took the place of dog sleds and snowshoes, and where Eskimos guided instead of Dogrib Indians. Yet descendents of the caribou those early hunters pursued still roam unimpeded over the treeless expanses, and echoes of the same Arctic winds still blow free.

Mid-August 1998. North again, toward that vast domain that encompasses one-third of Canada's land mass, the Northwest Territories. My route took me over familiar Wisconsin roads into Minnesota and the Kenora District of Ontario. I picked up Highway 16 at Winnipeg and angled northwest through Manitoba and Saskatchewan past immense fields of wheat that rippled like golden waves into the distant blue. The grain country continued into Alberta where my route began heading north toward the Peace River. The weather and the country continued delightful, calling for a leisurely pace. I camped wherever the end of day found me.

The grain fields began to give way to spruce forests north of the Peace River. Wilder country there, the road stretching desolate through an area of sparse habitation. A sign at the sixtieth parallel welcomed me to the Northwest Territories. I stopped to view Alexandra Falls on the Hay River, and Louise Falls a mile downstream, before reaching the banks of Great Slave Lake. At two thousand twenty feet, Great Slave Lake is the deepest lake in North America, and offers a setting reminiscent of a primordial seascape. Were it not for the modern vegetation, one could be looking at a Precambrian scene of nearly two billion years ago. Careful observers can discern early Proterozoic stromatolites along its shore.

The highway to Yellowknife, the territorial capital and my destination, crossed the Mackenzie River at the west end of the lake. There was no bridge. During winter the highway continues across the ice. A ferry serves during the months of open water.

Rare wood bison roam north of the Mackenzie River Crossing. A lone bull emerging from the nearby spruce forest highlighted my drive up the graveled highway. The great shaggy creature evidently held me in less esteem than I held it, for it paid me scant attention. I got very close, snapping pictures until he tired of the bother and laid down.

I left the wood bison to his rest and continued over the highway to the north side of Great Slave Lake. After a week and two thousand six hundred miles, Yellowknife at last showed in the distance, a surprisingly modern city of high-rise buildings in the midst of a vast wilderness. Eighteen thousand people live in Yellowknife, well over one-quarter of the sixty-four thousand people inhabiting the Northwest Territories 1.3 million square miles.

After making contact with my outfitter, Fred Webb, the sights of Yellowknife drew my attention. The Old Town section intrigued me, dotted as it was with gold-rush-era buildings and rustic streets such as Ragged Ass Road. I stopped in the original Wildcat Cafe, Yellowknife's oldest restaurant built in 1937, where the menu featured Arctic chowder and thinly sliced caribou with blackberry-lime gravy. Twenty-five dollars covered the bill for both. No doubt there was nightlife to experience, but an early morning flight suggested otherwise. I set up camp just before dark south of the city.

The floatplane base near Old Town was busy in the morning. I made the acquaintance there of the eight other hunters with whom I would be sharing camp. After loading our gear and ourselves, we became airborne in a Twin Otter, heading north over dark-green forests interspersed with sky-blue lakes and waterways. The forests thinned as the ground passed below and the tundra began to take hold. We entered the Barren Grounds, the Land of the Little Sticks.

Courageous Lake eventually took shape in the distance and the floatplane settled gently upon its surface. An impressive camp of nearly a dozen buildings lay along its shore. A Quonset hut offered shelter for the hunters, another one housed the guides, and a third accommodated the cook building. Other smaller structures answered for a variety of purposes. A four-strand electric fence surrounded the camp. Grizzly bear protection, we were informed. A generator charged the batteries for its use during the night.

Hunting was not permitted on the day of arrival in camp. We spent the afternoon organizing gear, sighting-in rifles, and getting acquainted with our guides. Mine introduced himself as Jorgen, an Eskimo, or Inuit, from Kugluktuk. The other guides were also Inuits, assigned one to two hunters. I fished a little before supper, and turned in shortly after eating for a six-o'clock awakening.

The morning dawned clear and warm. Jorgen and I set out in an eighteen-foot motorboat over calm waters. The early warmth soon gave way to a chilling breeze as we turned west across the broad expanse of Courageous Lake.

Rocks edged the shoreline, blending into the ground-hugging cover of the treeless terrain. Mile after mile of seeming emptiness stretched beyond the lake to a meeting with the sky. Small rises and stunted tundra bushes gave feature to the otherwise featureless expanse. The landscape exuded a stark wildness. Not a sign of life disturbed those barren grounds. A void seemed to be upon the land. Yet there was something compelling about the sheer emptiness, a sense of pristine wilderness existing as it had for the ages, pure and undefiled.

We traveled far down the lake. I watched both shores for a glimpse of caribou, but none were in evidence. Jorgen in due course turned toward the north shore. We beached the boat, shouldered packs, and I my rifle, then began picking our way through a jumble of rocks toward a small elevation.

An esker rose from the rocks, a ridge of gravelly drift formed by a stream under the last glacier, appearing like a raised railroad-track bed. It offered comfortable walking compared to the ankle-twisting rocks.

We hiked along the esker, pausing at intervals to glass the distant horizon. We saw caribou a mile in, but the binoculars revealed only a cow and a calf. Another mile, then two, before other caribou appeared off to our right. We sat down and focused them in our binoculars. A dozen altogether, half of them bulls, small to medium-sized. The herd drifted slowly across our front. We watched for an hour, enjoying the company of the caribou and searching for others. The herd in time disappeared behind a rise. No other caribou appeared. We retraced our steps along the esker, continually glassing, and arrived back at the boat at one o'clock. We ate lunch under a sky of intense blue framed by billowing clouds of white.

The afternoon continued pleasant as we searched along the lakeshore. We beached the boat where small rises held promise of caribou beyond, but our stalks over the rises only revealed empty tundra. Yet, empty as the tundra remained, it still offered a visual treat. A glorious fall palette had brushed the low green bushes with striking shades of red, orange, and yellow. The colors rivaled the brilliant autumn hues of a hardwood forest.

We continued our stalks and lakeshore searchings until the time to return to camp sent us skimming over the lake. The other hunters were already there when we arrived. Two bulls had been taken.

West again the following morning, watching the empty landscape pass in mile after mile sameness. We landed on the south shore this time where another esker offered easy passage through the tundra. We hiked a mile over its gravelly surface watching the morning unfold. Dots on a small lake off to our right materialized into a flock of twenty-plus white-fronted geese.

Nuckluck, Jorgen called them. He said they were by far his favorite. I sensed that had he a shotgun, he would have dined on the choice fowl that evening. We sat on the esker and watched the geese. They were a rarely encountered species and I studied them carefully through my binoculars. The geese were still feeding and preening when we resumed our hike over the esker.

Caribou finally appeared, two miles in. We spotted the last of five drifting over a rise half a mile ahead. Jorgen was sure there were no bulls but acceded to my wish to follow after them. A useless stalk proved him right.

Three loons rested on a small pond to the east of the esker when we returned. They seemed unconcerned with our passing. But another creature took great alarm at our sudden appearance. A wolverine, the pale band along the side of its dark brown coat betraying its presence, ran through the low cover edging the esker twenty-five yards to our left. I saw the wolverine briefly, for briefly was all the opportunity the scurrying animal gave me. We searched further for it, but the secretive carcajou had vanished into the brushy rocks.

We ate lunch at the boat under an overcast sky, after which we pushed off and followed along the south shore. A lone caribou far away to the left drew our attention. The binoculars revealed a most impressive, high-rising set of antlers. Jorgen beached the boat and we began a stalk. The bull remained unaware of our presence until a hidden cow spooked from below a small rise. The bull was still three-quarters of a mile away but the actions of the cow apparently convinced him all was not well. He took off in haste across the tundra, his great antlers skylined against the horizon.

We continued our routine of moving from point to point in the boat, then hiking inland to a rise that permitted further glassing. The tundra remained empty.

We crossed to the north shore and turned the boat east. The bank rose several feet in places with clusters of low-growing willows rising above the tundra. As we cruised along, antlers appeared above one of the clumps of willows. Two bulls were bedded in the clump, their bodies and heads hidden. We continued well past them, beached the boat, and began a stalk.

Jorgen led and I followed, matching his every movement. We entered the willows on our hands and knees, carefully moving leaves and twigs from our path and parting the willows with silent caution. The cover thinned as we drew closer to the bulls, turning Jorgen down a ten-foot incline to the edge of the lake. I eased down behind him. We crawled over the rocky surface, watching the antler tops holding steady above the willows. Closer we came. The bulls remained unalarmed. The willows obscured all but the tops of their antlers. On we crawled, angling back up the incline, moving with infinite care through the thick cover until the bulls took shape scarcely twenty yards away. We stopped. The slope blocked them partially from my view. Jorgen studied the bulls, then turned and shook his head. I eased back down to the bank. Jorgen came alongside and whispered that they were too small. We left them undisturbed.

Another medium-sized bull posed along the shore as we began our return to camp. He stood broadside a hundred yards from us, his striking white neck and tiny white upturned tail highlighted against the dark green of the tundra. I took his picture before he turned and trotted off.

Several other caribou came into view during our passage along the shoreline, cows and young bulls. We continued by them, returning to camp to find two more happy hunters in possession of fine bulls.

Rainy in the morning, the wind blowing a heavy chop and roiling the lake. We pounded over the water, the jarring threatening to shake rivets loose and restructure my spine. Southeast that day, down and across the lake on a shorter route than the preceding days. I hung on to my rifle and tried to roll with the back-jolting impacts.

It was a pleasure to again touch the earth. We pulled the boat high onto shore and climbed a modest hill overlooking a vast stretch of tundra. Several caribou were in motion a mile to the south. No bulls were among them. We dropped below the crest of the hill and sat in a light rain, glassing toward the misty horizon.

Droplets on the lenses distorted images through the binoculars. The rainy haze limited visibility. Half an hour passed with only the herd to the south giving evidence of life in the dreary landscape. Then, far off to our right, near the limit of clarity, three caribou appeared. It was difficult to determine size at that distance, but they definitely were bulls. The caribou moved slowly in our direction, drifting in and out of sight behind small rises. If they continued on their present course, the bulls would pass within easy range. We waited in the rain.

Time passed. Nothing else stirred. I gazed across the little inlet where we had beached the boat. A tundra wolf appeared, its white coat revealing against the dark rocks. I divided my attention between the wolf and the caribou. At least the wolf stayed in sight, trotting with an easy lope along the inlet onto a small jutting of land. The caribou went out of sight behind another rise. The wolf continued to the end of the peninsula, then turned around and followed it back before meandering north to fade into the mist. The caribou remained out of sight. Rain squalls came and went. Time passed, and with its passing came the realization that the bulls were no longer coming our way. We searched the surrounding tundra, but the caribou never reappeared.

Back onto the lake for another jarring ride in the rain. We landed where an esker gave easy passage for a mile through the tundra. Two small, bedded bulls in time rewarded our searching. They remained bedded while we glassed the vast opens around them. Not another animal was in evidence. The rain continued.

We returned to the boat and cobbled together a little shelter in the treeless terrain by draping a tarp over two oars jammed into the ground. We sat under the tarp and listened to the pelting rain while we ate lunch and shared a thermos of coffee. Wavelets broke along the shore, gently rocking the stern of the boat, their rippling murmurs the only sound accompanying the rain. The gray overcast tinted the reflecting waters a steely blue-black. A squall rattled over the tarp and dappled raindrops across the water as it hurried on down the lake.

With the passing of the squall, features of the distant shore began to take shape. Jorgen peered intently across the lake.

"There are two caribou there."

I looked in the direction of his gaze, but could see nothing.

"They are bedded. Only their antler tops are showing."

I pulled my binoculars from under my raincoat and focused on the opposite shoreline. The antlers gradually took definition, looking like branched willows above the tundra. When I lowered my binoculars, the antlers blended into the background.

We put the oars and tarp back in the boat and set out for the opposite shore. The lake had quieted some, smoothing our passage. The rise of the land began to hide the antler tops nearer to shore. By the time we landed, they were out of sight.

The wind quartered off the lake toward the bedded caribou. We walked steadily downwind along the shore. The antler tops remained hidden. A slight depression funnelled us inland. We moved rapidly but cautiously, watching to our right for a sign of the bulls. The antler tops of one of the bulls began to come into sight. We angled farther downwind, searching for a lower way around the bull. There was none. Onto our hands and knees, rifle slung across my back. The antlers held steady as a small rise began to hide us. When the antlers could no longer be seen, we arose and continued farther inland before turning into the wind and circling back toward the caribou.

One of the bulls lay bedded in a shallow depression. His antler tops began to appear. We started crawling toward him, slowly lowering to the ground and squirming forward over the rocky surface as we drew closer. The bull rested broadside to us, facing right. The second bull was not in sight. He must have wandered off during the stalk. I wriggled forward until I reached a clear shooting position with my rifle resting on my gloves cushioning over a small rock. Jorgen wriggled beside me.

"It is a fair bull."

I looked at the caribou through the scope, judging a hundred and fifty yards.

"Wait until he stands up."

"I'm comfortable with the shot."

"It would be better to wait until he stands up."

I waited. Forty minutes had elapsed during our stalk. Additional minutes began ticking slowly by while we lay watching the caribou. He rested unconcernedly on the barren ground, his double-shoveled antlers framed by the misty blue lake half a mile behind him. A squall blew in from the lake, spitting drops against the lens of my scope. I wiped it with my handkerchief then lay still again on the gravelly ground and watched the caribou while another squall scuttled across the lake. The minutes passed, dragging uncomfortably. I lay propped on my elbows, rifle at ready. The awkwardness started to tell. Muscle tension began suggesting that a shot delayed might not be the best. I looked at the caribou through the scope and debated. He rested on the tundra, oblivious to the time pressing on.

Then in a movement almost surprising, the bull stood up. The crosshairs followed him. He stared off in the direction he had been facing. The crosshairs settled low along his shoulder. The bull continued staring. The rifle roared and the impact echoed back to us. The caribou stood still for a few seconds, then collapsed to the ground. The time was near three o'clock.

The skies lightened a bit while we worked to cape the bull and debone the meat. I carried the antlers, head, and cape the half-mile to the boat while Jorgen packed the meat. We covered all with a tarp and set off for camp.

The rains had passed but a chop sent whitecaps across the lake. Jorgen's method of calming the troubled waters was to open the throttle full bore. We jolted over the wave tops, rattling my protesting spine.

Another boat came into view and Jorgen turned toward it. We pulled alongside Gary and Mark, and while Jorgen and the other guide conversed in Inuit, Gary and Mark congratulated me on my bull. They were still looking for their first one and had yet to see a bull that day.

We sat in the swell, holding the rocking boats side by side. Suddenly Jorgen interrupted his Inuit conversation to excitedly announce in English, "There's three!"

We looked to the far shore, and there indeed, walking slowly along the top of a rocky rise, were three respectable bulls. The hunters immediately started toward shore while Jorgen and I angled farther down, beached the boat, and turned to watch.

The rocky shore hampered the landing of the other boat. The caribou marched steadily on. Gary at last managed to get ashore. The bulls seemed a long distance off. Gary tried to close the range but the rocky terrain favored the caribou. They pulled steadily away. Gary scrambled to find a rock to rest his rifle over. His shot echoed back to us. We watched the bulls through our binoculars. The largest of the three faltered, then fell to the ground. The other two soon vanished over the rise.

Gary estimated the range at four hundred yards. Mark was hunting with a bow so there was no possibility of a shot for him.

We returned to camp to find a grizzly bear patrolling the perimeter. Earlier that afternoon the grizzly had tried to get to the building where the caribou meat hung. The electric fence held it at bay but the cook and three others in camp experienced a few anxious moments. The bear continued to hover less than two hundred yards off, skylined against the lake between some green willows. It seemed totally unconcerned about the gathering of hunters and guides along the fence. Cameras clicked relentlessly. The grizzly eventually ambled away, circling around camp, a beautiful animal, its back a striking grizzled white shading into the rich brown of its sides and legs.

The sighting of the bear elicited a chilling description of another grizzly encounter on a previous hunt at that camp. Gary, whom I had watched take the caribou earlier, his companion, and guide were strung out across the tundra. A grizzly unexpectedly loomed up out of a depression in front of Gary. Gary began backing away but the grizzly came on. As Gary continued retreating he tripped and started to fall. The bear closed. Gary managed a desperate shot as he fell and fortunately hit the bear between the eyes, dropping it in mid-stride. The authorities determined that the shooting was justified, but they confiscated the bear. In the aftermath, no one thought to take a picture.

The patrolling grizzly was gone in the morning, as was the rain. The day opened pleasant with a light breeze. The lake lay comfortably calm. Jorgen steered across the quieted waters toward a river he called the Jolliet. We followed only a short way up the rock-strewn channel before turning toward shore.

Hills rose a little steeper there and we crested the first one to come upon an unsuspecting flock of willow ptarmigan. I spotted several in the tundra brush, quite close. A male, sporting a bright red crescent over its eye, peered up from near my right foot in startled surprise before bursting into the air with the rest of the flock. They flew far over the tundra.

Caribou began appearing farther into the hills, two separate herds, one of which included two good bulls. We dipped out of sight below a concealing rise and walked rapidly toward their position. The morning continued pleasant and the walk over the tundra soon had us shedding our coats. We moved steadily, concentrating on keeping out of sight of the bulls, when we inadvertently came into sight of a herd of cows. They spotted us and trotted over another hill. We could only hope the others were not alarmed.

The contours gradually led us around to the hill shielding the herd. We began climbing the hill, slowing as the crest approached. Antlers appeared against the skyline. We crawled stealthily to the crest and watched the antlers materialize into a pair of fine bulls amid a dozen cows a hundred yards away. They fed unconcernedly.

I rested the rifle across the crest and contemplated the bulls. Both appeared larger than the bull of the day before. One perhaps more than the other. I isolated him in the scope.

Jorgen studied the bulls through his binoculars, then turned to me and shook his head.

I watched through the scope for a few more seconds, then lowered my rifle. We backed away from the crest and left the caribou undisturbed.

We moved over the tundra seeking other vantage points, swinging wide until the lake came back into view. The small herds in the hills remained the only caribou seen during the rest of the morning.

A willow-choked valley near the lake began to funnel us slightly away from our route toward where we had left the boat. We angled out of the willows to follow a rise a quarter of a mile above the blue-shimmering waters.

Movement along the lakeshore attracted us. A light-colored grizzly emerged from a low patch of willows. We reached for our binoculars.

The great bear ambled slowly along the lake. It gave no indication of searching for food but simply appeared to be taking a midday stroll. The grizzly loomed large and clear in the binoculars. We both agreed that this bear was not the same bear seen around camp.

The grizzly stayed in sight for nearly half an hour before it turned to disappear into the willow-thick valley we had been descending a little over thirty minutes previously. We contemplated the possibilities had we continued that route to the lake.

The afternoon passed with delightful weather but only the sighting of one other animal, a respectable bull bedded along the lakeshore. He posed for five pictures before we left to return to camp.

The other hunters were already there, some with very nice bulls. Five had now filled all their tags, two were still looking for their second bull, and Mark, the bowhunter, was still looking for his first. The open terrain was frustrating Mark but he nevertheless declined an offer of a rifle for the following day, our final day of hunting. I recalled another caribou camp where a hunter was determined to take a bull with a flintlock rifle. Unfortunately a week of constant wet weather dampened the powder in the rifle's flashpan, spoiling a couple of his opportunities. But he, like Mark, spurned the offer of a more reliable weapon. He went home without a caribou, but seemed comfortable with his decision.

Fifth and last hunting day. Overcast with no wind. The lake calm. Jorgen headed west planning to hunt the area we had hunted the first day, a favorite of his because of some exceptional caribou taken there.

Jorgen, I came early to understand, was a man who gloried in large-antlered bulls. He would be the consummate guide for a dedicated trophy hunter. I quickly grew accustomed to his head shaking at the sight of what to me appeared to be very nice caribou. It was either, "Tops too weak," or, "Bottoms too weak," or some such evaluation. We had yet to see a bull that Jorgen fully approved of. I fear I disappointed him somewhat with the bull I took the afternoon of the third day. I recall there was something too weak about it. But he consoled himself with the fact that at least it had double shovels.

We were halfway to our area when caribou on the south shore diverted us. A fair herd with some good looking bulls moved along a hillside. Between their movement and the motion of the boat, it was hard to gain a steady view through the binoculars. Jorgen turned toward shore for a closer look.

The caribou disappeared over the hill as we drew near a landing place. Within a few seconds of their disappearance, farther south along the same hill, a running animal came into view. A wolf! A beautiful white tundra wolf. Running in easy strides toward us with something in its mouth. We watched the wolf through our binoculars, trying to determine what it was carrying. Other than the fact the object was red, we had no idea.

The wolf loped closer, evidently unconcerned with the nearby boat. It constantly looked back, seeming hesitant and tentative. Several minutes elapsed as the wolf crossed nervously in front of us before turning to drift south and drop out of sight beyond another rise.

We beached the boat and began climbing the hill the caribou had disappeared over and the wolf had run down. The hill sloped gently upward. Jorgen led, watching ahead for the caribou. I followed, glancing left and right.

The weather continued overcast but pleasant. We soon removed our coats with the warming climb. The morning lay in a hush and our steps fell silently on the matted ground. The hills appeared empty except for three gulls that swooped low over the brush ahead to our left. I glanced at the gulls, then caught sight of a white flash through some low willow cover. I called Jorgen's attention to it, thinking it might be a wolverine. He looked through his binoculars and exclaimed, "Grizzly!"

I brought my binoculars to my eyes and beheld a rare sight. A grizzly bear, with the entire rear half of a caribou in its jaws, broke out of the willows and began running up the open slope within comfortable rifle range. We watched in fascination as the grizzly climbed effortlessly up the slope. The weight of half a caribou seemed to offer no impediment to the bear, but the dangling caribou legs kept getting caught up in the bear's legs, causing it to stumble at times. In spite of its stumbles, the grizzly climbed steadily, awesome in its power, and even with its awkward load, imposing in its bearing.

We watched the bear in continued fascination for fully ten minutes before it disappeared over a distant rise. Not once did it pause to rest or look back. The three gulls swooped down to feed on the remains.

We surmised that the wolf must have killed a caribou out of the herd we had seen, and the grizzly in turn had chased the wolf off. The red object in the wolf's mouth must have been a chunk of caribou, perhaps its sole reward for furnishing the grizzly with a meal.

We continued ahead, dipping into the willow cover the grizzly had run out of, and angling up the slope away from the direction the bear had gone. Scattered caribou began appearing, cows and small bulls.

We topped out on a flat stretch of tundra, richly colored with green, orange, red, and yellow bushes rising scant inches above the matted ground cover. The lake reflected blue-gray off to our right. The sky remained overcast, the temperature comfortable, warming some with our exertion. We walked over the colorful landscape, pausing often to glass.

Suddenly, from out of a small valley to our right front, a dozen caribou emerged. They were all bulls, some quite impressive. They saw us and began running toward the lake. When they reached the rise above it, they turned. But instead of turning away from us, they turned and ran between us and the lake. The bulls continued in a tight group until they reached a point two hundred yards or so away. There they stopped, and wheeling in almost perfect order, formed a single line, then dressed the line to the right as though on parade, and faced us. The storied Bengal Lancers could not have executed that maneuver with more style and precision. Nor could they have arrayed themselves more imposingly, compelling as that stalwart file was with alabaster necks and manes flashing against the multicolored background and sky-framed antlers rising like proud lances above the ranks. I half-expected them to advance, but they held their ground, as though in haughty challenge.

I marveled briefly at the spectacle, then dropped to a sitting position and studied the largest bull through my scope. He appeared to surpass my first bull. Still, the day was young. I debated, then took out my camera and captured that remarkable formation on film.

We left the bulls and returned through the thick-willowed valley. Two other gulls had joined the first three and all five were scavenging along the way the grizzly had dragged the caribou. We doubted the grizzly had returned but Jorgen asked me to chamber a round as a precaution. The dense willows offered an interesting passage with the thought of the grizzly hanging in the back of our minds. We reached the boat without incident, pushed off, and resumed our journey to the west.

Caribou appeared along the way, but none that tempted us. We continued over the gray-calm waters to the same landing place of the first day, beached the boat, and began walking through the jumbled rocks toward the esker. That welcome height was only a few steps away when a shot sounded to our left. We turned and saw three figures on a distant hill. A band of caribou ran ahead of them. A second shot rang out, then a third and a fourth, followed by a fifth. Then a sixth shot echoed over the tundra and one of the caribou faltered and fell.

The figures were too far away to identify. We presumed they were the two hunters looking to fill their second tags, and their guide. One of the hunters at least had been successful. An unexpected encounter and the only occasion others had been seen on the tundra since the start of my hunt.

We soon lost sight of the trio as the rolling terrain passed behind us. The esker provided comfortable walking and Jorgen, with his tundra-conditioned legs, began stepping out in quick-time. An observation point four miles in held promise and he was anxious to reach it. I was still pacing myself after a second coronary-bypass operation and felt no inclination to match his stride. I told him to go on ahead. I would join him at the observation point.

Off he went, leaving me to a more leisurely pace and a chance to enjoy the pleasant although overcast late morning. Jorgen eventually dipped below a small rise, and for the first time that week I was able to bask in solitude on the horizon-stretching tundra. I tried to envision that near featureless land in the depths of an Arctic winter, with its lakes and treeless expanses a frozen sea of white. Surely existence must be a fierce struggle for the creatures that spend those bitter months on the windswept opens. But now, in the soft days of autumn, the landscape was resplendent with glorious reds and yellows and oranges amid pockets of blue-sparkling ponds and lakes. Wildlife teemed. Caribou, grizzly bears, wolves and wolverines, ptarmigan, geese, loons, and ducks lived free and wild in these seemingly desolate spaces. But these spaces were far from desolate. They were alive. And they wove a captivating aura around the lone wanderer walking in quiet solitude there. I began to feel the allure that Jorgen had expressed for this, his homeland.

I came in time to the end of the esker and climbed a long, gentle rise. Jorgen appeared three-quarters of a mile ahead. He turned to make sure I was following, then disappeared below another rise. I caught up to him just over the crest where a large rock formation offered a prominent place from which to gaze out upon the sweeping tundra. Jorgen was busy with his binoculars and I was not long in joining him.

We glassed in silence for an hour, spotting scattered caribou but no above-average bulls. We each ate an apple for lunch, all that we had thought to bring with us, then resumed our glassing. Another hour passed. We hoped for other caribou to move into view or perhaps for a bedded bull to rise and reveal himself, but we hoped in vane. Time moved emptily along. Finally, Jorgen said we needed to start back.

We crossed a mile of tundra before reaching the welcome surface of the esker. We paused there to glass, facing back toward the observation point. Jorgen searched to the left while I searched to the right. Hardly two or three minutes went by before Jorgen uttered a low exclamation. I looked toward him.

"Three good bulls. One looks very good."

I found them in my binoculars. They did indeed look very good, but a far way off.

Jorgen reached into his pack, and for the first time that week, pulled out his spotting scope. He lay on his stomach and studied for a long time.

"Very good bottoms on the biggest one, but the tops are a little weak. Take a look."

The increased magnification pulled the bulls close. Any one of the three appeared to be a rare prize. The larger of the trio looked exceptional, certainly surpassing any of the number I had taken over the years, and perhaps surpassing any of the thousands I had seen.

Jorgen continued to study the bulls. They fed unhurriedly. The precious minutes ticked by. The last afternoon was passing.

"Do we have time to get to them?"

Jorgen continued to look through the spotting scope.

"Let's see which way they're going."

We sat on the esker, watching the caribou. They fed randomly across the tundra but were drifting generally south in the direction of the lake. Had they gone deeper into the north, daylight may have become a consideration.

Fifteen minutes slowly ticked by while we waited for the bulls to feed out of sight. At last the tundra hid them. Jorgen put his spotting scope away and we started.

The bulls had disappeared behind a distant rise to the northwest. We dropped off the esker and began a rapid walk across the tundra. Jorgen set a steady pace and I held tight behind him. The tundra appeared flat, but shallow depressions and gentle rises offered areas where hidden approaches were possible. We followed through one of those depressions, pushing rapidly but cautiously along, stopping at intervals to scan the distant rise the caribou were presumably behind.

Time passed forgotten as we stalked deeper into the tundra. The great expanses swept around us but we had eyes only for the far-off rise. The distance closed in weary stages until the shallow depression we were following began to trend south, swinging away from the rise. We halted. Jorgen squirmed to a vantage point from which to glass, then motioned me alongside.

"They're bedded down. On this side of the rise."

I looked through my binoculars.

"There are only two."

"Yes. But one of them is the big bull."

We studied the ground. The depression hiding us continued south. Half a mile beyond, another small rise offered the possibility of a way around to the opposite side of the rise the caribou were bedded on. A cautious stalk over that rise should put us almost among them.

We continued along the depression, needing to stoop as it began to level out. We paused again. The bulls remained bedded.

Then a freshening from the direction of the lake sent a breeze across our backs. The wind had been cooperative up until that moment. We waited, hoping for the breeze to die down, but it steadied. Our planned route around the caribou would take us across their front. No hope now with the breeze.

We looked downwind. The depression we were in would shield us for a short distance, but after that open ground extended nearly back to the esker before another small depression to the north with low-growing willows and tundra bushes offered any hope of concealment. The bulls lay on the far rise, facing south. Jorgen looked toward the distant depression.

"If we drop back far enough, we might be able to circle around."

Back we went, hurrying. The depression brought us to the open stretch of ground. We looked toward the bulls, then across that barren open. No reasonable way around. No other choice.

We started. I settled into a hunched-over gait alongside Jorgen, trying to be his shadow, concentrating on forming a single silhouette, letting Jorgen keep track of the bulls.

We followed down with the wind, trusting that even should the caribou spot us they would only see an indistinct form moving away. The open ground seemed glaringly revealing, but the cover of the willow depression slowly drew closer.

We stopped for a moment while Jorgen checked on the bulls. They remained bedded. We continued on, angling in the direction of the depression. Jorgen watched the bulls while I watched toward the depression. The willows growing there barely rose above the edge of the shallow concave, except for a couple that branched up higher. I glanced at the branched willows. Recognition registered. I touched Jorgen on the shoulder. He stopped and looked at me. I nodded toward the willows. He looked, then eased slowly to the ground. I followed suit.

A bull caribou lay bedded there.

It most likely was the third bull. He evidently bedded down in the willows while the other two fed on before bedding down on the rise. But no matter, we were stuck. We had to stalk in front of him to get to the big bull. One whiff of us and he would be gone, alerting the others.

We lay flat on the open tundra watching the antler tops turn from time to time. The minutes ticked frustratingly by. Jorgen touched my arm and nodded toward some low bushes to our left. He started bellying toward them and I followed. We slipped into their meager cover and resumed waiting.

The bushes we lay in obscured the bulls on the rise. Time dragged along as the antlers in the willows held our undivided attention. They turned frequently, exposing tops that perhaps even Jorgen would admit were not too weak. The rest of the animal remained out of sight.

Then he arose. A grand creature appearing almost magically from the wispy willows. A most impressive bull.

He began walking toward us. We scrunched into the tundra. The bull fed along the bushes we lay scantily hidden in, almost within reach. Surely he would see us or catch our scent. But he fed past us, nipping greens from the ground we had lain upon before seeking the cover of the bushes. The proximity of the grand bull was stirring. Jorgen and I looked at each other and smiled. Then Jorgen shook his head, thinking perhaps I might be tempted. But strangely I was not. The bull was a superb animal, and right there beside me. I simply watched in fascination as the magnificent creature passed a few feet away.

The lone bull finally fed far enough past us to permit our squirming into the depression. We found a place to cautiously lift our heads to check on the bedded bulls. We looked. They were gone.

We rose slowly from the stunted cover. The bulls remained out of sight. We looked back for the third bull. He likewise had vanished into the tundra. Jorgen searched through his binoculars.

"They must have crossed over the rise they were bedded on. We would have seen them if they went south."

We set off at a steady but cautious pace up the rise. The crest drew near and we stepped and stared our way along. The far western expanse slowly came into view. It was empty.

We turned to look north and instantly lowered ourselves to the ground. The two bulls were there, feeding a few hundred yards beyond the willow depression we had just left. They had fed around the backside of the rise while we lay pinned down by the lone bull.

Down the rise we squirmed, angling for the depression. The two bulls fed casually across the tundra. A light breeze wafted across the rise, quartering away from the bulls.

On our hands and knees through the willows and low bushes, my slung rifle catching irritatingly on the protruding growth. I shifted the rifle to my right hand and crawled awkwardly along. The bulls continued feeding.

The edge of the depression brought us to the open tundra. The bulls fed a quarter of a mile away moving from our left to the right. Two small ponds with a connecting streamlet between them funnelled the bulls east. The ground lay perfectly level with the multicolored tundra bushes rising just high enough to interfere with a prone shot. Small rocks lay scattered across the ground. A larger rock, a hundred and fifty yards away, rose several inches above the bushes. I turned to Jorgen.

"I'm going to try to get to that rock and use it as a rest."

He nodded.

I began crawling low across the ground. The caribou fed unconcernedly. From time to time one or both would raise an antlered head and scan their surroundings, bringing me, and Jorgen who crawled behind me, tense into the tundra. I carried my rifle in hand, setting it forward then pulling myself to it, pressing as low to the ground as possible. The caribou remained unaware of our presence. The distance to the rock slowly closed. The bulls continued drifting east. A final push brought me to the rock. I took my gloves out of my coat pocket and folded them into a cushioned rest over the rock. The rifle held steady above the bushes. The bulls fed tight together.

The pair locked into my scope. The second bull fed beside the large bull, shifting ahead, then behind, then ahead again. I blocked out all but the magnified circle, waited until the large bull stood clear, centered the crosshairs on the front shoulder, let my breathing slow, held half a breath, and cautioned myself to squeeze, squeeze, squeeze.

Ka-BOOM!

The great bull fell to the ground.

I lay there watching the downed bull, holding the rifle in readiness, vaguely aware of the second bull running around to the right. He circled out of sight and the tundra was still. I watched a moment longer, then rose slowly to my feet and walked the two hundred and sixty paces to the bull. He truly was a splendid animal, by far my finest caribou.

Jorgen came alongside and stood in silent admiration for a few seconds. Then he congratulated me. And I congratulated him.

We took a few pictures before beginning the task of getting the animal out. We shortly had the bull caped and the meat deboned. Jorgen lifted a muscle-straining pack of meat onto his back while I struggled with lifting the head, cape, and antlers, along with my rifle, onto mine. We adjusted our loads and set off across the tundra for the distant esker.

Far away on the horizon, the two bulls, whom along with my bull had formed the original trio, came together. They paused along the skyline, facing us, towering antlers rising in bold relief, the embodiment of that wild land. They watched us briefly, then turned with an elegant air and vanished into the broad expanses of the Barren Grounds.

We were at least three miles from the boat, probably more. I led for a change, Jorgen's heavier load telling as he dropped slightly behind. We toiled along, resting frequently before reaching the welcome esker where the easier footing enabled us to walk side by side for longer intervals. The section of jumbled rocks before the lake slowed me some. Jorgan pushed on ahead and was waiting beside the boat to take my picture as I topped the last rise.

The wind had freshened anew and the ride across the lake had us fighting through whitecaps that broke disconcertingly above the bow. We bent into the chilling spray. Camp offered a welcome beacon through the darkly pounding waves. Supper hour was long past by the time we arrived, but the cook had kept two plates warm. We ate ravishingly, then I made my weary way to bed.

We flew out the next morning, stopping at the Department of Renewable Resources office in Yellowknife to pick up export permits for the successful hunters. All had filled their tags except Mark, the bowhunter.

Several mounted specimens of native Northwest Territories wildlife adorned the office. The centerpiece was a most impressive full-body-mounted grizzly bear. We commented on the bear and were informed that an American hunter had shot it in self-defense a few years ago. As the story unfolded, we discovered that the grizzly was in fact the grizzly that Gary had told us about in camp. He belatedly had a chance to have his picture taken with the bear and add a most remarkable ending to his story.

And a letter a few months later added a most gratifying ending to my hunt.

Boone and Crockett Club

Dear Mr. Howard,

The file for your trophy listed on the enclosed certificate is complete, and is entered in the record archives, as well as the 24th Awards Entry Period.

Barring unforeseen circumstances, your trophy will be listed in the Awards records book, Boone and Crockett Club's 24th Big Game Awards, and the all-time records book, Records of North American Big Game, 12th edition.

Thank you for your interest and participation in the program, and congratulations on a fine trophy.

Chapter 23

Newfoundland

They came in ships of oaken keel with planks of pine and trunnels of peg-formed linden. Burr-secured iron rivets were their fastenings and twisted animal hairs soaked in pine tar their caulking. Course woolen cloth was woven into a single square sail. Their rigging lines were cut from walrus hide. Near sixty feet long and fifteen feet at the beam was one of their knarrs, partly decked forward and aft and carrying thirty people along with several head of cattle and provisions.

Vikings they were, sailing boldly from their Scandinavian homes to discover far-flung countries they called Iceland, Greenland, Helluland, Markland, and Vinland. Their names are legendary. Eric the Red, Leif Ericsson, Thorvald, Karlsevni. And of course, Biarni Heriulfson, the first European to set eyes upon America.

But eyes were all Biarni set upon the new-found shores. He did not land. It was Leif Ericsson, setting forth in Biarni Heriulfson's knarr in the summer of 1001, who first landed on Baffin Island five years after Biarni saw it. He named it Helluland—Country of Flat Stones. Lief pushed away from those rocky shores and crossed to the Labrador coast, which he named Markland—Land of Forests. From there to Belle Island, and then to a larger island where a stream flowed out of a lake through an extensive meadow.

They wintered there where cattle could graze outdoors all season and large salmon came easily into their nets. Vinber, or wineberries, grew in abundance. When spring came and they sailed away, Lief named the country in keeping with its most enticing feature. He called it Vinland

Five centuries later the English arrived on Vinland in John Cabot's ship *Mathew*. They knew nothing of the Vikings, for the Vikings had long vanished from the land. The English considered the island newly discovered. They called it the Newe Founde Launde. Those who dwell there now call it the same.

Newfoundland ranks as the tenth largest island in the world. This rugged Atlantic wilderness spreading over forty-two thousand square miles is home to one hundred twenty thousand moose, the densest moose population in North America. Seventy thousand woodland caribou also roam the tuckamore bogs and forests. And black bears of grizzly-sized proportions have been verified. Wildlife officials have captured and released a black bear weighing six hundred and eighty-seven pounds.

Early hunters left intriguing accounts of their Newfoundland expeditions. Frederick Selous, the first European to venture deep into the interior in search of game, hunted on the island three times. His last hunt in 1905 took him to King George IV Lake over an arduous canoe and foot passage. The lake was considered to be so remote at the time that Selous was granted a special permit to shoot as many caribou as required to keep himself and the two Newfoundlanders who accompanied him in fresh meat.

Selous's accounts, along with others, had long kept the Newfoundland fires burning in my mind. The waning days of September 1999 saw me at last on a parallel journey.

Familiar highways carried me east toward the Maritime Provinces in the dawning days of autumn. The glorious New England fall colors were weeks away from their splendor, but the Green Mountains of Vermont and the White Mountains of New Hampshire still showcased their grandeur clothed fair in verdant green. Maine's northern forests funnelled me into New Brunswick, where I crossed the St. John River on the longest covered bridge in the world, a 1,282-foot span into downtown Hartland.

An impressively longer bridge, uncovered, crosses the nine-mile straight from New Brunswick to Prince Edward Island. Heavy rains lashed the area as I approached the bridge. Portions of the highway lay underwater. Doubts arose about being able to continue, but I eased cautiously through the flooding to the bridge and crossed the roiling, angry waves below buffeted by a slashing, wind-driven rain.

Prince Edward Island passed in continuing wind and rain. The ferry ride across the fourteen-mile straight to Nova Scotia was not a landlubber's delight. The ship pitched and yawed in the heaving, rolling seas.

The storm subsided during my drive through Nova Scotia to North Sydney, the end of a two thousand one hundred mile segment of my journey. I camped along the way wherever night found me, sleeping in my new van which I had finished inside similar to my former Blazer.

My Blazer was gone, victim of an encounter with a deer while returning from a moose hunt in Ontario the previous year. A very nice white-tailed buck, as it turned out, just across the border into Minnesota. The deer died. But alas, the Blazer died with it. A fitting end perhaps for a vehicle that had served as my hunting and fishing home away from home for twenty-three years.

The one hundred mile ferry crossing from North Sydney to Port Aux Basques, Newfoundland, takes six to eight hours at night. That time and more was spent in the boarding area at the terminal. I sailed stand-by, belatedly finding out about the crowded nature of the ferry's schedule. Mine was the final vehicle loaded. I would have been delayed for at least another day had the vehicle in front of me not been too long to fit in the last remaining space.

The ferry slowly got underway and the shores of Nova Scotia faded into the dusk. I stood on the forward deck and watched the darkness close down upon the ocean. Calm had returned to the seas and the massive ship rose and fell gently in the swells. I thought of Vikings and their braving of the stormy North Atlantic in open ships tossed by the whims of the elements. The dark before a tempest must have been profound when a strong sea began to form. I stayed on the deck, caught up in the grand isolation of a ship alone on the vast ocean. The lights of Nova Scotia one by one blinked away. Soon there was only the intense night, the dull vibration of the engines, the rhythmic rising and falling, and the endless, endless dark reaching down into the deep.

Eleven o'clock. The ferry docked at Port Aux Basques after a seven-hour crossing. I followed a long line of taillights northeast on Highway 1 looking for the Hungry Bear Restaurant where my outfitter, Gerry Pumphrey, was to meet me in the morning. The restaurant at last came into view. All was dark. I pulled into a corner of the parking lot and slipped wearily into my sleeping bag. The remainder of the night passed unnoticed.

Gerry arrived at ten o'clock the following morning. I transferred my duffel to his pickup and within an hour we came to a helicopter landing area. The inevitable waiting began and one-thirty passed before the helicopter lifted off. The flight held me fascinated as we skimmed over trackless expanses of forests and lakes set low against the backdrop of the Long Range Mountains.

King George IV Lake began to pass beneath us and I could not help but think of Selous struggling his final three days by foot to this same lake nearly a century before, having abandoned his canoe in the nearly impassable river approaches.

The helicopter hovered a moment over the south shore of King George IV Lake before settling down into a small clearing sandwiched between the lake and the forest. A cabin stood there. The plywood structure housed a kitchen and dining area in the center with two double-deck bunk rooms on each side, one side for the hunters, the opposite side for the guides. The cook slept in a small room off the kitchen.

The four guides were in camp but the other three hunters were not due until the next day. The afternoon passed pleasantly in getting settled and watching a beautiful black mink with a small white diamond mark on its chest scurry about grabbing scraps from a moose quarter hanging in a tree, a gift from the previous week's hunter. Two of the guides set to work building a live-trap.

The following day, Sunday, was a non-hunting day and the guides enjoyed a free Saturday night in camp celebrating the cook's sixtieth birthday. Modest libations had been arranged for the occasion. A wilderness party ensued. While Sheldon, Jason, and Edward the cook stomped the floor to a Newfoundland jig, Gilbert, his brother Jake, and I sat on the front porch of the cabin where I sipped lightly from a small tumbler of rum, listened to the whoops of the celebrators ringing out over the darkened lake, and commented in turn as Gilbert discoursed at great length on the state of human affairs, the ways of the Almighty, the wonders of that wild, unspoiled island, and the stalwart nature of the fine, God-fearing men living proud on its windswept shores.

Heavy rain, driven by a strong north wind, began around midnight and continued into the morning. By ten o'clock the rain had stopped but the strong wind continued, raising white-caps on the lake. The weather cleared enough by noon for the helicopter to bring in the other three hunters, Bryan and Barry from Wisconsin, and Chuck from New Jersey.

The black mink reappeared after everyone was settled. It had tripped the live-trap during the night but remained too wary to be captured. Edward served a delicious moose roast with all the trimmings for supper.

Monday morning. Breakfast in the dawn's awakening. Eager talk of the coming hunt.

We left the cabin at daybreak. The other hunters and their guides scattered across the lake in boats while Jake and I set off to the south on foot. We followed game trails through the tuck-amore, more appropriately known as tanglefoot, that Newfoundland scourge formed when harsh island winds bend and twist new-growing black spruce and balsam fir into dense, nearly impenetrable jungles of interwoven roots, trunks, and branches. The spruce and fir are dwarfed and twisted by the flagging effect of the wind and resemble ground-hugging bushes rather than the stately trees rising tall in the sheltered areas. The resultant evergreen tangle makes even a tag-alder swamp seem like a thoroughfare.

Game trails guided us through the tuckamore until a half-hour brought us to more favorable ground and the heart-rushing sight of two caribou disappearing into distant spruce. Too fleeting to determine whether they were stags or does, the designation used for caribou in Newfoundland, bull and cow being reserved for moose.

We began a cautious stalk toward the spruce when the bawling of a cow moose wafting from a dense fir thicket to our right halted us.

Here was a pleasant dilemma. Two caribou ahead and a cow moose presumably advertising her loneliness to a bull. We debated. The caribou were there, although unidentified. The bull moose was only a possibility. Jake's comment that moose were a little more challenging to come across in this area decided it. Jake pulled his call from his pack and a competing bawl drifted toward the dark fir.

Silence settled over the morning. We sat in conformity with it. Only the occasional harsh note from Jake's call disturbed the quiet. Fifteen minutes passed. Movement to the far left drew our attention. We locked our gaze upon it. A caribou emerged from the spruce where we had seen the pair, a large animal carrying a small rack. We watched for others as it passed from view. None appeared.

Jake called again. No guttural response from a bull and no further sounds from the cow. If the cow had already lured a bull to her our chances of enticing him away were slim. Still the slim odds held us for another hour while Jake teased his plaintive call across the warming morning.

The sun slowly rose above the copses of spruce and fir. A few scattered clouds drifted gauzy white across an intense blue sky. The morning came clear and glorious. But the moose did not come with it. Ten minutes after a final pleading bawl, Jake put his call away and we turned south again.

A doe caribou appeared in the spruce we had seen the first two in, possibly one of the pair.

We continued a couple of miles past the doe to a high knoll. Binoculars came into use and we searched through a grand country of low-lying tuckamore bogs amid rolling hills covered with spruce and fir. Sparkling bodies of water glinted like blue diamonds in a jeweled crown of emerald green. The sun shed its warming light on the scene.

We searched in quadrants, patient in the lazy warming. A flock of twenty Canada geese joined us vocally for a few minutes, passing noisily overhead in a wavering vee bold against the sky. A sparrow hawk hunted nearby, soaring on a strong north wind. Its endeavors proved as futile as ours and the little hawk left us to fade into the distance.

I finally picked up a small band of four caribou showing white against the green background a mile back along the way we had come. I looked eagerly, but no antlers were visible. The band held my attention for several minutes before it drifted out of sight.

Midday passed but no other animals passed within view. We left the knoll and began hunting back along our route of the morning, coming in time to another knoll that overlooked the fir thicket where we had heard the cow moose. A flash of white in the woods two hundred yards to the northwest drew our attention. Movement coming in our direction. Too indistinct to make out in the evergreens.

We dropped off the skylining knoll and tucked ourselves into a small depression surrounded by scrub brush. The wind blew strong in our faces. Time passed in silent watching. More white appeared in the shielding greenery, off to our left, coming closer. I waited expectantly.

Movement again in the evergreens, becoming distinct. Taking form. Becoming a doe and a fawn caribou who walked into the open and passed in steady rhythm behind the knoll barely a hundred yards away.

Then a brown flash through the trees, deeper in the evergreens. Antlers perhaps, or perhaps a wish for them. A fleeting glimpse. Hidden in the denseness. Watching intently. But watching only greenery. The brown never flashed again.

We decided to observe from there for a while, the movement of caribou and the remembrance of moose offering double hope.

I ate a sandwich while we waited. An hour passed without further activity. The wind continued strong. During one of its lulls we heard a single shot echoing from a series of high hills several miles to the west.

Another hour with impatience beginning to take hold when movement fully a quarter of a mile away banished it. We focused on the trees and watched flickers of forms filter through the spruce and fir. Closer they came, showing white. Then showing antlers flashing brown as they came out of the trees. A small stag and a doe, following along where the doe and fawn had passed earlier.

The sighting offered inducement to stay in place. We were rewarded forty-five minutes later with the glint of antlers through the trees. I watched in anticipation as a small stag passed one hundred and twenty-five yards away, but no others followed.

The day continued pleasant. Comfortable temperatures under a brilliant sky. Minutes drifted lazily along as the afternoon passed. The westward-setting sun began dipping behind the trees, bringing hope of moose moving in the coming dusk, but the sun settled low with only another small stag treading silently by a hundred yards behind us.

At six o'clock we began hunting back toward camp. We saw nothing along the way and the only sound that disturbed the silence was a distant shot. When we arrived at camp, Edward, the cook, informed us that he had seen a young bull moose along the lake just ten minutes before.

The other hunters reported excellent success. Each had seen between twenty and thirty caribou and Chuck had also come across a bull moose with a cow. Bryan and Barry had taken nice stags, Bryan a most impressive one. Chuck likewise had a very nice stag caribou along with a small bull moose, the one he had seen with the cow. Chuck's success was unfortunately marred by a sorely injured leg. He decided to cut his trip short and fly out the next day.

We dined well again that evening.

Fog in the morning. Eerie quiet on the lake. Jake and I, along with Bryan, Barry, and their guides, loaded into a boat and set off across the still waters.

We wove through the fog on a crossing to a river flowing out of the lake. Bryan and his guide, Jason, parted from us there and we turned once more into the fog.

More dark water passed beneath. Closer terrain became distinct as the fog thinned and wisped away. We landed in a small cove. Barry and his guide, Gilbert, set off for a high hill two miles away. Jake and I turned toward a lower hill a mile off and trod easily across the tuckamore-free ground.

A tangle of spruce slowed us at the base of the hill, but by eight o'clock we had climbed to a level area beneath a secondary crest where we decided to glass.

We sat just below the crest gazing out over a grand wilderness scene. The fog had dissipated except for a few stubborn patches that clung low along the lake a mile away. The blue waters of the lake reflected the clearing morning sky. Small ponds of varying size dotted the low-lying country, adding a blue sparkle to the brown marsh grass of the bogs. Black spruce grew in numerous thickets and copses throughout. The sun highlighted the scene in a cloudless sky. The morning came calm.

We hardly began glassing when a fair-sized stag and a doe emerged from a spotty growth of spruce half a mile back toward the lake. They walked steadfastly without a pause from our right to our left, across the tracks we had left on our route to the hill. Evergreens hid them frequently as they plodded steadily on. We considered a stalk, for the stag looked quite good. But their steady pace combined with the realization that once off the hill we would loose sight of them in the labyrinth of evergreens decided us against it. They rapidly passed out of sight in the sheltering spruce.

An hour passed without the sight of any more game. We climbed to the top of the hill and came into view of an extensive valley stretching off to a low range of hills a few miles away.

We sat down again in the warming sunshine and searched the new country. It offered an extension of the pond-dotted bogs of our previous lookout. Low-growing spruce gave hints of tuckamore. A few scattered junipers showed their cedarlike lacework. Next to one of those junipers, half a mile away, I picked up a lone caribou in my binoculars. It resolved itself into a doe. She fed slowly out of sight.

Another doe startled us half an hour later when she suddenly appeared from behind us to our right. We held quiet and watched her pass seventy-five yards away, then resumed our glassing. The morning continued pleasant.

Noon was an hour off when we tired of our stationary vigil and began still-hunting around the hill. We dipped through small ravines thick in their bottoms with low-bush spruce. Junipers masked our movement in places and open bogs exposed us in others. Stretches of flat rock broke regularly through the thin soil cover, silencing the soft swish of our steps through the course grass faded dull brown between them. We stole along beneath a wind-gentle, cloudless sky.

Less than thirty minutes had passed when movement two hundred yards ahead stilled us. No need for binoculars. Antlers rose distinctly from a striking stag showing nearly pure white in the distance. He climbed steadily uphill, weaving in and out of juniper-covered draws.

I knelt down on the irregular hillside and tried to hold the caribou steady in my scope, but his continuing movement and my awkward position caused the crosshairs to shift erratically.

Jake knelt beside me.

"It's a long shot. Do you want to try and get closer?"

"No. He's moving too fast. We'll loose him in the trees. Let me use your pack for a rest."

Jake quickly slipped out of his backpack. I positioned the pack over a scrub juniper and laid down behind it. The rifle rested satisfyingly steady. The stag continued his march up the hill. Junipers hid him at times and I tried to hold in front of them and catch the stag in the scope when he reappeared. But he wove distractingly through their screening. I twisted on the ground to keep the stag in the scope. Finally he stopped for a second in a small clearing. I brought the crosshairs hastily to his shoulder and began the trigger squeeze. The rifle recoiled and a satisfying whoomp drifted back, but the stag gave no indication of a hit and moved slowly off behind some junipers.

We waited a minute, watching for movement. The junipers revealed none. I stood up. Jake shouldered his backpack and we began walking toward the stag's last position. Movement fifty yards in front of us brought a startle. A doe and fawn caribou trotted out of the evergreens and made off toward the boggy valley. We resumed our stalk toward the junipers.

The cover confused us for several minutes until the white of the caribou revealed the downed stag in a tangle of low spruce. He was a strikingly colored animal. The white of his mane and neck carried up into his cheeks and ears. Even his nose was white, leaving the deep brown of his face and muzzle showing like a mask. He carried an average right antler, but the left side, which had been away from me, failed to match it.

We dressed the stag, finding that my bullet had neatly pierced the top of his heart. The work of quartering went smoothly under Jake's well-practiced hands. We packed the meat in white sacks and carried the sacks downhill to a level clearing where, I pleasantly discovered, a helicopter would later pick up the meat and fly it directly to a processing plant, saving us a long pack back to the boat and camp, and freeing up an extra afternoon of hunting.

We rested after our labors and ate lunch before climbing back to the top of the hill and setting off for an area known to hold moose. The time was one o'clock.

The day continued warm and pleasant under a cloudless sky. We shed our jackets as we trod lightly across the hilltop. We followed the hill around until yet another extensive valley lay below us. There we halted and sat down to glass.

Small lakes and bogs filled the landscape. Striking country and a striking day, although a bit too pleasant perhaps to expect moose to be moving in the open.

Caribou were moving though. A herd of eight appeared on a bog a mile away. They lazed along, candidates for a stalk were my tag not filled. Then a rising wind gusted across our necks and those wishful thoughts vanished, although the distant herd never did seem to catch our scent. The caribou moved slowly through the bogs and spruce before drifting out of sight.

The afternoon passed in languid scrutiny. No other caribou came into view, nor did a moose. A little after four o'clock we spotted Barry and Gilbert crossing an outlying bog. Gilbert balanced a set of moose antlers across his shoulders. Barry had evidently met with success on the far hills. We climbed down from our spotting position to meet them and returned to the boat.

A crossing of the lake brought us to the river outlet where Bryan and Jason were waiting, also with a moose rack. A very nice one. We loaded all in the boat and were back at camp by five-thirty. I walked a short distance along the lakeshore to watch where Edward had seen the bull the day before, but dusk settled down without the bull making another appearance.

Heavy fog in the morning. Jake and I pushed off the boat and were soon lost in the soupy mist. Jake motored cautiously, keeping his bearing in a fashion beyond my understanding. A shore began to take dim shape in the haze. Jake began patrolling the edge, searching for a recognizable landmark. The fog shifted about in confusing patterns.

The vapor slowly dissipated as we probed the shoreline. Jake spotted a familiar marking and we turned toward shore, landing at the base of a very steep and very high hill, a fitting landmass in the Long Range Mountains. The boat was beached and securely tied, then, with Jake leading the way, we began an angling ascent of the mountain-pitched hill.

Large sections of the hillside revealed scars from earlier logging operations. The spruce and fir had been clear-cut but the loggers had left a number of mature birch. They stood like white-uniformed guardians above the dark second growth. The logging slash, blowdowns, bogs, and second growth made our climb up the steep hill a slow and wearisome one.

We reached after a sharp ascent the remnants of a logging road, overgrown and indistinct but a welcome path after the rigors of the lower slope. We climbed quietly up the faint roadway, detouring around occasional deadfalls, pausing often to peer into the surrounding cover.

An overlook halted us for a brief rest. We gazed out over a grand vista of fir and spruce forests encircling blue-tinted lakes reflecting the clearing sky. The early morning fog had given way to another sun-blessed day.

We resumed our climb, watching ahead and to our sides. A section of unlogged spruce grew up and down a steep area of the hillside. We moved cautiously through it. At one point Jake took a backward glance, then stopped and whispered excitedly, "Moose!"

I turned to look, but could see nothing.

"Two moose on the downhill slope. I can't see 'em now."

We carefully retraced our steps. Alert. Peering intently into the evergreens. They revealed only more evergreens.

We climbed a short way up the opposite slope to gain a better look into the cover. If the moose remained there, they remained well-concealed.

We hunkered quietly into some second growth. Jake produced his call and sent a plaintive note wafting down the hillside. No response. He called again. The forest echoed silence.

Movement ahead to our left drew our excited attention. A brown form slipped through the dense evergreens, going away, lost in an instant.

We peered with intensity into the deep shadows. The closed forest remained impenetrable. Not a sound disturbed the hushed morning. We waited in the silence until the realization of nothing before us finally settled in. The moose had evidently headed down the hillside. Hopeless to try and follow in the dense tangles.

We again resumed our climb, a bit disappointed but nevertheless encouraged by the presence of moose. The time was a little after nine o'clock.

The logging road in places had been carved into the hillside, offering excellent vantage points from which to view the far-reaching forests and lakes below. We came shortly to one of those overviews when Jake again brought me to a halt with an excited whisper.

"There!" he said, pointing down the hillside.

I looked and saw a small meadow surrounded by dense evergreens nearly a quarter of a mile away at the base of the steep hillside. The meadow was the only opening in the otherwise impenetrable forest. And standing broadside along the near edge of the meadow were a cow and a bull moose.

"You can hit him from here."

It was a statement rather than a question. Jake had evidently been impressed with my earlier shot on the caribou.

But this was better than twice the distance, and no possibility for a prone resting shot. In fact, no possibility for a rest at all.

I knelt down and steadied my left arm over my left knee. The bull and cow stood in the clearing, obviously unaware of the two hunters watching them excitedly from the hillside above. They had stopped in the only possible place they could be seen in that vast evergreen forest.

I turned my variable scope to six-power and centered the crosshairs on the front of the bull. They held comfortably on target. I tried to estimate the range and the effect of the forty-five degree downward slope on the bullet's trajectory, and positioned the crosshairs accordingly. At least there was no wind. The bull stood in place as I held and practiced squeezed with the safety on. Then I released the safety, maintained my hold with the crosshairs slightly above the shoulder, and squeezed again.

A sharp report shattered the silence. The sound of the bullet striking disturbed the silence again. The bull broke into a straight-ahead run, angled a little left, and disappeared into the evergreens. The cow ran to the left and was quickly enveloped by the spruce. I chambered another round, but there was no hope of a follow-up shot.

"You hit him. He should be easy to track."

Down the hill we went, picking our way through a maze of wasted timber, cutoff treetops, and blowdowns, struggling on the steep slope through dense tangles of second growth, the only favorable aspect being that we were going down instead of up.

We reached the meadow, determined where the bull had been standing, and began a patient circle looking for blood. There was none. We widened the circle, stooped over in intense scrutiny of the grass-covered ground. Not a trace of the moose existed.

We began searching along the path the bull had presumably taken, but neither blood nor tracks indicated his passage. More circles. More frustration.

Back again to the point of the shot. More futile circles. We split up and began searching into the dense evergreens surrounding the meadow. I followed a suspected pathway, weaving through a dark, dense canopy. A hundred yards brought me to a tiny rivulet. A few tracks showed in the mud, but they were crusted.

I retraced my steps and followed another possible route. The evergreen cover closed tight. Needles littered the hard-packed earth. The ground revealed neither blood nor tracks. Back again, exhausting other possibilities, conferring with Jake whose searching met with a similar lack of success. Circling back again over the same ground, crossing each other's tracks, but finding no fresh tracks to point us in the right direction.

An hour passed as we combed the meadow and forest. Not a trace of the moose could be found. We met again and reluctantly concluded that the bull had been lost. A sore disappointment. Only one other time in forty years of big game hunting had I failed to recover a hit animal, a black bear shot at dusk leaving a good blood trail that I followed until dark. Had I a flashlight, I could have continued, but when I resumed trailing at dawn, the blood trail petered out. A morning spent in searching proved fruitless.

We stood in the little meadow and dejectedly considered where to continue hunting. From atop the hill we had observed a small lake edged with spruce that shaded into a bog. The lake lay in the direction we had seen the bull take when he had been hit. It seemed a likely place to possibly run across him or another bull. We started in that direction.

Jake led, choosing a way through the evergreens that corresponded with the presumed general route of the wounded bull. At one point a juncture offered two possible passages through the dense cover. Jake pondered, then said if the moose had come this way, it probably would have chosen this route. We turned and followed it.

We traveled slowly, studying the ground for sign, but found nothing to offer encouragement. Another double possibility through the growth halted us. Jake pondered again, then choose. On we walked, still searching, but resigned to failure.

The evergreens grew crowded, leaving dense little openings here and there filled with brush and tall grass. We wended through the shadows. My searching gradually grew desultory with the sense of lost hope. Jake continued ahead. Close-growing spruce trees narrowed our passageway. Jake parted a low spruce bough and came to a sudden halt. An excited exclamation startled me.

"Here he is!"

And indeed, there he was. The grand creature who had eluded our careful search lay wonderfully concealed in the nearly impenetrable conifers. We whooped and hollered in an unseemly display, having gone from the depths of despair to the heights of exhilaration in the space of a few footsteps. The forest rang.

We examined the bull. The bullet had hit near the shoulder, pierced both lungs, and exited the opposite side. I was using my .270 Winchester with one hundred and fifty grain Nosler bullets. Even after determining the path the moose had taken, we could not find a single drop of blood along his route. Nor, for that matter, could we discern a track.

We skinned and quartered the bull, enclosed the meat in protective white sacks, and packed them to the meadow for later pick up by the helicopter.

A slow struggle back up the tangled hillside brought us to a more comfortable walk down the logging road to the lakeshore and the boat. We enjoyed a pleasant ride across

476 ——————————————————— The Hunting Time

the sparkling waters back to camp, basking in the afternoon sun and the warm glow of success.

The helicopter came later in the afternoon and made short work of carrying out the meat. A novel method but wonderfully efficient, and most welcome when I contemplated packing the moose up that tangled, mountain-pitched hillside.

We had enjoyed a most successful hunt. Four caribou and four moose in two and a half days, with an excellent camp and guides, and wonderfully cooperative weather.

The time at last came to leave and another helicopter ride over the dazzling wilderness held me fascinated. A car was waiting to transport me back to the Hungry Bear Restaurant and my van.

As we drove over the blacktop highway, two small animals came into view, running down the middle of the road in the direction we were traveling. We drew closer to discover a black mink in close pursuit of a snowshoe hare. Each frantic dodge of the hare was matched by the mink who seemed to be gaining rapidly. The hare was substantially larger than the mink and one would have thought that sheer size alone would have won the day had the hare turned to fight. But there are the pursued, and there are the pursuers.

The car pulled alongside the two animals. I watched in fascination as the chase unfolded next to me. So intent on their deadly contest were the pair, they appeared oblivious to the car's presence. Then the hare, perhaps sensing potential safety in the shelter of the vehicle, darted beneath it and ended the chase under the left rear wheel.

We stopped at the processing plant where I picked up the deboned hind quarters of the moose along with the tenderloins.

The rest of the moose and the caribou traveled home with Jake. My freezer still held caribou from the previous year's hunt.

Another nighttime ferry crossing. I slept most of the way, wanting to get a fresh start on my two thousand mile drive home. I had another quick thousand miles to drive after that. The season in Wyoming was already underway.

Chapter 24

The Fortieth Season

Warm under the western sun. My van kicked up a plume of dust on the north-running dirt road. The turn into the ranch house tempered the dust as the rutted, mile-long drive slowed me. Chuck came out of the screen door as I pulled up.

"You're late this year. I wasn't sure you were comin'."

"I always show up. You know that."

"Yeah. I guess. Come in. Have some coffee."

I sat down on a side chair alongside the kitchen table. Chuck busied himself with the coffee pot, then returned to the table and sat down.

"Where you comin' from this year?"

"Newfoundland."

I watched him search his mind trying to place it.

"What were you after there?"

"Moose and caribou."

"You went after them last year didn't you?"

"I did. But in different places."

"Where was that again?"

"Ontario for moose and the Northwest Territories for caribou."

He searched his mind once more, then got up, went to the stove for the coffee pot, and filled two cups.

"Didn't you say somethin' about New Mexico last year?"

"I may have. I went there for elk and then to Colorado for deer the year before after I left here."

He nodded in acknowledgement of familiar places.

"They got a big deer here earlier. There's still plenty around."

"Any other hunters?"

"No. I had eleven but they're all gone."

"How'd they do?"

"They got some other deer besides the big one but the antelope hunters did poor. Only got one. But I expect you'll do okay on both. You always seem to."

"I've been fortunate. I've done well every year except that year I got rained out."

Chuck got up and topped off his cup. He held the pot out to me. I shook my head. He returned the pot to the stove and sat down.

"You shot some big ones I recall."

"I have. And some not so big. Depends on how the hunt's going."

"Most are always sayin' they only want big bucks but after a few days they don't seem so particular. Specially now with antelope. There ain't that many on the ranch anymore. Coyotes and eagles are killin' off the fawns. But there's plenty of deer. Big ones too if you're lookin' for one."

"I've taken my share of big bucks. But that's not why I come. I'm here simply because I like to hunt. A big buck can sure enhance the hunt but it doesn't make or break it for me. Most of the time a fair-sized animal fairly taken satisfies the hunting impulse just fine."

"It seems to for most from what I see. But they still like to go on about the big ones."

"We all like to dream."

"I suppose."

I looked outside. The day was passing. I finished my coffee.

"Do you want some more?"

"No. I think I'll head out."

"You might want to try down by the dam where that new rig's up. There was a buck antelope by there yesterday."

"Thanks. I will."

There is this advantage to coming out with only a few days left in the season. Nobody else is around.

I followed the dirt road north past a section that interrupted Chuck's land. A young buck and doe antelope stood close to the road. An encouraging sight even though they were out of bounds.

The track to the dam turned east off the dirt road. I followed the track until a dip hid the van, then left it and walked across the prairie. Red-winged grasshoppers scattered in profusion from the tall grass along the way. I came in time to the earthen dam and its small impoundment of water without sighting any antelope. Seven coots bobbed across the impoundment away from my unwanted intrusion. Five mallards flushed from an edging of reeds and soared westward over the prairie.

I climbed a hill above the dam and began to glass. The afternoon sun shone warmly in a cloudless sky. The temperature hovered in the high seventies. A lazy afternoon.

The rains had been good that summer and the grass grew tall. Chuck must have been holding that section for winter feeding. My searching eventually picked up a doe mule deer and two fawns bedded a hundred and fifty yards away in the tall grass. They lazed in the afternoon sun on the open prairie, miles away from the nearest tree. And miles away, apparently, from the nearest antelope, for my careful glassing revealed not another animal.

I sat on the hill enjoying the pleasant afternoon, a dramatic contrast from the year before when my arrival in Wyoming coincided with a raging two-day blizzard. The fierce storm knocked out the power for the entire county for eight days and stranded me along with many others in Lusk. The highways were closed. Even had they been open, none of the gas stations could pump gas without electricity. Most of the town was shut down. The Silver Dollar Tavern managed to stay open by candlelight. Essential services always find a way. The state quickly sent emergency generators and the highways were soon opened, but I still lost four days before the back roads and prairie dried out enough to get to my hunting area. Even then the gumbo took its toll in time. My planned follow-up hunt to Colorado for elk and mule deer had to be put off.

The weather on my earlier hunts that year had not been much better. Twenty-five big game hunting days with near continuous absence of the sun, starting with my annual spring black bear hunt in Ontario where I woke up to two inches of snow on June second. The snow and rain followed me relentlessly through the seasons. The sun above my perch on the hill shone in balmy contrast.

I made a final sweep with my binoculars, then came down off the hill and walked back to the van. I followed the track out to the road, crossed it, and headed west over the rolling prairie. A draw hid the van. I left it and set out on foot. A climb out of the draw and down a shallow ridge soon put the van out of sight. I walked along under that grand illusion of an endless prairie rolling away unbounded toward a never-attainable horizon.

Would that it were so, but fences inevitably shatter the unbounded illusion. Yet there is little else to detract from the impression of unrestrained country, and the slow walking through it gives a fine sense of its seeming limitlessness. And turns the pursuit of antelope into a hunt instead of a shoot.

Antelope roamed this rolling country in considerable numbers during my earlier seasons. Multiple herds of twenty, thirty, forty, and more were common. Chuck and I on several occasions sat on his front porch and watched herds of that size feeding within sight of the ranch house. But a long drought severely affected the herds on the ranch. They had yet to fully recover, and perhaps, as Chuck remarked, predation on the fawns hampered that recovery. Still, some were always present. They could be found in time.

But the time was obviously not that afternoon. The prairies remained empty of even a suspicion of antelope. A wide circle brought me back to the van with just time enough to get into my mule deer area before dark.

The familiar track south past the ranch house took me toward the timbered hills. My old route through Sawmill Canyon was no longer passable. It had washed out. An offshoot track turned away from the steeper part of the canyon and dropped into the dry creek bed over a formerly unpassable bank. When the canyon track washed out, Chuck had a rough track cut down the bank. A shorter approach, although a problem should it rain. But than so was the canyon.

I eased down the bank and followed through the scattered evergreens. A clump of three tall junipers near a steep bank offered concealment for the van. I backed in. The forest green of the van became nearly one with the dark green of the junipers. Dusk was settling. An owl hooted. A rare sound in these hills. Then the familiar yip of a coyote joined in. My time for hunting had passed but the night hunters were awakening. I ate supper, read awhile, and turned in.

A roar of wind woke me in the night. It channeled down the dry creek bed, bellowing through the junipers and rocking the van. Rain became a concern, but the sky remained clear.

Five a.m. No wind. Clear sky. Forty-five degrees. Breakfast and hot coffee while I stare into the dark.

I have camped along this dry creek bed for twenty seasons, half of all the seasons I have hunted in Wyoming. No one else ever camped back in these hills. It was rare even to see other hunters during the beginning years. But I see them more lately. Early in the season. I began coming later when they are gone.

I lingered over coffee, enjoying the dark and the solitude and the hush of the morning night. I awoke earlier than necessary, wanting to be well in place for the dawning.

The stars began to fade. I shouldered my day pack and my rifle and walked through the silent junipers, across the creek bed, and up the south bank to where the prairie blends into the timbered hills. I angled southeast across the dark prairie toward a far draw that fingered down from the hills. I once watched the biggest buck I ever saw on the ranch come out of that draw on his way to the timber. He had two choices. Right would have brought him through the area I was watching. Left offered me no chance. He turned left.

I since have begun my morning watching at that draw. A few fair bucks have fallen there, but the big buck that drew me out of the hills had yet to make a second appearance.

Six-thirty. Calm in the breaking dawn. A little shiver from the cool air and, dare one admit after all these years, from the rising primal excitement at the start of the hunt. It has always been thus. When it ceases to be, then will I cease to hunt.

Seven o'clock approached with the sighting of a doe and two fawns filtering through the timbered edge of the hills a quarter of a mile away. Still not full light. They tracked dimly through my binoculars. Five minutes passed. Three more deer appeared near the same spot. Large bodied, but shadowy forms against the dark timber. I could not make out any antlers.

It might have been better to have stayed in the hills. The deer were funnelling in from farther south. I debated about moving then spotted a lone deer dropping into the draw a third of a mile to the east. Too fleeting to discern antlers. But a large deer. And alone. I waited.

The dawning came and a crackling, trumpeting sound came with it. Harsh in the still quiet. I looked up to see three sandhill cranes scouting ahead of a vee formation of forty or fifty. A second vee of thirty or more followed. The two vees joined as they passed over me heading south and in quick succession absorbed the three scouts into a single wavering vee. They passed on paralleling the rising sun.

An hour drifted by without the sighting of any other deer. Where the deer in the draw had gone remained unclear. It should have come by me by then.

I left my stand beside a pine and began still-hunting along the rim of the draw. Evergreens traced through the bottom. A few climbed up the sides. Cottonwoods grew farther to the northeast where the draw flattened out. The morning remained still with only a hint of a breeze. The rising sun became a bother. I tipped my hat brim to shield my eyes.

The draw bent around to the northeast. I followed the turn and startled three does. They ran up the side of the draw and stopped on the rim a hundred and fifty yards away. We stared at each other for a good minute until the does bolted. They ran along the rim a short distance before dropping back into the draw where a grove of cottonwoods screened them. I started forward again and followed into the cottonwoods, but saw neither the does nor any other deer.

The rising sun warmed my back as I turned and followed another draw west toward the hills. My wool jacket soon ended up in my day pack. The sunlight highlighted little pockets in the draw.

Deer drifted through these draws in the morning heading into the timbered hills after a night on the open prairie. Interception offered the best early chance, but I have taken surely as many still-hunting later in the hills.

The draw led me into the timber. I climbed slowly through the junipers, thick in the lower reaches between the ridges. Pines sheltered in the rocky upper areas.

Slow through the pines. Pausing often and long. Trading vantage points with cautious passages between. Two hours passed. The overhead sun shortened the shadows.

I left an overlook and began walking north through a more open area. A small, rocky prominence came into view sixty to seventy yards away on my right. I glanced toward it and came to an abrupt halt.

A deer rose from the rocks. A buck. A second deer rose. Another buck. The first buck bolted to his rear. I hurried with my rifle. He vanished as the scope came into position. The second buck followed the first, disappearing behind the rocks as the scope captured an image of neck, head, and antlers in the instant when I shot. A sense of an impact. But too fleeting for certainty.

I chambered another round and approached the rocks. The buck lay dead behind them. Shot through the neck.

The late morning sun beat warmly as I worked my way out of the hills with the buck in tow. The drag rope bit sharply into my shoulders on the uphill pulls. In time the last downward slope brought me to the creek bed. I left the deer, walked to the van, then drove it up the creek bed to the buck, loaded him into the van, and followed the creek bed and the track out of the hills.

The locker plant in Lusk was not as rushed as earlier in the season. I filled out the forms to donate the deer to the local food pantry, which I had been doing for several years since my freezer was generally well-stocked with moose and caribou, paid the processing fee, then headed north back to the ranch.

I passed the drive to the ranch house and continued toward the dam. The same young buck and doe antelope seen the day before grazed off to the west of the road. Still in the same section. Still out of bounds.

The seven coots were bobbing on the impoundment when I stalked up to it, but the mallards were gone. So was the mule deer doe and her fawns. I sat on the hill glassing. The afternoon continued warm and the prairies continued empty of antelope.

Back to the western rolling hills with another long circuit before the setting sun brought an end to my day. I camped there on the prairie, seemingly the only living creature around. A coyote yipped in the night dispelling that fantasy. The stars glimmered bright above.

A later arising. Letting the day start before setting out on another circuit. Brisk in the early light, and quiet, until a far-off murmur began trumpeting louder. Another flock of sandhill cranes croaked boisterously south across the sky. A hundred perhaps.

I turned in their opposite direction and set off across the prairie. The morning was fine. Another pleasant day.

I followed the contours, keeping low except for careful approaches over ridges. I watched ahead, occasionally turning to re-examine the country behind me. One of those turns brought me slowly to the ground. Three antelope were crossing a ridge a quarter of a mile away. Two does and a nice buck.

They spotted me and began running along the ridge. I flattened to prone. They stopped, staring in my direction. I lay still on the ground. They turned and dropped out of sight.

I arose and jogged rapidly toward the ridge. The country beyond it began to come into view. I slowed, stepped cautiously forward, then lowered myself and squirmed to the crest. The three antelope stood in the middle of an extensive flat, looking in my direction.

I nestled into the scope. The antelope showed four hundred yards plus. The buck was bunched tight between the does. I waited.

The trio broke and sprinted parallel to the ridge, then stopped with the buck a little behind the does. I tried to steady the crosshairs. Before I could, they ran again.

The antelope come to another halt and stared in my direction. I nestled again into my rifle. The buck held briefly in the scope. I began the trigger squeeze. The antelope bolted and ran farther onto the flat. I eased my finger off the trigger and lay there waiting.

Several minutes passed. The three antelope stood out of range, staring intently at the ridge. I lay watching them.

The trio stood like statues for several more minutes, then seemed to relax. They began feeding, drifting back in my direction. They kept the ridge under scrutiny but continued closing before drifting to the left. Another small ridge eventually hid them.

I squirmed back, stood up, and began a rapid walk toward the ridge. Another careful crawl brought the trio into sight. They fed three hundred and fifty yards away. I crawled behind a small rock outcropping, crumpled my hat over it, and rested my rifle on the hat.

The three antelope remained closely bunched. I waited. The two does finally opened a gap. I locked into the sight picture and fired. The buck dropped and the does broke into a run. The pair vanished over another ridge as I rose from the ground.

I began the walk to the buck. Half-a-hundred times and more have I made such a walk across the prairie, feeling always the familiar sense of primal fulfillment, yet feeling again that moment's uniqueness. It is ever old. And it is ever new.

I reached the buck and looked long over the sage-covered expanses. So many times have I been a part of this drama and still the primal impulse draws me ever back to these prairies, and with undiminished eagerness I begin each stalk. I hunt because it is ever new, and because it answers a compelling atavistic need, and because I glory in the freedom of it. And because, when the seasons come, the wild and the far-off places send out their siren's call.

-2-

It is late November, the Saturday before Thanksgiving, and I am doing what I have done on this day for the past forty seasons. I am in Wisconsin. I am deep in the North Woods. I am standing beside a tree. And I am waiting for a deer.

The predawn darkness surrounds me and the wet and the fog of the night have settled into a damp chill. Strange weather for opening day in these northlands. The woods are dripping instead of crackling from the cold.

Half an hour passes before the first shot echoes off to the north. The familiar tingle starts. I cautiously look at my watch. It is quarter to seven and I still cannot see into the dark morning. Another shot follows the first, and a third shortly thereafter. All from different directions. They must be watching forest openings.

There is no snow this year. The dark forest looms darker without the white background. Six-thirty is legal shooting time but it takes half an hour longer before the overcast sky sheds enough light to see into the closer second growth and brush. Still, compulsion draws me always into the dark of the morning to await the dawn. The magic of first light is still the most magical of all the magical times.

A red squirrel scurries about nearby. The bustling little creature has a cache only a few feet from where I stand and it is busy running through the damp leaves, hurrying to gather food, then returning to bury it in the same secret depression. The squirrel finally notices an unusual shape by the tree and dashes up a nearby hemlock where it investigates me thoroughly while chuckling softly through its throat. The flicking tail telegraphs every soft chuckle. I try to appear a part of the forest, hoping the squirrel will not break into its noisy alarm chatter. At last, apparently satisfied, the squirrel scampers down the hemlock and races away to resume its business of the morning.

Intermittent shots break the silence. Three behind me echo closer than the others. I watch a trail running from that direction but see only two ravens in silent passage overhead.

A weasel dashes through the leaves twenty yards in front of me dressed in its striking winter coat of ermine white. I trace the white ermine through the dark leaves for a long time. The diminutive creature remains in constant motion. Hunting. Hunting. For it, the essential life impulse.

The dawning shades into the morning, overcast but warming some. Sixteen deer passed this way last year in six separate sightings. Fifteen continued on undisturbed. Sign shows that many are still around. I wait through the hours for one of them to come.

Eleven o'clock. The little red squirrel returns but nothing else makes an appearance. I grow weary of standing and begin still-hunting. The damp leaves provide a silent passage through the forest. The day has warmed considerably, unseasonably so. The temperature must be approaching forty. I remove my down vest and stuff it into my day pack, then eat a sandwich while watching along a narrow, overgrown logging trail. Fresh tracks show in a stretch of muddy ground, the oversized imprints of a very large deer, dewclaws drilled deeply an impressive space away from the long, broad wedges of the split hoofs. I follow the tracks and the trail until they both become lost in a large, open marsh. Recent buck rubs show prominently along the way. Buck rubs are also in evidence around my stand. One on a small pine indicates some serious attitude.

I leave the marsh and hunt through the overcast forest back to my hemlock stand. Time passes, but no deer pass with it.

The sun breaks through, warming the afternoon and bringing a breeze that steadies from my back. I turn away from the stand into the breeze and still-hunt to another area where the wind is less troublesome. The late afternoon drifts by in warming silence. I watch into the breeze. Nothing appears. The dark at last turns me away.

Supper is my special-recipe caribou chili.

A steady south wind continues the unseasonably warm temperature Sunday morning. The walk to my stand nearly tempts me to shed my coat.

The morning dawns clear with the south wind strengthening. The wind quarters toward a tag-alder swamp that borders the area I am watching. Dense conifers grow into a nearly impenetrable labyrinth around the swamp and behind me, blending into a new-growth area of thick pines. I watch from an elevated thicket into a tract of mixed forest and scrub brush. A well-traveled trail runs through the tract between the pines and the swamp, with several crossing and offshoot trails. My stand is a nondescript spot alongside one of the hemlocks where the forest debris has been kicked aside to allow me to stand and turn silently on the bare earth. Nothing else distinguishes it.

Clearing skies through the morning. The wind continues steady, quartering across me away from the trailed tract. Deer may be moving on some of the farther trails but the lack of snow has turned the brown brush into perfect deer camouflage. If they are moving, they are moving as invisible as the wind.

Four hours pass. I begin still-hunting west. The damp forest floor silences my passage but the snowless woods reduce visibility through most of the stretches. I probe suspected bedding areas and come in time to a favorable spot for a later stand.

A long circuit brings my morning stand back into view. I wait on it for a while watching the presumed same white ermine of yesterday hunt through the dark forest litter. He appears to be no more successful on this second day than I. The red squirrel does not make an appearance. The temperature swelters at near fifty degrees. The warmest north country deer season I can recall.

The final two hours find me on the new stand. It proves no more productive than the other. I leave in the dark under a full moon. A large-bodied deer jumps out in front of me, its flashing white tail drifting through the moonlit shadows like a ghost.

Light rain Monday morning. Chilling in the damp. I walk in the dark to the hemlock and wait for the dawning. The red squirrel comes with it, busy at the start of day. Woodpeckers also come and the rat-a-tat-tat of one turns my gaze upward. A pair of downy woodpeckers are busy in the hemlock searching for beetle grubs and insect eggs. A hidden songbird keeps melodic cadence with the rat-a-tat-tat drumming while a pair of ravens croak in backup chorus. A springtime serenade on a late November morning.

I wait, clinging to the remembrance of last year's deer activity, expecting with hope its repeat. The sign still shows promise. But the morning passes empty again.

I still-hunt east through fresh country, treading silently over the dampened earth. A cedar swamp pulls me in. Dark and deep here. Trails crisscrossing. Buck rubs on stripling cedars. Beds in evidence. Quiet in the deep. And quiet do I drift through it, sensing and tensing and easing over mossy blowdowns farther into deeper shadows until rising ground thins the cedars and the swamp edges onto an open hardwood ridge and I leave the swamp for the longer vision.

The faint remains of a logging trail offers silent passage through the hardwoods. I circle slow through the still and empty woods back to the hemlock with two hours remaining in the day. The dampness seeps in as evening descends. The barely penetrable brush fades slowly into impenetrableness. The crosshairs loose their definition and I turn and walk the dark way out from the hemlock.

A misty Tuesday morning, settling into a steady rain an hour after I reach the hemlock. I huddle tight against its trunk. The evergreen canopy starting a few feet above my head gives me a leaky but still serviceable umbrella.

The hours pass. The rain turns to sleet and then to snow, heavy and wet. The dark ground turns white and I watch with rising hope as the falling snow opens up the thick brush. Then the wet snow begins to cling to the brush, slowly filling the spaces between, and gradually the barely penetrable brown brush transforms into an impenetrable wall of white.

A wind comes, shifting around to the north, angling the flakes before it. I shift to the leeward side of the trunk and let myself become immersed in the elements. Time passes in near forgetfulness as the dark forest transforms into an alabaster wonderland. Brown disappears. The wet snow clings to all except the lee of the trees. The wind rises, gusting now and harder, the snow driving before it. The raw wilderness closes around. I stand in the storm, watching it envelope me, part of the grandness of it, glorying in the tempestuous wildness.

I can barely see into the snow. The wind blows through the noon. I shield my back to it and open my day pack for a sandwich. My gloves are damp from the snow. I exchange them for a dry pair.

Another hour passes. It is no longer possible to see into the trailed area. I shoulder my pack and turn away from the hemlock.

Deer have been moving in the storm. I cross a set of tracks, then a second, and a third before I have covered sixty yards. All three deer came through the area I had been watching heading into the new-pine growth and the thick cover beyond. The snow-covered brush hid them perfectly.

Another twenty-five yards reveals two more sets of tracks. Both heading into the new pines. I continue to the downwind side of the tracks, find a tree to prop my rifle out of the driving snow, tuck myself tight beside it, and watch as far along the edge of the new pines as the storm will let me.

The wind drives the snow into my face. It is hard to see. The snow continues unabated through the afternoon. I turn to white, resisting any movement to brush myself off. I watch and wait for other hopeful deer to follow the five into the new pines. If they followed, they followed beyond my vision.

A foot of fresh snow slows my progress Wednesday morning. The forest is a solid sea of white. I decide to forgo my hemlock stand since the snowed-in brush of yesterday could hardly have improved overnight.

I walk along the edge of the lake toward a trail that will allow some open movement without getting drenched from the wet snow. The lake edges are frozen now.

Motion along the shore ice halts me. A mink comes into view. Unceasingly busy. Probing here and there. For what in the snowy ice I cannot tell. The mink continues its frantic activity as I turn down the trail.

Two grouse erupt from the snow, startling me with a heart-stopping explosion. I recover and continue on.

The morning is grand. The wind has stilled. I plow through the snow. But to what avail, I wonder? Visibility is limited to the narrow trail ahead. The snow-plastered brush obscures all else.

I follow the trail around to a small clearing and watch there for no other reason than that I can see. An hour passes in silent whiteness. I follow through more open woods toward my hemlock stand. A tiny shrew scurries across the snow in front of me, looking like a brown thistle blowing in the wind. It should be burrowed deep lest the mink be tempted.

I approach the backside of my stand and cross a large set of deer tracks in the snow. They lead me with growing intrigue directly to the hemlock. The tracks pass as close to the right side of the tree as I have been standing all these days on the left.

The dark ground shows fresh in the bottom of the tracks. The furrowed impression continues into the trailed area. I cannot see into it.

I drop off the little elevation and track after the deer. It is hopeless. I can see only feet ahead in the snow-covered brush. I follow for a short distance then accept the reality and turn back to the hemlock and hunt from there to the spot I watched from last evening.

There are fresh tracks in the snow.

I wait through the morning, surrounded by a fantasy world of white. The snow I hoped for has come with a vengeance, cancelling the vision into the dark brush it normally provides. Still the pleasure of the woods and the promise of the tracks holds me into the early afternoon. Then it is time to go. I have two hundred and fifty miles to drive in order to be home for Thanksgiving.

I walk through the silent forest, transformed in a day nearly beyond recognition. The open pathways through the conifers and hardwoods have closed into narrow corridors of white. But the trees and the brush will clear in time, and when they do the dark woods will open, and the deer will no longer leave their tracks in hiding.

I returned to the snow-flocked North Woods after Thanksgiving to close out the final weekend. The forest had opened some but my fortieth Wisconsin whitetail season ended as did my first. I did not get a deer.

The seasons have passed yet there are more beyond the years. The hunting time continues to fill the same special place it always has. I look with nostalgic pleasure on hunts past, but look with greater pleasure on hunts to come. Where those hunts will find me only the seasons will tell. Yet this I do know. When the snows of late November come, I will be where I have been since the seasons started. I will be in Wisconsin. I will be deep in the North Woods. I will be standing beside a tree. And I will be waiting for a deer.

I have come down once more from the mountains,
I have returned from north of the north,
I will rest me now for a winter's while,
Till the Red Gods again summon me forth.

PART IV

The Rifles

I seem always to have been a rifleman. My first real rifle, after my BB guns, was a .22 caliber Mossberg. I bought it when a teenager because I enjoyed shooting. Many a box of fifty rounds was shot through that rifle at targets and in general plinking. In time, fitted with a peep sight, that Mossberg became my first hunting rifle. I shot squirrels and rabbits with it, and, if memory serves, a game bird or two before my first shotgun was acquired.

I later purchased a .22 Winchester Magnum and mounted a Weaver four-power scope on it. I fancied that little magnum as a long-range squirrel and varmint rifle, and used it, among other things, for hunting fox in the winter.

When big game hunting took its hold, I agonized long over the proper caliber. I was strongly influenced by the writings of Jack O'Connor in *Outdoor Life* magazine and because of that influence settled on a used pre-64 Winchester Model 70 in .270 caliber with a Lyman peep sight. The peep sight was soon replaced with a Weaver 2.5X-8X variable scope. I shot my first and well over a hundred other head of big game with that Model 70. It remains my favorite rifle.

When I bought the rifle I also bought reloading equipment, mainly to save money. No doubt I still spent too much money on shooting but I got considerably more shooting for what was spent. And also considerably more enjoyment. Handloading became an integral part of my shooting hobby. It seemed for a while that the only reason I was shooting was to try out new loads.

I tested, in all likelihood, every make and weight bullet made for the .270 caliber. I settled mainly on 130- and 150-grain Sierra boat-tails for antelope and mule deer, and 150-grain Noslers for caribou. For whitetails in brush, 150-grain round-nosed bullets were preferred. For black bear, elk, and moose, I loaded both 150-grain Noslers and 170-grain Speers. But I was always trying different loads and did not hold hard and fast to those particular bullets.

One experiments with various bullets because it is the bullet, after all, that does the job in the hunting field. Rifles and cartridges and cases and primers and powders only launch the missile. Above all else, it is the bullet and the bullet's placement that determines the outcome. Caliber cannot make up for poor shot placement, but good shot placement can usually make up for less than ideal caliber and bullet.

I became enamored for a while with the thought of a special brush rifle for use on whitetails and black bear. I bought a customized German military 8MM Mauser and fitted it with a Weaver 2.5X scope with a post reticle and a quick-detachable mount that incorporated a peep sight. At the time Winchester made a 200-grain round-nosed bullet for that caliber. Conventional wisdom held that a large-diameter round-nosed bullet loaded to moderate velocity would treat brush as air. It may or it may not have. The few targets I shot at through brush neither proved nor disproved the theory. But that rifle and my handloads did account for a goodly number of whitetails and black bears in the typically brushy country I hunted them in. Winchester eventually quit making the 200-grain bullet. None of the replacement bullets I loaded ever seemed to be as effective.

My fascination with specialization did not end with a brush rifle. At one time I had a separate shotgun for every game bird and animal I hunted. I also determined a special antelope and mule deer rifle was needed. (I know, I had one with the .270, but we are not talking about rational thought processes here.) A new Winchester Model 70 in .243 caliber with a Weaver variable scope struck my fancy. It was indeed a fine caliber for those animals and a fair number of them fell to my handloads before it became my son's rifle.

When grizzly bear hunting passed from fancy to fact, I bought from a gunsmith his personal Winchester Model 70 in .338 Winchester Magnum caliber with a Redfield 1X-4X variable scope. (The gunsmith replaced his .338 with a .375 H & H Magnum.) I have used this rifle on moose, elk, caribou, mule deer, whitetail, and black bear with expected good effect. But except perhaps for a few occasions involving the larger animals, with no better effect than my .270. The only big game animal I ever lost, a black bear, was unfortunately shot with this rifle. Obviously it was not the rifle's fault.

I also acquired a Winchester Model 70 in .220 Swift caliber with an Unertl target scope, which I felt was the ultimate varmint cartridge. It was also the most accurate rifle I have ever owned. Ten-shot groups under an inch at one hundred yards were not uncommon. Perhaps I could have tightened the groups further from a bench rest. I actually did very little varmint hunting with the Swift but shot thousands of rounds at targets. I became more interested in fine-tuning my handloads and spent many a pleasant afternoon with that rifle at local gravel pits.

In addition to rifles I did a considerable amount of squirrel and rabbit hunting with a .22 caliber Ruger revolver. I took to carrying the revolver along with my rifle or shotgun when I was hunting small game and used it if the opportunity presented itself. In the deep snows of December and January, I often hunted rabbits with just the revolver. Usually they could be spotted sitting. Only occasionally did I shoot at them with the revolver when they were running.

For several years I also hunted whitetails and black bear with a bow. Archery hunting in the days I hunted with a bow was, except for a dedicated few, more of a novelty than the sole method of choice it has since become for many. Its main appeal for me was another deer season. I bought a forty-five pound Bear recurve bow and became quite proficient with it shooting instinctively. I still have the original carton the bow came in. The bow itself is retired to a prominent place on the wall as a reminder of some pleasant Wisconsin whitetail and Ontario black bear hunts.

I make these brief notes because hunters are typically interested in a hunter's choice of arms. These are the rifles I have used, and, in the case of my .270 and .338, still use for my big game hunting.

A Big Game Hunter's Library

Hunters have shared their experiences through the ages. One can almost visualize our Cro-Magnon ancestors sitting around the evening's fire relating their hunting exploits. Those long-ago hunters left no written words, but they did leave a number of intriguing cave art impressions.

Their earliest known pictographs, Paleolithic paintings in the Grotte Chauvet in France dating back thirty-two thousand years, are of animals. Various symbolisms have been ascribed to these animal paintings, but their true meaning can only be surmised. One thing that is evident, however, symbolism aside, is that the great majority of these paintings depict animals that were hunted. Those early Cro-Magnon artists must have been communicating, in some fashion, about the hunt.

All the writing systems ever devised evolved from pictures. It is instructive to note, therefore, that the earliest of these pictures, and hence by extension the earliest of writing, concerned itself with hunting.

I have always been a reader. Books, especially, have held a fascination since childhood. I have read and collected books for as long as I can remember. When hunting began to become important, it seemed only natural to seek out books on the subject. Through the years I have built up the hunting, fishing, and natural history section of my library to over sixteen hundred volumes.

My first hunting books were of a how-to nature, but over time the books describing hunting experiences became of greater interest. I began reading and collecting them in earnest. No country or game escaped my attention, but it was the books giving accounts of North American big game hunting that ended up holding my attention the most.

Along with my enjoyment of the narratives, I take an interest in the older hunting accounts because of my curiosity about the beginnings of things. No doubt an extension of my interest in ancient history.

The earliest known records of North American big game hunting are found in the manuscripts of the Aztecs. These vivid Mexican hieroglyphics depict the slaying of jaguars and ocelots along with the snaring of deer. The great king, Montezuma, had a private hunting preserve on an island where, among other game, he hunted deer.

Hunting is frequently mentioned in the early explorers and colonists writings. Illustrations eventually began to accompany these accounts. Captain John Smith's *Description of New England*, published in 1619, contains the first picture of North American colonists hunting and fishing for sport, an engraving which shows, among a myriad of hunting activities, a lone horseman following a hound in pursuit of a deer.

New Yorkers may be interested to learn of Daniel Denton's notice in 1670 of a great hunting place called Long Island, where among an extensive list of other "Wilde Beasts, there is Deer and Bear."

There are numerous mentions of North American big game hunting in a variety of books throughout the sixteen- and seventeen-hundreds, but it was not until 1830 that the first North American sporting book with accounts of big game hunting was published.

The Cabinet of Natural History and American Rural Sports was first issued as a monthly magazine and later bound into three volumes dated 1830, 1832, and 1833. The 1830 volume contains an early natural history of the white-tailed deer along with fascinating descriptions of an unsuccessful moose hunt during which a three hundred pound deer was killed, an encounter with a cougar while on an 1817 deer hunt, "An Extraordinary Wolf Hunt," a black bear hunt, an "Encounter with a Panther," a buffalo hunt, and a story of a cougar and bear fight. The bound volumes are quite rare and my copy of the 1830 volume is one of the prize books in my library.

The next American published book with good descriptions of big game hunting is Lieut. Col. P. Hawker's *Instructions to Young Sportsmen in all That Relates to Guns and Shooting to Which is Added the Hunting and Shooting of North America.* First published in England in 1814 without the North American portion, this book went through numerous editions. It is the 1846 edition published in Philadelphia that contains the North American hunting section, comprising over half of the book and including sixteen articles on deer, caribou, elk, moose, buffalo, black and grizzly bear, cougar, and wolf, with many descriptive accounts of their hunting.

Some early personal memoirs bring the hunting scenes of that erstwhile era wonderfully to life. Philip Tome's *Pioneer Life; or, Thirty Years a Hunter,* published in 1854, contains classic accounts of deer, elk, and black bear hunting in Pennsylvania from 1795 through 1823; and Meshach Browning's *Forty-four Years of the Life of a Hunter,* published in 1859, includes extensive accounts of deer and bear hunting in Maryland early in the nineteenth century. Browning's black bear hunting exploits are remarkable. He killed between three hundred and four hundred. Some with a knife.

A younger contemporary of those two hunters, Oliver Hazard Perry, kept a wonderfully detailed journal of his deer and elk hunting experiences in Ohio and Michigan from 1836 through 1855, although the journal was not published until 1899, thirty-five years after his accidental death. Only one hundred copies were printed for family and friends under the title *Hunting Expeditions of Oliver Hazard Perry.* It is obviously very rare in that first edition. A second edition was published in 1994 by St. Hubert's Press. Of all the early hunting chronicles, it ranks in the top group of my favorites.

John James Audubon left some nicely detailed descriptions of cougar and bear hunting in the south in the 1820's, part of his sixty sketches on early nineteenth-century American life collected together for the first time under the title *Delineations of American Scenery and Character,* published in 1926. William Elliott's *Carolina Sports by Land and Water,* published in 1846, includes some rousing tales of deer hunting with hounds in South Carolina in the 1830's; and Frederick Gerstaecker's *Wild Sports in the Far West,* originally published in German and first published in English, I believe, in 1854, contains deer and bear hunting episodes in Arkansas in the 1840's. Gerstaecker's book went through a number of printings, as did Elliott's.

With the exception of Perry's, these books treat a variety of other subjects beside big game hunting, but they contain the best descriptions of big game hunting available from that period. They are collector's books for the most part, and while I enjoy the collecting aspect, I rarely acquire books solely for that reason. I buy books to read. It is a rare book on my shelves that is there purely for its collector's value, although I have paid some goodly collector's prices upon occasion just to read a book.

Some of those goodly sums were spent for books authored by Frank Forester, a pseudonym for Henry William Herbert, a transplanted Englishman who became the first professional hunting and fishing author in North America. Herbert spent his first eight years in America teaching school, then resigned and made his living writing. His list of hunting and fishing works is extensive. One of his most popular books, *The Field Sports of the United States and British Provinces of North America,* first published in two volumes in 1849, contains a one hundred and fifty page section on North American big game, including incidents of their hunting. A number of his other books contain information on big game hunting.

Frank Forester's *The Deerstalkers,* which first appeared as a four-part magazine serial in 1845 and was published in book form in 1849, is the first American big game hunting novel. The hunting scenes have a decidedly British tone, but it is still an engrossing tale as is his story of a caribou hunt found in *The Wigwam in the Wilderness.* The latter story is included in the *Life and Writings of Frank Forester,* published in 1882.

Another novel from that period, Charles Whitehead's *Wild Sports in the South; or, The Camp-Fires of the Everglades,* published in 1860, contains nicely detailed descriptions of deer hunting in Florida. The book was reissued in 1891 and again in 1897 under the title *The Camp-Fires of the Everglades; or, Wild Sports in the South.*

A visiting Frenchman, Benedict Revoil, in his *Shooting and Fishing in the Rivers, Prairies, and Backwoods of North America,* first published in English in 1865, relates entertaining narratives of caribou and moose hunting in New Brunswick and Quebec along with chapters on deer, bison, grizzly, and black bear. Revoil was an unabashed plagiarist, so it is difficult to ascribe his writings. His caribou story, for instance, is lifted almost verbatim from B. P. Wallop's earlier account in Hawker's book. But with that as a caveat, one can still enjoy the hunting descriptions. The book is rare in the 1865 two-volume edition. A single volume of the hunting material was published in 1875 under the title *The Hunter and the Trapper in North America.*

Most of these early hunting accounts take place in the east. Accounts from the west were mostly of exploration, although a number of those western explorers did leave descriptions of their hunting. One of them, the English Captain John Palliser, after completing his report for Her Majesty and the Parliament, wrote a detailed chronicle of his hunting experiences in the American west. *Solitary Rambles and Adventures of a Hunter in the Prairies,* first published in 1853, includes much early Americana along with the descriptive hunting narratives.

Two other Englishmen left good accounts of their big game hunting in the west. Parker Gillmore authored several books on North American hunting. His *Prairie and Forest,* published in 1874, includes most of his western hunting. John Mortimer Murphy's *Sporting Adventures in the Far West,* published in 1880, includes all the western big game with numerous descriptions of their hunting.

While many of the early western accounts were written by English authors, American authors were also hunting in the new frontier. George Oliver Shields, who became editor and publisher of *Recreation* magazine, wrote two interesting books on western hunting: *Rustlings in the Rockies,* 1883, (later reprinted as *Hunting in the Great West,* 1890); and *Cruisings in the Cascades,* 1889. The latter book is most attractively bound and illustrated. Shields also edited *The Big Game of North America,* 1890, a likewise attractively bound and illustrated volume containing chapters on all the North American big game by various authors.

Another anthology that contains good descriptions of big game hunting was issued in 1896 as part of the out-of-door library and titled *Hunting*. The chapters originally appeared as articles in *Scribner's Magazine*.

An intriguing book published in 1893 recounts fourteen expeditions after North American big game by Lewis Lindsay Dyche, a professor of zoology in the Kansas State University. *Camp-Fires of a Naturalist* is unusual in that the professor, unlike all the other authors mentioned, did not write his own book. Clarence Edwords compiled these accounts from the professor's field notes.

We come now to surely the best known big game author of that period, Theodore Roosevelt, a writer who bridges the nineteenth and twentieth centuries and whose books are still eminently readable. His first book, *Hunting Trips of a Ranchman*, published in 1885, is almost wholly devoted to western big game hunting, unlike his next book, *Ranch Life and the Hunting Trail,* 1888, which devotes only about one-third to hunting. *The Wilderness Hunter,* first published in 1893, contains accounts of hunting all the big game of North America except those of the far north.

Roosevelt's books were reprinted many times, both individually and in combination. For example, *Big Game Hunting in the Rockies and on the Great Plains,* 1899; *Hunting Tales of the West,* 1907; and *Roosevelt's Hunting Adventures in the West,* 1927; are simply *Hunting Trips of a Ranchman* and *The Wilderness Hunter* bound together. *Hunting the Grizzly and Other Sketches,* 1900, and *Hunting Trips on the Prairie and in the Mountains,* 1900, are reprints of portions of those same two books.

There were two new books, however, published while he was president. *Outdoor Pastimes of an American Hunter,* 1905, and

Good Hunting, 1907, the latter a big game hunting book geared toward the younger reader. All of Roosevelt's books are worthy additions to any big game hunter's library.

An author who along with Theodore Roosevelt bridges the nineteenth and twentieth centuries, although with a decidedly different writing style, was Thomas Martindale. He wrote four books which contain interesting accounts of big game hunting. *Sport Royal, I Warrant You,* 1897, and *Sport Indeed,* 1901, contain much on moose and caribou hunting in Maine and New Brunswick. Like Roosevelt, some of his writings have been recycled. *Sport Royal, I Warrant You* is reprinted nearly in its entirety in *Sport Indeed,* with additional new material added. *With Gun and Guide,* 1910, contains more on Maine and New Brunswick along with "A Hunting Trip in Northern British Columbia." *Hunting in the Yukon,* 1913, describes a lengthy hunting trip to that area. Martindale's books are as much travelogues as hunting accounts. The three latter books are most attractively bound with colored pictorial game covers.

A series of big game hunting books that similarly bridge the nineteenth and twentieth centuries are the books of the Boone and Crockett Club, an organization founded by Theodore Roosevelt. The earliest of the club's books consists of a seven-volume series on big game and conservation. The best of these, from the standpoint of North American big game hunting accounts, are *American Big Game Hunting,* the first club book published in 1893; *American Big Game in Its Haunts,* the club's fourth book published in 1904; and *Hunting at High Altitudes,* the club's fifth book published in 1913. Well over half of the latter book relates the grizzly bear hunting experiences of Confederate Army Colonel William D. Pickett from 1876 through 1883.

One final book highlighting the nineteenth century is John E. Howard's *North American Big Game Hunting in the 1800's,* published by Amwell Press in 1982, a comprehensive compilation of accounts of big game hunting taken from many of the books mentioned above. This book came about as a result of my interest in reading and collecting nineteenth-century hunting books. After twenty years of additional collecting, I would make only a few additions to that anthology. A selection or two from Hawker's and Perry's books, neither of which I owned at the time.

I have touched on only a very small percentage of the books in my library that are from the 1800's, mainly the ones that, in my judgement, contain the better accounts of big game and its hunting available through those early years. Short of an annotated bibliography, it would simply be too unwieldy to mention all the books containing big game hunting from that century. No doubt later reviews of my library will suggest several others that I should have included.

The twentieth century ushered in the era of hunting and adventure books that often found a single volume describing a single hunting trip. Two early works on Alaska fall into this category: Colonel Claude Cane's *Summer and Fall in Western Alaska,* 1903; and C. R. E. Radclyffe's *Big Game Shooting in Alaska,* published by Roland Ward in 1904 and dedicated to Theodore Roosevelt. Both books contain accounts of sheep, bear, and moose hunting. Radclyffe notes that in 1903 the total number of sportsman hunting moose on the Kenai Peninsula was ten—five Englishmen, four Americans, and one German. The largest antlers taken measured two inches over six feet.

William T. Hornaday, director of the New York Zoological Park, left interesting accounts of his hunting trip to British Columbia in his *Camp-Fires in the Canadian Rockies,* 1906, and of a later trip to the Pinacate region of Mexico in his *Camp-Fires on Desert and Lava,* 1908.

The great hunter-naturalist, Charles Sheldon, left early twentieth century big game hunting accounts that have become classics: *The Wilderness of the Upper Yukon,* 1911; *The Wilderness of the North Pacific Coast Islands,* 1912; and *The Wilderness of Denali,* 1930. The latter book was published after his death in 1928 and contains his Alaskan journals of 1906 through 1908, a classic on Dall sheep. His southwestern journals of 1912 through 1922 were published in 1979 under the title *The Wilderness of Desert Bighorns & Seri Indians.* The first three books have been reprinted a number of times. The latter was issued in a numbered limited edition of one thousand copies. Sheldon's interest in hunting and natural history led him to collect books on the subject. His library of hunting and natural history books numbered nearly seven thousand volumes.

An Englishman who hunted with Sheldon, and whom Theodore Roosevelt called "the greatest of the world's big-game hunters", Frederick Courteney Selous, left accounts of two hunting trips in the Rocky Mountains in *Sport and Travel,* 1900, and of hunts in the Yukon and Newfoundland in *Recent Hunting Trips in British North America,* 1907.

Two books along with Selous's that contain early records of Newfoundland hunting are J. G. Millais's *Newfoundland and Its Untrodden Ways,* published in 1907; and H. Hesketh Prichard's *Hunting Camps in Wood and Wilderness,* published in 1910. Prichard's book also contains chapters on mainland caribou hunting and moose hunting in Quebec, as well as South American and European hunting.

Some good early descriptions of far north hunting for moose, sheep, goat, caribou, black and grizzly bear are in Daniel J. Singer's *Big Game Fields of America North and South,* 1914.

His book is noteworthy as it also contains a rare record of early jaguar hunting, along with accounts of hunting on the Rio Bonito and cougar hunting in Sonora.

The above books give a good representation of big game hunting from the far north to the far south in the first decade and a half of the twentieth century prior to the First World War. A number of them are quite scarce. Three of Sheldon's books, as I have mentioned, have been reprinted, as has Selous's. Prichard's book had more than one printing. The others may have to be found in their original editions, although a number of publishers, from time to time, reprint some of the more obscure titles.

The period immediately after the First World War saw a continuation of big game hunting trips being published in books. J. A. McGuire's *In the Alaska-Yukon Gamelands,* copyright 1921, relates a trip after sheep, moose, and caribou in the White River country. Nevill A. D. Armstrong's *After Big Game in the Upper Yukon* gives very good accounts of hunts for those same species in the MacMillan River area in 1925 and 1926, along with an earlier hunt in 1914, although the book was not published until 1937. It was reprinted in 1995 by Premier Press.

John W. Eddy's 1924 Alaskan hunt for sheep, moose, and bear is recorded in a small volume titled *Hunting on Kenai Peninsula,* dated that same year although copyrighted in 1925. Eddy also describes a later bear hunt along the shores of the Bearing Sea in *Hunting the Alaska Brown Bear,* 1930.

Two other Alaskan titles giving personal hunting accounts from that era are Wendell Endicott's *Adventures in Alaska and Along the Trail,* 1928; and Theodore R. Hubback's *To Far Western Alaska for Big Game,* published by Roland Ward in 1929. Some of the material describing one of the two hunts in

Hubback's book was originally published in serial form in the March, April, May, and June 1921 issues of *Outdoor Life* magazine under the title *Ten Thousand Miles to Alaska for Moose and Sheep*. A fifteen-page booklet of that material was published in 1921 and subsequently reproduced in very small printings in 1966 and 1974 by Shorey Publications.

One of the classics of Alaskan hunting is G. O. Young's *Alaskan Trophies Won and Lost*, 1928. The book recounts a hunting trip undertaken by three strangers from McCarthy, Alaska, to Whitehorse, Yukon, in 1919, an arduous undertaking that claimed the life of one of the hunters not long after his return home. The author was apparently not fully satisfied with the first edition and had a new edition with more pictures and text published in 1947 under the title *Alaskan-Yukon Trophies Won and Lost*. The later edition has been reprinted a number of times.

The best early book on big game in the Canadian province to the south of Alaska is *Game Trails in British Columbia*, 1926, by A. Bryan Williams, who for thirteen years was head of the provincial game department. All the big game is covered, with numerous illustrations.

We will briefly leave the big game of the west and the far north for more prosaic game in the east and the deep south. Archibald Rutledge, the poet laureate of South Carolina, shot one deer short of three hundred during his seventy-eight-year hunting career. It seems likely that he wrote a story about every one of them. Most of his stories were first published in magazines and later collected in books. One of his early collections, *Plantation Game Trails*, 1921, contains several deer hunting accounts. A later book, *An American Hunter*, 1937, also includes many deer hunting chapters. A listing of all his books that contain deer hunting stories would be extensive. Rutledge preferred hunting deer with hounds, reminiscent of another Carolina hunter, William Elliott, writing near a century earlier. Rutledge's deer hunting stories are mixed in with other hunting stories, but you are not likely to be disappointed with any of his hunting reminisces.

Joseph Stowe Seabury's *Reflections of a Moose Hunter,* privately printed in 1921, gives some early twentieth-century accounts of moose hunting in New Brunswick. The attractive little book is well-illustrated with sharp reproductions and interspersed with droll humor.

Paul Brandreth's *Trails of Enchantment,* 1930, is a nice blending of natural history and deer hunting adventures set in the Adirondacks in the early 1900's. Well over half the book records most interesting descriptions of whitetail hunting that some might say come close to rivaling Rutledge. The book is illustrated with many period photographs and with striking colored endpapers that match the dust jacket. It should be noted that the author was writing under a quasi-pseudonym. Her real first name was Paulina.

Moving west again, John Cudahy's *Mananaland,* 1928, provides a rare early account of hunting desert sheep in Mexico in 1923. The book also includes hunts for antelope and cougar south of the border.

Farther to the north, William Sheldon, son of the great hunter-naturalist, Charles Sheldon, was following in his father's footsteps. His *Exploring For Wild Sheep in British Columbia in 1931 and 1932* is reminiscent of his father's earlier adventures. Although the hunts took place in the 1930's, the accounts were not published until 1981 by Amwell Press. The book also includes a ten-day sheep hunt in Alberta in 1930.

Still farther north, Harold McCracken was recording his adventures in *Alaskan Bear Trails,* 1931. The title is a little misleading for the book also contains accounts of his adventures with sheep, moose, and caribou. McCracken's interests eventually shifted from hunting with the gun to hunting with the camera. As would be expected, his book is well-illustrated with photographs.

Another good work of that period, *Sheep and Bear Trails,* 1933, gives descriptions of sheep hunting in Alaska and grizzly bear hunting in the British Columbia Coastal Range. John P. Holman, the author, was editor of *Forest and Stream* magazine.

Like Holman, Montague Stevens was a grizzly bear hunter. But Stevens's accounts in *Meet Mr. Grizzly* are in dramatic contrast to Holman's. Stevens was a hound man. He also lost an arm in a hunting accident. The reminisces of this one-armed hunter riding to the hounds in pursuit of grizzly bears is most intriguing. Although published in 1943, the hunting episodes took place during the late 1800's and the early 1900's in the Rocky Mountains of New Mexico.

The above books are obviously a very small representation of the hunting books published in the 1900's up to the beginning of the Second World War. But most of these titles represent some of the best depicting that classic period of North American big game hunting. As must inevitably be the case, some other worthwhile titles will come to mind after this is published.

The great adventure hunts of the nineteenth and early twentieth centuries, where getting to and from the hunting grounds was often as much if not more of an adventure than the hunt itself, passed with the improvement of wilderness roads and automobiles and the advent of airplane travel. And the great books chronicling those adventures passed with them. No longer were weeks and months needed just to get to the hunting area, almost mandating a lengthy hunt to justify the travel. Frederick Selous, for example, after a long ocean voyage from England to Newfoundland, took ten additional days by steamer, canoe, and foot simply to reach his hunting grounds at King George IV Lake in 1905, a trip I made in 1999 in less than half an hour by helicopter, although not over the same route. Just his ten-day journey into the lake, during which he saw caribou every day and kept himself and his two companions well-supplied with fresh caribou meat, would be considered an extensive hunt by the majority of modern hunters.

This very ease of transportation opened up those distant hunting lands, making them more accessible and somewhat more common. And because the hunting became more common, the accounts of a single or a few hunts seemed not to justify a whole book. There were some-such books still being written, of course, but big game hunting accounts were for the most part being published as magazine articles. If an author had enough articles published in magazines, he might collect them into a book. Not a new thing, of course. Frank Forester was doing the same back in the mid 1800's, as was Archibald Rutledge in the early 1900's.

The post-World War II period ushered in a budding crop of new gun and hunting editors for the major outdoor magazines who went on extensive big game hunts, often paid for by the magazines, and wrote articles about them for their respective publications. Books followed.

One of the best known and most respected of these magazine editors was Jack O'Connor, a professor of journalism at the University of Arizona, who became gun editor for *Outdoor Life* magazine in 1939. O'Connor was a noted big game hunter and a superb writer. He was also very prolific. I have twenty-two editions of O'Connor's books in my library, and I do not have them all. His first hunting book was published by Derrydale Press in 1939. *Game in the Desert* covers the southwestern white-tailed deer, mule deer, elk, desert bighorn sheep, and antelope, with some descriptions of their hunting in the 1920's and 1930's. The book was reprinted in 1945 under the title *Hunting in the Southwest.* His earliest collection of big game hunting accounts, *Jack O'Connor's Big Game Hunting,* 1963, contains some African and Asian hunting, but is mostly on North America.

Three contemporary editors of O'Connor's also left records of their North American big game hunting. Elmer Keith, former shooting editor of *Guns & Ammo* magazine, weaves hunting accounts into his discussions of all the big game of North America in *Elmer Keith's Big Game Hunting,* 1948. Warren Page, long-time shooting editor for *Field & Stream* magazine, was a worldwide big game hunter. Eighteen of his North American big game hunts appear as chapters in *One Man's Wilderness,* 1973. John Jobson, who became camping editor of *Sports Afield* magazine in 1962 and later its hunting editor, was much admired by Jack O'Connor for his writing skills. A number of his articles were collected in 1982, three years after his death, in *The Best of John Jobson,* published by Amwell Press. The book includes nine chapters on North American big game and a seven-chapter section relating his hunting trip to Bonnet Plume Lake in the Yukon.

The majority of the hunting books from this era leaned more toward the how-to and technical than to personal hunting accounts. This is not to say there was an absence of good narratives being recorded. Russell Annabel, whose name will always be synonymous with Alaska although he moved to Mexico in his later years, wrote most entertaining stories of Alaskan big game hunting. *Tales of a Big Game Guide,* 1938, and *Hunting and Fishing in Alaska,* 1948, give captivating portrayals written in Annabel's inimitable style. His collected writings have recently been published by Safari Press in a five-volume series.

James H. Bond, in his *From Out of the Yukon,* 1948, authored a book that harkens back to the adventure hunts of earlier times with his account of a fifty-seven-day trip in the Ogilive Range of the upper Yukon in 1947, a pioneer hunt in that part of the country where he saw over two thousand head of caribou, moose, sheep, and grizzly.

Twenty-five hundred miles to the south of Bond's hunting area, Frank C. Hibben hunted cougar, grizzly, and black bear with hounds in Arizona and the southwest. He left nicely written descriptions of these hunts in *Hunting American Lions,* 1948, and *Hunting American Bears,* 1950. His first book contains a rare account of a jaguar hunt, and his second book also includes Alaskan bear hunting.

Another good title from that time period on Alaskan brown bear is Jim Woodworth's *The Kodiak Bear,* 1958. The book contains descriptive hunting accounts of a professional Alaskan bear guide.

Grancel Fitz, a man important in the development of the Boone and Crockett Club's measuring system for North American big game, and the first person to successfully hunt all the big game of North America, recorded his hunts in *North American Head Hunting,* 1957, a book title that perhaps could have been better phrased, but a worthwhile volume nevertheless.

Fred Bear, a bowhunter extraordinary and the man most responsible for popularizing bowhunting in North America, left detailed journals of fifteen of his worldwide big game hunts in the 1950's and 1960's in *Fred Bear's Field Notes,* 1976. There is much on brown and grizzly bear in the Yukon, Alaska, and British Columbia. All of his big game hunting was with a bow.

A most interesting volume published in 1978, with the intriguing title *Hard Hunting*, recounts a two-month backpack hunt after sheep, goat, moose, caribou, and grizzly in British Columbia in 1973. Patrick Shaughnessy and Diane Swingle, the coauthors and hunting companions, left a well-illustrated, memorable record of their wilderness experiences.

John Batten's name is as synonymous with sheep hunting as Fred Bear's name is with bowhunting. Batten left a record of his worldwide sheep hunting in *Skyline Pursuits*, 1981. Over half the book is on sheep hunting in North America from 1928 to 1975. Two other books by Batten contain his accounts of hunting the rest of the world's big game. *The Formidable Game*, 1983, includes a sixty-four-page section on hunting North American bears. *The Forest and the Plain*, 1984, includes in the first half hunts for the rest of North America's big game.

Thomas McIntyre gives us some thoughtful descriptions of hunting in *Days Afield*, 1984, and *Dreaming the Lion*, 1993. As with Batten's books, the North American big game hunting chapters are combined with African hunting chapters, (and with Asian and European hunting in Batten's case), but that is simply a nice excuse to read of other lands.

Eastern Canadian moose hunting is portrayed by Herbert F. Goodwin in *Moose Stew*, 1987. Goodwin and his companions took forty-five moose over thiry-five seasons beginning in 1947. The author was an avid aviator and his book includes considerable discussion of floatplanes and flying in the Quebec and Ontario back country.

The Life of the Hunt, 1995, by John Barsness contains some fine accounts of North American big game hunting as does Walt Prothero's *The Hunting Adventures of Me and Joe*, 1995.

Prothero's title is somewhat of a misnomer as much of his hunting was done on his own. It was in the dedication of Prothero's book that I learned of the death of Roger Dowding, the bush pilot who flew me in and out of the Brooks Range on my 1990 Dall sheep hunt. As seems not uncommon with this uncommon breed of men, Roger Dowding did not return from his last flight.

And so, on that unintentionally somber note, I will bring this two-century review to a close. I have said more than once throughout that there are a great many good titles not mentioned here. I have been especially brief on the more recently published books as I believe the older works may be the ones least familiar.

Certainly there is no shortage of books to add to one's library. M. L. Biscotti's *A Bibliography of American Sporting Books,* 1997, lists some five thousand volumes on American game mammals and birds and their hunting published between 1926 and 1985. And John C. Phillips's *American Game Mammals and Birds,* 1930, of which Biscotti's fine work is a continuation, lists some seven thousand additional volumes published between 1582 and 1925. For those interested in pursuing the subject further, these two volumes are indispensable.

A complimentary volume, Richard A. Hand's *A Bookman's Guide to Hunting, Shooting, Angling, and Related Subjects,* 1991, lists prices current at the time for over seven thousand titles. Another complimentary volume, *Wegner's Bibliography on Deer and Deer Hunting,* 1992, lists with annotations over eleven hundred titles on this most popular North American big game animal. A number of other specialized bibliographies on hunting books have also been published.

I have chosen here to review only books that I own and therefore have read which are similar to the type of book I have written. My thought being that the reader of this book might have an interest in other books relating personal North American big game hunting experiences.

While I take great pleasure in reading hunting books, I discovered long ago on a solo black bear hunt in Wisconsin that a hunting camp is a poor place for me to enjoy one. I took a copy of Clyde Ormond's *Bear!* along on that trip. Perhaps it was too much of a good thing.

I since have gone to other sections of my library when selecting books to take on a hunting trip. On another solo black bear hunt, this time in Ontario, incessant rain kept me tent-bound long enough to complete *Caesar's Commentaries on the Gallic and Civil Wars.* Over the seasons I also read Will and Ariel Durant's eleven-volume *The Story of Civilization,* along with other works on ancient and military history, anthropology, philosophy, and a host of related subjects, types of books that work for me in a wilderness setting. But reading, of course, is an individual thing. One person's eagerly read volume is another person's drudgery. One will take along on their trips those books that interest them. And maybe that will be a good hunting book.

Were it not for my interest in hunting books, I would not have written this one. Reading about the experiences of hunters past has filled many pleasurable hours over the years and it just seemed a natural extension to write down some of my experiences. There is little that I have done that has not been done and written about before. But like those other accounts, these accounts are unique for the simple reason that they happened to a particular person at a particular time. I leave them as a hopeful remembrance of one man's search for the wild places, and for the magnificent creatures that roam those splendored lands.

John E. Howard

John Howard was born in Oak Park, Illinois. Shortly after his birth his family moved to Dubuque, Iowa, where they resided briefly before settling in Beloit, Wisconsin.

John enlisted in the Wisconsin National Guard concurrent with his education and served for six years with Company L, 3rd Battalion, 128th Infantry Regiment, 32nd "Red Arrow" Division.

Following a few years with various corporations, Mr. Howard began his career in the insurance business as an agent for the Prudential Insurance Company. He became manager of the Beloit office and was subsequently transferred to the Regional Home Office in Minneapolis and to a number of other field management positions in the Midwest.

Mr. Howard attained the Chartered Life Underwriter designation (CLU) and was an instructor for that course and other industry courses. He was on the task force that designed the basic training program for Prudential agents. He received numerous industry and company awards.

After a thirty-two year career, Mr. Howard retired from the Prudential Insurance Company and formed St. Hubert's Press.

Mr. Howard's previous books include *North American Big Game Hunting in the 1800's*, and *Strayed Shots and Frayed Lines*, both published in 1982 by Amwell Press. He edited and wrote the introductions for *Wegner's Bibliography on Deer and Deer Hunting*, 1992, and *Hunting Expeditions of Oliver Hazard Perry*, 1994, both published by St. Hubert's Press.

Jack, as he is known to family and friends, resides in DeForest, Wisconsin, with his wife Ginny. He has two children and seven grandchildren.

John Rice

John Rice was born in Oneida, New York. He graduated from Syracuse University with a Bachelors' degree in Fine Arts.

Following graduation, Mr. Rice began a career as an illustrator and fine-arts artist. His illustrations have appeared in many books and magazines including *Field and Stream, Alaska Magazine, Salt Water Sportsman, McClanes' Game Fish of North America, Sport Fishing Aquatic Resources Handbook,* and *The Bird Watcher's Diary.*

Mr. Rice's works have also been commissioned by a number of conservation and natural resources organizations including Duck's Unlimited, Trout Unlimited, The Massachusetts Division of Fisheries, The New York Zoological Society, and the New England Coast Conservation Association.

His illustrations have also appeared in textbooks by Harper Collins Publishing, Macmillan/McGraw Hill, Harcourt Brace Jananovich, and Boyd Mills Press, among others.

Mr. Rice's landscapes, seascapes, and sporting paintings, which capture the peace and solitude often present in nature, can be found in many private collections nationwide. His artistic talents also find expression in fine wood carvings of waterfowl and game fish.

Mr. Rice currently lives and works in New York City.

Hubert Of Aquitane
(656-727)

Hubert of Aquitaine, a nobleman at the court of Germany's King Theodoric III, acquired a reputation as a vain man devoted to worldly pleasures. Legend records that while hunting one day, Hubert came upon a stag with a glowing cross between its antlers. A voice warned him that if he did not mend his ways he would be doomed. Heeding the warning, he abandoned his life at court and became a monk.

Hubert was later ordained a priest and traveled throughout the Ardennes Forest converting pagan hunting tribes. He eventually became bishop of the town of Luttich. He died in 727 and was buried there, but because of his early attachments to the hunters of the Ardennes, his body was transferred to that area's Andain Monastery, now known as St. Hubert's Abbey.

Following Hubert's death, legends grew concerning the miraculous healing powers of his bishop's key. By the tenth century, he emerged as the patron saint and guardian of hunters. His feast day is November third, and for many years hunters observed the custom of suspending the deer stalking season on that day in his honor. In parts of Europe, traditional "Hubert Hunts" are still held invoking the good saint's blessing.

The hunting tradition is as old as mankind. Always throughout that tradition hunters have invoked the Unseen Powers to aid them in their quest. The vagaries of the hunt, the uncontrollable factors that so often complicate it, sway the hunter's mind toward the Red Gods. From the Cro-Magnon hunters of thirty-two thousand years ago, communing with their animal paintings on the cave walls at Grotte Chauvet, to the hunter of today who offers a silent prayer to St. Hubert for luck, the tradition continues.

St. Hubert's Press continues another tradition—sharing the hunter's tale around the evening's fire. When the season ends and the hunters disperse, we go to our books to continue the tales. Our books are gracious friends, patiently awaiting our call and always receptive to our bidding. And like good friends, we can never have too many.

ST. HUBERT'S PRESS
Publisher of classic works
on the ancient and noble art of the chase.

Chronology Of The Chapters

The Hunting Time
was designed by
John E. Howard

Typeset in
13-point Adobe Garamond by
Chris Pike

Printed and bound by
Sheridan Books

Printed on acid-free paper